Instructional Technology for Teaching and Learning

Designing Instruction, Integrating Computers, and Using Media

PRE

Instructional Technology for Teaching and Learning

*Designing Instruction, Integrating Computers,
and Using Media*

Second Edition

Timothy J. Newby
Purdue University

Donald A. Stepich
Northeastern Illinois University

James D. Lehman
Purdue University

James D. Russell
Purdue University

Merrill,
an imprint of Prentice Hall

Upper Saddle River, New Jersey   Columbus, Ohio

Library of Congress Cataloging-in-Publication Data

Instructional technology for teaching and learning : designing
instruction, integrating computers, and using media / Timothy J.
Newby . . . [et al.]. -- 2nd.ed.
  p. cm.
  Includes bibliographical references and indexes.
  ISBN 0-13-914052-2
  1. Instructional systems--Design.   2. Educational
technology--Planning.   3. Computer-assisted instruction.   I. Newby, Timothy J.
  LB1028.38 .1587 2000
  371.3--dc21   99-35614
                                                          CIP

Editor: Debra A. Stollenwerk
Developmental Editor: Gianna M. Marsella
Editorial Assistant: Penny S. Burleson
Production Editor: Mary Harlan
Copy Editor: Robert L. Marcum
Design Coordinator: Diane C. Lorenzo
Text Design and Project Coordination: Carlisle Publishers Services
Cover Design: Janoski Advertising
Cover Art: © SuperStock
Photo Coordinator: Anthony Magnacca
Production Manager: Pamela D. Bennett
Illustrations: Carlisle Communications, Ltd.
Director of Marketing: Kevin Flanagan
Marketing Manager: Meghan Shepherd
Marketing Coordinator: Krista Groshong

This book was set in New Century Schoolbook by Carlisle Communications, Ltd. and was printed and bound by Banta/Harrisonburg. The cover was printed by Banta/Harrisonburg.

Photo Credits: All photos by Scott Cunningham/Merrill except the following: Courtesy of Apple Computer, Inc., p. 41; The Bettmann Archive, p. 248; Computer-Based Education Research Library, University of Illinois, p. 251; IBM Archives, p. 250; Missouri Historical Society, p. 248; John Underwood, Center for Instructional Services, Purdue University, pp. 21, 87, 101 (left); UPI/Bettmann, p. 247; Anne Vega/Merrill, pp. 117, 142.

Printed in the United States of America

10 9 8 7 6 5 4 3

ISBN: 0-13-914052-2

Prentice-Hall International (UK) Limited, *London*
Prentice-Hall of Australia Pty. Limited, *Sydney*
Prentice-Hall of Canada, Inc., *Toronto*
Prentice-Hall Hispanoamericana, S. A., *Mexico*
Prentice-Hall of India Private Limited, *New Delhi*
Prentice-Hall of Japan, Inc., *Tokyo*
Prentice-Hall (Singapore) Pte. Ltd., *Singapore*
Editora Prentice-Hall do Brasil, Ltda., *Rio de Janeiro*

PREFACE

VISION AND GOALS OF THE TEXT

As we began to create and then revise this textbook, we were guided by the following vision: *"Instructional Technology for Teaching and Learning* will show preservice and inservice teachers how to increase learning by designing lessons that use instructional technology, including computers and other media." Within this vision, we focused on three goals. Those who teach (whether in public school or elsewhere) need to

1. be proficient in selecting, modifying, and designing instructional materials. They need to know how to plan instruction that addresses and solves complex learning problems for individual students.
2. have a repertoire of instructional methods and media from which to draw in order to select and utilize those which most effectively and efficiently impact student learning.
3. be familiar with the computer as a tool for development and management of instructional materials, as well as a means by which students can effectively learn.

ORGANIZATION OF THE TEXT

One theme of this book is that the principles of designing instruction, the selection and use of methods and media, and the effective use of computers are intricately intertwined. To facilitate this integration, the text is designed around the PIE—*Plan, Implement, Evaluate*—model. Following introductory chapters that provide needed background on learning, instructional theories, and the computer (Chapters 1–3), the book focuses on helping the reader discover how to **plan** effective and efficient instructional materials and activities. While providing guidance on gathering the needed information about the learner, content, setting, and what is needed to create an instructional plan (Chapter 4), it also introduces the most commonly used instructional methods and media (Chapter 5) as well as how to select and/or create methods, media, and materials (Chapter 6).

The **implementation** phase focuses on how students actually experience instructional materials and activities. Here, we discuss proper utilization techniques for various forms of methods and media (Chapter 7). The utility of the computer is again emphasized to show how students can effectively learn using this electronic medium (Chapter 8). We then explore the computer's value for accessing information via the Internet and technology's role in distance education (Chapter 9).

Chapter 10 examines both the **evaluation** of instructional materials and the assessment of student performance. We examine how teachers can use evaluation to continuously improve not only the abilities and skill of their students but also the effectiveness of their instructional materials. Throughout this chapter we discuss the role of the computer in storing, organizing, analyzing, and managing evaluation data. The final chapter (Chapter 11) focuses on the key issues confronting the field today, what has been attempted, what current solutions are being tried out, and what possibilities the future holds.

STRUCTURING THE COURSE

Traditionally, preservice teachers have needed to take separate courses in instructional planning and design, media utilization, and computing to gain these competencies. *Instructional Technology for Teaching and Learning* has been designed as a single, integrated source that introduces preservice and inservice teachers to the basic principles of effective instructional material planning and development, to different types of media and how to best utilize them, and to the computer as a powerful tool that can be used to plan and develop as well as deliver effective instruction.

There are at least three ways courses can be structures to accomplish these goals:

▶ *Emphasize the development and use of the instructional plan.* Covering the text's chapters in order will accomplish this task. Begin with the general chapters on learning, instructional technology, theory, and the computer as a tool to develop and execute the plan. The remaining chapters (based on the steps of the PIE model) show how one *plans, implements,* and continually *evaluates* in order to learn and teach effectively.

▶ *Emphasize the learning experience itself.* You may want to begin with the chapters that focus specifically on methods and media (Chapter 5 through 7) and their role in the learning process. This can be followed by how the computer, the Internet, and distance education (Chapters 3, 8, and 9) can facilitate the learning experience. Finally, chapters on designing (Chapter 4) and evaluating (Chapter 10) can then be addressed to help your students learn how to develop and improve such learning experiences.

▶ *Emphasize the computer as a powerful tool that can improve learning.* You might begin by looking at background materials on computer hardware (Appendix A), followed by how and why the computer can be effectively used by both teachers and learners (Chapters 3 and 8). You may then wish to investigate the "power of the computer" and its use with the Internet and distance education (Chapter 9). Coupled with a lab component, this focus gives extra emphasis on the computer as a key tool for students and teachers and demonstrates its effectiveness within the classroom setting.

SPECIAL FEATURES

This text includes the following special pedagogical features:

▶ *Planning the Chapter Content.* The opening paragraphs of each chapter consist of an advance organizer that will prepare you for the chapter content. We highlight relevant sections of the text's vision, and we recall and synthesize critical information from previous chapters.

▶ *Toolboxes.* Throughout the text we include Toolboxes, special features that present relevant, useful pieces of information. These toolboxes are of three types: tips, tools, and techniques. For example, a *Toolbox Tip* might include a short section on the care of computer hardware or use of software, a *Toolbox Tool* might include a description and use of a specific tool such as Internet search engines, and a *Toolbox Technique* might include information on how, when, and why to use analogies within a set of instructional materials. These toolboxes occur throughout the text, positioned close to relevant text materials in each chapter.

▶ *Reflective Questions.* To help readers think about the ramifications and application of many of the principles that are discussed, we have inserted periodic reflective questions. These are designed to help readers generate ideas and consider possible benefits and problems related to issues discussed in the text. In many cases, these questions ask you to think about the content in terms of their own experiences.

▶ *Applications in the Learner-Centered Classroom.* Within each chapter we explore how teachers can engender a learner-centered approach in their classrooms. Following the main content of the chapter, this section is devoted to identifying critical aspects of the learner-centered classroom and applying the chapter's information within such a context. In this section we also include the story (carried through each of the chapters) of one teacher, Ms. Janette Moreno, and how she applies these principles and creates a learner-centered environment for her students.

▶ *Reflective Activities.* Each chapter concludes with selected activities that suggest how the chapter's information relates to your life experiences.

SUPPLEMENTS AND RESOURCES FOR STUDENTS AND TEACHERS

▶ *Companion Website.* We have developed a companion website for this text, located at **http://www.prenhall.com/newby,** to inform users of this text of changes in the field, and to provide additional resources and materials that could not be included in the text. Professors will enjoy the use of an online syllabus builder and online course management tools. Professors and students alike will benefit from additional discussion topics, self-assessment tools, reflective activities, and related web sites of interest (see pages xii and xiii for more details.)

▶ *Instructor's Guide.* An accompanying Instructor's Guide is available to professors upon adoption of this text. For each chapter, the guide includes (a) ideas on how to model the use of the various technological tools; (b) ideas for introducing each of the main concepts of the chapter; (c) an integrated application section with suggested applied activities for individuals, cooperative activities for both small and large groups, discussion starters, case studies, and suggested topics for a concurrent computer lab; (d) suggestions for assessment and feedback, ideas for portfolio projects, minute papers, and the use of reflective journal entries; and (e) a set of overhead transparency masters.

▶ *Computerized Test Banks.* Customizable test banks on disk are available for both Macintosh and Windows users. To request a complimentary copy of the test bank disks or the instructor's guide, please contact your Merrill/Prentice Hall representative.

▶ *Live Telelectures and Internet Chat Sessions.* As authors, we are available for live telelectures or Internet chat sessions if you so desire.

CONTACTING THE AUTHORS

We believe wholeheartedly in communication and feedback. If you have a question or suggestion, let us know. Both students and professors are encouraged to send us e-mail messages and to visit the companion website.

Tim Newby
e-mail: newby@purdue.edu
telephone: 765-494-5672
address: 1442 LAEB, Purdue University,
    W. Lafayette, IN 47907-1442

Don Stepich
e-mail: D-Stepich@neiu.edu
telephone: 773-794-6297
address: Northeastern Illinois University,
    5500 N. St. Louis Ave., Chicago, IL 60625

Jim Lehman
e-mail: lehman@purdue.edu
telephone: 765-494-5670
address: 1442 LAEB, Purdue University,
    W. Lafayette, IN 47907-1442

Jim Russell
e-mail: jrussell@purdue.edu
telephone: 765-494-5673
address: 1442 LAEB, Purdue University,
    W. Lafayette, IN 47907-1442

ACKNOWLEDGMENTS

Throughout the preparation of this edition various individuals have contributed to its successful completion. In particular, we would like to thank the following persons:

Our families, who have once again been patient as we spent extra time at the office, glued to the word processor.

Our students, who frequently challenge our work and look for ways to help us improve. Watching them succeed at learning has given us the motivation to continually look for ways to improve this text.

Our inservice classroom teachers and friends, who continually remind us of the need for better teacher training—all the while giving us great examples of why instructional technology must be integrated within the classroom setting.

Debbie Stollenwerk, our senior editor at Merrill/Prentice-Hall. She kept things in perspective. Her insights and encouragement helped us to make this edition the best it could be.

Gianna Marsella, our developmental editor. She really is the epitome of an instructional evaluator. Each time we sent in "perfect" ideas and manuscripts, her insights and thoughts helped us see ways to make them better. At the same time, she continually encouraged us and kept us excited about the challenge of this revision.

Robert Marcum, our copy editor. He made valuable editorial contributions by taking four different writing styles and making them read as written by a single author. It was enjoyable to watch this expert craft the manuscript.

Kathy Davis, our project editor at Carlisle Publishers Services. Even under great time constraints, she has always been pleasant and cheerful as she guided the work from copy editing to final product. Her input was invaluable to the success of this project.

Finally, all of our reviewers of this and the previous edition. We asked for their opinions and insights and they delivered. Their ideas and suggestions are found throughout this edition. The reviewers for this edition were

David Bullock, Portland State University
Leslie K. Curda, University of Toledo
Sue Elwood, Texas Tech University

Joan Hanor, California State University,
    San Marcos
Bonnie H. Keller, Valdosta State University
F. R. Koontz, The University of Toledo
S. Kim MacGregor, Louisiana State University
Janice Sandiford, Florida International University
Charles G. Stoddard, Utah State University

We hope this text will provide both preservice and inservice teachers with a solid foundation for planning, implementing, and evaluating instruction. By integrating the principles of instructional design, by selecting and utilizing relevant instructional methods and media, and by making appropriate use of the computer, the teaching-learning process can become more effective, efficient, and appealing.

Tim, Don, Jim, and Jim

ABOUT THE AUTHORS

Tim Newby is a Professor of Educational Technology at Purdue University. He teaches introductory courses in instructional design, computing, and media, as well as advanced courses in instructional design research, foundations of instructional design theory, and instructional strategies. His primary research efforts are directed toward examining the impact of learning and instructional strategies on students' learning and toward defining/investigating instructional conditions that foster and support the development of expert learners. Tim is particularly interested in the use of analogies and their impact on learning and memory. Thus, throughout this book, you will note the use of something familiar to explain something new. Tim's other life consists of chasing four active children and trying to keep up with an overly committed wife. Watching, coaching, and cheering for little kids as they learn to catch, throw, hit, and kick various forms of "ball" is a passion.

Don Stepich is currently an Associate Professor in the Human Resource Development Program at Northeastern Illinois University in Chicago, where he teaches courses in instructional design, instructional media, and presentation skills for both graduate and undergraduate students. As an instructional designer, Don is interested in the use of interactive strategies to help students learn and in the improvement of instructional materials through continuous evaluation. He is particularly interested in the impact of analogies on learning and their effective use in instructional materials. In a former life Don was a professional social worker in a mental health center and in private counseling practice. In fact, it was his counseling work that led him into education. He found that he was spending a lot of time teaching assertiveness, active listening, and communication skills, which led him back to school to study learning and instructional design.

Jim Lehman is a Professor of Educational Technology and Co-Director of the Technology Resources Center in the School of Education at Purdue University. He teaches classes on the educational applications of personal computers, integration and management of computers in education, computer software design, interactive multimedia, and distance learning. He was honored as the Outstanding Teacher in the School of Education in 1997. His research interests include integration of computer technology into subject matter instruction especially in the sciences, interactive multimedia design and implementation, and computer-mediated communication for distance education. He works extensively with colleagues in the K–12 schools on the integration of computers and related technologies. In his spare time, Jim is raising two daughters, Lauren and Katie, and he likes gardening.

Jim Russell is Professor of Curriculum and Instruction at Purdue University and a Visiting Professor at Florida State University. A former high school mathematics and physics teacher, Jim teaches courses on media utilization, instructional design, instructional delivery systems, and principles of adult education. His recognition as a fellow of the Purdue University Teaching Academy in 1998 honors him for exemplary work. Jim is also involved with Purdue's Center for Instructional Excellence, where he conducts workshops on teaching techniques for faculty and graduate assistants. His specialty areas are presentation skills and using media and technology in classrooms. When away from the university, Jim enjoys building plastic model race cars and is an announcer for the Nationwide Demolition Derby circuit. His wife, Nancy, is a parish nurse; their married daughter Jennifer, a former high school teacher, is currently devoting her full attention to nurturing Jim and Nancy's granddaughter, Lauren.

Discover the Companion Web-site Accompanying This Book

www.prenhall.com / newby

The Prentice Hall Companion Website: A Vitrual Learning Environment

Technology is a constantly growing and changing aspect of our field that is creating a need for content and resources. To address this emerging need, Prentice Hall has developed an online learning environment for students and professors alike–Companion Websites–to support our textbooks.

In creating a Companion Website, our goal is to build on and enhance what that textbook already offers. For this reason, the content for each user-friendly website is organized by topic and provides the professor and student with a variety of meaningful resources. Common features of a Companion Website include:

For the Professor

Every Companion Website integrates Syllabus Manager™, an online syllabus creation and management utility.

▶ **Syllabus Manager**™ provides you, the instructor, with an easy, step-by-step process to create and revise syllabi, with direct links into Companion Website and other online content without having to learn HTML.

▶ Students may logon to your syllabus during any study session. All they need to know is the web address for the Companion Website and the password you've assigned to your syllabus.

▶ After you have created a syllabus using **Syllabus Manager**™, students may enter the syllabus for their course section from any point in the Companion Website.

▶ Class dates are highlighted in white and assigned due dates appear in blue. Clicking on a date, the student is shown the list of activities for the assignment. The activities for each assignment are linked directly to actual content, saving time for students.

▶ Adding assignments consists of clicking on the desired due date, then filling in the details of the assignment—name of the assignment, instructions, and whether or not it is a one-time or repeating assignment.

▶ In addition, links to other activities can be created easily. If the activity is online, a URL can be entered in the space provided, and it will be linked automatically in the final syllabus.

▶ Your completed syllabus is hosted on our servers, allowing convenient updates from any computer on the Internet. Changes you make to you syllabus are immediately available to your students at their next logon.

For the Student

▶ **Topic Overviews**   outline key concepts in topic area

▶ **Electronic Blue Book**   send homework or essays directly to your instructor's email with this paperless form

▶ **Message Board**   serves as a virtual bulletin board to post—or respond to—questions or comments to/from a national audience

▶ **Web Destinations**   links to www sites that relate to each topic area

▶ **Professional Organizations**   links to organizations that relate to topic areas

▶ **Additional Resources**   access to topic-specific content that enhances material found in the text

To take advantage of these and other resources, please visit the *Instructional Technology for Teaching and Learning* Companion Website at www.prenhall.com/newby

BRIEF CONTENTS

CONTENTS

SPECIAL FEATURES

INTRODUCTION TO INSTRUCTIONAL TECHNOLOGY

Read Me First!

Have you opened a computer software package lately? If so, you may have noticed a section entitled "READ ME FIRST," included because the authors want to tell you about the materials *before* you head off into some trial-and-error learning process. In similar fashion, we think it is important for you to know a few things about this text before you dive into the initial chapters.

First, it would be helpful to know *why* this textbook was put together. We believe that many individuals, especially those within teacher education, need to know (1) how instruction is designed, developed, and improved; (2) the types and uses of different media formats—especially the use of the personal computer; and (3) how the design of the instruction and the media are integrated to promote student learning. Meeting these three needs requires integrating the three general areas of instructional design, instructional media, and instructional computing. Traditionally, these have been taught through individual texts and separate courses; however, teachers must apply them in an integrated fashion to have maximum impact on student learning.

Second, it is useful to know that this text is organized around a simple Plan, Implement, Evaluate (PIE)

model. The main sections of the text (Sections II, III, and IV), are all based on this model. The different aspects of instructional design, media, and computing are discussed within this structure.

Third, there are a number of special features within this text designed to facilitate your learning. This text focuses on instructional technology, especially on the tools that can increase the effectiveness, efficiency, and appeal of instruction. We have created a "toolbox" feature, which highlights important hardware, methods, techniques, and other tips. Also included are examples to encourage their use.

Of special interest within this text is the emphasis on a learner-centered classroom. We include a section within each chapter that addresses this, and also include throughout the text the story of Janette Moreno, a classroom teacher who has found ways to improve her performance, and the performance of her students, by integrating technology into her teaching.

Throughout this text, we frequently ask questions, present ideas for you to ponder, and describe problems that need thoughtful analysis and synthesis in order to be adequately worked through. This is our attempt to get you involved and to help you to remember and apply the information.

IF WE WERE STUDYING THIS TEXTBOOK, WE WOULD . . .

A few years ago, one of our students asked, "If you were going to study for this exam, how would you go about it?" In response, we created a set of notes that began with the statement, *If we were studying for this exam, we would . . .* The goal was not to provide a list of specific items to memorize; rather it was to guide them so they could draw their own conclusions. These notes worked so successfully, we decided to include a similar set here. So, *If we were studying this textbook, we would . . .*

▶ *Read and reflect on the subtitle of the text.* The purpose of this textbook is to show how instructional design, instructional media, and instructional computing become powerful teaching and learning tools when they are integrated. Throughout the book you should note the goal of integrating all three to increase instructional effectiveness, efficiency, and appeal.

▶ *Pay close attention to the plan, implement, and evaluate model.* Whenever you approach learning (from either a teacher's or learner's perspective) you need to think about how the planning will occur, how the learning will be experienced, and how assessment measures will indicate what worked and what needs improvement. The inside cover of this text and the list of questions offered there will help you recall important features of each part of the model.

▶ *Realize that learning is not a simple process.* There are no set prescriptions to ensure that it will consistently occur. You must be prepared to solve unique problems and to draw solutions from a repertoire of possible techniques, strategies, approaches, and media. If you see that one method or tool is not overly helpful, try to determine what would be more effective.

▶ *Reflect on how the textbook material can be applied to your own experiences.* We have included hundreds of examples throughout the text. Think about what you can learn from each of them.

▶ *Realize that this book has been designed to serve as a foundation.* It will not teach you everything. This book will give you the fundamental knowledge and skills you need for your own learning and future teaching.

▶ *Do not underestimate the power of the computer.* Unlike many media formats that are mainly used to present information, the computer can be used by both learner and teacher during the planning, the implementation, and the evaluation phases. The computer can combine a number of different methods and media formats (e.g., multimedia) to enrich learning experiences.

▶ *Learn to appreciate the power of the computer as a teaching and learning tool, but do not be overwhelmed by it.* Don't fall into the trap of thinking that the computer is the savior of education. The computer is not the most important tool in *all* learning situations. It is one of many tools that can facilitate your work. In addition, don't think that the computer is such a complex tool that you cannot master it.

▶ *Reflect and question.* Take time to reflect on what is presented in this text and, more important, how you can *use* it. When a principle is presented, imagine how, when, and why you might apply it.

▶ *Ask for help.* As you reflect and question, feel free to contact us directly. Our desire is for you to be challenged by what is here, not to be frustrated or overwhelmed. If you have questions or problems or suggestions, please contact us. Our e-mail addresses, phone numbers, and mailing addresses can be found in the Preface.

▶ *Be excited about learning!* Learning should be a marvelous adventure, whether you accomplish it personally or assist in helping others experience it. As you learn about instructional technology and begin to see its potential we hope you will become as excited as we are.

SECTION I OVERVIEW

This first section of the text, entitled "Introduction to Instructional Technology," is an introduction to the field of instructional technology and the supporting contributions of instructional design, media, and computing. Central to Chapter 1 is the concept of learning and how you can enhance it through the use of instructional technology.

In Chapter 2 we explore the theoretical foundations of teaching and learning. We look at learning from a number of different angles to enable you to consider which teaching and learning orientation might be best, given a particular topic, situation, and/or type of learner. To increase the usefulness of this theoretical background, realize that the emphasis is not simply on knowing the different perspectives of learning but on understanding how each perspective applies to real students in actual classrooms.

Finally, we have designed Chapter 3 to supply important prerequisite information about the computer and how it can be used to enhance learning. This is a powerful machine, and is intricately involved in the design, development, implementation, and evaluation of learning experiences.

C H A P T E R 1

Learning, Instruction, and Technology

KEY WORDS AND CONCEPTS

Learner-centered instruction
Learning
Instructional effectiveness, efficiency, and appeal
Instruction
Instructional plan
Instructional media
Instructional computing
Instructional technology

OBJECTIVES

After reading and studying this chapter, you will be able to

▶ Describe learning and explain why understanding the learning process is important for both teachers and learners.
▶ Describe the changing roles of teachers and learners in the learning environment and the need for a variety of instructional methods, media, techniques, and activities.
▶ Identify relevant questions that both teachers and learners should generate and investigate during the planning, implementation, and evaluation phases of learning.
▶ Identify the potential contribution to learning of various instructional tools and technology, including computers and other media.

PLANNING FOR THE CHAPTER CONTENT

Welcome to the second edition of *Instructional Technology for Teaching and Learning*. We, the authors, want you to know from the beginning that we are excited about this book's contents. We live in a time when phenomenal tools allow for more rapid access to and manipulation of information than has ever been possible in the past. It is an exciting time to learn about learning. In this text we will explore ways to design instruction incorporating computers and related technology to increase learning within the classroom. We encourage you to begin early on to look for the applications that are relevant to you.

In this chapter, we will share the vision of the book—where we are going and why. We will define and share examples of learning and technology, and more importantly, we will begin to discuss integrating the two. How can technology affect learning? What obstacles do we face? What are the roles of teachers and learners? We will consider these and similar questions as you venture through this chapter.

INTRODUCTION: THE EXPERT CABINETMAKER

To begin, let's think about experts and how they perform. Have you ever had the opportunity to watch a professional at work? Perhaps you have observed a master chef prepare a delicious entrée, or an artist turn a blank canvas into a portrait, or perhaps you have seen a wrecked car restored to a like-new appearance. In each case, expertise has been demonstrated.

If you have ever attempted to replicate such fine work, you undoubtedly realized that it was not a simple task. Many of us can follow the processes experts use, but the "art" of their expertise escapes us. For example, if you observe an expert cabinetmaker build a customized bookcase and then compare a novice's attempt to make the same thing, you will likely note one or more of the following differences. First, before ever touching a tool, the expert typically spends time planning and preparing. Although this effort is not always recorded on paper, the expert plans not just the end result but the process of creation as well—what materials he will need, which tools will be most useful, how and when to use those tools, and even what to do if he encounters certain problems. To some degree novices may also plan their work, but experts take more time, are more creative and thorough, and plan more effectively.

A second difference regards the expert cabinetmaker's overall knowledge of the available tools and how to use them in creative ways. Experts seem to know exactly which tool is correct for every situation. If they run into an unexpected problem that renders their first choice ineffective, they can quickly determine the next-best alternative. The customized

An expert craftsperson evaluates a piece of wood.

bookcase, for example, may have a unique recessed panel design the expert can create with the standard router and blade; however, he may realize that a stationary wood shaper would provide a cleaner, more precise cut. The novice, on the other hand, may select a familiar, favorite tool and use it even if it doesn't work quite right.

One additional difference—and perhaps the biggest—is the way experts continually review and monitor how their work is progressing. Experts don't wait until little problems become big headaches. For example, if the initial pieces of the bookcase are not properly squared, serious problems will result later with misaligned joints and uneven shelves. As projects near completion, experts also spend time reviewing—what steps they took, how closely the final products match the original conception, what problems they encountered, and what they could have improved.

VISION OF THE TEXTBOOK: WHERE ARE WE GOING?

At this point you may be wondering why a text on instructional technology begins with an example of building a bookcase. Our primary interest is not woodworking, but how the transition from novice (student) to expert occurs and how you can help this transformation by effectively using instructional tools and technology. The purpose of this text is to describe what these tools are, as well as how, when, and why you can use them to support learning. Our vision is that

> *Instructional Technology for Teaching and Learning,* will show you how to increase learning by designing lessons that use instructional technology, including computers and other media.

As you read this statement, note the emphasis on "learning." We want you to understand what learning is, what it requires, and what is needed to shift toward a higher level of learning. Focusing on learning will help you become a more skilled learner yourself, and will enable you to more effectively help your students.

As shown in Figure 1–1, learning is the central focus. To learn about learning, we must examine the roles of the learners, the teacher, and the instruction.

Also note within our vision statement an emphasis on technology. We live in an age in which technology, specifically the computer and other electronic tools, has made a tremendous impact.

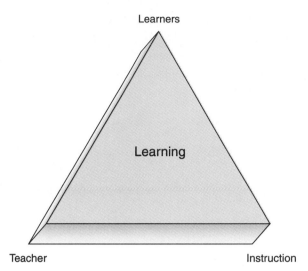

FIGURE 1–1   Relationship among learners, teacher, instruction, and learning

From providing quick access to huge amounts of information, to performing high-speed, accurate calculations, the computer has changed our lives. This tool has the potential to readily impact how one learns and how one assists others as they learn. Review Figure 1–1 again, and think of the ways in which technology can impact the teacher, the learner, the instruction, and the learning experience. (For example, through a multimedia computer simulation, students can encounter more lifelike experiences, which lead to greater knowledge transfer; or, teachers may automate management tasks and thus spend more time coaching their students.) In this text we will explore the many possibilities that technology provides.

The final element of our vision is knowing when, why, and how to design an effective, technology-enhanced learning experience. We will explain the key principles of designing instruction, and will discuss the methods, strategies, and techniques needed to ensure reliable learning.

In sum, our vision is for you to become an instructional expert capable of helping others to learn. To begin, we examine learning itself, and the key elements of the learning process.

THE CHANGING FACE OF EDUCATION

A Traditional View of Teaching and Learning

For a moment, think about the "traditional" classroom setting. For most, this will conjure up thoughts of a room with rows of desks and chairs. As depicted in Figure 1–2, the traditional view of teaching and

FIGURE 1–2 Traditional view of teaching and learning

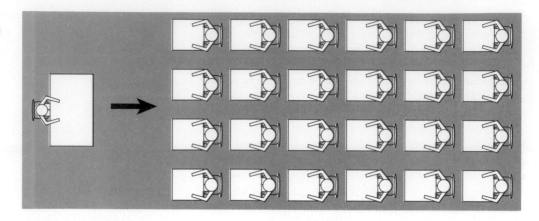

learning is one in which the teacher stands and delivers the content, while students sit and receive.

This view places the control of all planning, implementation, and evaluation in the hands of the teacher. It assumes only a slight diversity in the manner in which most students assimilate information. For some types of learning, mostly those dealing with basic rote skills, this traditional viewpoint has proven quite efficient.

The Changing Learner

In today's world, however, demands on the learner have increased substantially. Where once it may have been sufficient to learn rote responses within given working environments, now the real world demands individuals use high-order reasoning skills to solve complex problems. Access and accountability for solving complex problems are no longer left to the few; all individuals whether they are working on an assembly line, or in a corporate think tank, need problem-solving skills. As stated by Driscoll (1994), no longer can learners be viewed as "empty vessels waiting to be filled, but rather as active organisms seeking meaning" (p. 360). Learners must now be viewed as proactive participants in learning, actively seeking ways to analyze, question, interpret, and understand their ever-changing environment.

From another viewpoint, think about the average classroom from 90 years ago and the demands placed on the classroom teacher. The majority of students, and teachers as well, came from homogeneous backgrounds (e.g., grew up in the same town, raised in two-parent families with a mother who stayed at home with the kids). Today, the diversity among class members is much greater. With that diversity comes the challenge of different learning styles, greater differences in background experiences, varied home life settings, and so on. Classrooms of today are much

more diversified, leading to more complex learning problems for teachers and students alike.

A Shift Toward Learner-Centered Instruction

Today we live in an age of lightning-fast information transfer. Technology has allowed individuals to obtain, assemble, analyze, and communicate information in more detail and at a much faster pace than ever before possible. One consequence of this is the ever-increasing demand on education to help all learners acquire higher-level skills that allow them to more readily analyze, make decisions, and solve complex "real-world" problems. According to Bruer (1993), learners must rise above the rote, factual level to begin to think critically and creatively. These increased demands dictate changes in the way teachers interact with students; moreover, these changes must be grounded in an understanding of how a diverse population of individuals learns.

Throughout this text, we give examples of many techniques, methods, and technologies for helping learners acquire new knowledge. We understand that at times you will engage your students in lower-level, rote learning, and as needed we describe techniques to help learners acquire factual information. (For example, we highlight the use of mnemonics or specific drill and practice techniques for basic-level learning.) In such cases, the teacher-centered "traditional" view of teaching may prove most efficient and effective.

Of particular importance, however, will be teaching the higher-order skills now in demand and the manner in which students acquire them. Therefore, a major emphasis throughout the text is on problem solving and transfer. We emphasize the use of such methods as simulations, discovery, problem solving, and cooperative groups for learners to experience and solve real-world problems. In these cases, you will note a shift in the manner in which the learning experience is planned, implemented, and evaluated. Instead of the traditional teacher's total control and manipulation, we emphasize the importance of the learner's role in planning, implementation, and self-evaluation. As shown in Figure 1–3 learners engaged in **learner-centered instruction** proactively engage with various sources of potential information (e.g., the teacher, technology, parents, media) to gain insights into a problem and its possible solutions. The teacher's role shifts to one of guide and facilitator who assists learners in achieving their learning goals.

Table 1–1 highlights several key changes in the roles of the teacher and the learners within a learner-centered environment. As you reflect on these changing roles, imagine the impact they have on the manner in which you plan and carry out instruction. We want to emphasize that because of the diversity in both learners and information, a single approach to all instruction will not work: A

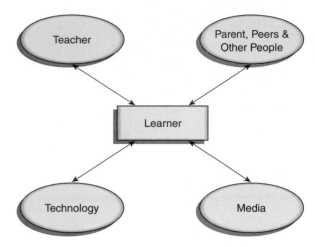

FIGURE 1–3   Learners engage proactively with various sources of information

number of different methods and media exist for designing and developing learning experiences, and the roles of learner and teacher shift based on the situation, the content, and the special needs of the individuals involved.

TABLE 1–1   *Key Teacher Role Changes In a Learner-Centered Environment*

For the TEACHER	
A shift from:	**A shift to:**
Always being viewed as the content expert and source for all of the answers	Participating at times as one who may not know it all but desires to learn
Being viewed as the primary source of information who continually directs it to students	Being viewed as a support, collaborator, and coach for students as they learn to gather and evaluate information for themselves
Always asking the questions and controlling the focus of student learning	Actively coaching students to develop and pose their own questions and explore their own alternative ways of finding answers
Directing students through preset step-by-step exercises so that all achieve similar conclusions	Actively encouraging individuals to use their personal knowledge and skills to create unique solutions to problems

For the STUDENT	
A shift from:	**A shift to:**
Passively waiting for the teacher to give directions and information	Actively searching for needed information and learning experiences, determining what is needed, and seeking ways to attain it
Always being in the role of the learner	Participating at times as the expert/knowledge provider
Always following given procedures	Desiring to explore, discover, and create unique solutions to learning problems
Viewing the teacher as the one who has all of the answers	Viewing the teacher as a resource, model, and helper who will encourage exploration and attempts to find unique solutions to problems

Reflective Questions

▶ Why has the way teachers today perceive learners changed from the early 1900s? Have economic, societal, and/or technological developments increased or decreased the extent of these perceived changes?

▶ As teachers' views of learners change, how might this impact their role as instructional experts?

LEARNING

The transition from novice to expert depends on learning. Therefore, a central focus of this text is on human learning and how it is accomplished. Even though most of us are quite familiar with the "learning experience" and we know we have "learned" in the past, there are still important questions to address:

▶ What exactly is learning?
▶ Why is the study of learning important?

What Exactly Is Learning?

It is relatively easy to cite examples of learning. For instance, reflect on the past few days or weeks and think about something you learned. Maybe it was something that required concerted time and effort, such as learning how to write a specific type of research paper. Or you learned something that needed less effort or time, such as the location of the closest parking facility for your new night class. Or possibly your learning occurred without you consciously realizing it, such as when you learned verbatim two full verses of an obnoxious jingle in a television commercial. The time, effort, and purpose involved in each of these examples varied considerably. However, in each case, learning occurred.

Learning is such a broad concept, and occurs across such a variety of subjects, that defining it concisely is not simple. Compare the following definitions:

▶ Learning is a "persisting change in human performance or performance potential [brought] about as a result of the learner's interaction with the environment" (Driscoll, 1994, pp. 8–9).

▶ "Learning occurs when experience causes a relatively permanent change in an individual's knowledge or behavior" (Woolfolk, 1998, p. 204).

The key word in these definitions is *change*. To *learn* is to change (or have the capacity to change) one's level of ability or knowledge in a permanent way. Typically, learning is measured by the amount of change that occurs within an individual's level of knowledge, performance, or behavior. To qualify as learning, Woolfolk (1998) explains, "this change must be brought about by experience—by the interaction of a person with his or her environment. Changes simply caused by maturation, such as growing taller or turning gray, do not qualify as learning" (p. 205). So, for example, as novice cabinetmakers change their behaviors and begin to consistently use wood shapers instead of routers at specific appropriate times, then we can say they have "learned." More than 60 years ago, Thorndike (1931) emphasized the importance of change by writing, "Man's power to change himself, that is, to learn, is perhaps the most impressive thing about him" (p. 3).

Why Is the Study of Learning Important?

The study of learning is important for both those who will be learning and those who will be guiding the learning of others because specific actions, techniques, and technologies can have an impact on the quantity and quality of what is learned. By understanding learning we can better design and develop strategic learning experiences.

Our emphasis is on what learners and teachers can do to positively impact learning. As shown in Figure 1–4, such things relate to the following:

▶ The *planning* required to ensure that instruction is developed and sequenced in a manner that the learner can effectively process
▶ *Implementing* the instruction
▶ *Evaluating* both the instruction and the student's resultant learning

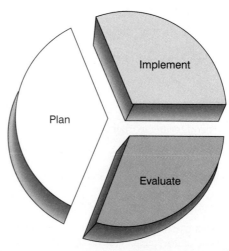

FIGURE 1–4   Plan, implement, and evaluate. The phases of learning

This emphasis can be compared to the approach of the expert cabinetmaker discussed at the beginning of the chapter. The expert is noted for planning, for understanding the strengths and weaknesses of various tools given different situations and expected outcomes, and for reflecting on and evaluating the effectiveness of the tools throughout the entire design and construction process. Throughout this text, we place a similar emphasis on *planning, implementing,* and *evaluating.*

In planning, the focus is on what students are to learn, how it might be accomplished, when, and why. The result is an outline, lesson plan, or blueprint of the learning experience that will bring about the desired goal. This plan helps to delineate learners' *present* knowledge and abilities, as well as what their knowledge and skills *should* be, and it suggests ways to reduce the difference between the two. This plan influences the manner in which you develop and present information and the learner experiences it. Section II of this text (chapters 4–6) focuses on planning.

Implementation focuses on putting the plan into action based on what situational constraints exist, using selected instructional materials and activities. For learners, implementation is when, where, and how they experience learning. For the teacher, implementation includes monitoring and managing the instruction, groups of learners, and individuals with special needs. Section III, chapters 7–9, explores implementation in greater detail.

The emphasis during evaluation is on the assessment of two things: (1) the effectiveness of the materials, and (2) the overall learning students achieved. This is a time to reflect on what was accomplished, to compare that with your desired goal, to suggest changes in future planning and implementation, and to complete suggested revisions and fix-ups. Section IV, Chapter 10, focuses on evaluation.

In Section V, Chapter 11, we explore instructional technology's current trends and possible future directions of development.

Another related question addressing the importance of the study of learning focuses on the benefits. Are the potential outcomes worth the investment of effort? The positive outcomes listed below can justify the study of learning and the use of strategic instruction.

▶ Increased **instructional effectiveness.** In this case students actually learn in a better way than they would without the experience. Increased effectiveness includes greater recall accuracy, longer retention, and better transfer and generalization of skills and knowledge to similar or dissimilar situations.

▶ Increased **instructional efficiency.** Here the focus is on time. You may gain efficiency through reducing the time required to design and develop the instruction, or through better or quicker means of instructional delivery. Efficiency may also relate to the manner in which students acquire skills and knowledge, reducing the amount of time they need to learn new information.

▶ Increased **instructional appeal.** Another outcome—often neglected and forgotten, but critical to the success of instruction—is its appeal to both teacher and student. Increasing the appeal enhances the possibility that students will devote time and energy to the learning task and increases the likelihood they will return to review and work on the material at other times. Appeal is strongly associated with learners' attitudes toward the information and their motivation for studying the subject.

Reflective Questions

▶ What role does the learner play in the planning, implementation, and evaluation phases of learning?

▶ In what ways do planning, implementation, and evaluation potentially contribute to the effectiveness, efficiency, and appeal of the instructional experience?

TECHNOLOGY

Technology is an important concept that is addressed throughout this text. Formally stated, **technology** is defined as "the systematic application of scientific or other organized knowledge to practical tasks" (Galbraith, 1967, p. 12). In this sense technology performs a bridging function between research and theoretical explorations on the one side and the real-world problems faced by practitioners on the other (see Figure 1–5).

The space industry offers a good example. Numerous practical problems have been encountered as humans have traveled in space (e.g., How does one breathe in a place devoid of oxygen?). To solve such problems, contributions from physics, materials science, and other fields of research had to be translated to practical applications. In many cases the results were tangible products such as the space shuttle, space suits, and advanced telecommunications capabilities. In other situations, the resultant tools and products have taken not-so-tangible forms such as enhanced safety procedures, formulas for

FIGURE 1–5 The bridge of technology between research and practical problems

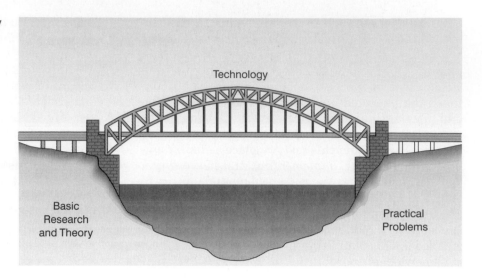

reentry projections, and backup contingency plans. In each instance, scientific knowledge was reviewed and applied to answer specific practical problems.

What Exactly Is Instructional Technology?

Just as there is space technology, engineering technology, and medical technology that bridge basic research and practical problem areas in these specializations, there is also instructional technology. Generalizing from the previous definition, **instructional technology** has been defined as "applying scientific knowledge about human learning to the practical tasks of teaching and learning" (Heinich, Molenda, & Russell, 1993, p. 16). Specifically, instructional technology is the bridge between those who conduct research on human learning (e.g., psychologists, linguists) and those who are teaching and learning (see Figure 1–6). That is, instructional technology translates and applies basic research on human learning to produce instructional design principles and processes as well as hardware products that teachers and students can use to increase learning effectiveness.

In today's language, when most people use the word *technology,* they are referring to so-called "high-tech" equipment or hardware, such as computers, CD and DVD players, cellular telephones, even satellites. And indeed, these tangible items are part of our definition of instructional technology. But view Figure 1–7 and then review our vision statement for this textbook (p. 5). As the figure shows, instructional technology is a means of connecting the teacher, the instructional experience, and learners in ways that enhance learning. The use of "high-tech" hardware is one way to make these connections; another is to use instructional media such as textbooks,

overhead projectors and transparencies, and audiotapes. A third way is through the use of less tangible tools, such as instructional design principles and instructional strategies, methods, and techniques. These less tangible instructional technologies are sometimes referred to as **process technologies.**

Just as expert cabinetmakers view their tools as being necessary for the successful completion of many tasks, so must students and teachers come to view available instructional tools. This text will explore these uses of instructional technology and demonstrate how, when, and why they are relevant to both learners and teachers when planning, implementing, and evaluating learning. It is our desire to show that just as cabinetmakers can increase their level of performance by correctly selecting and using tools of their trade, students and teachers can elevate their level of performance with the proper use of tools designed for the improvement of human learning.

Now that we have defined learning and instructional technology, it is time to address the three points on our triangle: The learners, the teacher, and the instruction. We will discuss these participants and aspects of learning using the plan, implement, and evaluate structure that chapters 4–10 are based on.

THE ACTIVE EXPERT LEARNER

As can be expected in any learning task, the individual doing the learning plays a central role. Although some view the learner as an empty, passive vessel waiting to be filled, others see the learner as one who actively constructs and processes new information (Ertmer & Newby, 1993). Of central concern here is what individuals can do that will facilitate their overall learning. Through the observation and study of various "strategic" or "expert" learners (Weinstein

FIGURE 1–6 The bridge of instructional technology between research on learning and practical teaching and learning problems

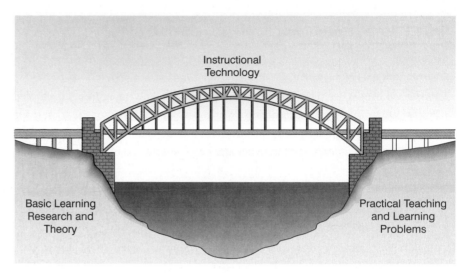

FIGURE 1–6 The bridge of instructional technology between research on learning and practical teaching and learning problems

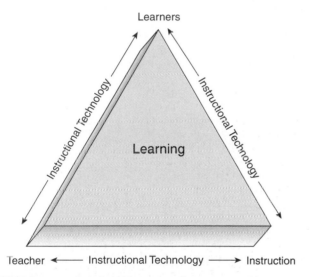

FIGURE 1–7 Relationship among learners, teacher, instruction, and instructional technology

& Van Mater Stone, 1993), we can highlight several important actions learners take that assist their own learning.

First, when given a new task to learn, the strategic learner, just like an expert craftsperson, frequently spends time **planning** and preparing a course of action. This preparation often includes the review of personal resources. For instance, learners can use past strategies and tactics to learn and remember new information (e.g., using simple rehearsal techniques for memorizing passages of information; using analogies to highlight how the new information is similar to what they already know), or use familiar motivational strategies to maintain interest and levels of effort (e.g., determining reasons for learning the new material). Additionally, learners

can analyze the task and the environment to determine if the task requires a specific type of strategy or technique (e.g., summarizing the main idea of each paragraph, paraphrasing new definitions) or if the environment contains any obstacles they must overcome to accomplish the task (e.g., distracting background noises, insufficient lighting).

Learners all plan differently depending on their abilities and previous experiences. Although experts may readily review their resources and select appropriate strategies based on past experience, many young, novice, or less sophisticated learners may have few resources to draw on, little experience in analyzing what a new task requires, and/or inadequate ability to match current resources with the needs of the task. As shown through the work of Weinstein and Van Mater Stone (1993), novices can learn these strategies and selection mechanisms to become more strategic learners. In this case their focus is not just on learning task content but also on *learning how to learn*.

A second important action occurs while **implementing** the learning experience. Here strategic learners concentrate on the task and on using and monitoring the effects of selected learning and motivational strategies. During this phase learners monitor learning and motivational progress, revising selected strategies as obstacles are encountered. Additionally, they monitor the means used to present the task content, the amount, sequence, and speed of information presented, and how successfully the presentation maintains their attention and motivation.

Finally, strategic learners spend time **evaluating** the impact of the experience and the effectiveness of the employed strategies. This is a period of reflecting and revising as needed. Learners who have

---

TABLE 1–2   *Questions Learners Should Ask During Each Instructional Phase*

Planning

- What is the goal of this task (i.e., What am I supposed to learn?)?
- What will I need to learn this task (e.g., learning strategies, assistance from others, time, effort)?
- In what ways can my previous learning experiences help?
- What obstacles and problems could hinder me from learning this task?
- How will my motivation and effort in this task be generated and maintained (e.g., Am I good at this kind of task? Do I like this kind of work?)?
- How should I approach this task in order to learn effectively while maintaining my motivation and overcoming presented obstacles (e.g., Does this type of activity require a great deal of concentration?)?

Implementation

- How do I assemble or create what I need to carry out the plan?
- How do I begin and follow the planned learning strategies?
- Is this going the way I planned?
- Do I understand what I am doing?
- What outside materials or resources should I add?
- What should I look for to tell if I am in fact learning?
- How can I tell if my task motivation is being maintained?

Evaluation

- Did I learn everything I needed to, as thoroughly as possible?
- What obstacles did I encounter, and what strategies were or were not effective in overcoming those problems?
- What did I do when selected tactics and learning strategies didn't work?
- What have I learned from this experience that I could use at other times for different tasks?
- What improvements could I make for future learning tasks?

---

not reached their learning goals may choose to plan and implement new strategies.

As shown in Table 1–2, students can ask key questions during planning, implementation, and evaluation to focus on how they can facilitate their learning. We suggest you consider these questions as you attempt to learn the content of this text. Additionally, you can use these questions to prompt and cue novice learners in your own classroom as they encounter new tasks. (These questions also appear on the inside cover of this book for easy access and review.)

THE TEACHER AS INSTRUCTIONAL EXPERT

In most educational settings, another key ingredient for learning is the teacher. Although teachers frequently serve in roles from administrator to surrogate parent, the most important function is that which Woolfolk (1990) refers to as the "instructional

expert." In this capacity teachers plan, implement, and evaluate instructional activities. The instructional expert's involvement can range from little actual interaction with students (e.g., when devoting time and effort to developing learning activities) to a high amount of group or individual interaction (e.g., when presenting new materials to students in a lecture or discussion format).

Over the years the functions of teachers as instructional experts have remained relatively constant. Whether direct or indirect, good or bad, teachers heavily influence what students experience and subsequently learn in the classroom. Even in situations where students have more control (e.g., a discovery/exploratory environment, individualized instruction), the teacher selects or arranges the activities and gives guidance and clarification. Because of this critical role, *this text will focus on what you as an instructional expert should know and do so that your students can learn.*

TABLE 1–3   *Questions Teachers Should Ask During Each Instructional Phase*

Planning

- What task must students be able to do, and how can I determine when it has been accomplished?
- What do students already know that will assist in learning this task?
- What is the best medium to assist students in learning the new information?
- What information should the instructional materials or activities include?
- What relevant instructional materials (or parts thereof) already exist? Which materials will I need to adapt? Which materials will I need to create?
- What resources, facilities, and equipment are available and accessible?
- In what order should I arrange the learning activities?
- Based on need and practicality, what approaches and media should I include or have students include in the instruction?
- What is the most effective, efficient, and appealing manner in which students can learn the task?
- What can be done to help this learning be transferred to other similar situations?

Implementation

- How will I manage the instructional experience and activities?
- How will I manage groups of learners as well as individuals with special needs during their learning experience?
- During the learning process, how will I maintain students' attention and motivation?

Evaluation

- How can I determine how well students have learned the material?
- How will I teach and encourage student self-evaluation and regulation?
- What types of remediation or enrichment activities may be necessary?
- In what ways can I improve these instructional materials and activities for repeated or adapted use?
- How will I monitor these needed changes throughout students' learning experience?

Similar to those principles outlined for learners, instructional principles for teachers are based on planning, implementing, and evaluating. As defined by Reigeluth (1983), **planning** involves "the process of deciding what methods of instruction are best for bringing about desired changes in student knowledge and skills for a specific course content and a specific student population" (p. 7). Teachers identify students' instructional needs by identifying existing gaps between current and desired levels of skills and knowledge, then select instructional methods and strategies to meet these needs. Other considerations at this time include the type of learners they are dealing with and the teacher's own personal style of teaching. The principal result is a plan or blueprint of instruction, which includes learning content, which strategies and activities to use, when to use them, and how to structure them. Table 1–3 identifies key questions that teachers should ask during this stage. (These questions also appear on this text's inside cover.) Note that the questions do not dictate a single role for the teacher. In some cases the teacher plans, presents, and controls the instruction, but in others it may be controlled totally by individual learners.

Another frequent teacher role is as **implementer** of instruction. After teachers assemble or produce needed instructional materials, they then orchestrate the instructional experience. Ideally, teachers follow a previously completed plan or one suggested by other teachers or curriculum experts, and the needed instruction is brought together or developed into a finished product, in the form of lecture notes, videotapes, reading assignments, small-group activities, computer programs, guided discovery activities, or a mixture of all of these.

At this point the teacher becomes a "director of learning activities" (Ausubel, Novak, & Hanesian, 1978). This may require the teacher to personally disseminate information through some form of expository lecture, inquiry discussion, or demonstration, to serve as manager of other learning vehicles (e.g., video presentation, small-group discussion), or to become a guide/coach who encourages and helps

Toolbox: Tools, Tips, and Techniques

As you venture through this text, note that we have inserted special short features called "Toolboxes." Just as a cabinetmaker's toolbox holds valuable things that allow him to successfully complete his job, our toolboxes contain items that will play a role in your success as both teacher and learner.

Similar to the builder's toolbox, the ones in this text contain a variety of items. Each one of these will be designated as a "tool," a "tip," or a "technique." Toolboxes appear strategically throughout the text because of our desire for you to immediately see their value and worth. Instead of giving you a long list of tools in an appendix, for example, our goal was to locate individual toolboxes where their need was apparent and where we could illustrate an example of its use. In that manner, you can read about the tool, tip, or technique in the inserted toolbox on the same page that you can see its value and potential usefulness.

The **TOOL** toolbox will generally focus on hardware or software that you will find helpful in specific situations. We might, for example, discuss scanners, digital cameras, or graphic software that could help as you develop instructional materials.

The **TIP** toolbox will be devoted to giving you insight on things that the authors and others have learned through experience that warn you of potential problems and help you accomplish your job in a more professional and efficient manner. Examples include, "How to use visuals in instructional materials." and "Care of computer systems."

The **TECHNIQUE** toolbox will be devoted to different types of instructional techniques that have been shown effective in improving learning, for example, mnemonics, analogies, reflection, and debriefings.

We could not, of course, include everything you will need for all learning situations. We had to be very selective. This is our way of helping you begin to develop a toolbox of your own. Some of these items you may find you need and use daily, others you may use only on a very limited basis. It is important for you to understand that this is just a beginning. Throughout this text and as you venture on through your career, you will continue to add relevant tools, tips, and techniques to your learning toolbox.

students experience learning on their own. The primary outcome is that the student experiences the instruction.

The final role for the instructional expert is that of **evaluator** of both student learning and the overall effectiveness, efficiency, and appeal of the instruction. Teachers traditionally have done this by examining how well students completed the lesson and by determining if they have attained the desired level of performance. Increasing attention is now being focused on providing continuous evaluation throughout all stages of learning (Stiggins, 1997). Evaluation should also be a time to reflect on successes achieved and problems encountered. The evaluation's result is a description of the strengths and weaknesses of the program, which teachers may then use for instructional improvement.

For most teachers, planning, implementing, and evaluating instruction are all ongoing processes. On any given day a teacher may plan and develop several future lessons, monitor current topics to ensure that they are being properly addressed, and reflect on completed lessons and the results they produced.

THE ROLE OF INSTRUCTION

Instruction is "the deliberate arrangement of learning conditions to promote the attainment of some intended goal" (Driscoll, 1994, p. 332). In this text, the role of instruction is to use instructional technologies in ways that maximize students' learning. The extent to which these technologies enhance teaching and learning is determined by the degree to which you properly select individual teaching and learning tools and learn to use them interdependently.

In many cases individuals take one course to learn how to design and develop instructional materials, another course to learn about different forms of media and how to use them properly, and still another to learn how to use the computer in the classroom. Although such a disjointed approach may give students a solid background in all three individual areas of study, it may limit their ability to see how each area may expand the effectiveness of the others. We feel that such an approach, while better than not having any courses, can be improved by emphasizing the relationships among these areas. It is only

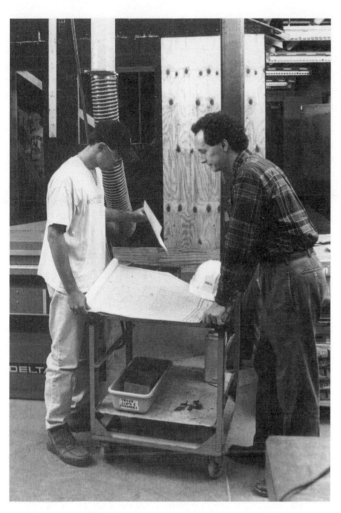

Blueprints are critical for successful planning and development.

through an integrated approach that teachers can identify and solve the more difficult problems of human learning. Through such an integrated approach teachers may readily see how computers can contribute to designing the instructional plan and developing the instructional materials, how the design directs the media selection, and, likewise, how using the media affects students' interpretation and acceptance of the designed instructional message. Although you could study instructional design, media, and computing independently, viewing them as an interrelated whole magnifies their potential for teacher and student alike.

Instructional Design

Designing instruction is the process of translating principles of learning and instruction into plans for instructional materials and activities (Smith & Ragan, 1999, p. 2). The emphasis is on creating a plan for developing instructional materials and activities

that increase an individual's learning. Reigeluth (1983) compared this task with that of an architect. The architect produces a blueprint or plan that effectively integrates the needs of those who will purchase and use the facility, the environment in which it will exist, the costs involved, the appropriate materials, and other design specifications for functionality, safety, and aesthetics. Similarly, instructional experts incorporate learning principles into plans for instructional materials and activities based on analyses of the learners, the situation, and the task or content to be learned.

Although a builder may attempt to build a structure without using the architect's plans or blueprints, he may encounter problems he could have avoided by using a plan—walls may be in the wrong location, electrical outlets forgotten or misplaced, or improper materials purchased. As with any plan, the major benefit of an instructional plan is the guidance it gives. This does not mean that all instruction should be designed based on a single set of plans (like a subdivision of one-style homes), but rather that specific principles can be used to solve different instructional problems and to produce unique solutions in a variety of situations.

Power of the Plan

The overall **instructional plan** plays a critical role in directing the selection and use of all other tools within the learning environment. Just as the cabinetmaker uses a plan to determine what materials and woodworking tools to select and use, so too the teacher and learners should use an instructional plan to determine the methods, techniques, and media they will use. Additionally, the plan helps to determine how and when to present specific sets of information and when additional information is required.

Even though a plan gives teachers direction, it should not be perceived as a rigid structure that dictates regimented, systematic procedures. Whenever learning is required, different types of learners, tasks, and situations all interact, requiring flexibility. The plan provides a means to review alternative possible solutions to instructional problems, assess their potential, and then confidently select the best. If and when those alternatives do not produce desired levels of learning, the plan can be revised and additional alternatives selected. Robinson (1981) notes that expert fishermen usually outperform those of lesser ability, not because they know the best bait for a given fish on a specific day, but because they also know the second- and third-best alternatives. Similarly, the power of the instructional plan is that it

TABLE 1–4   *Types of Instructional Tools: Methods, Techniques, and Activities*

Instructional Methods (Chapters 5 and 7)	Instructional Techniques	Instructional Activities (Chapter 4)
Cooperative learning	Focusing questions (Chapter 2)	Motivation activities
Discovery	Highlighting (Chapter 2)	Orientation activities
Problem solving	Analogies (Chapter 2)	Information activities
Instructional games	Mnemonics (Chapter 2)	Application activities
Simulation	Imagery (Chapter 2)	Evaluation activities
Discussion	Concept maps (Chapter 4)	
Drill and practice	Embedded questions (Chapter 4)	
Tutorial	Feedback (Chapter 4)	
Demonstration	Case studies (Chapter 5)	
Presentation	Role playing (Chapter 5)	

suggests alternatives and a means whereby they can be investigated and evaluated before investing time and money in developing the final products.

Aspects of instructional design include

▶ the overall instructional plan—what to include and how to arrange the components
▶ various analysis techniques and methods that help determine both learners' current skill levels and those needed to accomplish the task
▶ analysis techniques to determine what information students are to learn and what should receive the focus of the instruction
▶ a repertoire of methods, techniques, and activities that can be used to increase student learning (Table 1–4)
▶ strategies for sequencing instructional materials so that learners get the proper amount of information when needed
▶ an emphasis on evaluation to ensure that the instructional materials and procedures resulted in students achieving the desired goals

This text explains how to design instruction so that learners and teachers all may benefit.

Process Technologies   Table 1–4 lists process technologies, instructional tools that aid in instructional design. These include methods, techniques, and activities teachers may use to create and augment successful instructional materials. We discuss these process technologies in greater detail throughout the text.

Specific chapters have been devoted to the discussion of instructional methods (chapters 5 and 7) and instructional activities (Chapter 4). Instruc-

tional techniques are integrated throughout Section II within various Toolbox: Technique features.

Instructional Media

Instructional media are "a means by which information can be delivered to a learner" (Heinich et al., 1993, p. 5). In one case the selected medium may be videotape, in another it may be audiotape, in still another it may be computer software. Each medium represents a means of connecting learners, the teacher, and the instruction. Table 1–5 lists several forms of media, each with its own set of unique attributes. Important questions involving the manner in which learners experience information include the following:

▶ What forms of media are available?
▶ What impact do the different media formats have on learning?
▶ Under what conditions can this potential impact be altered?
▶ How is each media format most effectively used?

When investigating the answers to these and similar questions, research in the areas of perception, cognition, communication, and instructional theory comes to the forefront. For every learner and teacher, the central concerns are how information is structured and what happens once individuals have perceived and experienced it. Research shows that various forms of media and their respective selection and utilization processes directly impact what learners perceive and how they retain and recall information (Kozma, 1991).

TABLE 1–5   *Types of Media with Attributes and Examples*

Instructional Media	Key Attributes	Example
Real objects and models	Actual item or three-dimensional representation	A living animal A plastic model of the human eye
Text	Written words	Biology textbook Written material from an electronic encyclopedia
Video	Moving pictures	Instructional video on the procedures to insert memory chips in a computer Video on how to seek shelter during a tornado
Audio	Sound	Audio CD of an inspirational speech Audiotape of directions for completing a process
Graphics (visuals, slides, overhead transparencies)	Pictures, line drawings, maps	Projected overhead transparency of the state of South Carolina Map of the organizational structure of a school corporation
Multimedia	Combination of various media forms	Computer program on comparative culture that incorporates pictures, textual descriptions, native music, and short videos of individuals speaking different languages

Students learn through various media formats.

Instructional media for teachers and learners can be used to

▶ present materials in a manner learners readily assimilate (e.g., a video can clearly illustrate how cells divide in the early stages of reproduction)
▶ deliver materials independently of the teacher, thus allowing students some control over how much of the material they will experience and when (e.g., students can rewind or fast-forward portions of a video- or audiotape to match their own learning needs)
▶ allow learners to experience materials through various senses (e.g., seeing projected slides, reading textual materials, and hearing a verbal description of the same content)

▶ provide learners with repeated and varied experiences with subject matter to help them construct their own understanding or meaning
▶ gain and maintain learners' attention on the subject matter
▶ motivate students toward a goal
▶ present information in a manner that individual learners otherwise could not experience (e.g., events can be speeded up or slowed down, objects can be decreased in size [e.g., the universe] or increased in size [e.g., an atom])
▶ accommodate varying sizes of audiences

Power of the Learning Experience

Review the list of media forms presented in Table 1–5. Teachers can use all of these to help students learn. The question is, "Why do we need all of the different types of media?" For example, isn't an overhead projector an effective medium for delivering information to students? Why then are videos, computer software, textbooks, and so on also used? The answer lies with the learning experience itself. Various levels of content, types of learners, and learning situations dictate that some media formats are at times better suited or more feasible than other formats.

Each medium has its own set of unique characteristics, and how people interact with a message is shaped by the medium's particular attributes. For that reason, it is important to understand what each medium can contribute to the learning environment.

For example, readers make use of the stable quality of information presented in the traditional textbook. When they encounter a difficult passage, learners can slow down, reread portions, skip back and forth, refer to pictures or diagrams, and so on. As learners struggle to create meaning from information in a textbook, their interaction with the *book* is dependent, to a great extent, on the characteristics of that medium.

Throughout this text we will emphasize the importance of correctly selecting and utilizing these various forms of media. *It is critical to keep in mind that no matter how good the medium, learning will be hindered if the message is poorly designed. Learning also will be obstructed if the message is well designed but delivered in such a fashion that the learner can't understand or interpret it correctly.* The power of the learning experience very much depends on the learners' experiences. The media format dictates how the instruction will be delivered and how learners will subsequently experience it. Clearly, media play a critical role in the overall learning process.

Instructional Computing

The computer has made a tremendous impact throughout our society, and that impact has been particularly strong within the field of education. **Instructional computing** is defined as the use of the computer in the design, development, delivery, and evaluation of instruction. The computer's power within education is due to its versatility as both a production and a presentation tool. Although it is a form of media and should be considered as such, the computer's capability to be *both* a presentation and production tool sets it apart from other media formats (e.g., slides, videos). For example, in a single day a classroom computer may be used to write a creative short story about a character from the Wild West, to monitor on the Internet the current shape and velocity of a tropical storm off the coast of Florida, to store scores from the last social studies assignment, and to look up information on Nelson Mandela and listen to parts of his major speeches. These examples illustrate the power of the computer in teaching and learning.

Because of its current impact and tremendous potential, it is imperative that classroom teachers understand the power of the computer and how they can use and adapt it for learning. Throughout this text, we devote sections to explaining how you may use the computer, when and why it is a valuable asset, and how to integrate it in the classroom to ensure the maximum effect on your teaching and on your students' learning.

Instructional computing for teachers and learners can be used to

- enhance the quality of instructional materials using the electronic capabilities of the computer
- reduce the time required to design, produce, and reproduce instructional materials
- increase the overall effectiveness of instructional materials through enhanced presentations
- combine graphics, video, audio, and textual forms of media into single, integrated instructional presentations
- store and quickly access huge amounts of information and data
- communicate with others at both near and distant locations
- function as a learner, in which the student programs the computer to complete a task or to solve a problem
- function as an instructional expert, in which the computer makes decisions about levels of student learning, suggests media and learning experiences to students, and then selects and presents those media and experiences.

Power of the Machine

The real power of the computer is in its versatility. At times it becomes an assistant, helping to manage classroom and instructional development efforts. At other times, it can become the actual way through which students experience the instructional activities and learn content. In still other cases, it becomes the means by which students attempt to solve complex problems. This versatility, coupled with its power to store, access, and manipulate huge amounts of information, is why so much attention has been devoted to computers in education.

What is the role of instruction in the learning process? This question and others like it (Table 1–6) can help you focus on how to use the tools of instructional design, instructional media, and computing when planning, implementing, and evaluating your teaching and your students' learning. (See similar questions inside front cover of this text.)

Reflective Questions

- In what ways can the instructional plan influence implementing and evaluating learning?
- How do process technologies relate to high-tech hardware and other media technologies? Is it important to differentiate among these different types of technologies?

TABLE 1–6   *Questions Teachers Should Ask About Instruction and Instructional Technology During the Phases of Learning*

Planning

• In what ways can instructional technology effectively impact how students address a learning task?

• In what ways can instructional process technologies (e.g., methods, techniques) and high-tech and other media technologies effectively impact how I design and create instructional materials?

• How can I or my students improve learner attention and topic motivation with instructional technology?

• How can instructional technology improve the efficiency of my preparation and/or my students' learning?

Implementation

• How can instructional technology assist and impact the manner in which students experience instruction?

• How may I use instructional technology to teach more efficiently?

Evaluation

• How can I use technology to determine the degree of student learning that has occurred?

• How can I use technology to collect student feedback?

• In what ways can I use technology to measure the effectiveness, efficiency, and appeal of implemented instructional materials?

Elementary school children develop a class web page.

APPLICATIONS IN THE LEARNER-CENTERED CLASSROOM

In this section of each chapter, we will discuss how you may apply selected principles discussed in the chapter to a learner-centered classroom environment. This section is designed to generate ideas and questions, and give relevant application examples, to help lead you to higher levels of learning for yourself and your future students.

In these application sections we will focus on one or more key assumptions about the learner-centered classroom. We will highlight and give examples of ways in which instructional technology (including high-tech hardware, media, and process technologies) can facilitate the development of such a learning environment. We will conclude most chap-

ters by telling the continuing story of one teacher and her attempts to create a learner-centered environment for her students.

In this first chapter, it is key for you to understand the relationship between learning and **instructional technology.** Technology supplies teachers and students tools to increase the effectiveness, efficiency, and appeal of the learning experience. *Within the learner-centered classroom engendering learner activity and exploration is of paramount importance. Learning requires exploring possible avenues to uncover potential solutions.* As stated by Jonassen, Peck, and Wilson (1999, p. 3), "Knowledge is embedded in activity." Focusing on the learner means that you, the teacher, design experiences in which learners frequently face problems that require their active exploration to solve. Information is not just transmitted to passive students; they must actively seek it and find ways to adapt it to create personal meaning.

To facilitate learner exploration through the use of instructional technology, students first must have the following: (1) a means whereby to explore, (2) motivation to explore, and (3) some way to organize gathered information to gain understanding. Could access to huge amounts of information via multimedia CD-ROMs, the Internet, libraries, and so on give students the means to explore? Could immediate access via electronic data retrieval mechanisms increase their motivation and exploratory behaviors? How may you provide examples, nonexamples, or modeling to help students organize their data into potential solutions?

The Standards and this Textbook

What is it that you really know about the computer? So much information is coming out each day about new developments, new uses, new software that it can get overwhelming. What is it then, that teachers need to be able to do with this technology, so that they can really function in the classroom of the twenty-first century? These are questions that many teacher preparation colleges and professional educational organizations are asking. In an effort to help prepare teachers, professional standards are currently being developed. Teachers can use these standards to help plan learning experiences, as well as evaluate progress in developing needed teaching tools.

The National Council for Accreditation of Teacher Education (NCATE) is the official body for accrediting teacher preparation programs. The International Society for Technology in Education (ISTE) is the professional education organization responsible for recommending guidelines for accreditation to NCATE for programs in educational technology teacher preparation.

ISTE has defined the following major standard categories for all preservice teacher preparation programs:

A. *Basic Computer/Technology Operations and Concepts.* Candidates will use computer systems to run software; to access, generate, and manipulate data; and to publish results. They will also evaluate performance of hardware and software components of computer systems and apply basic troubleshooting strategies as needed.

B. *Personal and Professional Use of Technology.* Candidates will apply tools for enhancing their own professional growth and productivity. They will use technology in communicating, collaborating, conducting research, and solving problems. In addition, they will plan and participate in activities that encourage lifelong learning and will promote equitable, ethical, and legal use of computer/technology resources.

C. *Application of Technology in Instruction.* Candidates will apply computers and related technologies to support instruction in their grade level and subject areas. They must plan and deliver instructional units that integrate a variety of software, applications, and learning tools. Lessons developed must reflect effective grouping and assessment strategies for diverse populations.

In this textbook, we address the Basic Computer/Technology Operations and Concepts standards in chapters 3 and 8, Appendix A, and within Toolbox features throughout the book. Information pertaining to the Personal and Professional Use of Technology standards appears in chapters 8 and 9. We address the Application of Technology in Instruction standards in chapters 2, 4–7, and 10. We have looked closely at the ISTE standards and have attempted to provide information and examples to help you to achieve and exceed them.

Appendix C lists the full set of foundation standards in technology for all teachers. You can also check for updates at the ISTE Website (http://www.iste.org/Resources/Projects/TechStandards)

ONE TEACHER'S STORY

by Janette Moreno

Let me introduce myself. I am Janette Moreno, and I have been teaching high school Spanish for eight years. I want to provide my students with challenging, stimulating, and enjoyable learning experiences, so I continually evaluate their interest and performance and seek innovative ways to improve those areas that seem weak. Over the last few years, I've turned more and more to the instructional technology literature for ideas regarding course enhancements. In particular, my efforts have resulted in what I would call a more learner-centered classroom. I'd like to share with you some of the things I have learned and describe how I have gradually integrated a number of new technologies into my Spanish Conversation class. I hope that you will enjoy, and benefit from, my story.

Although my class is Spanish Conversation, one of my goals is for students to gain cross-cultural experiences. I feel that such experiences help my students understand why native language speakers respond the way they do, use different types of word intonations, body language, and facial expressions as they converse. An appreciation and understanding of each of these are critical before full communication can occur. These are tough parts of communication—but they are critical to full understanding.

Ms. Janette Moreno is teaching students in her Spanish Conversation class.

When I explained this desire to my class, one student suggested that it might help if the class first studied the word intonations and nonverbal behaviors in their own culture then expand that to the study of Spanish-speaking cultures. This activity quickly developed into one in which small groups of students videotaped friends and relatives and then compared and analyzed the interviews. Some students began searching for information to help them interpret facial expressions and other nonverbal forms of communication. They were able to quickly locate relevant information via the Internet and the local city library.

After this activity, I began to show students short segments of videos and multimedia CD-ROM software with video clips of native Spanish-speaking individuals

conversing. Students quickly began to examine the different types of nonverbal communication that were occurring. They were not only able to perceive many different expressions, they also began to question whether specific expressions meant the same thing for those individuals speaking Spanish as they did within their own culture. They discussed ways to interpret them and why the differences could exist.

I found the use of multiple types of media, the Internet, and methods such as discussions and small cooperative groups all to be very effective. Moreover, these technologies and processes enhanced students' opportunities to explore and attempt to establish personal meaning from the materials. My goal was for my students to communicate more effectively, and their attempts at exploring nonverbal communication elements helped them to achieve this goal.

SUMMARY

In this chapter we have introduced several initial key concepts. We defined *learning* as a change in or potential to change one's level of skill or knowledge, and it is of central concern for both students and teachers. We emphasized that the design and use of effective, efficient, and appealing instruction can enhance learning.

Learning is difficult to measure and to consistently achieve because of the inherent differences in learners, content, and contexts. Facilitating learning requires an active knowledge of a variety of tools and techniques plus an understanding of how, when, and why they should be appropriately used. Instructional technology, includes tangible tools (high-tech hardware such as computers, and instructional media such as overhead transparencies and video tapes) as well as process technologies (methods, techniques, and activities) for planning, implementing, and evaluating effective learning experiences.

Learners, teachers, and instruction all play key roles in the learning process. Furthermore, each of these roles shifts as the instructional focus changes from planning, to implementing, and to evaluating instruction.

REFLECTIVE ACTIVITIES

▶ Reflect on things you have learned in the past and note the impact of the technologies used. What planning was involved? What hardware or media were used? What went especially well

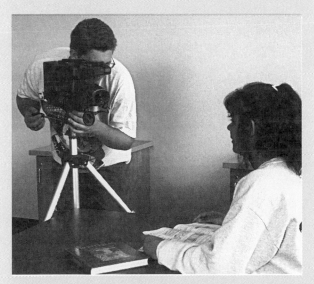

Some of Ms. Moreno's students are videotaping conversations and interviews to analyze nonverbal behaviors.

(e.g., What did you grasp from the very beginning?)? What other methods could have been as effective, if not better?

▶ If you were asked to give a talk (e.g., on the care of pets) to a class of third graders, what questions would you ask yourself while planning, implementing, and evaluating your presentation?

▶ Convince a skeptic of the benefits of reflecting on and evaluating instructional materials. Explain why this effort is necessary.

▶ Keep a notebook/diary for the next two weeks on the instructional technologies that you encounter. Note the type of instruction, how it was planned and sequenced, what type of media was used in the delivery, and what forms of evaluation you believe were used. Also note the level of effectiveness you felt the instruction achieved.

SUGGESTED RESOURCES

Driscoll, M. P. (1994). *Psychology of learning for instruction.* Boston: Allyn & Bacon. (Chapter 1)

Jonassen, D. H., Peck, K. L., & Wilson, B. G. (1999). *Learning with technology: A constructivist approach.* Upper Saddle River, NJ: Merrill/Prentice Hall. (Chapter 1)

Seels, B. B., & Richey, R. C. (1994). *Instructional technology: The definition and domains of the field.* Washington, DC: Association for Educational Communications and Technology. (Chapter 1)

Smith, P. L., & Ragan, T. J. (1999). *Instructional design.* Upper Saddle River, NJ: Merrill/Prentice Hall.

Woolfolk, A. E. (1998). *Educational psychology.* Boston: Allyn & Bacon.

C H A P T E R

2

Theory into Application

OUTLINE

INTRODUCTION

THE VALUE OF THEORY

LEARNING THEORY

Behavioral Perspective

Information Processing Perspective

Constructivist Perspective

SELECTING THEORETICAL PRINCIPLES

APPLICATIONS IN THE LEARNER-CENTERED CLASSROOM

SUMMARY

REFLECTIVE ACTIVITIES

SUGGESTED RESOURCES

KEY WORDS AND CONCEPTS

Theory
Learning theory
Antecedent
Behavior
Consequence
Attention
Encoding
Retrieval

OBJECTIVES

After reading and studying this chapter, you will be able to

▶ Explain *theory* and describe its practical value.
▶ Discuss the role of the instructional expert from three theoretical perspectives on learning.

PLANNING FOR THE CHAPTER CONTENT

Instructional Technology for Teaching and Learning, will show you how to increase learning by designing lessons that use instructional technology, including computers and other media.

This chapter focuses on the concept of *learning*. In Chapter 1 we defined learning and discussed how understanding it will make us all better learners and better teachers. In this chapter we discuss learning from three different theoretical perspectives: behavioral, information processing, and constructivist. We take a practical approach, describing applications of each learning theory.

INTRODUCTION

Cynthia, a friend of ours, has been a teacher for a number of years. Over lunch one day our conversation turned naturally to the subject of teaching. We mentioned that a lot had been written about educational theory over the years and asked her what theoretical principles she found most useful. Cynthia laughed and said, "The only thing I remember about any theory is that I'm supposed to bribe the kids with candy." She went on to explain that in the "real world" teachers have too much to do to spend much time thinking about theory. "Not only that," she said. "There are so many conflicting theories out there and the theories are so abstract and artificial that they don't seem relevant to what goes on in my classroom. They just don't seem to offer much in the way of practical advice."

TABLE 2–1   *Examples of Professions and Their Theoretical Foundations*

Profession	Theoretical Foundations
Music	Harmony
	Tonality
	Rhythm
Medicine	Biochemistry
	Anatomy
	Physiology
Teaching	Learning theory
	Motivational theory
	Communication theory

Cynthia has raised a legitimate issue about practical relevance: Is it important for teachers to understand learning theory? Initially, you might think the answer is "No." After all, teachers are practitioners who are rightly concerned with what happens in real classrooms with real students. And as Cynthia said, theory often seems too abstract and artificial to apply to the practical concerns of classroom life. In addition, sorting through the apparently conflicting claims of different theories is a time-consuming challenge. With all the demands on their time, is it really necessary for teachers to take the time to study theory?

Our answer is an unqualified "Yes." We believe that theory has practical value that will more than compensate for the time spent studying it. As Table 2–1 illustrates, every profession, including teaching, is built on a foundation of theoretical knowledge that allows practitioners to adapt to the unique characteristics of a particular situation.

This chapter focuses on the theoretical foundations for the profession of teaching. You must keep three essential points in mind as you read the chapter. First, the purpose of teaching is learning. Second, as we noted in Chapter 1, the teacher's primary role in learning is that of instructional expert. Third, theory informs practice and, as a result, helps teachers effectively fulfill this primary role.

THE VALUE OF THEORY

A **theory** is an organized set of principles explaining events that take place in the environment (Gredler, 1997). Theories evolve from observations. As observations about causes and their effects accumulate, a theory attempts to explain those ob-

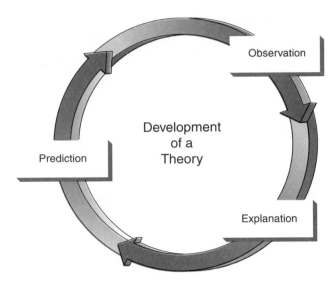

FIGURE 2–1 Development of a theory

servations. Based on that explanation, the theory makes predictions, or hypotheses, in the form of "If *x, then y*" statements that can be tested, resulting in more observations, which lead to additional predictions, and so on (Figure 2–1). As an example, the theory of immunity was Edward Jenner's attempt to explain why milkmaids in early nineteenth-century England were less likely to catch smallpox than were most other people (Asimov, 1984). Jenner noticed that the milkmaids were *more* likely to catch cowpox, a similar but relatively minor disease. He hypothesized that individuals exposed to cowpox develop a natural immunity to the disease that also protects them from smallpox. To test his theory, he injected a young boy with cowpox. Two months later he injected the same boy with smallpox. The boy did not get sick, which confirmed Jenner's theory.

That's what a theory is. But the question is, *What is the practical value of theory?* Effective professional practice requires more than knowing what tools and techniques are available and how to use them. The hallmark of your professional practice is your ability to select and use tools and techniques to devise a solution that meets the demands of a particular situation. This requires the flexibility and adaptability that come from understanding at the deeper level of theoretical principle rather than at the more superficial level of technique.

Theory informs practice in every profession. For example, physicians now routinely provide vaccinations as protection against infectious diseases such as diphtheria, measles, and the flu. The relevant principle from biology is that the body naturally

develops immunity to many of the diseases it encounters.

Similarly, theory informs practice in the classroom. For example, in Chapter 1 we introduced Ms. Moreno's high school Spanish Conversation class, in which she sought better ways to help students master a growing repertoire of Spanish words. One problem she encountered was that students practicing together progressed slowly because they gave one another poor feedback. The relevant principle from learning theory is that students learn best when they have frequent practice followed by *immediate* and *accurate* feedback. Applying this principle, Ms. Moreno devised a number of activities, using both videotape and a multimedia CD-ROM, to encourage students to practice frequently and to provide them with accurate feedback about pronunciation and usage. While Ms. Moreno devised new and better learning activities, she invariably based them on the same theoretical principle.

In summary, theory is not simply a collection of abstractions that are not relevant to the real world. Theory has *practical* value for teachers. As with other professions, you can translate into practical guidelines the principles that form the theoretical foundation for teaching. For the remainder of this chapter we describe theories that inform instructional practice and discuss the practical guidelines derived from them.

Before we begin, however, we have two caveats. First, we haven't tried to include all of the theories that inform teaching practice. We focus on learning theory. While motivational theory, communication theory, and others are important, we believe learning theory is critical because the way we teach is governed by what we know about how people learn. Second, our purpose here is *not* to provide a definitive statement of any theory. We want to outline some key features of several learning theories, and emphasize how they inform instructional practice. Thus, we briefly describe each theory in terms of its background, its central principles, and its practical applications.

LEARNING THEORY

A **learning theory** is an organized set of principles explaining how individuals learn; that is, how they acquire new abilities and/or knowledge. But we can't simply describe learning theory as a single entity. Learning has been studied for hundreds (perhaps thousands) of years, and many theories have been proposed to explain it (see Driscoll, 1994; Gredler, 1997). Of these theories, we have selected three broad theoretical perspectives: behavioral, information processing, and constructivist. These perspectives represent major trends or themes in the way learning is conceptualized and provide some distinctly different practical guidelines for instructional practice.

It is important to note that we present these perspectives in roughly historical order rather than in a presumed order of importance. Each perspective is alive and well today and has both theoreticians and practitioners as adherents.

Behavioral Perspective

Imagine Ms. Moreno's Spanish class. The students are working at computer terminals on a vocabulary lesson. The computer presents students with an increasingly difficult series of sentences in Spanish. Each sentence contains a blank space, and students are asked to enter a Spanish word or phrase that fits into the sentence, such as the following:

¿ _____ te llamas?

¿ _____ vive María?

¿ _____ Ud. de Mexico, señora?

After students respond, the computer gives them feedback about the appropriateness of their chosen word or phrase. The computer allows for a number of "correct" responses for each sentence. When the response is "correct," students move on to the next sentence. When the response is "incorrect," the computer gives them a hint regarding how to translate the sentence and asks again for a response. If the response is again "incorrect" the computer translates the sentence and provides several appropriate responses.

Why does this instructional technique work? In what ways is it informed by theory? Let's consider the background, principles, and applications of the behavioral perspective and then revisit this classroom.

Background

Behaviorism began in the early part of the twentieth century with the argument that "the subject matter of human psychology is the behavior *or activities of the human being*" (Watson, 1924, p. 3), rather than the mental phenomena, such as consciousness, that had been the subject of study during the latter part of the nineteenth century. In education, behaviorism is most closely associated with the work of B. F. Skinner. In contrast to other forms of behaviorism (such as Pavlov's classical conditioning), Skinner focused

on the voluntary, deliberate behaviors that he believed made up most of an individual's behavioral repertoire. These behaviors, which he termed "operants" because they are the individual's way of operating on, or influencing, the environment, are affected by what follows them, as well as what precedes them. Understanding this type of behavior, therefore, involves understanding all of the environmental events surrounding it. Skinner developed his theory during the 1930s and began applying it to an increasingly broad array of human problems, including education, during the 1950s. He believed that, by applying behavioral principles, "the school system of any large American city could be so redesigned, at little or no additional cost, that students would come to school and apply themselves to their work with a minimum of punitive coercion and, with very rare exceptions, learn to read with reasonable ease, express themselves well in speech and writing, and solve a fair range of mathematical problems" (Skinner, 1984, p. 948).

Theoretical Principles

The behavioral perspective focuses on behavior and the external environment's influence on it. Learning is described as a change in the probability of a particular behavior occurring in a particular situation (Ertmer & Newby, 1993). We may use an A → B → C model to explain how behaviorists view the learning process. The environment presents an **antecedent** (A) that prompts a **behavior** (B) that is followed by some **consequence** (C) that then determines whether the behavior will occur again (Woolfolk, 1990). Learning is said to have occurred when students consistently behave in the desired way in response to the specific antecedent, that is, when A consistently results in B.

Students learn without instruction, but instruction provides "special contingencies which expedite learning" (Skinner, 1968, p. 64). These contingencies are the antecedents and consequences that influence individuals' behavior. A process called *shaping* can help students learn complex behaviors. To shape a behavior, teachers gradually and carefully adjust contingencies to encourage students to behave in ways that are progressively closer to the goal. For example, when learning to parallel park a car, your driving instructor may have you begin by parking in a space that is much longer than your car. Gradually, the instructor reduces the size of the space until you can park in a space only slightly longer than your car. According to Skinner (1968), well-designed instruction allows teachers to concentrate on those aspects of the learning situation that

FIGURE 2–2 A learning cue (the graphic showing finger placement) in a CBT program
Source: *Stickybear Typing, Optimum Resources, Inc.*

are "uniquely human": diagnosing learning needs and providing encouragement, support, and guidance.

Reflective Question

▶ What is something you have learned via shaping (progressive improvement toward the final goal)?

Practical Applications

The emphasis in the behavioral perspective is on the external environment's role in determining behavior. Instruction, then, refers to the environmental conditions presented to students. From the behavioral perspective, the primary responsibility of the instructional expert is to arrange the contingencies (antecedents and consequences) in ways that will help students learn. To carry out this responsibility, the behavioral perspective suggests that teachers follow certain guidelines. First, teachers should state instructional objectives as specific learner behaviors that, when successfully performed, will indicate that learning has occurred. This involves identifying the goal and breaking that goal down into a set of simpler behaviors that can be used to shape student behavior.

Second, teachers should use cues to guide students to the goal (Figure 2–2). Initially incorporating a cue, or hint, into the antecedent will help ensure students' success by guiding them to the desired behavior. The teacher should then gradually withdraw the cue to make sure the behavior is clearly linked to the appropriate antecedent.

Third, teachers should use consequences to reinforce desired behavior. Reinforced behaviors are more likely to reoccur. Using consequences effectively involves two tasks. The first is to select reinforcers. Unfortunately, this is not always easy. Reinforcement is defined solely in terms of its effects on an individual student's behavior and can often be determined, therefore, only after the fact. In addition, different things reinforce different students, and, to make matters even more complicated, the same student may be reinforced by different things at different times. Common reinforcers include praise, tangible rewards (good grades, certificates, etc.), and time spent on enjoyable activities. The second task is to arrange the selected consequences so that they reinforce the desired behavior. Timing is critical. To be effective, the consequence should immediately follow the behavior it is meant to reinforce. Otherwise it may reinforce an unintended behavior that doesn't help students progress toward the goal.

Student responsibility within the behavioral perspective is essentially passive, responding to the cues provided by the environment.

Now let's revisit Ms. Moreno's Spanish classroom. Her students are working through a structured computer program developed by an instructional expert to help them increase their Spanish vocabulary. Each frame in the program presents students with a

TABLE 2–2 *Practical Applications of Principles from the Behavioral Perspective*

Theoretical Principle	Practical Applications
Learning is inferred from the behavior of the students.	State the objectives of the instruction as learner behaviors.
Behavior is determined by the antecedents that precede it.	Use initial cues to guide students to the desired behavior.
Whether a behavior will be repeated depends on the consequences that follow it.	Select consequences that will reinforce the desired behavior. Arrange the consequences to immediately follow the desired behavior.

problem in the form of a sentence to complete (antecedent). Students enter a word or phrase that they think will complete the sentence (behavior), and the computer tells them immediately whether they are "correct" (consequence). If the initial response isn't "correct," students receive a cue in the form of help translating the sentence and are asked to enter a new response. Students can be said to have learned a new set of Spanish words when they can consistently use them correctly in sentences.

Table 2–2 summarizes theoretical principles and practical applications from the behavioral perspective.

Information Processing Perspective

Ms. Moreno's Spanish Conversation students are working on another vocabulary lesson, but this time they are using a printed workbook. For each new Spanish word, the book presents an English translation and, to help students remember the meaning, a visual image based on a familiar English word that sounds like part of the Spanish word. For example, the Spanish word *silla* (chair) sounds similar to the English word *sea* (*silla* is pronounced "see-ya"). A simple picture of a chair floating on the sea quickly associates the Spanish word with the similar-sounding English word and the English translation (Figure 2–3). For the first set of new words, the workbook provides the images. For subsequent sets of words, students are asked to create their own images and draw them into their workbooks. At the end of each set of words, students are quizzed on the meanings. As part of the directions for the quiz, students are advised to use their images to help them remember the meanings of the new words.

Why does this instructional technique work? In what ways is it informed by theory? Let's consider the background, principles, and applications of the information processing perspective and then revisit this classroom.

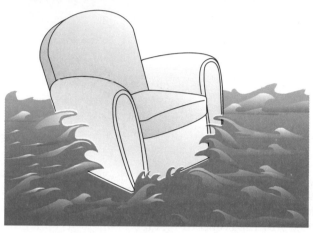

SILLA

FIGURE 2–3   Using a visual image as an aid in remembering the English translations of Spanish words.

Background

Behaviorism developed as a reaction to the study of mental phenomena, such as consciousness, that had characterized nineteenth-century psychology. In a similar way, cognitive psychology developed as a reaction to behaviorism. Cognitive psychology "was officially recognized around 1956" (Gardner, 1985, p. 28), in large part because of a growing dissatisfaction with behaviorism's inability to adequately explain complex behaviors such as language acquisition. For example, at a 1948 symposium on "Cerebral Mechanisms in Behavior," Karl Lashley argued that when people use language their behavior is so rapid and continuous that it could not possibly be controlled by external prompts alone, as behaviorism would suggest (Gardner, 1985). Their behavior must be organized and planned in advance using processes that occur internally in the mind. Lashley used language as his primary example, but he argued that most human behavior is similarly complex and governed by mental processes.

The perceived limitations of behaviorism led to a search for new ways of explaining human learning. At the same time, rapid technological advances led to the development of the high-speed computer as a mechanism for swiftly manipulating large amounts of information. As these two trends came together, one result was the development of the information processing view of human cognition, using the computer as a model for the way humans think. While this view isn't the only one that has developed from cognitive psychology (see Driscoll, 1994, for descriptions of other cognitive theories of learning), it has been a prominent view that has influenced instructional practice. Like a computer, the mind takes information in, organizes it, stores it for later use, and retrieves it from memory. With the growth of cognitive psychology the focus was again on the mind, as it had been before the advent of behaviorism. However, using computer models and other laboratory methods (e.g., reaction-time tests), cognitive scientists were now able to quantify mental functions with much more scientific rigor than before.

Theoretical Principles

The behavioral perspective emphasizes the influence of the *external* environment. In contrast, the information processing perspective has an *internal* focus. Learning is described as a change in knowledge stored in memory. The central principle is that most behavior, including learning, is governed by internal memory processes rather than external circumstances. Understanding behavior, therefore, requires understanding how memory works.

Human memory has two essential characteristics. First, it is organized rather than random. As an illustration, try this simple exercise: Ask several people to write down the names of as many of the 50 United States as they can. Give them about 15 seconds and then examine the results. The lists are likely to be different, but virtually all of them will be organized in some way. The most common organizing schemes are alphabetic (Alabama, Alaska, Arizona, Arkansas, etc.) and geographic (Washington, Oregon, Idaho, California, etc.). Some lists may be organized in a way that isn't readily apparent and may make sense only to the person who wrote the list (Florida, Virginia, Wyoming, Kentucky, etc.—states the list-maker has visited on vacation). But each list will be organized in some way (Figure 2–4). The same can be said for all the knowledge we have accumulated.

The second essential characteristic of human memory is that it is active rather than passive. Memory doesn't simply receive information. It actively synthesizes and organizes information, integrating it with knowledge already stored in memory. Memory as an active synthesizer involves three processes: attention, encoding, and retrieval (Bell-Gredler, 1986). **Attention** refers to the process of selectively receiving information from the environment. **Encoding** refers to the process of translating information into some meaningful, memorable form. **Retrieval** refers to the process of identifying and recalling information for a particular purpose. Learning is said to have occurred when individuals encode new information or recode existing information in some new way. In both cases, individuals can easily recall information from memory and effectively use it in a particular situation.

As a way of understanding how these memory processes work together, imagine a library receiving new books and subsequently making them accessible to its patrons (Stepich & Newby, 1988). A library continually receives information about new books and selects some of those books for addition to its collection (attention). When a library receives new books, they are cataloged using a classification scheme such as the Dewey Decimal System (encoding). This places the new books into coherent categories and allows related books to appear on the shelves near one another. It also provides a search cue to help one find the books later. To locate a particular book in the library, an individual begins with the search cue (the catalog number) and searches the shelves for the desired book, perhaps at the same time scanning the shelves for other relevant books (retrieval).

Memory works in a similar way (Figure 2–5). Humans are constantly bombarded with information from the environment and select only some of it to remember (attention). New information is considered in light of what is already known and integrated into existing information whenever possible (encoding). This creates a coherent organization that makes new information more meaningful and allows related information to be linked together. It also provides a "search cue" that makes it easier to find information at a later time. In order to recall information from memory, an individual begins with the "search cue" provided by the organizing scheme and searches memory for the desired information, perhaps at the same time "scanning" memory for other relevant information (retrieval).

There is, of course, at least one significant difference between memory and a library. A library keeps physical objects (books) in specific places (shelves). In contrast, the facts and ideas that make up memory aren't physical objects, and we can't yet pinpoint where in the brain specific memories reside. However, the processes involved are similar.

Practical Applications

The emphasis of the information processing perspective is on students' cognitive processes and on the

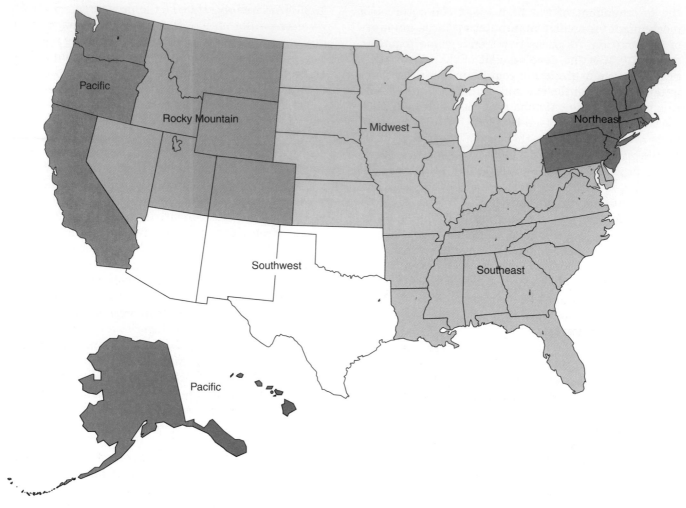

FIGURE 2–4   A geographic organizing strategy

critical role memory plays in helping them translate new information into a meaningful form they can remember and use. Instruction, then, involves a deliberate effort to guide and support these cognitive processes. The primary responsibility of the instructional expert is to create conditions that will help students attend to, encode, and retrieve information. To carry out this responsibility, the information processing perspective suggests that teachers take specific steps.

First, organize new information and make the organizing scheme explicit to students. Because humans actively seek order in information as a way of making sense of it, new information will be easier to encode, and therefore easier to retrieve, if it is also organized in some explicit way.

Second, carefully link new information to existing knowledge. New information linked to existing knowledge will be more meaningful and students

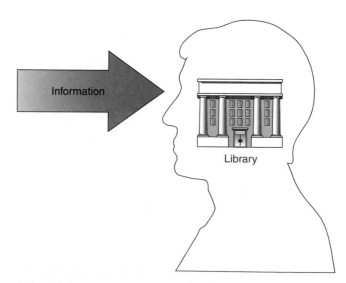

FIGURE 2–5   Memory is like a library

will therefore more easily and effectively learn it. Two techniques facilitate this linking. The first is to make sure students notice possible connections between the new information and something they already know. The second is to form multiple links between the new information and students' existing knowledge as a way of "cross-referencing" the new information (Ormrod, 1995).

Third, use techniques to guide and support students' attention, encoding, and retrieval. Teachers may use a variety of techniques (see Baine, 1986). We briefly describe a few here. To guide students' attention, use focusing questions and highlighting. To guide students' encoding and retrieval, use analogies, mnemonic devices, and imagery.

▶ *Focusing questions.* A **focusing question** is used, typically at the beginning of a lesson, to direct students' attention to particularly important aspects of the new information. For example, at the beginning of a lesson on the American Revolution, you might ask students, What were the arguments supporting the revolution? Who made those arguments? What were the arguments against the revolution? Who made those arguments?

▶ *Highlighting.* **Highlighting** refers to various emphasizing techniques designed to direct students' attention to certain aspects of information. You can highlight written information by using **bold-face,** underlining, or *italics.* You may highlight pictorial information by using color, labels, or arrows. You may emphasize verbal information by speaking more loudly or more slowly, by repeating important words or phrases, or by using signal phrases such as, "What you should remember is . . ." or "There are several important characteristics. These are . . ."

▶ *Analogies.* An **analogy** likens something new to something familiar. Analogies are typically used either to make abstract information more concrete or to organize complex information. For example, imagine that you wanted beginning biology students to learn the function of red blood cells. You might use the following analogy: "Red blood cells work like trucks, carrying needed materials from a central distribution point for delivery throughout the body" (Stepich & Newby, 1988a, p. 136). This analogy uses familiar objects (trucks) to direct students' attention to the critical (at least for this lesson) feature of red blood cells: their function as carriers of essential materials. In addition, the analogy uses the familiar objects as a guide to

help students encode new information about red blood cells. Finally, the analogy provides students with a retrieval cue, allowing them to recall their new knowledge about red blood cells. This retrieval process might begin with the analogy itself (red blood cells are like trucks). Students might then recall how red blood cells are like trucks (they carry things), and this might be followed by their recalling what red blood cells carry (oxygen).

▶ *Mnemonics.* In general terms, any practical device used to make information easier to remember can be called a **mnemonic.** To illustrate some of the many different mnemonics, answer the following questions:
   a. How many days does March have in it? Perhaps, like many people, you answered this question by thinking, "Thirty days has September, April, June, and November . . ." This is an example of using a **rhyme** as a mnemonic.
   b. What are the names of the five Great Lakes? One way to answer this question is by thinking of the word "HOMES" (Huron, Ontario, Michigan, Erie, Superior). This is an example of an **acronym,** in which a single word is made up of the first letters of a group of words.
   c. What are the names of the lines on the musical staff? This question can be answered by thinking of the sentence, "Every good boy deserves fudge." This is an example of an **acrostic,** in which letters in the new information (E, G, B, D, F) are used as the first letters of the words in a sentence or phrase.

▶ *Imagery.* **Imagery** refers to using mental pictures to represent new information. Visual images may take various forms, such as pictures, drawings, maps, and so on. In each case the image represents important aspects of the new information and serves as a cue for retrieving that information from memory. Visual images can be used with various types of information. They can be used with concrete objects. For example, information about the concept "dog" (a furry, four-legged animal with a tail and a long snout) can be encoded into memory by using a picture of a particular dog. Visual images can also be used with abstract ideas. For example for learners who are familiar with U.S. symbolism, information about the concept "freedom" (not subject to arbitrary power or restriction) can be encoded into memory by using a drawing of the Statue of Liberty.

Using Analogies

At the beginning of Chapter 1 we referred to the way a master cabinetmaker continually plans, implements, and evaluates his or her work. This is an example of the instructional technique of analogy. Its purpose is to help you learn by comparing a new concept with something familiar. An analogy consists of four parts:

1. the information to be learned (the subject)
2. the familiar thing to which the new information is compared (the analog)
3. the means by which the subject and analog are compared (the connector)
4. a description of the similarities and differences between the subject and analog (the ground)

In the cabinetmaker analogy, we used the differences between how expert and novice cabinetmakers would go about creating a bookcase (the analog) to describe the phases of learning (the subject). In both cases, experts plan their work, implement the plan, and evaluate the results (the ground).

Analogies have repeatedly been found to be effective in learning all types of subject matter (West, Farmer, & Wolff, 1991). To facilitate your own use of analogies, consider the following ABCDE method of constructing an analogy (adapted from Kearny, Newby, & Stepich, 1995).

A	Analyze the subject	What is it you most want the learners to understand about the subject?
B	Brainstorm potential analogs	What concrete items share the important feature(s) you have identified?
C	Choose the analog	Which candidate analog has the best combination of the following characteristics:
		▪ Familiarity—Will learners recognize the analog?
		▪ Accuracy—Does the analog accurately reflect the identified feature?
		▪ Memorability—Is the analog vivid; will learners remember it?
		▪ Concreteness—Is the analog something learners can directly perceive?
D	Describe the ground	How are the subject and analog alike? How are they different?
E	Evaluate the analogy	Does the analogy work with the intended audience?

Reflective Question

▪ From an information processing perspective, how would you explain the function of the "PIE" chart in Figure 1–4?

Students' responsibility within the information processing perspective is to actively synthesize information, using cognitive supports provided by the environment or that they develop for themselves. The way students use these cognitive supports will depend, in part, on their age and experience. Teachers should develop and present these supports for younger students. However, as stu-

dents mature, they can learn to develop their own cognitive supports.

For example, consider three biology classes learning the function of red blood cells (the cells in the blood that carry oxygen throughout the body). For the first class, made up of younger students, the teacher may present an analogy. "A red blood cell is like a truck. It carries oxygen to different parts of the body." For the second class, of somewhat older students, the teacher might state the two objects in the analogy and ask students to fill in their similarities: "Think about a red blood cell as being like a truck. In what ways are they alike?" For the third

TABLE 2–3 *Practical Applications of Principles from the Information Processing Perspective*

Theoretical Principle	Practical Applications
Knowledge is organized in memory.	Organize new information for presentation.
Learning is influenced by students' existing knowledge.	Carefully link new information to existing knowledge.
Learning is made up of the component processes of attention, encoding, and retrieval.	Use a variety of techniques to guide and support students' learning processes, including focusing questions, highlighting, analogies, mnemonics, and imagery.

class, of still older students, the teacher may simply say, "Think of something familiar that is like a red blood cell in some important way." Faced with this question, students might come up with a variety of analogies:

▶ A red blood cell is like a postman carrying mail to different houses.
▶ A red blood cell is like a book bag carrying books to school.
▶ A red blood cell is like a bee carrying pollen from flower to flower.

An analogy students develop for themselves may be more familiar to them and they may therefore more easily remember it. In addition, students who develop analogies for themselves are more actively processing the new information. The result is that student developed analogies may actually be more effective aids to learning than those teachers present.

In a similar way, students can gradually learn to develop their own schemes for organizing new information, methods for linking new information to existing knowledge, mnemonics, and imagery.

Now, let's revisit Ms. Moreno's Spanish classroom. The students studying with the workbook are using a type of mnemonic called a **keyword** (Ormrod, 1995) to learn the meanings of new Spanish words. Creating a keyword involves two steps. First, the unfamiliar word is linked to a similar-sounding familiar keyword. Then the keyword is used to create a visual image that incorporates the meaning of the new word. Like other types of mnemonics, keywords help students encode new words for easier retrieval at a later time.

Table 2–3 summarizes theoretical principles and practical applications from the information processing perspective.

Constructivist Perspective

Once again we are visiting Ms. Moreno's Spanish Conversation class. She has placed students in small groups, and each group is acting out a real-life sce-

Role plays provide students with complete, realistic problems.

nario in Spanish. There are no set scripts; Ms. Moreno has given each student a description of a situation and a role to play. The students' task is simply to make themselves understood, using only Spanish, and successfully play out their scenario. Situations include students finding a lost child who speaks only Spanish, asking a policeman in Madrid for directions, and convincing an airline baggage assistant at the Mexico City International Airport that the bag they have claimed is indeed their own.

Why does this instructional technique work? In what ways is it informed by theory? Let's consider the background, principles, and applications of the constructivist perspective and then revisit this classroom.

Background

Constructivism is a relatively recent term used to represent a collection of theories, including (among others) generative learning (Wittrock, 1990), discovery learning (Bruner, 1961), and situated learning (Brown, Collins, & Duguid, 1989). The common thread among these theories is the idea that individuals actively construct knowledge by working to solve realistic problems, usually in collaboration with others (Duffy, Lowyck, & Jonassen, 1993).

While the label is relatively recent, the ideas that make up constructivism have been around for a long time. As early as 1897, for example, Dewey argued that "education must be conceived as a continuing reconstruction of experience" (1897, p. 91) that occurs through "the stimulation of the child's powers by the demands of the social situations in which he finds himself" (1897, p. 84). In the middle of the twentieth century, the idea that knowledge is constructed through social collaboration shows up in the theories of Piaget, Bruner, and Vygotsky (Driscoll, 1994).

Theoretical Principles

The constructivist perspective describes learning as a change in meaning constructed from experience. On the surface this seems the same as the information processing definition of learning, but there is a critical difference in the way the two perspectives define knowledge (Jonassen, 1991). The information processing perspective defines *knowledge* as an *objective representation* of experience, whereas the constructivist perspective defines it as a *subjective interpretation* of experience.

An analogy will help to illustrate this critical difference. In the information processing perspective, the mind is like a mirror, accurately reflecting the objects and events in our experience. The assumption is that knowledge is objective and can be described as separate from the knower. In other words, regardless of whose mirror is used, the picture in the mirror is essentially the same. Learning, then, refers to the *acquisition* of new representations. In the constructivist perspective, on the other hand, the mind is like a lens. When we look through our lens, some aspects of our experience are in sharp focus, some are fuzzy, and some can't be seen at all. The assumption in the constructivist perspective is that knowledge is constructed *by* the knower and therefore cannot be separated *from* the knower. In other words, the picture we see is determined by the lens we use. Learning, then, refers to the *construction* of new interpretations.

Thus, knowledge construction is a process of thinking about and interpreting experience. And because each individual has a unique set of experiences, seen through a unique lens, each individual constructs a unique body of understanding. Learning is said to have occurred when our knowledge has changed in a way that allows us to interpret our experience in a more complete, complex, or refined way; that is, when our lens allows us to see something we couldn't see before or to see things in sharper focus.

There is some debate about exactly how this knowledge construction occurs (Phillips, 1995). Some constructivist theories focus on the individual learner, suggesting that constructing knowledge is a matter of individual interpretation. Other theories focus on social interaction among individuals, suggesting that constructing knowledge is a matter of dialogue leading to a shared interpretation. In general, however, this is a matter of degree and most constructivist theories incorporate both individual and social perspectives.

Practical Applications

According to the constructivist perspective, learning is determined by the complex interplay among students' existing knowledge, the social context, and the problem to be solved. Instruction, then, refers to providing students with a collaborative situation in which they have both the means and the opportunity to construct "new and situationally-specific understandings by assembling prior knowledge from diverse sources" (Ertmer & Newby, 1993, p. 63). Various authors have described the characteristics of constructivist instruction (Brooks & Brooks, 1993; Cognition and Technology Group at Vanderbilt [CTGV], 1993; Driscoll, 1994; Honebein, Duffy, & Fishman, 1993). Two characteristics seem to be central to these descriptions, learning in context and collaboration.

Learning in Context   According to the constructivist perspective, knowledge is like a muscle; it grows when it's used. Therefore, constructivist instruction asks students to put their knowledge to work within the context of solving realistic and meaningful problems. The idea is that when they work to apply their knowledge to a specific problem, students will naturally explore their knowledge, and this will, in turn, lead to the continual refinement of that knowledge. However, not all problems are equally effective. To be effective, a problem should

▶ be seen by students as relevant and interesting. Students are likely to invest more effort in problems that they perceive as relevant or that stimulate their curiosity.
▶ be realistically complex. Complex problems mirror the complexity of actual experience and, therefore, help students come to a fuller understanding of their experience. In addition, complex problems are more likely to trigger the different experiences of students and, therefore, promote different approaches to solving the problem.
▶ require students to use their knowledge. As with a theory, students construct knowledge as they use it to explain what has happened and to make and test predictions about what will happen.

Collaboration   From the constructivist perspective, students learn through interaction with others.

This collaboration has two basic aspects. The first involves the relationships among students. Students work together as peers, applying their combined knowledge to solving the problem. The dialogue that results provides students with ongoing opportunities to explore alternative interpretations and to test and refine their understanding.

The second aspect of collaboration involves the role of the teacher. Constructivist instruction has been likened to an apprenticeship in which teachers participate *with* students in solving meaningful and realistic problems (Collins, Brown, & Holum, 1991; Rogoff, 1990). This doesn't mean that the teacher knows "the answer" to the problem. In fact, the problem may be just as new to the teacher as it is to the students. However, teachers are probably more familiar with the processes of solving problems and constructing knowledge. Teachers, therefore, serve as models and guides, showing students how to reflect on their evolving knowledge and providing direction when they are having difficulty. Learning is shared. Teachers are likely to learn as much as students. Responsibility for instruction is also shared. As much as possible, students determine their own learning needs, set their own goals, and monitor their progress. The amount of guidance teachers provide depends on students' knowledge levels and experiences.

The emphasis in the constructivist perspective is on students' evolving knowledge and the critical role dialogue plays in helping students interpret their experiences. From a constructivist perspective, the primary responsibility of the instructional expert is to create and maintain a collaborative problem-solving environment. To carry out this responsibility, the constructivist perspective suggests that teachers do the following:

▶ Provide opportunities for learning in context. Learning occurs as students apply knowledge to solving problems that are realistically complex and personally meaningful.
▶ Create group learning activities. Learning occurs via social dialogue in which students and teacher explore and apply their combined knowledge.

▶ Model and guide knowledge construction. Students and teachers work together to solve problems, with teachers using their more extensive experience to provide direction consistent with students' experiences and knowledge levels.

Reflective Question

▶ How has your experience as a learner influenced your interpretation of the learning process?

Students' responsibility within the constructivist perspective is to work like scientists, trying out what they know about a subject while investigating a problem, noting what happens, and using their observations to expand their knowledge (note the similarity to the evolution of theory, described at the beginning of the chapter). Similar to the techniques described in our discussion of the information processing perspective, teachers' specific application of the constructivist perspective may vary according to students' age and experience. Teachers may guide younger students step by step through solving the problem. They may provide older students with a general problem-solving outline as a reminder and let them carry it out in the way they think best. Still older students may be presented with a problem and left to their own devices. Frequently case studies are used to introduce such problems (see Toolbox on next page).

Let's visit Ms. Moreno's Spanish class again. Students who are involved in role-playing scenarios, are engaged in a lesson that meets the criteria for an effective problem: The situations stimulate their curiosity and interest, the problems are complex enough to allow for a number of different conversations, students must use their knowledge of Spanish vocabulary and pronunciation to make themselves understood, and accomplishing the task requires cooperation.

Table 2–4 summarizes theoretical principles and practical applications from the constructivist perspective.

TABLE 2–4 *Practical Applications of Principles from the Constructivist Perspective*

Theoretical Principle	Practical Applications
Learning occurs through applying knowledge to solving problems.	Provide opportunities for students to solve realistic and meaningful problems.
Learning occurs through interaction with others.	Provide group learning activities.
Constructing knowledge can be thought of as an apprenticeship process.	Model and guide the process of constructing knowledge within the context of mutual problem solving.

TOOLBOX

TECHNIQUES

Toolbox Techniques: Case Studies

The case study is a teaching approach that requires students to actively participate in real or hypothetical problem situations that reflect the types of experiences actually encountered in the discipline under study. After you read the following case study examples, reflect on the type of problem-solving lesson you could generate by using them.

You are a botanist working to preserve the waters of Everglades National Park in Florida, the nation's third-largest national park, established in 1947. You have already documented the extent of the damage from surrounding farm chemicals that run off into the Everglades' vast swamps, saw grasses, and coastal mangrove forest. But recent attempts to reach agreement on the part of government and farmers' organizations have failed. How can you work to preserve these natural wonders of the country? (Barell, 1995, p. 126)

Aurora is experiencing an increase in the crime rate. Currently, 30 percent of the cases admitted to hospital emergency rooms are victims of violent crimes, compared with a rate of 25 percent two years ago. What steps should the city take to find a solution to the problem? (from Gallaher, Stepien, & Rosenthal, 1992, as cited in Barell, 1995, p. 126)

The case "report" contains relevant (but not conclusive) data. You may present it to students, or they may develop it themselves. Individual or groupwork follows the case presentation, allowing students to analyze data, evaluate the nature of the problem(s), decide on applicable principles, and recommend a solution or course of action. A case discussion follows, which is useful in developing critical-thinking, problem-solving, and interpersonal skills. Although case methods may have strategies in common with other teaching techniques (particularly simulations and instructional games), the focus in all case methods is a specific set of circumstances and events. Whereas case methods are generally motivating to students due to the high level of involvement and can help bridge the gap between the "real" world and life in the classroom, they tend to be time consuming and require good management skills on the part of the discussion leader.

TABLE 2–5 *Comparing the Three Theoretical Perspectives of Learning*

	Behavioral Perspective	Information Processing Perspective	Constructivist Perspective
What is learning?	A change in the probability of a behavior occurring	A change in knowledge stored in memory	A change in meaning constructed from experience
What is the learning process?	Antecedent → behavior → consequence	Attention → encoding → retrieval of information from memory	Repeated group dialogue and collaborative problem solving
What is the teacher's primary role?	Arrange external contingencies	Arrange conditions to support memory processes	Model and guide
What can the teacher do to carry out that role?	▶ State objectives. ▶ Guide student behavior with cues. ▶ Arrange reinforcing consequences to immediately follow students' behavior.	▶ Organize new information. ▶ Link new information to existing knowledge. ▶ Use a variety of attention, encoding, and retrieval aids.	▶ Provide opportunities to solve realistic and meaningful problems. ▶ Provide group learning activities. ▶ Model and guide the process of constructing knowledge within the context of mutual problem solving.
What is the student's primary responsibility?	Respond to cues	Actively synthesize information	Explore like a scientist

FIGURE 2–6   A heuristic guide for selecting principles from the three theoretical perspectives on learning
Note. © 1993 by the Learning Systems Institute, Florida State University, Suite 4600 University Center, Bldg. C, Tallahassee, FL 32306-2540. Reprinted by permission from Performance Improvement Quarterly.

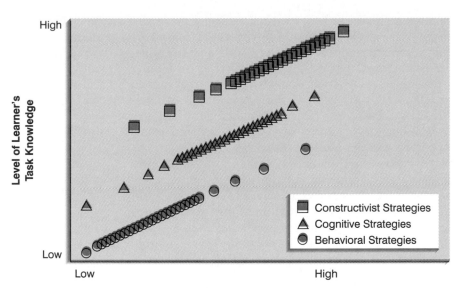

SELECTING THEORETICAL PRINCIPLES

Learning theory has been defined as an attempt to explain how people acquire new knowledge and skills. We have presented three perspectives on learning, summarized in Table 2–5. Because these three theoretical perspectives view learning in distinctly different ways, you might ask, *Which theory is best?* While this is a natural question, we believe it isn't the right one to ask. It is similar to asking, Which food is best? The inevitable answer is that no one food is best. We should eat a variety of foods, because each one contributes something to good nutrition. Similarly, we believe that teachers should understand a variety of theoretical perspectives because each perspective contributes something to good instruction.

Principles from the different theories can be applied in virtually any learning situation. For example, reinforcement (from the behavioral perspective), organized information (from the information processing perspective), and learning from one another (from the constructivist perspective) are principles that will be useful in virtually every instructional situation. At the same time, however, some theories fit some learning situations better than others. Ertmer and Newby (1993) suggest that this fit depends on two critical factors: students' knowledge level and the amount of thought and reflection required by the learning task. As Figure 2–6 shows, students with little content knowledge are likely to benefit most from learning strategies based on the behavioral perspective. As students' knowledge grows, the emphasis may shift to the information processing and then the con-

structivist perspective. Learning tasks requiring little thought and reflection (e.g., memorizing facts, following a rote procedure) also are likely to benefit most from behavioral learning strategies. As the amount of thought and reflection required by the learning tasks increases (e.g., finding unique solutions to "old" problems, inductive reasoning, creative thinking), the emphasis may shift to the information processing and then the constructivist perspective.

The shift from behavioral to information processing to constructivist strategies involves an important shift in the extent to which the students direct their own learning. With behavioral strategies, responsibility lies almost entirely with the teacher. Students learn by responding to cues the teacher builds into the environment. In contrast, with constructivist strategies, teacher and students share responsibility for directing learning. Students learn by collaborating with one another and with the teacher to solve mutually determined problems. Information processing strategies occupy a middle ground. Teachers may present the cognitive supports that facilitate effective information processing or students may develop them for their own use.

APPLICATIONS IN THE LEARNER-CENTERED CLASSROOM

We began this chapter with a conversation with our friend Cynthia, a teacher who expressed doubt about the usefulness of learning theories. She questioned their value in helping her solve the practical learning problems she daily faced with her students. In the chapter, we explained that a key value of theories is the prescriptive guidelines they offer. For example, one such constructivist guideline focuses on having learners develop their knowledge by working on problems that are realistic and meaningful. We discussed this under the heading "Learning in Context."

When developing your learner-centered classroom you can promote learning in context in several ways. First, think about ways you can teach subject matter (math, English, social studies) in integrated/thematic units instead of in isolation. Most real-world problems require a combination of strategies drawn from different subject areas instead of from a single area of study. Traditionally, however, these subjects are taught in isolation. Consider, for example, the study of whales. Students could explore the degree to which different countries protect these creatures, how their size and weight is determined, what ecological problems they face, and what role these giants have played within literature and culture.

Second, specific instructional methods (see chapters 5 and 7 for more details) can help learners experience problems "in context." These include simulations, case studies, and role plays. In each case, learners are put in situations similar to real-world settings, such as having high school students role play being parents to a newborn child. To some degree, these students would experience what it would be like to have someone totally dependent on them and their actions.

Third, media, particularly multimedia, can help learners experience input simultaneously from different sources. Visual, aural, and tactile input can make problems more realistic.

Finally, when possible, have students experience apprenticeships within the real world. For example, those studying math may work with an engineer on a bridge construction project to experience applied math concepts. Likewise, an elementary school art class may work in a studio setting with a resident artist and develop a class sculpture that later becomes a centerpiece in their school entryway.

SUMMARY

As a teacher, your primary role, that of instructional expert, is based on a theoretical foundation. In every profession, including teaching, theory informs practice. This means that theory offers a set of consistent principles teachers may use to create solutions to a variety of unique problems. As in other professions, understanding theory allows teachers to select the tools and techniques that will work best with specific students and learning goals, apply those principles in a coherent manner, and adapt instruction as students' needs change.

Instructional practice is built on a diverse theoretical foundation, with learning theory as the critical cornerstone. In this chapter, we have described three broad categories of learning theory—behavioral, information processing, and constructivist—in terms of their central principles and their practical applications to your role of instructional expert. Just as different foods contribute to good nutrition, different learning theories contribute to good instruction.

REFLECTIVE ACTIVITIES

▶ Write a letter to a skeptical friend explaining why the time you spend studying theory will help you become a better teacher.
▶ Consider, from the behavioral perspective, a class you have recently attended. Were objectives stated as learner behaviors? What cues and consequences did the instructor use? How might the class be made more consistent with the behavioral perspective?
▶ Consider the same class from the information processing perspective. Was new information organized? Was it clearly linked to existing knowledge? What techniques did the instructor use to make information processing easier (e.g., focusing questions, analogies, mnemonics, imagery)? How might the class be made more consistent with the information processing perspective?
▶ Consider the same class from the constructivist perspective. Were relevant, interesting, and realistically complex problems presented? Was collaborative learning emphasized? Did the teacher serve as a model and guide? How might the class be made more consistent with the constructivist perspective?

SUGGESTED RESOURCES

Driscoll, M. P. (1994). *Psychology of learning for instruction.* Boston: Allyn & Bacon.

Ertmer, P. A., & Newby, T. J. (1993). Behaviorism, cognitivism, constructivism: Comparing critical features from an instructional design perspective. *Performance Improvement Quarterly, 6*(4), 50–72.

Information on the learning theories discussed in this chapter is available at the San Diego State University College of Education Website: http://edweb.sdsu.edu/courses/edtec540/perspectives/perspectives.html

CHAPTER 3

Computer Tools for Teaching and Learning

OUTLINE

KEY WORDS AND CONCEPTS

Word processor
WYSIWYG
Graphic
Pixel
Desktop publishing (DTP)
Presentation software
Database
Field
Record
Spreadsheet
Modem
Electronic mail (e-mail)

OBJECTIVES

After reading and studying this chapter, you will be able to

▶ Describe educational applications in which the computer can be classified as a teacher, an assistant, or a learner.
▶ Define and describe each of the major categories of software tools discussed in this chapter (word processor, graphics/desktop publishing, presentation software, database, spreadsheet, and computer telecommunication).
▶ Describe two or three examples of teacher and/or student uses of each of the software tools discussed in this chapter.
▶ Identify at least one problem or pitfall to consider when implementing each of the software tools discussed in this chapter.

PLANNING FOR THE CHAPTER CONTENT

Instructional Technology for Teaching and Learning, will show you how to increase learning by designing lessons that use instructional technology, including **computers** and other media.

In chapters 1 and 2, we introduced you to instructional technology, and we presented fundamental concepts of learning and the theories that help us to understand it. In order to plan instruction to increase your students' learning, you must be aware of the various tools that are available to help you and your students. In this chapter, we introduce the computer, a multifaceted tool that can be of benefit to you and your students in many different ways. We present an overview of computer applications in teaching and learning, focusing on those tools that can assist you or your learners with common tasks. This information will prepare you to move on to Section II of this book, where we explore planning instruction. Later in chapters 8 and 9, we will focus on implementing computers and the Internet with your students.

INTRODUCTION

An acquaintance of ours is an expert model builder. She constructs all sorts of models: plastic replicas of product packaging (e.g., the bottle for a new perfume), model buildings to illustrate architectural plans, and various other creations from plaster, fiberglass, and just about any other material you can think of. Not long ago, she was asked to create models of an alien city of the future that were to be used in a science fiction movie. Like most expert artisans, such as the cabinetmaker we discussed in Chapter 1, she uses a variety of tools to make her models. She has one special tool, however, that she uses more than the others. It is called a rotary multi-tool.

A rotary multi-tool is a device, sort of like a drill, that spins a shaft at very high speeds. The user can attach a variety of different implements to the end of the shaft, such as drill bits, a small circular disk to cut wood, metal, and other materials, or a sanding drum to smooth rough wooden surfaces. Various grinding attachments can be used to mold the contours of wood, plaster, or fiberglass surfaces. In short, the multi-tool, as its name implies, does a lot of different things.

What our friend likes so much about the multi-tool is its versatility. Rather than needing a lot of different tools, she can use one tool to perform different model-making tasks, simply by changing its attachment to one appropriate for the job at hand. With this one versatile tool, she can accomplish many of her aims.

The computer is a multi-tool for teaching and learning. It is a machine that can help with many different teaching and learning tasks. Rather than having separate tools for common tasks such as writing, drawing, filing, and calculating, in the computer you have one tool that can do them all. In this chapter, we take a closer look at this remarkably versatile tool.

The basic capabilities of the rotary multi-tool are determined by its physical characteristics—the spinning shaft and the attachments. The computer's capabilities are defined, enabled, and constrained by the hardware and software that comprise a particular computer system. The physical components of the computer system are termed **hardware.** The hardware sets absolute limits on what the computer can

FIGURE 3–1   In education, the personal computer can be used as a teacher, as a "learner," or as an assistant.

do. With only a monochrome display screen, for example, a computer cannot display multicolor images. A multi-tool changes function when the attached implement is changed. In a computer, function is changed by changing the software. **Software** is the term for the programs or instructions that tell the computer what to do. The software unlocks the capabilities of the hardware. A computer is capable of performing an amazing variety of tasks, but each task requires appropriate software.

In popular terms, the word *computer* refers to a machine that processes information according to a set of instructions. When most people picture a computer, they think of a desktop device that has elements such as a keyboard, a disk drive unit, and a monitor. In reality, this is a **computer system,** a collection of components that includes the computer and all of its **peripherals,** the devices used with the computer that realize or extend its capabilities. The **computer** itself is the device responsible for processing information. The other components and peripherals are usually responsible either for putting information into the computer **(input devices)** or getting information out **(output devices).**

There are three generally recognized categories of computer systems. The members of the largest and most powerful class are known as **mainframe computers.** They have very large storage capacities, very fast processing speeds, and support large numbers of users simultaneously. Mainframes are expensive and generally are used by businesses, universities, and governments for large-scale processing tasks. The most powerful and fastest mainframes are called **supercomputers.** The members of the second class of computer systems, **minicomputers,** feature intermediate storage capacities and processing speeds and simultaneous use by several to dozens of users. They are often used by small businesses and larger schools.

The members of the third class, **personal computers** or *microcomputers,* are the smallest, least powerful, and least expensive. Personal computers are intended for use by individuals. Since their proliferation began in the late 1970s, they have become the focus of much of the computing industry. In addition, as personal computer capabilities have grown, the distinctions between personal computers and the more powerful classes of computers have begun to blur. We will focus our attention on personal computers because they are such useful and widespread tools for both educators and learners. Figure 3–1 shows a personal computer system. For an overview of common components and terminology, see Appendix A, "Understanding Computer Systems." Refer to the "Toolbox Tips" in this section for some important tips on the care of your computer system.

COMPUTER TOOLS

For many years, teachers have planned and implemented instruction using the tools available to them—typewriters, pencil and paper, lesson

Care of Computer Systems

As with any tool, it is important that you care for and maintain computer hardware and software to keep the system in good working order. Care for system hardware in the following manner:

1. Use electrical surge protectors to protect against power fluctuations.
2. Use antistatic devices to prevent problems from static electricity.
3. Regularly clean the exterior, keyboard, and monitor according to manufacturer directions.
4. Occasionally clean the computer's interior by blowing out dust with compressed air or by vacuuming with an attachment made for computers.
5. Clean disk drives, printer heads, and so on, using a kit made for the purpose, if problems arise.

Computer disks are vulnerable to damage from a variety of sources. It is important to protect them by taking the following basic precautions:

1. Keep disks away from magnetic fields; magnets can erase disk data!
2. Avoid exposing disks to temperature extremes (below about 50°F or above about 125°F).
3. Keep disks away from dirt, dust, and other contaminants.
4. Do not open the metal shutter on floppy disks; that exposes the disk surface to contaminants. If the disk surface is exposed, don't touch it.
5. Avoid dropping disks; the hard plastic case can break, and the metal shutter can pop off.
6. Never force disks into or out of disk drives.
7. Keep disks write-protected by opening the write-protect tab when copying to avoid accidental erasure.
8. When you are not using disks, store them in boxes or cases made for that purpose.

It is also important to keep the software on your computer operating correctly. Utility software helps you maintain the integrity of applications software and the workings of your hard disk. One type of software that you should use regularly checks for and corrects hard disk problems. Large-capacity hard disks containing thousands of files are subject to occasional problems with file storage and retrieval. Over time, little errors can build up to create big problems. Programs such as *Norton Utilities Disk Doctor, First Aid, Check-It,* or *Windows ScanDisk,* used regularly, can identify and fix many disk problems.

Program files and documents are stored on a hard disk in chunks that may often be physically located in many different spots. Over time, disks can become fragmented with portions of the same program or document scattered across the greater part of the disk. This fragmentation causes your computer system to run more slowly and increases the likelihood of errors. To reduce fragmentation, use a program designed for this purpose, such as *Norton Utilities Speed Disk* or *Windows Defrag.* Be sure to check your hard disk for errors and back up your data before using one of these programs.

Finally, one of the most important ways to protect yourself from problems is by backing up your work. Make sure that you keep at least two copies of every file. If one should be lost, for whatever reason, you'll have the other to fall back on. You should regularly back up *all* key hard disk files by using a tape backup system, large-capacity removable disks (e.g., Zip, Jaz, SuperDisk), or other storage options. Hard disks do fail! If you are prepared for problems, your difficulties will be minimized when disaster strikes.

---

planning books, calculators, and so forth. Students, too, have used traditional tools. In many cases, these tools remain popular today. But we also have newer, computer-based tools that can help teachers plan, implement, and evaluate instruction and help students during their learning. It is important to understand what these new tools do and how both teachers and students can use them. We begin by considering the following classroom vignette.

Waste, Pollution, and the Environment Unit Scenario

Judy Wood is a sixth-grade teacher who does an exciting lesson unit on waste, pollution, and the environment. She begins by showing students a videotape about the environment and the global problems of waste and pollution to give them background and arouse their interest. Then, she makes a presentation to the class to focus the students' attention on local waste and pollution issues to help them see that they have a responsibility for helping to keep the environment clean. In the past, Ms. Wood lectured and displayed or passed around the room pictures for her students to examine. Today, she uses Microsoft *PowerPoint,* electronic presentation software that allows her computer to function like a slide projector. The program is easy to use, and she can embed her pictures in the presentation—scanned headlines about the landfill from the local newspaper, photographs of the playground showing litter around the trash receptacles, a computer drawing of the school mascot urging recycling—so that everyone can easily see. It helps to set the tone for the rest of the unit, a student-centered exploration of local waste and pollution issues.

In the unit, teams of students investigate different aspects of local waste and pollution problems. To help them get background information, Ms. Wood sets up a couple of tutorial programs on CD-ROM, one about natural resources and another about ecology, as learning stations on the computers in her classroom. Students use these programs, in addition to their science textbook and materials from the school library, to learn basic concepts concerning natural resources, natural cycles, and the effects of pollution on plants, animals, and people.

Last year, one of the teams decided to investigate how much trash the team members' homes produced. Each student kept track of how much and what their household put in the trash that week. The team used a spreadsheet program to compile the data and make a graph that showed how much paper, plastic, metal, and so forth were produced. The kids were really surprised to see how much they threw away, and they were concerned about what it meant for the environment.

Another team got interested in wastewater. The students in that team were able to go out and collect water samples from upstream and downstream of the local wastewater treatment plant. They ran tests on the water to see whether the water from downstream of the plant was more polluted than the water collected upstream. With a little help from Ms. Wood, the kids found a site on the Internet where they could check the EPA standards for water quality and compare their findings with them.

Near the end of the unit, Ms. Wood arranged a field trip to the local landfill, so that her students could see and learn about how solid waste was disposed. She used her class database and her word processing program's mail merge function to send personalized letters to parents to recruit chaperones for the trip. Her letters got enough volunteers in no time. It was a great trip. The people at the landfill went out of their way to explain to the students how the waste was handled and what the landfill did to avoid creating pollution problems.

At the end of the unit, each student team presented the results of their investigations to the class. Some of the teams made posters of their results, some used *HyperStudio,* a multimedia authoring program, to create multimedia presentations, and one group even made a video of their investigation. As a final step, the students acted on what they had learned. They wrote letters, using the word processors on the classroom computers, that they sent out to members of the community. The wastewater team sent their results to the local plant. Some students wrote and thanked the landfill personnel for the field trip. Other students wrote to the mayor urging that the city do a better job of recycling. The class started an in-school program to recycle paper and aluminum cans. It is still going strong today!

Reflective Questions

1. How did Judy Wood use computer-based tools? How did her students use them?
2. What other ways might Ms. Wood have used computer-based tools to help the students learn?
3. Could Ms. Wood have used traditional media in place of computer-based tools in her unit? Which traditional media and in what situations?

Computer as Teacher, Assistant, and Learner

The computer is a powerful machine with a number of different uses in the field of education. This diversity is reflected in a popular categorization scheme developed by Robert Taylor (1980). Taylor's "tutor, tool, tutee model" divides the educational applications of computers into three broad categories: computer as teacher, computer as assistant, and computer as learner. In the first category, the computer presents instruction to the learner. In the second, the computer aids the teacher or learner in performing routine tasks such as writing, calculating, or presenting information. In the final category, the computer becomes the "student" and the learner "teaches" the computer to perform some task. While new developments have often blurred the distinctions between categories, this model remains a simple but useful way to look at different computer uses in education.

The Computer in the Role of Teacher

Of course, you may use computers to present instruction directly to students. In this mode, the computer engages in activities traditionally associated with human teachers or tutors. It presents instruction, provides instructional activities or situations, quizzes or otherwise requires interaction from learners, evaluates learner responses, provides feedback, and determines appropriate followup activities. As teaching machines, computers can be highly interactive, individualized, and infinitely patient. In the previous vignette, tutorial programs on CD-ROM provided instruction to students to help them learn basic concepts about natural resources and the environment. Applications that utilize the computer for teaching are usually labeled **computer-based instruction (CBI), computer-assisted instruction (CAI),** or **computer-assisted learning (CAL).** There are a number of common categories of computer-based instruction: drill and practice, tutorial, simulation, instructional game, and problem solving. We will discuss these in more detail in Chapter 8.

The Computer in the Role of Learner

When the computer functions as the learner, or in what Taylor (1980) called "tutee" mode, the traditional roles of computer and learner are reversed. The computer becomes the learner; the user becomes the teacher. The goal is for the user to "teach" the computer to perform some task. To achieve this goal, the user must learn how to perform the task and then must communicate this to the computer in a way that the computer will "understand." In other words, the user must program or direct the computer to make it do something. This requires logical thinking and problem-solving skills, and, as a result, many experts believe that this is one of the most valuable ways to use a computer in education. Activities of this sort can involve traditional computer languages such as Logo, BASIC, and C as well as newer multimedia/hypermedia authoring tools such as *HyperStudio, Toolbook, HyperCard,* and *Director.* In the vignette, student teams used *HyperStudio* to create multimedia presentations of their projects. We will look in more detail at the computer as learner in Chapter 8.

The Computer in the Role of Assistant

As assistant, the computer aids the teacher or learner in performing routine work tasks. It can function as a typewriter, a manual filing system, a financial worksheet, an artist's canvas, a drafting table, and much more. Software programs (commonly called **applications**) for these uses include word processors, graphics packages, presentation software, databases, spreadsheets, and telecommunications programs. Teachers often employ computers as labor-saving devices to produce instructional materials (e.g., printed matter, graphics, presentations) and manage their instruction (e.g., to maintain records and calculate student grades). Of course, learners can also employ the computer as an assistant. Students can use the computer to produce materials (e.g., term papers, presentations), and can use software tools in ways that help them learn (e.g., for research and calculations). In the vignette, Ms. Wood used her computer as an assistant for developing and making her presentation to the class and for locating parent volunteers for the field trip. Students used the computer as an assistant to do research, tabulate data, create graphs, and write letters to people in the community.

The computer, indeed, is a multifaceted tool that teachers and learners can use in many different ways in the classroom. It is so versatile that we cannot discuss all of its uses in detail here. We will look further at the computer as teacher and as learner in Chapter 8, when we discuss implementing instruction with learners. For the remainder of this chapter, we will focus on the computer as assistant. In this role, the computer aids teachers in planning and managing instruction, and aids students in organizing and presenting their work. Software that allows the computer to function as an assistant falls into the following broad categories: word processors, graphics tools and desktop publishers, presentation software, database management programs, spreadsheets, and telecommunications programs.

WORD PROCESSORS

Word processors are generally conceded to be the most widely used computer tools for personal productivity. A **word processor** is a computer application that allows you to enter, edit, revise, format, store, retrieve, and print text. Most word processors today also permit you to include graphic and tabular materials along with text. Popular word processors for personal computers include Microsoft *Word and* Corel *WordPerfect* as well as the word processors in integrated packages such as Microsoft *Works* and *AppleWorks* (formerly *ClarisWorks*). There are also particularly easy-to-use word processors designed specifically for school use, such as *Bank Street Writer* and *Write This Way.*

Word processors are tools for writing. They eliminate many of the difficulties associated with editing and producing a mechanically correct printed version of written work. As you enter text, it appears on the computer's **monitor,** or display

TABLE 3–1   *Common Features of Word Processors*

Text Entry and Editing	Formatting	Special Features	Storage and Retrieval
• *Word wrap.* Automatic shifting of whole words to a new line during text entry. The Return or Enter key denotes the end of a paragraph. • *Cursor control.* Using directional movement keys or mouse to position the cursor within a document. • *Insertion.* Automatic entry of text at the cursor's location. • *Deletion.* Deleting text at the cursor's location. • *Text selection.* Selecting or "highlighting" a portion of a document for subsequent editing or formatting. • *Block operations.* Copying, moving, formatting, or otherwise manipulating a selected block of text in a document. • *Search and replace.* Finding and/or replacing a word or phrase throughout a document. • *Undo.* Reversing an editing or formatting action; it lets you recover from an error.	• *Fonts.* The appearance of the text itself, typefaces in various sizes. Common ones include Times, Helvetica, and `Courier`. • *Type styles.* Attributes of text including **boldface,** *italics,* <u>underline,</u> and others. • *Margins and tabs.* Margins on all four sides of a document can be set. Tab stops can be set with respect to the margins. • *Text alignment.* Text can be centered or left, right, or fully justified. • *Line spacing.* Single and double line spacing, as well as line and a half spacing, can be set easily. • *Paging.* Paging is automatically handled although users can set their own page breaks. • *Graphics.* Pictures can be embedded in a document. • *Tables.* Tabular material may be embedded in a document. • *Others.* Other formatting features include headers, footers, and footnotes. • *Printing.* After formatting, documents can be previewed for final appearance and finally printed.	• *Spelling checker.* Software that identifies words it does not find in its built-in dictionary. • *Grammar checker.* Software that identifies a range of grammatical and format errors. • *Thesaurus.* Computer version of the popular library tool for the writer in search of synonyms. • *Outliner.* An automatic outlining feature.	• *Storage.* Documents can be saved to floppy diskette or hard disk. A "Save As" option permits a document to be modified and saved under another name. • *Retrieval.* The document can be copied from disk into working memory. • *File import and export.* One can store or retrieve files in other word processing and text formats. Nearly all word processors can save and retrieve ASCII or plain text files. Many can read and write HTML, the Web document format.

screen. If you make an error, it is simple to correct it before printing your work. More complex editing, such as moving or inserting entire paragraphs, is not much more difficult than correcting a single mistyped letter. You can align and format text as you wish, and can check both your spelling and grammar. Finally, after revising and laying out, or *formatting,* your text as desired, you can print a "clean" copy. You can then store your word processed text on computer disk for later retrieval, revision, and reuse.

Features of Word Processors

The most important word processing functions fall into four basic categories: (1) text entry and editing,

(2) text formatting and page layout for printing, (3) special assisting features, and (4) document storage and retrieval. Table 3–1 summarizes common word processor features in these four categories.

Word processors greatly simplify entering and editing text. They also provide a high degree of control over its appearance on the printed page. Although the degree to which text's appearance on the computer monitor accurately reflects its appearance, the printed page varies from one word processor to another. Today nearly all aspire to a standard called **WYSIWYG** (*what you see is what you get*). In other words, word processors today try to display on the monitor exactly what you will see when you print the document (Figure 3–2).

FIGURE 3–2 A screen from Microsoft *Word* showing WYSIWYG. *Screen template and text reprinted with permission from Microsoft Corporation. Illustration by Tom Kennedy.*

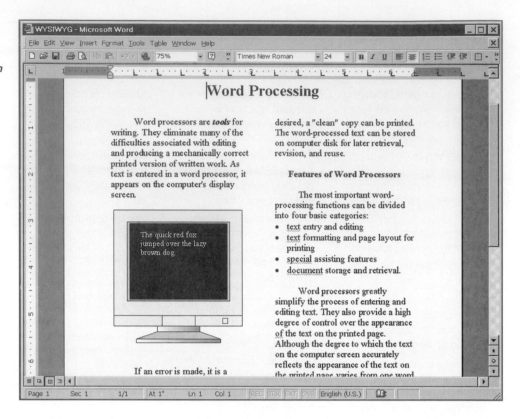

Special assisting features make your writing task easier and more nearly error free. Nearly all word processors have spelling checkers. Some work "on the fly" as you enter text, and some even do basic grammatical checking (e.g., subject-verb agreement). Of course, word processors support disk storage and retrieval. No longer must you create student handouts from scratch any time you change course content. You simply retrieve the old version of the handout from disk, edit it to reflect the new content, and print it. Word processors make it easier to avoid "reinventing the wheel."

Example Uses for Teachers and Students

Both teachers and learners can use word processors in a variety of ways. Examples follow.

Teachers' Uses

▶ Preparing lesson plans, handouts, worksheets, and other instructional materials
▶ Recording ideas during in-class brainstorming sessions
▶ Creating quizzes, tests, and other forms of evaluation
▶ Writing letters, permission slips, newsletters, and other forms of communication with parents, students, and administrators

Students' Uses

▶ Writing papers and other assigned written work
▶ Performing prewriting activities such as brainstorming, note taking, and idea collection
▶ Typing handwritten notes to reinforce learning or when studying for an exam

Problems and Pitfalls

Word processors, while wonderful tools, are not without potential problems. Users must learn specific routines to ensure that their text displays and prints properly. Some usage errors are relatively common, such as basic formatting problems, including inconsistent formatting among paragraphs, adding unwanted spaces or lines, and using spaces instead of more reliable tabs to position text. Global search and replace problems are common as well. Indiscriminately replacing "tree" with "pine" can also change "Main Street" to "Main Spinet." This problem can be overcome by searching by whole word only (e.g., for "tree "—tree with a space after it) to avoid finding matches embedded in other words.

Teachers may encounter other problems as well. In the early grades, some teachers fear that reliance on word processors may have a detrimental effect on students' handwriting skills. Certainly, word processing should not substitute for handwriting practice. As students learn to use word processors, keyboarding becomes important. Students who lack keyboarding skills may be hampered by slow typing speeds. There is also a danger that students may become overreliant on the word processor. For example, students relying on spell checkers can miss contextual errors (e.g., "there" instead of "their"). Students still must pay attention to the *content* of their writing.

It is important to keep in mind that word processors alone do not confer magical benefits. Users must pay attention as they write, and must learn to properly use their program's features. Teachers must integrate word processor use into a cohesive process approach to writing for maximum effectiveness.

GRAPHICS TOOLS AND DESKTOP PUBLISHERS

While word processors are primarily tools for manipulating text, graphics tools relate to pictorial information. Any computerized pictorial representation of information—chart, graph, drawing, animated figure, or photographic reproduction—is called a **graphic.** While different types of graphics may look different, they are usually one of two basic types: bitmapped or vector. Graphic images on the monitor appear composed of many tiny dots, much like photographs in a newspaper. Each screen dot is referred to as a picture element, or **pixel** for short. In **bitmapped graphics** (sometimes called *paint* or *raster* graphics), each pixel directly maps, or corresponds to, a portion of the image. The computer must keep track of position and color information for each pixel. In **vector graphics** (also called *draw* graphics), on the other hand, the computer "remembers" the steps involved in drawing a particular graphic image. This information is independent of a particular screen location or a graphic's size. So, vector graphics can be *scaled* (changed in size) without any loss of quality. Bitmapped graphics, on the other hand, become jagged looking when scaled to larger sizes. Some graphics tools are designed for working with bitmapped graphics, some for vector graphics, and some for both.

Although most word processors today can embed graphics in the text, this was not always so. In the mid 1980s, a new category of software arose in response to demand for control over both text and graphics on a printed page—desktop publishing. **Desktop publishing (DTP)** programs give users a high degree of control over the composition and layout of material on a printed page, including both text and graphics. This category of software remains important today both in the publishing industry and for such educational applications as school newspapers.

Features of Graphics Tools

A variety of computer graphics tools have been developed to meet many different graphical needs. Tools are available to help you with creative arts, business and scientific, mechanical drawing, print, and desktop publishing graphics tasks.

Creative Arts

Graphics packages that permit you to produce original artwork or modify existing artwork fall into this category. In most, you work with a mouse or drawing tablet and have available a variety of simulated tools intended to mimic what an artist might use, such as a pencil, a paintbrush, a color palette, and an eraser. You can draw perfectly straight lines, squares, circles, and polygons, as well as curves and irregular shapes. You can move or rotate portions of graphics as well as cut, copy, and paste them. You can select and control colors, and fill shapes with colors and/or patterns. More advanced packages let you apply special effects such as blurring, textures, and the illusion of embossing. Popular graphics packages include Adobe *Photoshop,* Adobe *Illustrator,* Corel *Draw,* MetaCreations *Painter,* and Microsoft *PhotoDraw 2000.* Graphics packages oriented for elementary students' use include Brøderbund *Kid Pix* and Davidson *Kid Works.* Figure 3–3 shows a screen from *Kid Pix.*

Business and Scientific Graphics

Programs that produce graphics common to business or scientific environments—charts and graphs—fall into this category. These programs accept data, from within the program or from another source (such as a spreadsheet program), and produce a chart or graph according to the user's specifications. Business graphics often include bar charts, pie charts, and line graphs. Scientifically oriented programs focus on line graphs as well as trigonometric and other mathematical functions. Programs in this category include *Cricket Graph, Graphers, Graphical Analysis, Harvard Graphics,* Microsoft *Graph,* and *The Graph Club.* In addition to these software packages for personal computers, there are now powerful graphing calculators that graph scientific data and mathematical functions. Graphing calculators are becoming very popular tools in mathematics and science classes.

Mechanical Drawing

Traditional drafting applications today rely on the computer. Computer-aided design (CAD) is

FIGURE 3–3 A screen from Brøderbund *Kid Pix,* a popular graphics program for elementary-age learners *Source: KidPix, © 1999, The Learning Company, Inc.*

used for the production of blueprints and factory floor layouts, for landscape architecture, for the design of machined parts, and so on. Popular programs of this type include *AutoCAD, PowerCADD,* and *IntelliCAD.*

Print Graphics

Although virtually all graphics programs support printing, this category refers to inexpensive programs that use built-in clip art to produce simple printed work such as signs and banners. The most well-known products in this category are *Printshop* and *PrintMaster,* which provide the user with a simple means to produce signs, greeting cards, and other graphically enhanced printed material.

Desktop Publishing

Desktop publishing (DTP) programs focus on the layout of text and graphics elements on a printed page. Page composition consists of identifying features such as the number of columns text will occupy, size and positioning of headlines or titles, text fonts used, spacing of text (both between lines and between individual letters), position of graphics, and how text wraps around graphics. Although word processors can do many of these things, desktop publishing programs typically afford greater control and precision. However, it is important to bear in mind that this high degree of control may be unnecessary for many

educational applications. Most desktop publishing programs include basic word processing and graphics functions. In addition, high-end DTP packages, especially, are designed to import text and graphics from other sources, such as word processing and graphics programs. Major desktop publishing programs include Adobe *PageMaker,* Quark *XPress,* and Ventura *Publisher.* Packages that are simpler to use and so more suitable for basic school uses include *Children's Writing and Publishing Center* and *Student Writing Center.* Figure 3–4 shows a page layout in Adobe *PageMaker.*

Example Uses for Teachers and Students

You can use graphics and desktop publishing applications in various ways in the classroom. Examples follow.

Teachers' Uses

▶ Creating handouts, worksheets, and other instructional materials for student use
▶ Creating signs or other graphical material for classroom display
▶ Maintaining graphical information (e.g., pictures of students) in a class database (see the section on databases later in this chapter)
▶ Designing and producing a class newsletter to send home to parents

FIGURE 3–4 A screen from Adobe *PageMaker,* a desktop publishing program *Source:* PageMaker, *Adobe Systems. Reprinted with permission.*

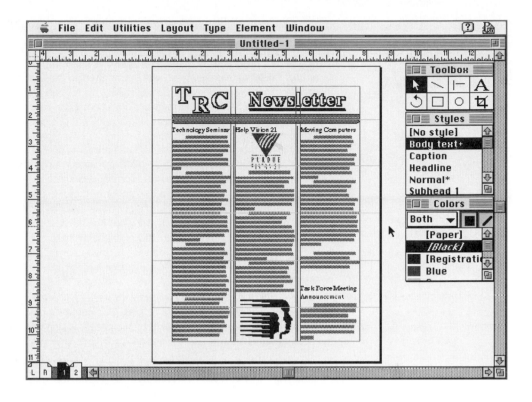

Students' Uses

▶ Making drawings for mini-books, reports, and other illustrated material

▶ Creating a graph of data collected in the science laboratory

▶ Producing major school works such as the school newspaper or yearbook

Problems and Pitfalls

One of the significant risks of using graphics and desktop publishing tools in school is that students may tend to emphasize form over substance. With page layout programs, students (and teachers!) often spend inordinate time fiddling with how a document looks. They may experiment with different fonts and page layouts at length while worrying little about the content. With graphics tools too, students often spend a great deal of time experimenting with various features, and they may want to use particular features of the software regardless of their applicability to the task at hand. It is important to recognize that the availability of computer tools does not substitute for good design. Bad design is bad design, whether done on the computer or not. Students need to apply sound design practices to their work and use features only when they are appropriate. See "Toolbox Tips: Guidelines for Designing Graphics" in Chapter 6 for tips about good visual design.

PRESENTATION SOFTWARE

Presentation software is designed for producing and displaying computer text and images, usually for presentation to a group. It is intended primarily to replace the functions typically associated with traditional media presentation tools such as slide and overhead projectors. Like other computer-based tools, it offers advantages over its traditional counterparts. Information is easily entered, edited, and presented. There is no need to set up or fumble with traditional media and equipment such as slides and slide carousels. With a presentation package, it is easy to produce very professional looking presentations complete with multimedia elements. Popular presentation packages include Microsoft *PowerPoint,* Adobe *Persuasion,* Lotus *Freelance Graphics,* Corel *WordPerfect Presentations,* and Gold Disc's *Astound.*

Features of Presentation Software

▶ *Slide format.* Most presentation software packages are organized around the concept of a *slide,* analogous to a photographic slide. What appears on a single computer screen is treated as though it were a photographic slide. Individual slides may have a number of different elements including text, graphics, bullets for emphasis,

TOOLBOX

TOOLS

Graphics Hardware

Most graphics programs today use the mouse as a drawing tool. However, there are alternatives. **Graphics tablets** are drawing devices that connect to the computer. Users commonly draw on the pad with a pressure-sensitive pen or stylus, much as an artist uses a sketchpad, while the resulting image appears on the monitor. Light pens allow users to draw directly on the computer screen. Many people prefer graphics tablets and light pens because the act of drawing is more natural than using a mouse (Figure A).

Because graphics usually require large amounts of disk storage space, developments in compact disc storage have made it possible to maintain large libraries of graphic images. CD-ROMs are often used to store collections of **clip art,** images designed to be copied from an original collection and pasted into a document or graphics program. Some clip art collections have tens of thousands of images to choose from, and include line art, paintings, photographs, and computer-generated artwork. In addition, Kodak has developed a CD format called the PhotoCD. A **PhotoCD** stores up to 100 high-quality images, in sizes and resolutions ranging from thumbnail pictures to large and very detailed images, which are scanned from 35-mm photographic negatives or slides. Many graphics programs now accept images stored in the PhotoCD format.

Probably the most significant developments in the area of graphics hardware in recent years have involved digitizing technologies. One common digitizing device is the optical **scanner,** which uses technology similar to a photocopying machine to take a printed image or a transparency and convert it into machine-readable form (Figure B).

FIGURE A A graphics tablet *Source: Photo courtesy of WACOM Technology Corporation, Vancouver, WA 98683.*

FIGURE B A scanner captures images on a printed page in a form the computer can use

TOOLBOX TOOLS
(continued)

You can manipulate scanned graphic images for desktop publishing applications or import them into graphics software. Scanners can also be used to capture text. In this case, the device scans the image of print on a page just as it would a graphic, but uses special *OCR* (optical character recognition) software to convert the image into editable text that you can import into a word processor.

Digital cameras represent one of the newest advances in the acquisition of graphic images (Figure C). These cameras take pictures just like ordinary cameras, but store the pictures on disk or on a memory chip for later transfer into a computer.

FIGURE C   A digital camera

and multimedia elements (see Figure 3–5). Once you have created individual slides, you can arrange the set just as a photographer would order her slides to create your presentation or slide show.

- *Slide templates.* Slide templates are usually provided to simplify the process of creating slides. These templates have preselected formatting, artwork, fonts, text styles, bullets, special effects, and so on. You simply select the desired template and enter the information; the program automatically applies the template's formatting.
- *Slide special effects.* To emphasize the points of your presentation, you may wish to add a bullet (•) before each text item. In many cases, bullets or text can be animated or made to appear point by point. When going from one slide to another, presentation packages allow for any one of a number of special effects, including dissolving, wiping, and fading.
- *Printing.* Presentation packages usually allow you to create a printed copy of your slides, either full size (one slide per page) or in a reduced format with multiple slides printed on each page.
- *Disk storage and retrieval.* Of course, like other computer tools, presentation software allows information to be stored on, or retrieved from,

disk. Large presentations can often be compressed and saved to multiple disks for easy transport.

- *Text entry and editing.* Because text is usually an integral element of most presentations, presentation packages provide basic text entry and editing features, including a variety of fonts and type styles. Basic word processor–like functionality is provided. Some packages provide a "chalk" function that allows you to use the mouse to write on a slide during a presentation like chalk on a chalkboard.
- *Graphics.* Graphics, too, are an important part of most presentations. Typical packages provide a basic set of drawing or painting tools. Chart and graph-production capabilities are common. Clip art is often provided. In addition, most presentation packages permit you to import graphics created in other packages.
- *Multimedia elements.* Most presentation packages support multimedia elements. These may include digitized audio, digitized video, hypermedia links, and control of external devices such as audio CDs. With full multimedia capability, presentation packages now include the functions of slide projectors, overhead projectors, tape recorders, and VCRs all rolled into one.

FIGURE 3–5 A screen from Microsoft *PowerPoint* showing various multimedia elements *Screen shot reprinted with permission from Microsoft Corporation.*

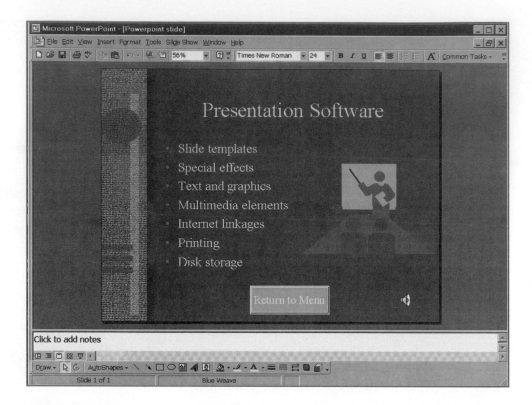

▶ *Internet compatibility.* The newest trend in presentation packages is compatibility with the Internet and the World Wide Web. You can embed links to Websites in your presentations. In addition, some applications let you save your presentations in Hypertext Markup Language (HTML), the language of the Web, which permits them to be placed on a Website for viewing online.

Example Uses for Teachers and Students

Teachers' Uses

▶ Supporting lectures or other presentations to groups in the classroom

▶ Making presentations to school boards, at professional meetings, or in other nonschool settings

▶ Displaying information at events such as parent open house nights; most presentation packages support timed or auto-run features that allow slide shows to run unattended

▶ Recording the results of brainstorming or other development activities in the classroom

▶ Preparing notes, pictures, or other material that can be printed, transferred to photographic slides, or converted for placement on the Web

Students' Uses

▶ Making in-class presentations or reports

▶ Preparing textual information, pictures, or other material that can be printed, transferred to photographic slides, or converted for placement on the Web

Problems and Pitfalls

As with graphics and other computer tools in school, a major risk in the use of presentation software is that students (and teachers) may emphasize form over substance. Presentation packages, especially when using prepared templates, can make almost any content *look* good. Unfortunately, the content itself may be awful. It is important that students realize that good content *must* come first. One way to emphasize this point is to require your students to first construct presentations using a blank template or in outline mode to discourage them from focusing on the flashy elements of the package—graphical templates, colors, pictures, animations, and so on. After creating the content, students then can focus on adding visual appeal. Caution students to avoid overdoing available effects when adding visual elements. Good design principles still apply.

Presentation software can greatly enhance the interest and visual appeal of lectures and other presentations. But, teachers who discover presentation software sometimes fall into the trap of wanting to turn everything into a presentation. It's easy and attractive, but the result can be too much of a good thing—lots of nice-looking lectures, but all lectures nonetheless. As we emphasize in this book, there are many methods and media for helping learners to learn. It is best to take a variety of approaches when trying to reach different learners and help them stay actively involved.

COMPUTER DATABASES AND DATABASE MANAGEMENT

A **database** is nothing more than a collection of information. We are familiar with many examples of databases that are *not* computerized: a telephone book, a recipe file, a collection of old magazines. These examples of noncomputer databases may be organized to a greater or lesser extent. Telephone books are well organized if you know the last name of the individual for whom you need a telephone number. A recipe file may be organized by type of dish: entrée, side dish, salad, or dessert. A stack of old magazines may be organized by date of issue. However, other ways of approaching this information may be very awkward. What if you have a telephone number and want to know what address it corresponds to? What if you want to know all of the recipes that use oregano? What if you want to find all of the articles in your magazines that relate to a particular topic? These tasks are very difficult with a noncomputerized database, but become simple when the database is computerized.

Computerized databases offer significant advantages compared to their noncomputer counterparts:

▶ *Flexible access.* While a telephone book is convenient if you know the name of the person you want to call, a computerized telephone directory can be searched by name, number, address, or any other information it contains. Any information category in a database can be used for searching. For example, you may search a library's electronic card catalog by title, subject, author, or key word without the need for separate catalogs.

▶ *Amount of information.* Electronic databases can provide access to huge amounts of information. A CD-ROM database can hold an entire encyclopedia. On the Internet, you can find the telephone number for just about anyone in the United States who has a public listing.

▶ *Ease of manipulation.* Electronic databases also make it easy to work with the information they contain. Schools that maintain student records, grades, and other administrative information in electronic databases can quickly generate grade-

point averages by class, or identify all of the teachers who should be notified of student absences because of an upcoming band trip.

Features of Computer Database Programs

In this section, we'll concentrate on database applications that run on personal computers. A program for working with computer databases is known as a **database management system (DBMS).** Database management software enables you to enter, edit, store, retrieve, sort, and search through databases. To understand exactly what DBMSs do, let's examine the structure of a typical computer database.

Suppose you want to put the name and address information from your Rolodex (or your address book) into computer form. How would you organize it? A computer database is organized in much the same fashion as a Rolodex. Each card in the Rolodex corresponds to an individual. On the card are various items of information: name, address, telephone number, and so on. In computer terminology, each individual category of information that is recorded is called a **field.** So there might be a name field, a street address field, a city field, a telephone number field, and so on. The whole collection of fields that corresponds to one Rolodex card—that is, to one individual—is called a **record.** Each record is designed to contain the same collection of fields. All of the records are collected into a **datafile.** The datafile corresponds to the entire Rolodex. In simple cases the database consists of only a single datafile. In other cases the database is a collection of datafiles that are interrelated in some way. For example, you might crossreference your name-and-address file with your recipe file to make sure that you prepare a different dish the next time you have certain friends over for dinner. The components of a computer database are depicted graphically in Figure 3–6.

Database management software allows you to create and work with databases in the following ways:

▶ Define fields.
▶ Organize the fields that comprise a record.
▶ Enter and edit the data in records.
▶ Sort the information in various ways (e.g., alphabetically by last name).
▶ Selectively search through the information (e.g., find all the individuals who live in a particular city).
▶ Generate various reports or summaries of the information and print these.
▶ Save the database to and retrieve it from disk.

FIGURE 3–6 Components of a computer database

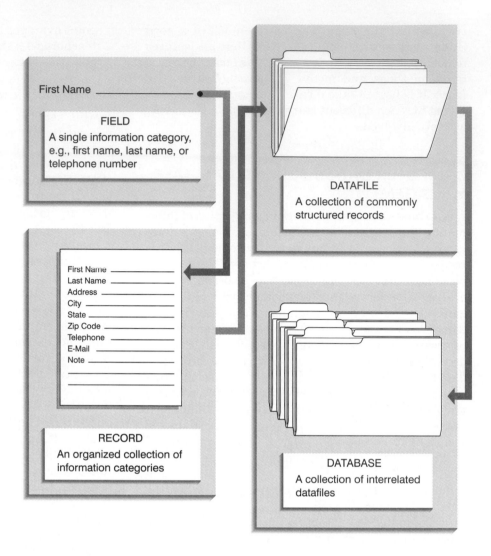

There are two basic varieties of traditional database management programs: simple or flat filers and relational databases. **Flat filers** limit their work to a single datafile at a time. Popular flat filers include the database components of integrated products such as Microsoft *Works* and *AppleWorks* (formerly *ClarisWorks*). **Relational databases** are more powerful but usually are more complex to use. They permit you to interrelate information across more than one datafile, as in the previous example of cross-referencing an address file with a recipe file. Programs such as Microsoft *Access, dBASE, FileMaker Pro,* and *Paradox* fall into this category.

With the rapid growth of hypertext and hypermedia, more and more computer databases are incorporating elements of these technologies. In a database on CD-ROM, for example, one might link from an article about the heart to one about the lungs simply by clicking on the word "lungs" in the text of the heart article. Of course, the World Wide Web represents the most dramatic example of this type of access to data. We'll look in more detail at this technology later in this chapter and in Chapter 9.

Example Uses for Teachers and Students

Teachers' Uses

▶ Creating and maintaining basic information about students in classes
▶ Developing bibliographic files of books and/or articles available in the school that support the curriculum
▶ Keeping records of media and materials available in the classroom or resource center
▶ Building a collection of test or quiz questions referenced by topic, book chapter, objective, and possibly other identifiers, such as level of Bloom's taxonomy
▶ Storing compilations of teaching methods, strategies, and lesson plans

FIGURE 3–7   Sample spreadsheet in Microsoft *Works* for calculating students' grades (cell H2 is highlighted) *Screen shot reprinted with permission from Microsoft Corporation.*

	A	B	C	D	E	F	G	H
	Name	Quiz 1	Quiz 2	Quiz 3	Quiz 4	Exam 1	Final	Overall
2	Butcher, Cheryl	83	76	91	94	86	90	87.20
3	Doe, Jane	98	89	94	100	95	92	94.22
4	Doe, John	73	60	86	89	77	74	76.10
5	Ferkis, Mary Ann	100	93	93	100	98	96	96.65
6	George, Ed	62	55	79	84	68	73	70.50
7	Lin, Ella	78	80	84	88	76	79	80.15
8	Mandell, Susan	91	90	95	95	89	94	92.38
9	Taylor, Dave	87	81	91	95	88	90	88.85
10	Ward, Aggie	76	65	82	80	75	81	77.18
11								
12	Class Average	83.11	76.56	88.33	91.67	83.56	85.44	84.80

Cell reference: H2 =Average(B2:E2)*.5+F2*.2+G2*.3

Students' Uses

▶ Locating simple information in prepared databases such as the school's electronic card catalog or a database of U.S. presidents

▶ Developing problem-solving and higher-order thinking skills by investigating the answers to complex questions through searching databases

▶ Developing original databases to maintain information of various kinds

Problems and Pitfalls

Students, especially younger learners, need to have a good concept of research before using a computer database to find information. Poor library research skills will translate into poor computer search skills. Examples and assistance may be needed for students to understand Boolean logic and more complex search techniques.

Students also need to understand the limits of databases. A student might approach database research with a particular hypothesis. Failure to find evidence in the database to support the hypothesis does not necessarily negate it. The query might not be appropriately constructed, the information in the database might be categorized in another way, or the database might not contain complete information relative to the question. The limitations of a database can have significant impact on its usability in particular situations.

When constructing databases, it is important to think about your information needs and to plan well. Some simple programs may not permit changes once you have defined the structure of the database. Some programs limit you in other ways. For example, the database components of many integrated packages permit only a limited view of the data when preparing printed reports. Careful planning can help to minimize problems.

ELECTRONIC SPREADSHEETS

Electronic **spreadsheets** are general-purpose calculating tools derived from the paper worksheets once used by accountants. A spreadsheet is like a large piece of paper that has been marked off into rows and columns to form a grid. Each intersection of a row and column, a single block in the grid, is called a **cell.** Individual columns and rows are labeled for reference. In the most common scheme, columns are lettered and rows are numbered. Thus each cell can be uniquely identified by its column and row reference (see Figure 3–7).

An individual cell normally contains one of three types of information: a number, a textual label, or a formula. Since spreadsheets are fundamentally calculating tools, it makes sense that cells can contain numbers. Numbers are the basic stuff that spreadsheets work with. Textual labels, as the name implies, are used to label parts of the spreadsheet. From the standpoint of calculations, they are ignored. **Formulas** are mathematical expressions that direct the spreadsheet to perform various kinds of calculations on the numbers entered in the cells. Formulas work on values in the spreadsheet by referring to the cells where the values are located.

Popular spreadsheets include Microsoft *Excel*, Lotus *1-2-3*, and Quattro *Pro*. In addition, spreadsheets are found in integrated packages such as Microsoft *Works* and *AppleWorks* (formerly *ClarisWorks*). The *Cruncher* is a spreadsheet program designed especially for school use. Spreadsheets offer several advantages over older paper-and-pencil methods of manipulating numbers, including built-in formulas, the ability to replicate or copy formulas from one spot in a spreadsheet to another, rapid automatic recalculation, the ability to quickly see the effects of making changes, and the capability to create a template—a spreadsheet "shell" with all of the appropriate labels and formulas in place but without the data.

Features of Spreadsheets

▶ *Mathematical functions.* Most spreadsheet programs support a range of built-in mathematical functions, usually including simple statistics, logarithmic functions, trigonometric functions, and common financial functions. These greatly simplify building formulas.
▶ *Formatting.* The information you enter in the spreadsheet can be formatted in a variety of ways. Text labels or numbers can be aligned. Numbers can be expressed to a certain number of decimal places or in different forms (e.g., dollar amounts or scientific notation). You can apply different fonts and type styles.
▶ *Graphing.* Most spreadsheet programs have graphing capability. After selecting appropriate parts of the spreadsheet, the program will produce a graph of the data in the highlighted cells. This feature makes it easy for you to visualize relationships among your data.
▶ *Database elements.* Although spreadsheets are basically calculating tools, many spreadsheet programs also include some database elements. For example, you can create a simple database in a portion of the spreadsheet by treating the cells in a particular column as a database field. You can then link the entries in the database to calculations performed by the spreadsheet.
▶ *Macros.* A **macro** is a shortcut for encoding a series of actions in a computer program. While not unique to spreadsheets, macros are very commonly used with them. Macros provide a means of performing a number of separate steps through a single command. They simplify complex actions. For example, in a gradebook spreadsheet, you might create a macro to automatically copy end-of-quarter grades to a new location, keep students' names, and blank out the grades area in preparation for the start of a new grading period.
▶ *Printing and disk storage.* Of course, spreadsheets also support disk storage/retrieval and printing. Because spreadsheets can grow quite large (e.g., tens of thousands of cells), some spreadsheet programs support horizontal or *landscape* printing to better work with continuous-form printer paper.

Example Uses for Teachers and Students

Teachers' Uses
▶ Creating a gradebook to maintain students' grades
▶ Keeping other information about students (e.g., a physical education teacher might maintain student performance in various exercises or sporting activities)
▶ Tracking costs of classroom materials (e.g., a chemistry teacher could maintain information about the costs of chemicals used in laboratory exercises)
▶ Demonstrating complex calculations to a class (e.g., a business teacher might build loan amortization tables varying by interest rate as a class illustration)

Students' Uses
▶ Maintaining financial records of a student organization (e.g., tracking candy sales by members of the pep band)
▶ Setting up and maintaining a personal budget
▶ Entering and analyzing data from science experiments
▶ Performing "what if?" simulation or hypothesis-testing activities (e.g., What would happen to my monthly cost of operating a car if an accident doubled my insurance rates?)

Problems and Pitfalls

Probably the most common problem when constructing spreadsheets is flawed formulas. It is easy to enter an erroneous formula either because of flawed logic or mistaken syntax. Flawed logic means that you or your students fail to correctly devise the way to get the answer to the problem at hand. Syntactical problems can occur, in part, because spreadsheets rely on a hierarchy when performing mathematical calculations (e.g., multiplication and division are performed before addition and subtraction). To reduce syntactical problems, use parentheses to enclose parts of the formula; whatever is enclosed in parentheses is calculated first. Flawed formulas are sometimes easy to spot because they give obviously incorrect values. However, sometimes errors can be quite subtle. It is important to always doublecheck spreadsheet formulas and to remain alert for the possibility of errors.

Spreadsheets can remove the burden of complex calculations and so allow students to focus on conceptual understanding of problems. In many cases, this is a good thing. However, it is important to recognize there can be problems. Students may have a poor grasp of the limitations of the information produced by the spreadsheet because they do not understand the underlying model or mathematics. When using spreadsheets in instruction, teachers need to strike an appropriate balance between eliminating unnecessary calculations and giving students adequate understanding to make sense of what the spreadsheet tells them.

COMPUTER TELECOMMUNICATIONS AND THE INTERNET

Today there are millions of personal computers, and they are becoming interconnected to other computers, both large and small, at an astonishing rate. We live in an era of global computer interconnectivity. As a result, there is literally a whole world of information available to the personal computer user through computer networking and telecommunication.

There are two basic categories of computer networks: **local-area networks (LANs)** and **wide-area networks (WANs).** LANs cover a limited geographical area, often within a single building or even in a single room within a building. They are common in offices and in school computer laboratories (or whole buildings). They permit the sharing of resources; for example, many users can share a printer via a LAN. In schools, many different software programs can be installed on the *network server,* the computer that manages the network, allowing users to easily access the software via the LAN without having to fumble with floppy disks.

Wide-area networks, as their name implies, cover a broad geographic area. The most extreme example is the Internet. The *Internet*—also known as the "Net," the "Information Superhighway," and "cyberspace"—is the vast collection of computer networks that links millions of computers and tens of millions of people worldwide. Computers on the Internet are linked together by a maze of interconnections sort of like a spider's web. This web is composed of many separately administered computer networks, including many different kinds of computers, that are linked together by

means of a common communications *protocol* (a set of common rules) known as **TCP/IP** (Transmission Control Protocol/Internet Protocol). Every computer on the Internet has a unique address, actually a number, called its *IP address.*

These computers communicate with one another over network connections, via a network adapter, or telephone lines, using a **modem,** a device that converts the computer's digital information into sound that can be sent or received. Information transmitted across the Internet is first broken into chunks called **packets.** These packets are routed to their destination, a specific IP address, by means of any available pathway. This system was originally created for defense utilization; if part of the network is knocked out, for example by a military strike or power outage, the remainder of the network still functions because the information is simply routed along another pathway. Hence, the Internet was built to overcome potential blockages.

The Internet provides teachers and students with unprecedented access to up-to-date information and resources. It provides access to text, graphics, and multimedia. It supports new forms of communication, such as electronic mail, Internet-based telephony, and even videoconferencing. It breaks down the barrier of the classroom wall and brings new opportunities and new challenges to schools.

Features of Computer Telecommunications

There are a number of applications of computer telecommunications and the Internet. The three most common functions today are electronic mail (e-mail), information retrieval, and information publishing. We briefly consider each here. We will discuss the Internet in more detail in Chapter 9.

Electronic Mail

Electronic mail (e-mail) is the most widespread application of computer telecommunications. It is analogous to postal mail but much faster and more versatile. E-mail allows private messages to be sent from individuals to other individuals or from individuals to groups. An e-mail message travels from the sending computer to the receiving computer, usually in seconds to minutes, and it is stored in the receiver's electronic mailbox until she is ready to access it. Once the message has been received, it can be stored, printed, replied to, or forwarded to someone else.

Today, people send e-mail all around the globe using the Internet. To send e-mail to someone on the Internet, you must have access to mail services on a computer linked to the Internet, and you must know the

FIGURE 3–8 Finding your way in cyberspace—a guide to e-mail and Internet addresses

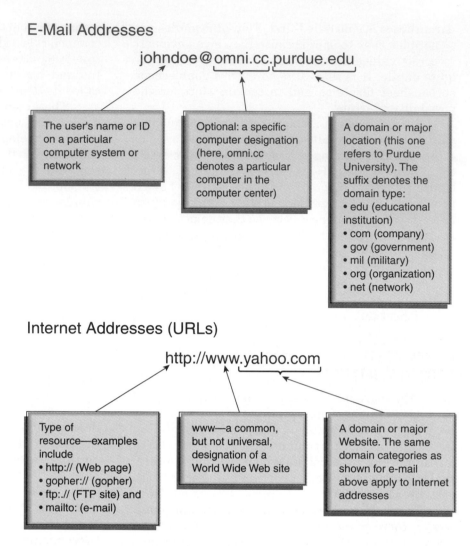

E-Mail Addresses

johndoe@omni.cc.purdue.edu

The user's name or ID on a particular computer system or network

Optional: a specific computer designation (here, omni.cc denotes a particular computer in the computer center)

A domain or major location (this one refers to Purdue University). The suffix denotes the domain type:
• edu (educational institution)
• com (company)
• gov (government)
• mil (military)
• org (organization)
• net (network)

Internet Addresses (URLs)

http://www.yahoo.com

Type of resource—examples include
• http:// (Web page)
• gopher:// (gopher)
• ftp:// (FTP site) and
• mailto: (e-mail)

www—a common, but not universal, designation of a World Wide Web site

A domain or major Website. The same domain categories as shown for e-mail above apply to Internet addresses

---

other person's **e-mail address.** Just as you have a postal mail address, everyone on the Internet has an e-mail address. The basic form of any Internet e-mail address is *username@location*. As one scans from left to right through an e-mail address, one moves from more specific to more general information just as a postal address on an envelope goes from specific to general as one moves down the address label. See Figure 3–8 for an overview of e-mail and Internet addresses.

In e-mail addresses, the *username* is usually the individual's assigned identifier on her computer system. The *location* refers to the other person's computer system. This may be a commercial online service (e.g., aol.com), a university (e.g., purdue.edu), a school-based network (e.g., wvec.k12.in.us), or some other computer system on the Internet. As noted in Figure 3–8, **domains,** or general location classifications, are identified by the suffix following the period (called the "dot") at the end of the address—for example *edu* indicates an educational institution, while *com* denotes a company. Other common domain identifiers are *gov*

(government), *mil* (military), *net* (network), and *org* (organization). Countries also have identifiers added to the end of the location name for international e-mail. Examples include *au* (Australia), *ca* (Canada), *fr* (France), *jp* (Japan), and *uk* (United Kingdom).

Information Retrieval

Information retrieval, especially for education, is one of the most important uses of the Internet. A source of vast information resources on the Internet is the **World Wide Web** (**WWW** or just **the Web**). The Web consists of millions of sites of information displayed in hypermedia format; it supports formatted text, graphics, animations, and even audio and video. Through the Web, one can visit the White House, tour exhibits from the Library of Congress, see the latest pictures from NASA's Hubble Telescope, and find information on just about any topic imaginable. All are accessible through a simple point-and-click mouse interface familiar to users of graphical operating systems.

FIGURE 3–9 Home page of the World Wide Web site for the White House *Source: The White House*

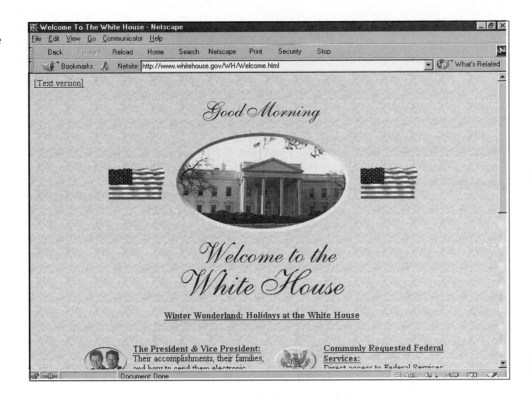

A software program used for accessing the Web is known as a **browser.** The two most popular browser programs today are Netscape *Navigator* and Microsoft *Internet Explorer.* Browsers allow users to navigate the Web, bookmark favorite sites, control how Web pages are displayed, and manage the behind-the-scenes interactions that take place when retrieving Web information. (See Figure 3–9 for a picture of the White House Website, first established by the Clinton administration in 1994, as shown in Netscape *Navigator.*)

Information on the Web is organized in units called **Web pages,** which are similar to printed documents but that contain hypermedia features. A **Website** consists of a set of interrelated pages usually operated by a single entity (e.g., a company, school, organization, or individual). The preliminary or main page of information for a particular site on the Web is called its **home page.** Most pages on the Web contain links to other information. Sometimes these links access information elsewhere in the Website, and sometimes they access information at another site altogether. To access the information, the user simply clicks on the *hot link,* which is usually represented by colored text, a picture, or an icon. There is no need to know where the link leads; the browser automatically makes the appropriate connection and retrieves the information.

Browsers also provide access to sites still supporting older forms of Internet information retrieval— Telnet, ftp, and gopher. *Telnet* is a way of making a connection with a computer at a remote location. *File transfer protocol (ftp)* is the standard way that files are exchanged over the Internet. *Gopher* is software, developed at the University of Minnesota, to "go for" information; gophers access information via a hierarchical menu system rather than the hypertext format of the Web. Today, these older methods of accessing information have been incorporated into most Web browsers. The browser automatically does whatever is needed to fetch the desired information, whether it is a Web page, gopher information, or whatever. It doesn't matter whether the information comes from a computer in the next room or one halfway around the world. It all looks the same. As a result, the Web effortlessly brings the world to the desktop.

Every site on the Internet has a unique address called a **URL (Uniform Resource Locator).** You can jump directly to any page (or identifiable component of a page) on the Web by entering its URL in the browser's location window. Figure 3–8 shows how to interpret Internet and Web addresses.

Throughout this book, we have listed the URLs of Websites of interest in the "Suggested Resources" section at the end of each chapter as well as in other places to alert you to valuable Web resources. When you know the URL for the information you want, it is easy to go right to it. However, sometimes finding the information that you want can be daunting. Websites shut down, page addresses change without notice, or you may not have complete URL information.

To help with the process of finding information, a number of so-called search engines are available. **Search engines** are sites on the Internet that maintain databases of Websites that you can search to locate information of interest. Most let you enter key search terms as well as apply simple Boolean (logical search) expressions. Different search engines rely on different methods for locating information of potential interest. Therefore, when trying to locate information it is usually a good idea to try several search engines or one of the metasearch engines (e.g., Metacrawler) that automatically sends your search parameters to multiple search engines.

Information Publishing

Increasingly, the Web is being seen as a place where organizations and individuals can display information for others to view and/or retrieve. So, many schools have created their own Websites, which teachers, students, and whole classes often use for display of projects as well as for dissemination of information about the school.

Web pages are written in **Hypertext Markup Language (HTML).** HTML is not a computer language in the conventional sense; it consists of plain unformatted (ASCII) text with embedded labels or **tags** that tell browsers how to display the information. The embedded tags allow for different type sizes, text styles, paragraphs, embedded graphics, links, and more. For example, the tag set <B> and </B> is used to mark the beginning and end, respectively, of boldfaced text.

You can create HTML documents using any text editor, such as a word processor. Alternatively, you can use one of the many tools now available specifically for developing Web pages, such as Adobe *PageMill, BBEdit,* Claris *Home Page,* Macromedia *Dreamweaver,* Microsoft *FrontPage, NetObjects Fusion,* Netscape *Composer,* and others. These programs permit you to design and lay out a Web page without writing HTML code, much like you would use a desktop publishing program, and then publish the resulting page to a Website. We consider Web page development in more detail in Chapter 9.

Example Uses for Teachers and Students

Teachers' Uses
- E-mailing other teachers in similar positions to exchange ideas and reduce teacher isolation
- Accessing online databases of teaching methods, strategies, and instructional plans
- Gathering up-to-date content from the Internet to plan and carry out lessons
- Setting up a classroom home page to let parents and community members know about class activities, children's homework assignments, upcoming field trips, and so on

Students' Uses
- Using e-mail for pen-pal exchanges with students at other locations to learn more about other places and cultures or to practice a foreign language
- Exchanging written work with students at other locations
- Sharing data from science experiments conducted at many locations
- E-mailing teachers to ask questions, get help, submit work, and so on
- Conducting research using resources available online
- Publishing class projects on the World Wide Web for access by other students, parents, and members of the community

Problems and Pitfalls

Computer telecommunications open many new and exciting avenues for teachers and students. But the information superhighway is not free of potholes! With its myriad technical details, computer telecommunications can sometimes be difficult to master. The basic problem is that it requires many separate components to work in concert: the computer, modem or network adapter, communication software, telephone or network line, and the remote computer. Sometimes they do not cooperate. If you have problems you can't resolve on your school computer, call on your school's technical support personnel. If you have problems at home, contact your Internet service provider, or ask a knowledgeable friend for assistance.

Many teachers are rightly excited by the opportunities available through access to the Internet. But there is a need for caution. Simple pen-pal projects or aimless searching of the massive Web resources available may accomplish little educationally. You need to think about productive ways to use the Internet. You should spend time to locate and check out useful resources in advance. This will help to make Internet-based activities more meaningful.

You also need to be aware that the Internet is unregulated. While there are many wonderful resources (e.g., Library of Congress, Smithsonian Institute, NASA), there are also many worthless sites. Students may waste time, or, worse, may find biased or inaccurate information. You need to help your students think about how to evaluate the information they find on the Internet. What makes information "good"? Is a source reliable? Can information be verified from other sources?

It is also important to point out that material unsuitable for children is available on many Internet sites. In addition, there have been reported incidents of adults using electronic networks to stalk or lure children. While software is available to block access to undesirable content or Websites, no software is perfect. If the Internet is available to students, close supervision is essential, and students need to be educated about responsible behavior on the Internet. Every school should have an Internet acceptable use policy that spells out its policies and procedures. We'll talk more about Internet usage issues in Chapter 9.

Reflective Questions

1. As a teacher, which of the computer tools discussed in this chapter do you think you will use the most? The least? Why?
2. How could you use these tools to help your students have more valuable learning experiences?
3. Can you think of ways not discussed in this chapter to use the software tools discussed for teaching or learning?

APPLICATIONS IN THE LEARNER-CENTERED CLASSROOM

We hope that this chapter has given you many ideas about how you might use the computer in your own classroom. Keep in mind that the computer with appropriate software is just a tool, albeit a very versatile one. Like the rotary multi-tool described in the beginning of the chapter, the computer can do a lot of different things. However, it is not appropriate for everything. Just as the multi-tool does a poor job of hammering a nail, the computer is not particularly effective in many learning situations ranging from helping students learn handwriting to assisting with some types of complex reasoning and problem solving. While the computer can do a lot, it isn't right for everything. In teaching and learning, as in model building, it is important to know when and how to use available tools appropriately. As we look closely throughout this text at the best ways to plan and implement instruction to help your students learn, we will highlight ways that computers can be useful tools for you.

There are no absolute rules for using computers in the classroom. Computers are relatively

recent innovations, and software is constantly changing. Teachers and schools are still struggling to find the best ways to make use of these wonderful tools. Don't be afraid to try things, and don't be fooled into thinking that you have to know everything to get started. Jump in! Within the learner-centered classroom, at times it may be very effective to *use the students in the "teacher" role as you take on the role of the "learner."* Moreover, *a key assumption within such classrooms is collaboration.* Using the computer with small groups of students who work together on a project may prove beneficial to learning new software, gaining experience with the computer, reducing computer technology fears and anxieties, and engendering exploration. You and your students will learn as you go along together. A spirit of adventure and openness is the best attitude to have when working with computers. As you learn and grow, you will find more and more ways that they can be of benefit in your classroom.

In the remainder of the book, we highlight applications of computers to the topics being discussed. In Chapter 8, we focus on many ways that students can use computers for learning, and in Chapter 9 we focus on the Internet and distance learning technologies. In other chapters, we highlight potential applications of the computer and allied technologies as appropriate. As you progress through this text, look for these applications and refer to the diagram in the front cover of the book for ways that the technology ties into planning, implementing, and evaluating your instruction.

ONE TEACHER'S STORY
by Janette Moreno

I just cannot believe what a change the computer has made to my teaching! When I first started teaching, I didn't use a computer at all. I had my typewriter, scissors, glue, and tape. That was how I put everything together. Now I can't believe I did it that way!

I can remember the start of my second year of teaching. I was talking to Sherry, who taught in the room next to mine. We had both decided to do a newsletter to hand out to parents for our upcoming open house. I went back to my room and started cutting and pasting some things together the old-fashioned way. A few minutes later, Sherry walked in the room, and she was done with hers! "How did you do that so quickly?" I asked. She said, "I had last year's newsletter on my computer. I just went in, changed the things I needed to update, printed out a new version for this year, and ran it off." Well, I can tell you, that sold me on what the computer could do!

I was a little nervous about it at first. You know, I didn't get much computer experience when I was in college. But, the district provided some inservice training, and later I took a class at the university. I just decided to dive in and see what I could do. Before long, I started using the computer for all sorts of things. My students also jumped in and helped me figure things out when I got stuck. I'm getting used to the idea that at times I have to go into "learner mode" while they do the teaching.

I made my newsletter on the computer, complete with some neat clip art I found on a CD-ROM. I also used *PowerPoint* to make a presentation for the open house. I built a database to keep track of information on the students in my class, and I set up a spreadsheet to figure grades. Just last week, I used e-mail and the Internet.

I'd been worrying about how to handle this one unit I teach. It's been difficult in past years, and I was looking for something new. Well, at a conference last year, I met this teacher named Ramona who teaches down south. We've been exchanging e-mail for a few months, mostly about recipes and other fun stuff. So, I thought I'd ask her if she had any ideas. I got onto my system, started my mail software, and sent her an e-mail note. She answered me before the end of the day. E-mail is so great!

Anyway, Ramona didn't really have any ideas for me. But she sent me the address of a Website of lesson plans that she knew about. So, I got back on my computer, launched Netscape *Navigator,* and found the site. It was incredible! There were thousands of lesson plans. I searched for my topic, and sure enough I found several plans that I think will work with my kids. I printed them, and I'm going to try my own version of one next week.

This has been so helpful for me. And, you know what? As I have learned new uses for the computer for myself, I have also started to see ways in which I can use it as a learning tool for my students. They are now working on various projects in small cooperative groups in which they gather information, assemble it, and produce very nice results with the computer as a key tool.

I just don't know how I ever got along without the computer before. It is the one tool I turn to for just about everything now. It's my little electronic teacher's aide!

SUMMARY

In this chapter we examined applications of personal computers for teaching and learning. The computer can be used in three ways: as a teacher, as an assistant, and as a learner. A number of different kinds of software tools are commonly used when the computer functions in education. These include word processors, graphics and desktop publishing tools, presentation packages, databases, spreadsheets, and computer telecommunications and the Internet. We described common features of each type of software, presented typical applications for both teachers and learners, and discussed potential problems and pitfalls.

REFLECTIVE ACTIVITIES

▶ Survey area schools regarding the computer systems that they use. What brands are common? What sorts of hardware and software do typical school computer systems have?

▶ Think about a recent assignment involving research and writing (e.g., a term paper). Did you use the Internet for research? If so, how? If not, how could you have used it? Did you compose the paper using a word processor? If so, what specific features did you find most useful? If not, what features would have been of particular use?

▶ Talk to a computer-using teacher. What computer tools does she use regularly? For what purposes? What tools do her students use regularly? For what purposes?

SUGGESTED RESOURCES

Grabe, M., & Grabe, C. (1997). *Integrating technology for meaningful learning.* Boston, MA: Houghton Mifflin.

Jonassen, D. H. (1996). *Computers in the classroom: Mindtools for critical thinking.* Upper Saddle River, NJ: Merrill/Prentice Hall.

Lockard, J., Abrams, P. D., & Many, W. A. (1997). *Microcomputers for twenty-first century educators.* New York: Longman.

Roblyer, M. D., Edwards, J., & Havriluk, M. A. (1997). *Integrating educational technology into teaching.* Upper Saddle River, NJ: Merrill/Prentice Hall.

Simonson, M. R., & Thompson, A. (1997). *Educational computing foundations.* Upper Saddle River, NJ: Merrill/Prentice Hall.

Taylor, R. P. (Ed.). (1980). *The computer in the school: Tutor, tool, tutee.* New York: Teachers College Press.

WEBSITES

Yahoo Computers and Internet: http://www.yahoo.com/Computers/

Yahoo Education: http://www.yahoo.com/Education/

PLANNING

Webster's *New World Dictionary* defines a *plan* as "any detailed method, formulated beforehand, for doing or making something." Planning is a natural part of life. We plan in order to exercise some influence over future events and to increase the likelihood that things will turn out the way we want. Although a plan doesn't guarantee success, not having a plan often ensures failure. Plans can take various forms:

- A recipe helps us make sure the food we are preparing includes the necessary ingredients and cooks for the right amount of time.
- An itinerary helps us make sure our vacation trip includes all the things we want to see and do, given our limited amount of time.
- A budget helps us make sure our income both covers our expenses and also allows us some spending money.
- A grocery list helps us make sure we purchase the necessary items when we go shopping.

This section is about planning for instruction and learning. Our purpose is twofold: to convince you that effective planning is a vital part of effective instruction, and to provide you with some practical guidelines for effective planning.

This is the first part of the PIE model described in Chapter 1. Your instructional plan directs what takes place during the implementation and evaluation stages of instruction. Once you have a plan for your instruction, you can move on to implement the instruction outlined in the plan. Once you have implemented your instruction, you can evaluate its effectiveness in helping your students learn. Planning instruction is made up of three parts:

1. *Developing the plan.* This involves identifying the important characteristics of your learners, specifying your intended objectives for the instruction, specifying the relevant features of the learning environment, and developing instructional activities that will ensure learning. We discuss each of these in Chapter 4.
2. *Identifying methods and media.* A variety of instructional methods and media exist that can impact how learners experience the learning situation. With the variety of content, as well as differences in learners and the practical constraints of time and budget, it is imperative that you become aware of the different methods and media available. We

discuss these options and the advantages and limitations of each in Chapter 5.

3. *Selecting, adapting, and / or producing instructional materials.* We explore in Chapter 6 the process of assembling and/or developing the instructional materials you will need to carry out your plan. We address the practical aspects of preparing instructional materials within your time and budget constraints.

In this exciting section of the book we encourage creativity, problem solving, and reflection. For many, the art of teaching is embedded in planning and developing what students will experience and how they will learn from those experiences. This section focuses on how you can create learning experiences that will ensure your students' success.

C H A P T E R 4

Developing a Plan

KEY WORDS AND CONCEPTS

Prerequisite
Objective
Knowledge
Intellectual skill
Motor skill
Attitude
Learning environment
Instructional activity
Declarative information
Conditional information
Reinforcing feedback
Corrective feedback
Heuristic

OBJECTIVES

After reading and studying this chapter, you will be able to

▶ Identify the important characteristics of a group of students
▶ Specify the objectives for a lesson of your choice
▶ Identify the relevant characteristics of a learning environment
▶ Specify the instructional activities for a lesson of your choice
▶ Describe the practical benefits of an instructional plan
▶ Develop an instructional plan for a lesson on a topic of your choice

PLANNING FOR THE CHAPTER CONTENT

> *Instructional Technology for Teaching and Learning,* will show you how to increase learning by **designing lessons** that use instructional technology, including computers and other media.

This chapter focuses on designing instruction. In Chapter 1 we introduced our PIE model, describing three interrelated processes that comprise both learning and instruction—planning, implementation, and evaluation. In Chapters 2 and 3 we presented foundation information about learning theories and computer tools. This chapter expands on the PIE model and describes a systematic process for developing instructional plans that help students learn. We describe the components of the plan, as shown in the following outline:

▶ Plan
  Students
  Objectives
  Learning environment
  Instructional activities
  Methods and media
  Instructional materials
▶ Implement
▶ Evaluate

In this chapter we describe the first four components of the plan (students, objectives, learning environment, and instructional activities). Chapters 5 and 6 will complete the plan by providing more information about instructional methods and media (Chapter 5) and acquiring instructional materials (Chapter 6).

INTRODUCTION

An instructional plan is like a recipe. Most people cook from recipes. Recipes tell cooks what ingredients they need and how to combine those ingredients to produce a particular dish. Cooks who don't have much experience, either in general or with a particular dish, tend to follow a recipe closely. They will carefully measure the ingredients, add them in the order listed, and cook the dish for the prescribed time to make sure it turns out as the recipe specifies. On the other hand, experienced cooks will often vary the recipe to fit the tastes and preferences of particular diners. They may substitute or change the amounts of ingredients or cook the dish for a different amount of time. In addition, they may adjust the recipe "on the spot," based on their repeated taste testing. Experienced cooks use a recipe as a flexible guide. They have made the dish often enough that they can prepare it without constantly referring to the recipe, and they've learned how they can modify the recipe without sacrificing the quality of the dish. For both novice and expert cooks, creating a dish involves identifying ingredients and specifying how to combine them to produce a satisfying eating experience.

Most teachers have a "recipe" or plan. The plan tells them what "ingredients" they need and how to combine them to produce learning in a particular group of students. Teachers who don't have much experience, either in general or with a particular topic, will probably follow a relatively detailed plan. They will outline the content in detail, carefully describe any activities, and follow their plan closely to make sure their instruction turns out the way they want. On the other hand, experienced teachers will often vary their plan to fit their students' existing knowledge and learning preferences. They may substitute or rearrange activities, or vary the amount of time spent on them. In addition, experienced teachers may adjust the plan "on the spot," based on their repeated evaluation of how the students are responding. Experienced teachers use a plan as a flexible guide. They have taught the lesson often enough that they don't need to constantly refer to their plan, and they've learned how they can vary from the plan without sacrificing the quality of the instruction. For both novice and expert teachers, developing a plan involves identifying "ingredients" and specifying how to present them to ensure a satisfying learning experience. This chapter presents our recipe for instructional planning.

DESIGNING INSTRUCTION

Recall from Chapter 1 that *learning* is the process of acquiring new knowledge and/or skills through the interdependent subprocesses of planning, implementation, and evaluation (refer to the "PIE" graph in Figure 1–4). *Instruction* is the process of helping students learn through the deliberate arrangement of information, activities, methods, and media. **Instructional design** is the process of developing plans for instruction through practical application of theoretical principles (some of which we described in Chapter 2).

Designing instruction is often described as a "systematic" process for developing an instructional plan, meaning that it is an orderly process with an internal logic, resulting in a coherent plan in which the components of the plan closely match one another. This often follows a "rational" or objectives-first process (Hunter, 1982) in which the components of the plan are put in place in a prescribed sequence, beginning with the objectives.

However, practicing teachers don't always follow an objectives-first process when they plan their instruction (Sardo-Brown, 1990). They may begin by specifying objectives. But they are just as likely to begin by considering the following:

- One or more practice activities for the students
- The content to cover
- The students' existing knowledge
- The means for testing students' understanding
- An instructional method or medium to use

Teachers often develop the remaining components of their plan in an equally varied sequence. To mirror this flexibility, we suggest a "recipe" for designing instruction in which the order for adding components to the plan isn't critical. What is impor-

FIGURE 4–1 Components of an instructional plan

tant is that each of the components appear in the finished plan (Figure 4–1).

Our recipe is "rational" in the sense that it represents a thoughtful, systematic process that results in a coherent plan with closely matched components. Like any system, the plan is dynamic and flexible. Decisions made while developing one component of the plan will affect decisions made about other components. This may mean examining, even changing, decisions you have already made. You may use our design process to plan a lesson, unit, course, or entire curriculum. We focus here on the *lesson* as the basic element of teacher planning.

Students

We begin our discussion with students because the purpose of instruction is to help particular students learn. As a teacher, your challenge is to help *all* students reach desired learning goals. However, individual students differ in a number of ways:

- Developmental level
- Intelligence
- Learning style
- Gender
- Ethnicity and culture
- Socioeconomic status
- Special needs
- Motivation to learn
- Existing knowledge and skills

This diversity makes planning for instruction more difficult. Even when you find a way to help some students reach certain learning goals, that way may not work for all students.

So, how do you solve this type of problem? The critical planning task is to take your students' diversity into account. This requires, first, understanding the ways in which students are likely to differ. We will only touch on these differences. A detailed discussion is beyond the scope of this book. Books on educational psychology, such as those by Ormrod (1995) and Woolfolk (1998), cited at the end of this chapter, are good sources of additional information.

Developmental Level

As they mature, children develop along a number of dimensions, including their motor skills and muscular coordination, thinking processes and abilities, ability to use language, ability to get along with others, emerging personality and self-concept, and understanding of right and wrong. For each of these dimensions, development progresses through a predictable sequence of stages, marked by recognizable milestones. For example, children learn to sit up before they can crawl, and they learn to crawl before they learn to walk.

While the sequence of developmental milestones is common to all children, within a group the same age, individual children are likely to be at different points in these progressions. For example, while walking is a developmental milestone that the average child reaches at approximately 1 year old, some start walking a little younger or a little older.

Both heredity and environment influence development. For example, physical development is influenced by genetic factors such as neurological and muscular development. At the same time, physical development is influenced by environmental factors such as the nutrition and exercise the growing child receives.

Intelligence

Intelligence has been described in numerous ways (Sternberg & Detterman, 1986). Common to all descriptions is the idea that intelligence involves the adaptive use of previously acquired knowledge to analyze and understand new situations (Ormrod, 1995). One common way to measure and report intelligence is through the use of IQ (intelligence quotient) scores, which refers to a score on a standardized test such as the Stanford-Binet Intelligence Scale or the Wechsler Intelligence Scale for Children (WISC). These tests compare a student's performance with that of other students within the same age group, with a score of 100 established as "average" performance.

The original purpose of IQ tests was to predict achievement in school and, to a certain extent, they accomplish this. Several important points should be kept in mind, however (Ormrod, 1995). First, the relationship between IQ and achievement is not perfect. While most students who do well on IQ tests also do well in school, some students' achievement is higher than we might expect from their IQ scores, while that of others is lower. Second, the relationship between IQ and achievement is not one of cause and effect. Intelligence may contribute to achievement in school, but so does motivation, parental support, and the quality of instruction students receive, among other things. By itself, intelligence does not *cause* achievement. Third, IQ scores may change over time as a result of students' experiences, including experiences in school. Finally, intelligence is culture specific. "Intelligent" behavior in one culture may not be considered so in another. Standardized IQ tests developed within the context of a single culture may not always be useful indicators of a student's intelligence.

IQ tests result in a single score, suggesting that intelligence is a single, general capability. However, some theorists suggest that intelligence is made up of multiple dimensions. For example, Gardner (1983) postulates seven different forms of intelligence:

- Linguistic intelligence: the ability to use language
- Musical intelligence: the ability to create and comprehend music
- Logical-mathematical intelligence: the ability to reason logically, especially in science and mathematics
- Spatial intelligence: the ability to mentally manipulate visual objects
- Bodily-kinesthetic intelligence: the ability to use one's body skillfully
- Intrapersonal intelligence: the ability to recognize one's own feelings, motives, and so on
- Interpersonal intelligence: the ability to recognize the feelings and motives, of others

Learning Style

Learning style refers to "preferred ways that different individuals have for processing and organizing information and for responding to environmental stimuli" (Shuell, 1981, p. 46). We must make a clear distinction between learning style and developmental level and intelligence. Students who are at the same developmental and intelligence levels may have different learning styles.

One commonly described dimension of learning style is field dependence/field independence. *Field dependence* refers to the tendency to perceive things in context, to focus on whole patterns rather than on elements within the pattern. Students who are field dependent have difficulty separating out the details of an event or observation. In contrast, *field independence* refers to the tendency to perceive things analytically, to focus on parts rather than wholes. Students who are field independent can easily separate events or observation into their component parts.

Field dependence and field independence are opposite ends of a continuum and it is important to note that neither end of this continuum is better than the other. They simply reflect different ways of processing information. Field-dependent students are better at some things, while field-independent students are better at others. Field-dependent students often perform better in tasks involving the social world in which the context is critical to understanding. They tend to see things wholistically and are sensitive to subtle environmental cues. In contrast, field-independent students often perform better in tasks involving the physical world in which analytical skills are critical to understanding. They tend to see things analytically and are adept at breaking things down into their component parts.

Gender

When they are young, boys and girls are more similar than different. However, as they mature, some differences appear. For example, the following are generally true:

▶ Boys tend to be taller and have more muscular strength than girls (especially after puberty at approximately 11 or 12 years of age).

▶ Boys tend to be more physically aggressive. Girls tend to be more affiliative, concerned with social relationships.

▶ Boys tend to explain their successes in terms of ability ("I'm smart") and their failures in terms of effort ("I didn't try very hard"). Girls tend to explain their successes in terms of effort ("I kept trying until I got it") and their failures in terms of ability ("I'm not very good in science") (Deaux, 1984).

▶ Boys become more interested in subject areas such as mathematics, science, and athletics while girls become more interested in areas such as literature, art, and music (Fennema, 1987).

▶ Boys tend to see themselves as competent in problem solving. Girls tend to see themselves as competent in social relationships (Bloch, 1983).

These differences are partly the result of biology (boys become stronger because of increased levels of the hormone testosterone). However, they are mostly the result of *socialization*—the process by which we learn the rules, norms, and expectations of the society in which we live. In general, boys and girls are treated differently by parents, peers, teachers, and mass media. As a result, they learn that some things are appropriate for males while others are appropriate for females. For example, boys may be reinforced for being independent, competitive, and logical. As a result, they may be drawn to subjects such as science and athletics in school and to occupations such as engineer and electrician after school. In contrast, girls may be reinforced for being cooperative, sympathetic, and emotional. As a result, they may be drawn to subjects such as social studies and art in school and occupations such as librarian and nurse after school. These gender-related stereotypes have been decreasing during the past 20 years, but they still exist and they affect students at all grade levels.

It is important to note that, even as they mature, few substantial differences in academic ability exist between boys and girls. As a group, their scores on IQ tests are comparable. While socialization may lead boys and girls to prefer different subject areas and different instructional methods, they have the same *ability* to achieve in *all* subject areas.

Ethnicity and Culture

An *ethnic group* is a segment within the larger population that shares a cultural background, indicated by a common language and common customs. Within the United States there are a number of ethnic groups, including African Americans, Hispanics, Asian Americans, Native Americans, and various immigrant groups, including Italian, Polish, Israeli, Indian, and many others.

For the most part, schools in the United States are based on a white, middle-class, American majority culture. Students from different cultural backgrounds are likely to experience a "cultural mismatch" (Ormrod, 1995), in which important discrepancies appear between their home culture and the school culture. This may result in confusion about what to expect or what is expected of them, which may, in turn, result in reduced achievement for these students. Teachers sometimes contribute to this cultural mismatch through the natural human tendency to view student behaviors through their own cultural window. The resulting misinterpretations may lead teachers to conclude that minority students lack ability and/or motivation. They may very well be wrong. Consider the following examples:

▶ During a conversation with the teacher, a student looks down rather than maintaining eye contact. The teacher interprets this to mean that the student is bored or isn't paying attention. However, the student may come from a culture in which eye contact with an adult is a sign of disrespect.

▶ A student seems to wait a long time before responding to a question. The teacher interprets this to mean that the student doesn't understand the question or know the answer. However, the student may speak a language other than English at home and need time to translate the question.

Socioeconomic Status

Socioeconomic status refers to a combination of factors that includes family income, parents' occupations, and the amount of formal education parents have received. Lower socioeconomic status is associated with several factors that can interfere with a student's progress in school (Ormrod, 1995):

▶ Students from lower-income families may be chronically hungry and, as a result, may have lower energy levels and exhibit little interest in school.

▶ Students from lower-income families may be worried about meeting their basic needs at home and, therefore, not be able to concentrate on schoolwork.

▶ Parents who have received little formal education themselves may not be able to help their children with their schoolwork. They may feel ill at ease when asked to discuss the progress their children are making in school.

Lower socioeconomic status is associated with lower achievement in school. Students from lower-income families are more likely to drop out of school. But, as with IQ and achievement, the relationship between socioeconomic status and achievement is imperfect. Many bright students come from lower-income families and, while they may initially lack basic academic skills, they easily acquire them. In addition, many parents whose education was limited recognize the value of education for their children and work hard to support their children's progress in school.

Special Needs

Students are individuals, and differ from one another in a variety of ways. Sometimes students are different enough from their peers that they require

special educational services to help them reach their potential. In recent years there have been increasing efforts to *mainstream* these students—to educate them as much as possible in regular classrooms with other students who do not have special needs—to ensure that all students have the same educational opportunities. At the same time, there have been increasing efforts to identify their special needs in order to provide them with school experiences that will enable them to reach their individual learning potentials.

Students may require special educational services for a variety of reasons:

▶ Learning disabilities, such as attention disorders, in which a student has difficulty concentrating on a single task for any length of time

▶ Communication disorders, such as stuttering, in which a student repeats a sound while pronouncing words

▶ Behavioral problems, such as overly aggressive behavior, in which a student has difficulty interacting appropriately with other students

▶ Physical or health problems, such as cerebral palsy, epilepsy, paraplegia, asthma, or AIDS

▶ Partial or total loss of vision or hearing

There is yet another category of special needs that is often not thought of as a "problem" that requires special attention—giftedness. *Giftedness* refers to an exceptional talent or ability in one or more areas. Students may be gifted in any academic area—science, music, creative writing, and so on. Gifted students are often frustrated or bored in school because the instruction does not challenge them or help them develop their special talents. In addition, they may become isolated from other students because of differences in their interests that may seem impossible to reconcile.

For each of these types of special needs, we must reemphasize that students are individuals, as different from one another as they are similar. For example, visually impaired students are similar in that they all may benefit from specially designed instructional materials (for example, large print or Braille books). Like other students, however, they are likely to differ in terms of their intelligence levels, cognitive styles, and cultural backgrounds. For a thorough discussion of special needs students and the issue of mainstreaming, see Salend (1994).

Motivation

Motivation refers to an internal state that leads people to choose to work toward certain goals and expe-

Individualized Education Programs (IEPs)

Considerable attention has been given to the needs of students with special needs. In the past, these students were separated from their peers and placed in special programs. Today the emphasis is on mainstreaming—including these students in regular classroom settings to the greatest extent possible. An important element of the education of special needs students is the **Individualized Education Program (IEP).** The IEP is an instructional plan for an individual student and is developed through a conference that includes the student's parents (or guardians), teachers, and (when possible) the student. Other individuals may also be involved, for example, the school psychologist and/or special education or gifted education teacher. Most IEPs include the following:

▶ A description of the student's current level of achievement
▶ A set of short-term and long-term goals
▶ A description of the methods that will be used to accomplish those goals
▶ Procedures and criteria that will be used to evaluate the student's progress toward those goals

The concept of the IEP arose as a result of the needs of special needs students. However, there is growing interest in many schools in using IEPs with all learners. The intent is to make education a truly individualized experience. Computer-assisted instruction and other computer tools may be a part of the overall plan for individual students. One day, every student may have an IEP that sets out a personalized program of study.

riences. It defines what people *will* do rather than what they *can* do (Keller, 1983). Motivation is a common influence on human activities. We are motivated to pursue certain relationships, to enter certain careers, or go to certain places. Motivation is, in turn, influenced by many variables, some internal (such as our perceptions, wants, and personal goals) and some external (such as opportunities and rewards). Motivation makes a direct contribution to learning by focusing students on certain desired learning goals and increasing the effort they expend in reaching those goals.

Motivation can be categorized as either intrinsic or extrinsic. *Intrinsic* motivation is generated by aspects of the experience or task itself (such as challenge or curiosity). *Extrinsic* motivation is generated by factors unrelated to the experience or task (such as grades or recognition). Intrinsic motivation is generally more effective. Students who are intrinsically motivated will work harder and learn more because of their natural interest in the material. In fact, while extrinsic motivators are often valuable, relying on them can sometimes interfere with learning by reducing students' sense of self-determination. Whenever possible, it is better to develop students' intrinsic motivation.

One valuable approach to describing student motivation is Keller's (1983) ARCS model. Keller describes four essential aspects of motivation: using the mnemonic ARCS (the mnemonic has given its name to the model):

Attention refers to whether students perceive the instruction as interesting and worthy of their consideration.
Relevance refers to whether students perceive the instruction as meeting some personal need or goal.
Confidence refers to whether students expect to succeed based on their own efforts.
Satisfaction refers to the intrinsic and extrinsic rewards students receive from the instruction.

Existing Knowledge and Skills

Existing knowledge and skills refer to what students already know. There are two related questions: Are the students ready to begin the lesson? and Have they already achieved the desired goals? To understand the first question, it is important to understand the concept of **prerequisites.** As we will see in the next section, objectives define the knowledge and skills students should have at the *end* of a lesson. Prerequisites, on the other hand, define the knowledge and skills students should have at the *beginning* of the lesson. When students don't have the necessary prerequisites, they will, at best, have a difficult time succeeding in the lesson. Learning is cumulative, and this means two things. First, it means that virtually every lesson has prerequisites. The objectives of one lesson often form the prerequisites for the next. Second, it means that, to be meaningful, instruction should build on what students already know.

FIGURE 4–2   An example of the concept of prerequisites

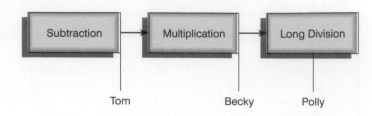

Imagine that you are planning a lesson on long division using the traditional algorithm. The prerequisites for long division are subtraction and multiplication; to learn long division effectively and efficiently, students must be able to subtract and multiply. Students lacking these prerequisite skills cannot learn long division. Figure 4–2 illustrates the order in which these prerequisites lead up to long division. It represents three students who differ in what they already know. The first student, Tom, has mastered subtraction but not multiplication. Long division is over his head; he isn't ready yet because he doesn't have all the prerequisites. He's likely to feel frustrated and lost. The second student, Becky, has all the prerequisites. She knows how to subtract and multiply but doesn't yet know how to do long division. She's ready to begin. The third student, Polly, has gone beyond the prerequisites. She knows how to subtract and multiply, and she knows how to do long division, at least in some situations. Like Tom, Polly is likely to be frustrated, but for a different reason; she's likely to be bored because the instruction is presenting something she already knows.

Dealing with Diversity

Clearly we've only scratched the surface of these dimensions that describe students. Each dimension is complex and much more information is needed to understand it completely. The important question for teachers is how to deal with this diversity in the classroom. Woolfolk (1998) offers three general principles that provide both guidance for responding to a diverse group of students and a framework for acquiring additional information about student diversity:

▶ Know your students. Get to know them as individuals—their backgrounds, interests, families and communities.
▶ Respect your students. Identify and support their strengths, talents, accomplishments, and cultures.
▶ Teach your students. Teach every student to think, create, and learn as well as to read, write, solve mathematics problems, and so on.

We would add to Woolfolk's third guideline the suggestion that you teach your students to respect one another and to appreciate the diversity among them.

Following these general guidelines will make it easier to understand any problems or concerns particular students are having and to plan instruction that will help overcome those problems. You will be able to do the following:

▶ Adjust an instructional activity to accommodate a student's developmental level
▶ Look for and support the different ways in which students are "intelligent"
▶ Organize new information and plan instructional activities based on students' cognitive styles
▶ Encourage boys and girls in subject areas that do not fit traditional gender-related stereotypes
▶ Adjust instructional methods to allow for responses that are appropriate in students' home cultures
▶ Provide additional support (social and emotional as well as educational) for students (and their parents) from lower-income families
▶ Help identify students' special needs and obtain services to help them meet those needs
▶ Develop strategies to increase students' intrinsic motivation
▶ Match the starting point for the instruction to students' existing knowledge and skills

Objectives

Objectives form the foundation of a lesson. They give direction to those designing the lesson, those delivering the lesson, and those receiving the lesson. They help everyone understand when and to what degree the purpose of the instruction has been accomplished. **Objectives,** as we define them, are what students should be able to do following instruction. It may be necessary to infer that students have accomplished objectives based on their completion of specified performances.

The Importance of Specifying Objectives

Imagine that you are taking a vacation trip. You will want to know where you're going so you can

▶ *Make reasonable decisions* about what routes and means of transportation to take, how long you will take to reach your destination, what you

TABLE 4–1   *The Practical Benefits of Specifying Lesson Objectives*

	Guidance	Communication
Teacher	Guides selection and development of lesson content and activities. Guides selection and development of assessment instruments.	Reminds the teacher of what the expected outcomes are.
Students	Guides students' studying.	Tells students what will be expected of them.
Others	Guides the development of the overall curriculum into which the lesson or course fits. Guides the delivery of instruction by substitutes.	Tells interested others (e.g., principals, parents, substitutes) what the students are learning and what is expected of them.

might want to see along the way, what you'll need to take with you, and so on

- ▶ *Manage your budget*
- ▶ *Monitor your progress* and *manage your time*
- ▶ *Tell concerned others* (friends and family) where you're going and what your itinerary is so they will know where you are

A lesson is an instructional "trip," and, like a vacation trip, you'll want to know where you're going so you can

- ▶ *Make reasonable decisions* about what instructional methods and media to use, how long your students will take to reach the "destination," what else you might want them to learn along the way, what materials, facilities, and equipment you'll need, and so on
- ▶ *Manage your budget*
- ▶ *Monitor students' progress* and *manage the time* allotted for the lesson
- ▶ *Tell concerned others* (students, parents, principals, other teachers, etc.) where you're going and what your itinerary is so they will know where you are

Reflective Question

Examine the objectives at the beginning of this chapter. As a learner, how can you use these objectives to help you accomplish your goals? As a teacher, how might you use these objectives to guide your instructional planning?

So, objectives are important because they define where you're going—the knowledge or skills the students should have at the end of the lesson. Table 4–1 summarizes the practical benefits of specifying lesson objectives. As the table shows, objectives provide a useful communication tool as well as practical guidance for teachers, students, and others. However, researchers have raised questions

about the value of specifying objectives in advance (Dick & Reiser, 1989; Yelon, 1991). Following are several of the most common criticisms, together with our responses.

Criticism: Objectives dehumanize the instruction by focusing on the requirements rather than on the students.

Response: Contrary to this common misperception, the purpose of objectives is to specify the knowledge and skills that are important for the students to achieve. This allows you to plan a way for *each* student to achieve your learning goals. In addition, clearly stated objectives tell students where they will be going. This helps motivate them, guides their studying, and allows them to plan and monitor their own progress.

Criticism: Specifying objectives takes up valuable time.

Response: Time spent specifying objectives is an *investment* rather than an expenditure. As with any other investment, clearly stated objectives have a significant dividend: they help assure that your instructional plan will match your students' needs.

Criticism: Objectives can't be specified for complex or intangible skills, such as problem solving or critical thinking. The result is a focus on low-level skills, such as memorization, which are easy to describe and measure but are not always the skills the students should be learning.

Response: It is easier to specify objectives for low-level skills such as memorization. However, objectives can be specified for all types of learning, including complex, high-level skills like problem solving or creative thinking. In fact, because of the greater complexity of high-level skills, specifying objectives for them may be more important than for low-level skills.

Criticism: Specifying objectives in advance "locks in" the curriculum and makes it difficult to change.

Response: Explicitly stating objectives doesn't necessarily mean they are written in stone. You can modify them as easily as you wrote them. Good teachers review the objectives periodically so they can modify those that are no longer relevant.

Criticism: Specifying objectives in advance leads to a rigid, mechanistic approach to teaching that reduces the teacher's ability to respond creatively and spontaneously to students and to the "teachable moments" that often occur in the classroom.

Response: When you're taking a vacation trip, having a destination doesn't mean you can't or won't take side trips to explore other interesting places. Similarly, on an instructional "trip," having objectives doesn't mean you can't or won't explore other interesting ideas.

Criticism: Specifying objectives in advance results in a tendency to "teach to the test."

Response: If your test accurately assesses your objectives, as it should, and you have designed your instruction to achieve your objectives, as you should, then your instruction will also help students succeed on the test.

Sources of Objectives

There are a number of sources to help you identify lesson objectives:

> *Curriculum guides.* General objectives are often provided in curriculum guides, competency lists, and content outlines that are set forth by state education departments, school districts, or professional organizations. You may then translate these general course objectives into objectives for specific lessons.

> *Textbooks and instructional activities.* Textbooks and commercially produced instructional activities often include suggested objectives that identify what students should learn. These objectives may appear in an accompanying instructor's guide.

> *Tests.* Objectives can be derived from the tests used in a course. When the objectives, instruction, and tests are parallel, tests will indicate what the students should have learned. This is true for standardized tests as well as for tests you develop. The general principle is that if it is important enough to be on the test, it is probably important enough to specify as a lesson objective.

> *World Wide Web.* More and more lesson plans and instructional activities can be found on the World Wide Web. These often include objectives.

> *Your own ideas.* You will often have your own ideas about what students should learn from a lesson, especially if you have taught the lesson

before or are familiar with the particular students.

Specifying Lesson Objectives

Objectives specify what the teacher wants the students to learn. Various methods for specifying objectives have been described (Jacobson, Eggen, & Kauchak, 1993). We suggest the method Mager (1997) describes, in which objectives include three components:

> *Performance:* what the students will do to indicate that they have learned
> *Conditions:* the circumstances under which the students are expected to perform
> *Criteria:* the standard that defines acceptable performance

Specifying the objectives for a lesson involves identifying each of these three components.

Specify the Performance.   What will students do or say that will indicate they have learned? We suggest specifying the performance first because it is often the easiest component to identify. Teachers usually know what they want their students to learn in a lesson, even if they haven't thought out all the details. The key is to specify a performance that is an observable indicator of students' capabilities.

Observable Performance. Assessing learning almost always involves inference. In some situations (e.g., learning to solve arithmetic problems) the inference is relatively straightforward, while in others (e.g., learning to think critically) the inference is more difficult. But in virtually every situation students must do something before you can infer their level of learning. To facilitate this inference, the objective should specify an observable performance. This will allow both you and your students to tell whether learning has occurred. One way to ensure the specification of an observable performance is to use verbs that describe observable actions—things you can see or hear students doing. Table 4–2 lists some observable action verbs, along with verbs you should avoid. This list is not exhaustive, but will give you an idea of the kinds of verbs to use when specifying lesson objectives.

Student capability. Teachers are naturally focused on what is going to happen during the lesson (Sardo-Brown, 1990). One result of this is a tendency for the teacher's plans to focus on the activities (either the teacher's or the students') that will take place during the lesson. Developing these activities is an important aspect of planning. But the purpose of specifying objectives is to clearly identify

TABLE 4–2   *Use Observable Action Verbs in Objectives*

Use Verbs Such As			Avoid Verbs Such As	
compare	construct	operate	understand	believe
translate	create	adjust	appreciate	become familiar with
describe	explain	replace		
measure	repair	compose	think	become aware of
identify	define	compute	know	be comfortable with
draw	administer	solve		
			recognize	

the results, or destination, of the lesson rather than the route students will follow to reach that destination. What should students learn? One way to make sure you describe a student capability is to use the phrase, "the student will be able to," before the action verb. Using this phrase will remind you that the objective of the lesson is a future capability of the student.

Specify the Conditions.   What are the circumstances under which students will be expected to perform? What will they be given to work with? The key is to specify conditions that will be in place *at the time* of the expected performance. One way to specify the conditions is to think about the questions students are likely to ask about the expected performance (Yelon, 1991). Their questions can be grouped into four categories:

▶ *Setting:* Where will they be expected to perform?
▶ *People:* Will they be working alone? With a team? Under supervision?
▶ *Equipment:* What tools or facilities will they have to work with?
▶ *Information:* What, if any, notes, books, checklists, or models will they have to work with?

For example, imagine that you want your students to describe the use of symbolism in *Macbeth*. The students might ask: Will we have to come up with the examples ourselves, or will we describe examples you give us (information)? Will this be an in-class assignment, or can we take it home (setting)? Can we use our books (information)? Can we work together (people)?

As shown in the following example, you can include your responses to these questions in the objective by using a word such as *given* or *using:*

▶ Given a scene from *Macbeth*, individual students will be able to describe the use of symbolism in the scene.

Specifying the conditions often helps you define what is important in the performance. For example, if you want your students to describe symbolism in *Macbeth*, you might consider the following questions: Is it important that they recall instances of symbolism, or is it enough that they can describe the identified symbolism? Is it important that they be able to perform under pressure, as in the classroom, or is it enough that they can perform in the more private and relaxed setting of home?

Specify the Criteria.   What is the standard that defines desired performance? How well must students perform? Some might argue that specifying the criteria for students' performance is part of developing a test. However, criteria, like conditions, are an important component of an objective because they help you identify what is important in the performance. Consider wanting your students to describe symbolism in *Macbeth*. Will you accept just any description? Probably not. You want students' answers to be "correct" in some way. Thinking about what "correct" looks like will help you devise a lesson that will guide students to the objective. There are a number of possible ways of defining a "correct" performance. As Table 4–3 indicates, these can be classified into three broad categories: time, accuracy, and quality (Mager, 1997; Yelon, 1991). Of course, not all of these criteria will be relevant in every situation. The key is to identify those that are critical for successful student performance in your particular lesson.

Of course, an objective may use more than one type of criterion, as in the following example:

▶ Given a topic, the student will be able to compose a letter that contains no more than two errors in grammar or syntax (accuracy: number of errors). The letter must be at least one page long (time: duration) and contain a combination of simp' and complex sentences (quality: essential characteristics).

TABLE 4–3 *Categories of Criteria for Defining Acceptable Performance*

Category	Description	Example
Time		
Time limits	Specifies the time limits within which the performance must take place.	Given a "victim" with no pulse or respiration, the student will be able to begin one-person CPR *within 15 seconds.*
Duration	Specifies the length of the performance.	Given a "victim" with no pulse or respiration, the student will be able to maintain one-person CPR *for at least 15 minutes.*
Rate	Specifies the rate or speed at which the performance must take place.	Given a "victim" with no pulse or respiration, the student will be able to administer one-person CPR *at a steady rate of 12 compressions per minute.*
Accuracy		
Number of errors	Specifies the maximum acceptable number of errors.	Given a topic, the student will be able to compose a letter that contains *no more than two errors* in spelling, grammar, or syntax.
Tolerances	Specifies the maximum acceptable measurement range.	With the aid of a dial gauge, the student will be able to measure the lateral roll-out on a disc *to within 0.002 inch.*
Quality		
Essential characteristics	Specifies the characteristics that must be present for the performance to be considered acceptable. Often signaled by words such as "must include."	Without reference to books or notes, the student will be able to describe the causes of the American Revolution. The description *must include at least two of the significant events leading up to 0the war.*
Source	Specifies the documents or materials that will be used as a gauge of the performance. Often signaled by words such as "according to," or "consistent with."	Given a computer with a hard drive and a new software application, the student will be able to install the software onto the hard drive *according to the procedure described in the software manual.*
Consequences	Specifies the expected results of the performance. Often signaled by words such as "such that" or "so that."	Given a flat bicycle tire, a patch kit, and a pump, the student will be able to patch the tire *so that it holds the recommended air pressure for at least 24 hours.*

Composing Objectives

Once you've considered each of the three components of an objective, you can put them together. You can simply list the components of the objective, as in the following example:

Performance: Solve simultaneous algebra equations
Conditions: Graphing calculators
Criteria: Accurate to two decimal places

Or, you can combine the components into a coherent sentence or two, as in the following example:

▶ With the use of graphing calculators, students will be able to solve simultaneous algebra equations. Solutions must be accurate to two decimal places.

Types of Learning

Look again at the examples of objectives in the previous section. Notice that they ask different things of stu-

dents. Solving algebra equations asks students to perform a mental activity, while administering CPR asks them to perform a physical activity. This illustrates the fact that objectives may define different types of capabilities to be learned. One way to classify objectives is to sort them into four major types of learning (often called *domains*): knowledge, intellectual skills, motor skills, and attitudes (Reiser & Dick, 1996).

Knowledge refers to the ability to recall specific information. This may involve recalling particular facts, such as the parts of speech, or the main points of some larger body of knowledge, such as the theory of relativity. In each case, the primary focus is on the ability to recall some specific information. Examples include the following:

▶ Stating the formula for the area of a rectangle
▶ Summarizing the functions of the three branches of the U.S. government

▶ Explaining the economic principle of supply and demand

While the primary focus of the knowledge domain is the ability to recall information from memory, this goes beyond simple rote memorization. Learning in this domain often involves recalling the substance or significance of ideas "in your own words."

Intellectual skills refer to a variety of thinking skills, including concept learning, rule using, and problem solving. *Concept learning* refers to the ability to determine whether something is an example of a particular concept. A *concept* is a label used to designate a group of things or ideas that have similar characteristics. Concepts may be relatively concrete (such as "computer" or "planet") or relatively abstract (such as "intelligence" or "prejudice"). *Rule using* refers to the ability to apply a given rule or principle in a given situation. For example, students who are asked to use a formula to determine the area of a rectangle or write a correct English sentence are using a rule. *Problem solving* refers to combining rules to solve a unique problem. For example, students who are asked to design a scientific experiment or write a poem are solving a problem. In each case, the intellectual skill goes beyond simple recall to the application of that information. Examples of intellectual skills include the following:

▶ Identifying examples of symbolism
▶ Solving algebra equations
▶ Planning a scientific experiment

Intellectual skills may be seen as closely related to knowledge. The distinction between them is in how the information is used. Learning in the knowledge domain focuses on the *simple recall* of information. In contrast, when learning intellectual skills, the primary focus is on the ability to *apply the information.*

Motor skills refer to the ability to perform complex physical actions in a smooth, coordinated manner. This may involve large muscles, as in sawing a board using a hand saw, or small muscles, as in tying a knot. In any case, motor skills go beyond simple actions such as pushing a button and focus on complex actions that require coordination of several muscle movements. Examples include the following:

▶ Playing a musical instrument
▶ Performing a dance step
▶ Slam-dunking a basketball

Motor skills often include a thinking, or intellectual, component that guides the physical action. For example, a beginner playing the guitar may think about where to place his fingers in order to play the notes. However, when learning motor skills, the primary focus is the ability to perform the physical action in a smooth and precise way.

Attitudes refer to feelings, beliefs, and values that lead individuals to make consistent choices when given the opportunity. Attitudes can't be seen directly; they must be inferred from the individual's behavior. We can reasonably infer that an individual has acquired an attitude when he chooses to behave in a consistent manner in similar situations. Examples include the following:

▶ Choosing to play sports
▶ Choosing to wait your turn
▶ Choosing to follow laboratory safety guidelines

Because attitudes are inferred from behavior, there is a close link between the attitude and the intellectual skill or motor skill that is evidence of the choice. However, when learning an attitude, the primary focus is on the choice rather than on the ability.

The Learning Environment

Simply stated, the **learning environment** is the setting or physical surroundings in which learning is expected to take place. At first glance this may seem obvious: learning takes place in the classroom. It is more complicated than that, however, for two reasons. First, classrooms are different; they vary in size, layout, lighting, and seating, among other things. Second, learning takes place in a variety of settings besides the classroom: the laboratory (computer lab, science lab, or language lab), playground, beach, backstage at a theater, or at home. In fact, learning typically involves some combination of environments.

We said earlier that instruction should match the students for whom it is intended and the goals defined in the objectives. It is equally true that instruction should match the environment in which it will occur. If it doesn't, the instruction may be theoretically valid but practically impossible (Tessmer, 1990). Sometimes this is obvious, as in the following example:

▶ A biology lesson that includes a laboratory experiment in which the students use microscopes to identify the structures of the cell requires enough lab equipment and supplies for all students. When lab equipment is limited, it may be necessary to change the experiment to a group activity. When lab equipment is severely limited, it may be necessary to use a demonstration as the instructional method.

Sometimes this problem isn't as obvious, as in the following example:

▶ A mathematics lesson on solving algebra equations that includes a commercial computer-based tutorial requires a site license authorizing use of the tutorial at multiple workstations. Without a site license, the students may have to use the tutorial one at a time, requiring a reorganization of the lesson.

Instructional planning, therefore, involves asking several questions about the setting:

▶ Where will learning occur? A classroom? A laboratory? Some other area of the school? On a field trip? Or at home?
▶ What are the characteristics of the environment(s)? How large is the space in relation to the number of students? How are the seats arranged? Can they be moved easily? What equipment do you need? What equipment is available? How much noise do you anticipate in the setting? What other distractions are there? Is the lighting adequate? Can you adjust the lighting?
▶ How will those characteristics influence instruction? Can the setting(s) be modified to accommodate instruction? If not, what constraints will the setting(s) impose on the nature of the instruction?

Developing Instructional Activities

As a way of describing the ingredients in an instructional plan, we will use the concept of an instructional activity (Yelon, 1996). Simply put, the term **instructional activity** refers to something that is done during a lesson to help students learn. Instructional activities have been described and combined in various "recipes" (Reiser & Dick, 1996; Hunter, 1982; Kauchak & Eggen, 1989; Sullivan & Higgins, 1983). Yelon describes five types of instructional activities that should, at least, be considered in planning any lesson:

▶ Motivation activities
▶ Orientation activities
▶ Information activities
▶ Application activities
▶ Evaluation activities

Motivation Activities

As discussed earlier, motivation refers to the internal interests that lead students to want to learn and to put in the effort required for learning. To develop a motivation activity for an instructional plan, consider the following questions:

▶ What strategies will you use to hold students' attention throughout the lesson?
▶ What strategies will you use to help students see the relevance of the information?
▶ What strategies will you use to increase students' confidence in learning?
▶ What strategies will you use to increase students' satisfaction in learning?

Orientation Activities

In general, *orientation* refers to knowing where you are in relation to your intended destination. In instruction, orientation refers to knowing where you are in terms of the intended objectives. Orientation activities go beyond the specific lesson. Any lesson fits into a sequence of lessons; it naturally follows some and leads to others. The purpose of an **orientation activity** is to help students see where they have been (what they have previously learned), where they are now (what they are currently learning), and where they are going (what they will subsequently learn). You use orientation activities to introduce a lesson and link it to preceding lessons, to move from one part of a lesson to the next and help students monitor their progress, and to summarize a lesson and link it to subsequent lessons. To develop an orientation activity for an instructional plan, consider the following questions:

▶ What will you do to help students understand the objectives of the current lesson?
▶ What will you do to link the lesson to previous lessons?
▶ What will you do to form transitions?
▶ What will you do to summarize the lesson and link it to future lessons?

Information Activities

Instruction generally includes some new ideas (facts, concepts, principles, procedures, etc.) and an opportunity for students to practice using those ideas. The purpose of an **information activity** is to help students understand and remember those new ideas. To be effective, information activities should focus on two different types of information, declarative and conditional. **Declarative information** refers to new ideas and the relationships among them (for example, "Here's how you do long division"). Declarative information is important but by itself is not enough. Students must be able to use that information, which requires conditional information. **Conditional information** refers to information about the potential usefulness of the new ideas (for example, "You can use long division when you want to . . .").

TOOLBOX

TOOLS

Concept Maps

Concept mapping is a visual organizational technique used to facilitate learning and recall. The map is designed to help visualize two or more concepts and their relationships to one another. You may effectively use the visual representation to introduce a topic to students or as a review of concepts and their relationships. Additionally, you may find concept mapping a useful organizational tool when planning instruction. Figure A is an example of a concept map.

To develop a concept map, use the following steps:

1. Select the major concepts to include. These may be generated during brainstorming, from other knowledgeable individuals, or by using outside reference materials.
2. Cluster the concepts according to two criteria:
   ▶ Group concepts horizontally if they function similarly (i.e., are at a comparable level or abstraction). In Figure A these would include the related concepts of "bleeding from artery" and "bleeding from vein."
   ▶ Group concepts vertically if they are hierarchically related (e.g., techniques for controlling bleeding → pressure points → pressure point in arm).
3. Arrange the concepts in a way that depicts their individual relationships. This may require rearranging, rethinking, reclustering, and adding prior knowledge.
4. Connect the concepts with lines and, if needed, label the connections.

Note: Not only has concept mapping been found effective as a study aid, but also having students build concept maps has been shown to be an effective means for them to gain insights and understanding of relationships among different concepts (Ault, 1985; Barenholz & Tamir, 1992).

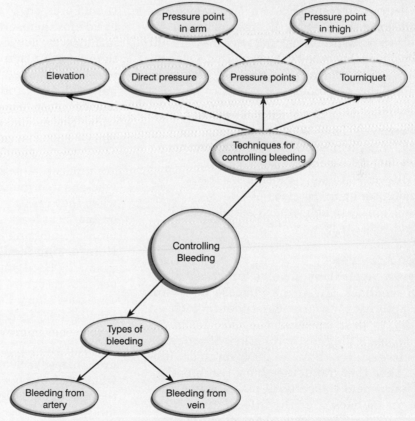

FIGURE A A concept map describing basic ways of controlling bleeding

Using Embedded Questions

One type of application activity involves the use of "embedded questions," questions placed within the instructional material. You may present embedded questions, or students can develop their own. In either case, embedded questions, strategically placed within the instruction, serve several purposes:

▶ They are effective at focusing students' attention (e.g., as an advance organizer identifying what warrants special attention).
▶ They encourage discussion and further inquiry of critical parts of the instruction.
▶ They prompt student self-monitoring and self-assessment to ensure that they have received, understood, and, in some cases, transferred critical information.

Here are examples of generic questions that both teachers and students can adapt for use with a variety of topics:

▶ What will happen next?
▶ Why is this considered true (false)?
▶ How might the events described here be explained?
▶ What was the purpose of this?
▶ What is the everyday relevance of this?
▶ How might this information be used in other situations?

Conditional information helps students internalize what they learn and transfer it to a variety of situations by showing them when the new ideas will be useful (the types of situations) and why they should use the new ideas (how they will help). To develop an information activity for an instructional plan, consider the following questions:

▶ What major content ideas will you present? In what sequence? Using what examples?
▶ What will you do to help students understand and remember those ideas?
▶ What will you do to help students see the relationships among the ideas?
▶ What will you do to help students understand when and why the ideas will be useful?

Application Activities

Application activities involve practice, guidance, and feedback. First, the purpose of an application activity is to provide students with an opportunity to practice what they are learning. Practice serves a diagnostic function. If students practice successfully, they can move on to evaluation. If, on the other hand, they have trouble, they might either repeat the activity, perhaps in a simpler form, or go back over the information, clarifying it as needed. To serve as an effective diagnostic tool, an application activity should ask students to demonstrate the performances called for in the objectives under the same conditions indicated in the objectives.

Second, an application activity may include varying amounts of guidance. In guided practice

students are given clues that suggest how they should proceed. In unguided practice students must decide for themselves how to proceed. Practice that includes more guidance is generally less difficult than practice that includes less guidance. You can regulate your guidance to meet the needs of individual students. Students who progress easily might benefit most from relatively unguided practice, while those who are having trouble might need more structured practice.

Finally, feedback is an essential component of an application activity. **Feedback** refers to giving students information about how well they are doing when they practice. Practice and feedback are inseparable, or at least should be. Feedback comes in two forms: reinforcing feedback and corrective feedback. **Reinforcing feedback** is like a pat on the back (for example, "Good job" or "I like the way you . . ."). You use it to recognize good performance and encourage continued effort. **Corrective feedback,** as its name implies, tells students specifically what they can do to correct or improve their performance (for example, "What if you . . ." or "Next time try . . ."). These two forms of feedback are often used together, reinforcing what students have done well and correcting what they could do better. Practice without feedback has limited value because it does not tell students whether they are progressing toward the objectives or what they can do to improve their progress. To develop an application activity for an instructional plan, consider the following questions:

▶ What will you do to give students an opportunity to apply their new knowledge or skill?

- How much guidance will you provide and what form will that guidance take?
- In what way will you give students feedback about their performance during practice?

Evaluation Activities

The purpose of an **evaluation activity** is to determine how well students have mastered the lesson objectives. Like practice, evaluation serves a diagnostic function. Students who "pass" the evaluation are ready for the next lesson, while those who don't "pass" may need some additional instruction before they proceed. We have purposely put quotation marks around the word "pass" to make a point. We often think of evaluation in terms of traditional paper-and-pencil tests. But, as we describe in Chapter 10, there are a variety of ways to evaluate how well your students have learned, and the meaning of "pass" will be different for these different evaluation methods. To develop an evaluation for an instructional plan, consider the following questions:

- What will you do to determine whether students have achieved the learning objectives?
- How will you give students feedback about their performance during the evaluation?

The Next Steps in Planning

At this point in the planning process, we've described the students, the objectives, the learning environment, and the instructional activities. Your next planning task is to select the methods and media you will use during your instruction. In Chapter 5 we will go into this task in detail, describing the characteristics of different instructional methods and media, along with tools for selecting them for a given unit of instruction. Once you have chosen your instructional methods and media, your next planning task is to acquire the instructional materials that you will use during instruction. In Chapter 6 we will go into this task in detail, providing information on how to find and choose instructional materials, modify existing materials, and create new materials.

INSTRUCTIONAL PLANS AS HEURISTIC GUIDES

We refer again to the recipe analogy that appeared at the beginning of this chapter as a way of making a point about the flexibility of instructional plans. Ask three people how they make spaghetti sauce. Chances are you'll end up with three different recipes. Now, ask three teachers to show you their instructional plans (they may call them *lesson plans*)

for a given topic. Chances are you'll end up with three different plans, even if the content is the same.

We've suggested an instructional "recipe." It is a recipe that is flexible and adaptable to a variety of teaching and learning situations. Remember that an instructional plan, like a recipe, is a decision-making guide. It helps you decide what ingredients to use and how to combine them to help your students learn. The instructional plan we have presented is designed to provide you with a set of **heuristic** guidelines; that is, it is a set of general rules that you can adapt to fit each situation, rather than a rigid procedure that you must follow in the same way every time. Our goal is to provide you with guidelines that are flexible enough to use with a variety of situations, yet structured enough to provide practical guidance. However, you must keep in mind that *there is no one "correct" instructional plan.* Instructional situations differ in terms of students' needs, interests, and experiences; the structure of the content; the available resources; and your preferences, interests, and experiences. Your task is to create a unique solution for the unique problem of helping your students learn; that is, you must develop a plan that helps your particular students learn the particular content. There are several ways in which instructional plans may vary from one situation to the next.

Combining instructional activities. We think the five instructional activity categories (motivation, orientation, information, application, evaluation) are basic ingredients that you should include in every lesson. However, that doesn't necessarily mean that each activity must be a separate entity in every lesson. For example, the purpose of an application activity is to allow students to try out their new knowledge or skill, and the purpose of an evaluation activity is to determine whether they have mastered the intended objectives. It is possible to present a sequence of application activities that will help determine whether students have mastered the objectives. In this case, you combine evaluation and application. The point to keep in mind is that each instructional activity has an important purpose in each lesson. Sometimes you can accomplish those purposes with greater efficiency by combining two or more instructional activities.

Emphasizing an instructional activity. Instructional activities are not all necessarily of equal importance in every lesson. For example, one lesson may present a lot of information and provide limited time for application, while another lesson on the same content may present a small amount of information and allow a lot of time for application.

The manager of an instructional activity. The manager of an instructional activity is the person or

FIGURE 4–3   Varying sequences of instructional
activities

Motivation > Information > Information > Application > Application
Motivation > Information > Application > Information > Application
Motivation > Information > Application > Motivation > Application

thing that is primarily responsible for carrying out that activity, dictating the pace of the activity, controlling the flow of information, and determining what to do next. We say "primarily" because learning is always a collaboration among students, teacher, and instructional materials, and all are likely to influence each instructional activity. However, to what extent do students, teacher, and materials control the pacing, flow of information, and decision making? Note that the manager may vary from one activity to the next. For example, in a given lesson the teacher may manage the orientation while the material manages the information and the students control the application.

Encouraging students to manage their own learning is a powerful technique (refer to the discussion of constructivist learning theory in Chapter 2). Students often learn more from an instructional activity when they manage it themselves. However, this is an acquired skill, and students—especially younger or less sophisticated ones—may require instruction and practice before they are able to do it well. Although teaching students to manage their own learning is beyond the scope of this book, we refer readers who are interested in learning more about this topic to Derry and Murphy (1986), Palinscar (1986), and Schmitt and Newby (1986).

The amount of detail or structure in the plan. You may describe an activity within an instructional plan with more or less detail or structure, depending in part on your experience with the technique being used. As indicated at the beginning of this chapter, teachers who are relatively inexperienced or who are using a new technique may want their plans to provide a lot of structure and will, therefore, describe activity content and materials in great detail. On the other hand, teachers using familiar techniques may need less structure and may therefore sketch out their activities rather than describe them in detail. Note that we're talking about individual activities rather than an entire plan. Different activities within a plan may be described at different levels of detail. For example, a teacher who has developed a new way to introduce a familiar topic may develop detailed motivation and orientation activities while briefly outlining the familiar information.

The order and number of activities. We have listed instructional activities in an order that seems logical, but that isn't the only "correct" order. For example, you may decide to place an orientation activity at the beginning of the lesson as a natural introduction. Alternatively, you may decide to place an orientation activity after an information activity as a way of clearly connecting the new information to previously learned information. Or you may decide that an orientation activity would be useful in both places.

This last point highlights the idea that a lesson often contains more than one of each type of activity and that the activities may be clustered together or spread throughout the lesson. As shown in Figure 4–3, a lesson may include multiple motivation activities, information activities, and/or application activities in various configurations.

Making Plans Parallel

Instructional plans are flexible, designed to guide decision making rather than dictate the way to present a lesson to students. However, one thing should be true of every instructional plan: the components of the plan should parallel one another. That is, the objectives should match the instructional activities, and the instructional activities should match one another. The objectives should accurately represent the knowledge and skills described in the information and measured in the evaluation. Conversely, the evaluation should measure the knowledge and skills described in the information and represented by the objectives. Students should be motivated to learn, and should be applying the knowledge and skills they will be evaluated on, and so on through all the combinations of instructional activities.

To illustrate the concept of parallel plans, consider the brief examples in Table 4–4. In Example A the objectives, information, application, and evaluation are all parallel. They all relate directly to learning how to solve algebra equations. In Example B, however, the objectives, information, application, and evaluation are all aimed at different aspects of algebra. Although they are all important, they are not parallel to one another.

TABLE 4–4 *Parallel Components in the Instructional Plan*

	Example A—Parallel	Example B—Not parallel
Objective	Be able to solve algebra equations	Be able to solve algebra equations
Information activity	Description of the notation used in algebra equations, followed by a demonstration of how to solve various types of algebra equations	Description of the historical development of algebra as a branch of mathematics
Application activity	Problems asking the students to solve the types of algebra equations presented in the information activity	Problems asking the students to interpret various types of algebraic notation
Evaluation activity	A set of algebra equations to solve	Questions about the importance of knowing how to solve algebra equations

Sample Plans

How might you combine instructional activities to form an instructional plan for a specific situation? The following two sample instructional plans (Figures 4–4 and 4–5) will help answer that question. The situations are related, but begin with a different planning component. As a result, the plans are different. Look over each of the two sample plans. What differences do you notice? How might you explain those differences? What does this suggest about the flexibility of the instructional plan?

Scenario A. Ms. Heinrich teaches a beginning Spanish class for fourth graders. A curriculum guide distributed by the school district specifies that students should be able to carry on simple conversations in Spanish and be able to use Spanish greetings (see Figure 4–4).

Scenario B. Mr. Delgado teaches a beginning Spanish class for fourth graders in a different school. His objective is also to have students be able to use Spanish greetings. He has read about cooperative learning techniques, and he likes what he has read. He wants to try cooperative learning in his class (see Figure 4–5).

Practical Benefits of Plans

An instructional plan is a decision-making guide. It allows you to make sensible decisions about how to carry out instruction, respond to the changing needs of students and the situation, and make continual improvements in the instruction you provide. The practical benefits of having a plan can be described in terms of the functions the instructional plan serves before, during, and after the instruction (Borko & Livingston, 1992; Kauchak & Eggen, 1989; Reynolds, 1992).

Before Instruction

Bridge The instructional plan serves two important linking functions. First, it is the *link between the curriculum goals and the students*. The plan is the vehicle you use to decide how to tailor the curriculum, which is often predetermined, to the needs of your particular students. Second, the plan is the *link among the objectives, instruction, and evaluation*. It is the means by which you can decide how to adapt the objectives, instruction, and/or evaluation to ensure that they match one another. The way these links are made depends on (1) the particular curriculum, (2) the students, and (3) your knowledge of the content, level of experience, beliefs about students and how they learn, and knowledge about teaching methods that will help students learn. By making these links, you can ensure students meet the prescribed learning goals, thus making your instruction more accountable.

Checklist The instructional plan encourages you to anticipate the specific materials, facilities, and equipment needed, as well as when you will need them. This helps you make sure that there will be enough materials on hand for all students.

Schedule The instructional plan allows you to decide what activities you will use to help students learn, to put them in a logical sequence, and to allocate sufficient time to the different activities.

During Instruction

Road Map. The instructional plan describes the destination you want to reach and the routes you plan to follow to get there. This road map function helps you make adjustments in the plan. This is important for two reasons. First, interruptions in the classroom are inevitable (for example, because of student absences or school assemblies). The

Students: Fourth Grade Spanish I   Topic(s): Greetings

Objectives:

▶ Say the Spanish equivalent to a given English greeting.
▶ Say the appropriate Spanish greeting when meeting someone.
▶ Say an appropriate Spanish response when greeted in Spanish.

Learning environment: Classroom Activities

1. Combined motivation–orientation activity

Present a series of situations, in English, calling for a greeting. Ask students what they would say. Show similar situations in Spanish on videotape. Present the objectives as steps toward being able to converse in Spanish. Emphasize the importance of practice.

Method: presentation
Medium: videotape

2. Information activity

Demonstrate common Spanish greetings and responses (both formal and informal) for morning, afternoon, and evening. Write the words on the chalkboard, say them several times. Emphasize the greeting/response pairs. During the demonstration, clearly explain when each greeting and response would be used.

Method: demonstration
Medium: chalkboard

3. Orientation activity

Before starting the practice activity, ask students when greetings are generally used and why. Then ask them when they would use the different types of greetings and why. Use this discussion to decide whether to review any of the previous information.

Method: discussion
Medium: audio (conversation)

4. Combined application–evaluation activity

Pair the students up with an audiotape recorder. Instruct students to practice on the tape and to listen to the tape to see how they sound. Spend a few minutes with each pair after they have recorded a practice greeting and response. Listen to the taped practice with students (ask them to evaluate what they hear on the tape). Point out specific strong points in their pronunciation and give specific pointers for improving pronunciation.

Method: drill and practice
Medium: audiotape

FIGURE 4–4   Instructional plan for teaching Spanish greetings and responses

instructional plan *helps you keep the instruction on track,* monitor students' progress toward the destination, and ensure the prescribed content is covered in the face of these inevitable interruptions. It does this by marking your place so you can return after the interruption. Second, students' needs and interests may change, and unanticipated learning opportunities may arise. The instructional *plan allows you to respond to these changing needs, interests, and opportunities* while continuing to progress toward the destination. The plan is designed to be flexible, to allow you to improvise based on the students' responses.

Outline   The instructional plan provides a set of guidelines to follow in the classroom, allowing the teacher to concentrate on interacting with the students rather than trying to remember what comes next.

Compass   The instructional plan provides you with a clear sense of direction, and this helps to increase your confidence and reduce the uncertainty and anxiety that often accompany not knowing where you're going. This may be especially important if you are relatively inexperienced and need something to provide guidance.

After Instruction

Diary   The instructional plan provides you with a place to record what happened during the instruction (McCutcheon, 1980). It is also a place to record your observations and comments about what worked and what didn't. You can then use these notes to improve your instruction.

Briefing Book   It is often important that others know what is happening in the classroom. The instructional plan provides a convenient way to do this.

Students: <u>Fourth Grade Spanish I</u>   Topic: <u>Greetings</u>

Objectives:

▶ Say the Spanish equivalent to a given English greeting.
▶ Say the appropriate Spanish greeting when meeting someone.
▶ Say an appropriate Spanish response when greeted in Spanish.

Learning environment: Classroom Activities

1. **Combined motivation–orientation activity**

   Greet students in English. Explain that all languages use similar greetings. Their task will be to learn greetings in Spanish. Each student will learn 1 greeting from audiotape and teach it to classmates. This is the beginning of being able to talk with people in Spanish. Once they've learned the greetings, they will be able to move on to other parts of conversation.

   Time: 5 minutes   *Add written materials showing*
   Method: presentation   *the words*
   Medium: audio (conversation)

2. **Information activity**

   Divide class into 3 equal groups for morning, afternoon, and evening greetings. Give each group an audiotape with the greeting and response for their time of day recorded on it. Review how to use the tape recorder.

   Directions—Each group is to practice their greeting and response so they can teach it to 2 classmates. Group members should listen to one another and help one another with pronunciation. *Encourage them to practice as much as they can*

   In about 15 minutes the groups will switch around and each student will teach their greeting to the students in their new group. Ask if they need help. Circulate around the room. Keep students on track.

   Time: about 15 minutes
   Method: tutorial
   Medium: audiotaped Spanish greetings

3. **Orientation activity**

   Reorganize class into groups of three—one member from each of the previous 3 groups.

   Directions—Your task now is to teach as much as you can. Help one another out. Everyone in the group is to learn each greeting and response. After about 15 minutes I will start calling students to the front of the room in pairs to show me what you have learned.

   Time: about 15 minutes
   Method: cooperative learning
   Medium: audio (conversation)

4. **Evaluation activity**

   Call students to the front in pairs. Give first student an English greeting on a card. The student is to greet their partner with the corresponding Spanish greeting. Partner is to respond in Spanish.

   Time: 15 minutes   *Find an alternative. Students*
   Method: drill & practice   *need more time for practice*
   Medium: Spanish/English flashcards

5. **Information activity**

   Debrief the lesson:

   ▶ Recall when each greeting and response is used.
   ▶ Ask who else students might teach these greetings to (parents, friends, etc.)
   ▶ Suggest using the greetings with one another around school.

   Time: 5 minutes
   Method: discussion
   Medium: audio (conversation)

FIGURE 4–5 Instructional plan for teaching Spanish greetings and responses using cooperative learning

TOOLBOX

TIPS

Finding Lesson Plans on the Web

The Web has been a real boon to teachers looking for good lesson plan ideas. Many Websites have collections of lesson plans, typically organized by topic and grade level. The sites listed here have a wealth of lesson plan resources.

▶ http://school.discovery.com/schrockguide/ (Kathy Schrock's Guide for Educators, part of Discovery school) (Figure B)
▶ http://henson.austin.apple.com/edres/lessonmenu.shtml (Apple Learning Interchange lesson plans)
▶ http://ericir.syr.edu/Virtual/Lessons (AskErRIC lesson plan collection)
▶ http://www.kn.pacbell.com/wired/bluewebn/ (Blue Web'n blue ribbon learning sites)
▶ http://www.classroom.net/resource/ (Classroom Connect Internet lesson plans and projects)
▶ http://www.mcrel.org/resources/plus/index.asp (Connections+ lesson plans and resources)
▶ http://www.lessonplanspage.com/ (The Lesson Plans Page)
▶ http://www.nytimes.com/learning/teachers/lessons/archive.html (*New York Times* Learning Network lesson plans)
▶ http://www.teachnet.com/lesson/index.html (TeachNet lesson ideas)

You may also locate lesson plans by using standard search engines. To locate lesson plans, use appropriate search terms to target the topics of interest. For example, to locate lesson plans in biology, use the keywords "lesson plan" and "biology." To find plans targeted specifically at the middle school level, add "middle school" as a qualifying keyword.

FIGURE B Sample Web page for locating lesson plans *Source:* Discovery Channel School, Discovery Communications, Inc.

APPLICATIONS IN THE LEARNER-CENTERED CLASSROOM

For example, the plan will tell substitute teachers what parts of a lesson have been completed and what is yet to be done. Similarly, the plan will help principals keep track of what is happening in all classrooms in their building.

We cannot overemphasize the importance of planning. Learning can happen without planning. However, for it to reliably occur across a variety of individuals, planning always plays a key role. Within the planning process, you first must know where you are and where you are going. Whether you are helping a single individual in a one-on-one tutoring situation, or working with dozens of individuals at a professional conference, you need to have the goal in sight. Second, to reach the desired goals, you need activities and learning experiences. Third, one of the best ways to learn is to plan for the learning of others.

Traditionally the emphasis in planning has been on the teacher determining the goals and the subsequent learning activities. However, students also can participate in this process. What are the benefits (and potential pitfalls) of having students plan learning experiences? Think about the following list of ways students may gain from being involved in planning instruction. As they plan, students learn the following:

- The need for knowing the goal and objectives of the instruction and ultimately where they are going
- The whole process, not just individual pieces
- To note the importance of sequence—how they must learn some things before others
- Different individuals have different needs, and individual learning styles and needs must be taken into account
- Motivation doesn't just happen—you have to consider what is relevant to students and how and why they would want to invest effort to learn
- How to determine if they have achieved the goal

For students to progress in levels of expertise, they need to have more than just an experience with well-designed and well-executed instructional lessons. They need to understand how they should plan to learn for themselves and others.

ONE TEACHER'S STORY

by Janette Moreno

The other day, I was thinking about some of the different experiences I have gone through with my students. One of the most enlightening that I think I have ever had was when a Mary Jacobs, a third-grade teacher from Lincoln Elementary, came and asked me to help her with a lesson. The students were studying Spanish and Mary thought maybe I could come and help them learn a few words and play some different games with them. As I thought about this, I decided that I would get some of my high school students involved.

For a class project, I had my students develop a plan for teaching some Spanish phrases to Mary's class. I

Ms. Moreno uses the word processor to plan an upcoming lesson.

told our students that it was up to them to determine what the goals, objectives, and activities would be for the 40-minute lesson. I wanted them to determine what was possible, what kind of information they would need to gather about the topic and about their students, what sources of information they could go to, what they would have to consider for getting and keeping the little kids' attention, how they would deliver the information, and how they would determine if anyone learned anything.

After creating the plan, my students walked away with quite a bit of new knowledge. They learned how much effort goes into planning, how important it is, how critical the information is about your learners, why you have to sequence things appropriately, how you can't take for granted that your learners are all going to "get it" the first time, and so on. Also, my students really learned the content of what they were going to teach. They had to— they couldn't find the right way to develop the activities and so on until they knew the content inside and out. For some of my students, this was the first time they had really fully understood some of the things that they were trying to teach.

Another thing that they learned was the need for examples and for finding out what others have done. Experienced teachers understand this and have experience exchanging ideas, but these novices soon found out that they needed help. They suddenly realized what help was out there, and through work in the library and on the Internet they were able to get some very good examples and activities that helped them plan their lesson.

This was a great experience for all of us. Maybe later we can talk about what actually happened as they presented it to Mrs. Jacobs's class. That was a whole new set of things that my students learned! Third graders can be really funny when you try to teach them—especially in a language they don't fully understand.

SUMMARY

An instructional plan is like a recipe. It describes the "ingredients" of instruction, indicates how they are to be combined for a particular lesson, and is used as a flexible decision-making guide. This chapter elaborated the P in the PIE model, describing the six basic ingredients of the instructional plan: students, objectives, learning environment, instructional activities, methods and media, and instructional materials.

First are the students. Individual students invariably bring to any instructional situation a unique set of characteristics. A major part of the teacher's task is to fit instruction to the students and that means gathering information about their general characteristics, what they already know, and their motivation for learning. Second are the objectives. Objectives specify the intended results: they define what the students should be able to do following instruction. Objectives have three components: a performance, conditions under which that performance is expected, and the criteria that define acceptable performance. Third is the learning environment. It is as important to match the instruction to where learning will occur as it is to match the instruction to who will be learning (the students) and what is to be learned (the objectives). Fourth are the instructional activities. Instruction is made up of varying combinations of five types of instructional activities: motivation, orientation, information, application, and evaluation. Fifth are the methods and media that will be used during the instruction. We discuss this topic more fully in Chapter 5. The instructional materials are the final ingredient. We explore materials in Chapter 6.

In instructional planning, the order in which components appear isn't as important as developing a plan whose parts are parallel. Such a plan offers a number of benefits before, during, and after instruction.

REFLECTIVE ACTIVITIES

▶ Think about your own background and experience. How do you think they influence your motivation for learning? How do you think they influence the types of instructional methods and media that work well for you?

▶ Read each of the following objectives and determine whether each one contains the three components described in this chapter. Rewrite any objective that doesn't include all three components.
  a. Identify the correct methods of financing the purchase of a new house.
  b. Summarize the benefits of specifying performance outcomes in instruction.
  c. Describe the relationship between f-stop and shutter speed. The description should include their effects on exposure.
  d. Explain why firms under competition will adopt least-cost technologies.
  e. Understand the importance of semiconductors in the microcomputer industry.
  f. Discuss from memory the five basic economic goals. The discussion should be consistent with the course textbook.
  g. Judge the extent to which the design for an electrode system meets a set of specifications.
  h. After completing the course, the student will be able to utilize a particular medium effectively.
  i. Given a computer, the students will improve their computer skills.
  j. Given a partner, an elastic bandage, and tape, the student will be able to wrap his or her partner's ankle effectively.

▶ Consider a learning environment you have been in recently. Visit it if you can. What are the characteristics of that environment? How do you think those characteristics might influence a lesson presented in that environment?

▶ Obtain an instructional plan from the Internet (see "Toolbox Tips: Finding Lesson Plans on the Web" on p. 86) and analyze it in terms of the types of instructional activities described in this chapter. Can you find evidence of each type of instructional activity? What alternatives can you identify for each type of activity?

▶ Develop an instructional plan for a lesson. Briefly describe how you would implement each instructional activity. Give your plan to another student and ask for feedback. Does the plan make sense? Does it seem coherent? Did you clearly describe the instructional activities? Are there alternative ways to implement each activity?

SUGGESTED RESOURCES

Clark, C. M., & Yinger, R. J. (1987). Teacher planning. In J. Calderhead (Ed.), *Exploring teachers' thinking* (pp. 84–103). London: Cassell.

Eisner, E. (1985). *The educational imagination: On the design and evaluation of school programs* (2nd ed.). New York: Macmillan.

Fennema, E. (1987). Sex-related differences in education: myths, realities, and interventions. In V. Richardson-Koehler (Ed.), *Educator's Handbook: A Research Perspective*. New York: Longman.

Keller, J. M. (1983). Motivational design of instruction. In C. M. Reigeluth (Ed.),

Instructional design theories and models: An overview of their current status (pp. 383–434). Hillsdale, NJ: Lawrence Erlbaum Associates.

Mager, R. F. (1997). *Preparing instructional objectives* (3rd ed.). Atlanta, GA: Center for Effective Performance.

Ormrod, J. E. (1995). *Educational psychology: Principles and applications.* Upper Saddle River, NJ: Merrill/Prentice Hall.

Woolfolk, A. E. (1998). *Educational psychology* (7th ed.). Boston: Allyn & Bacon.

Yelon, S. L. (1996). *Powerful principles of instruction.* White Plains, NY: Longman.

WEBSITES

http://www.geocities.com/Athens/Delphi/7862/
http://www.yahoo.com/Education/K_12/teaching/lesson_plans/

CHAPTER 5

Identifying Methods and Media for Learning

KEY WORDS AND CONCEPTS

Instructional methods
Medium/media
Interactive multimedia
DVD
Compact disc (CD)

OBJECTIVES

After reading and studying this chapter, you will be able to

▶ Identify an example of each instructional method discussed in the chapter.
▶ Identify examples of each type of media described in the chapter.
▶ Identify and explain combinations of methods and media commonly used in instruction.

PLANNING FOR THE CHAPTER CONTENT

Instructional Technology for Teaching and Learning, will show you how to increase learning by designing lessons that use instructional technology, including computers and other media.

In this chapter we discuss instructional methods, focusing on the tools and media teachers commonly employ when using these methods to design lessons. In Chapter 4 you learned how to develop a plan for increasing your students' learning. This chapter addresses the methods and types of media to use in your plan.

INTRODUCTION

Let's assume you are buying your first vehicle. Which type of vehicle you buy will depend on how you define your needs. Do you have a family? Do you go on frequent trips? If so, then you would probably look for a full-size car or van with a lot of passenger room and luggage space—maybe even one with a large towing capacity if you have a trailer or camper. Are you on a tight budget? If so, then you would probably look for a small, low-priced car that gets good gas mileage and is relatively inexpensive to maintain. Is safety a priority? If so, then you would probably look for a car with safety features such as antilock brakes, air bags, and side-impact protection.

After you define your needs, you should make yourself aware of the range of available vehicles.

Only after you learn the characteristics, advantages, and limitations of each are you prepared to choose the one that meets your needs

WHAT ARE METHODS AND MEDIA?

As discussed in Chapter 4, you select your instructional methods and media after determining your students' characteristics, identifying your instructional objectives and your learning environment, and planning your instructional activities. Methods and media are the tools you use to create learning experiences. **Instructional methods** are "the procedures . . . selected to help learners achieve the objectives" and **media** are "carriers of information between a source and a receiver" (Heinich, Molenda, Russell, & Smaldino, 1999, p. 8). The purpose of this chapter is to help you identify the methods and media most appropriate for your planned instructional activities. We first discuss instructional methods. Then, we explore instructional media.

INSTRUCTIONAL METHODS

Traditionally, instructional methods have been described as "presentation formats" such as lecture and discussion. Your methods are the procedures you select to help students achieve your stated lesson objectives. In Chapter 1 we introduced ten different types of methods (Table 5–1). We discuss them here, beginning with the more student centered and proceeding to the more teacher centered.

You can, of course, (and should) use a variety of methods in any instructional situation. However, some methods seem better suited for certain content or certain learners. You will learn which method or combination of methods is most effective only by trying them with actual students. You will undoubtedly

TABLE 5–1   *Instructional Methods*

Cooperative learning

Discovery

Problem solving

Games

Simulation

Discussion

Drill and practice

Tutorial

Demonstration

Presentation

Students learn interpersonal skills through cooperative learning.

find yourself using a variety of methods to keep instruction interesting.

Methods of instruction vary in their interactivity and typical group size. Presentations and demonstrations tend to be less interactive, while drill and practice and tutorials are highly interactive. While most methods lend themselves to small-group instruction, presentations and demonstrations are most effective for larger groups and tutorials and drill and practice tend to work best with individuals.

We now look briefly at each method, together with examples.

Cooperative Learning

Many educators have criticized the competitive atmosphere that dominates some classrooms. They believe that pitting student against student in attaining teacher-assigned grades is contrary to the societal requirements of on-the-job teamwork, and creates an adversarial relationship between students and teachers. Such competition in the classroom can interfere with learning.

Cooperative learning involves small heterogeneous groups of students working together to learn collaborative and social skills while working toward a common academic goal or task. Each student in the group is accountable to the group for a different and specific aspect of the content. Individual students cannot complete the task on their own, but must rely on others in the group. In this method, students apply communication and critical-thinking skills to solve problems or to engage in meaningful work together. A growing body of research supports the claim that students learn from each other when they work on projects as a team (Slavin, 1990a, 1990b).

Students can learn cooperatively not only through being taught with media but also by producing media themselves. For example, designing and producing a video or a *PowerPoint* presentation presents an excellent opportunity for cooperative learning (see "Toolbox Techniques: Using Student-Generated Instructional Materials"). You will work as a partner with your students in a true cooperative learning situation.

Cooperative groups have several uses including facilitating learning about a specific topic, promoting positive interactions and interdependence among groups of students, and teaching important social and communication skills. Another important reason for using such an approach is to teach individual accountability. When a group's success depends on the input of each individual in it, individuals learn to be accountable for their actions.

Example

In the science lab, groups of middle school students work together as detectives to determine the nature of an unknown substance. In each group, one student is assigned to search the Internet, another goes to the public library for background research, others focus on designing and running experiments on the substance, while others work to locate someone who may be familiar with the substance. Together they

Using Student-Generated Instructional Materials

Instruction has traditionally been planned, designed, produced, and delivered by an instructional expert. This expert, the teacher, knows the content, how to sequence the subject matter, what prerequisite knowledge is necessary, and how to best present the content. But is it always better to have teachers supply instructional materials for students?

There are several advantages to having students participate in designing, developing, and delivering instructional materials, perhaps through cooperative learning:

▶ Students bring their own experiences and backgrounds to the learning situation; therefore, they may tailor instruction to their individual understanding, thus increasing the likelihood of effective encoding and retrieval of information.

▶ In most cases, for learners to be able to effectively design and develop instructional materials, they must first achieve a high degree of understanding of the subject matter.

▶ Planning and designing effective instruction involves high-level problem solving. Not only do students learn subject matter, but they also gain experience analyzing and solving specific problems.

▶ Investing effort into relevant and creative endeavors can be highly motivating. Students may become more interested in content they help plan and develop.

▶ Students learn additional skills as they produce instructional materials. For example, students who create a multimedia presentation to help teach about different plants of the intermountain Northwest learn not only about plants but also about how to effectively design and script *HyperStudio* stacks.

---

pool their information to come to a combined, cooperative solution.

Discovery

The **discovery** method enables and encourages students to find "answers" for themselves. A principle of discovery learning is that students learn best by *doing,* rather than by just hearing and reading about a concept. With this method, your role is to arrange the environment so that "discovery" can occur.

Discovery uses an inductive, or inquiry, approach to learning; it presents problems students must solve through trial and error. The aim is to foster a deeper understanding of the content through active involvement with it. Instructional media can help promote discovery or inquiry learning. For discovery teaching in the physical sciences, students might view a video in which the narrator states a set of relationships and then go to the lab to discover the principles that explain those relationships. For example, after viewing someone saying, "Air has weight," they may then experimentally weigh a balloon before and after filling it with air, thus discovering that the statement is true.

Example

High school economics students "play" the stock market with $100,000 in pretend money. Students work in teams to gain the most from their "investments." Their

success or failure is determined by the rise and fall of the real stock market during the time they are "investing." Students discover how outside forces, such as the Federal Reserve, impact the value of stocks.

Problem Solving

In the problem-solving method, learners use previously mastered content and skills to resolve a challenging problem. **Problem solving** is based on the scientific method of inquiry. The usual steps are (1) define the problem and all major components, (2) formulate hypotheses, (3) collect and analyze data, (4) derive conclusions and/or solutions, and (5) verify conclusions and/or solutions. Learners must define the problem clearly (perhaps state a hypothesis), examine data (possibly with the aid of a computer), and generate a solution. Through this process learners are expected to arrive at a higher level of understanding of the content under study.

One way to distinguish problem solving from discovery is that in problem solving students are *using* previously learned content and skills to solve problems while in discovery students are *learning* the content and skills. One type of problem-solving method commonly used is the case study.

Examples

Students in a business class are given information about a situation at a small manufacturing firm and asked to

FIGURE 5–1 *Thinkin' Things* allows the student to create a feathered friend based on a specific pattern and sequence *Source: Thinkin' Things, Edmark Corporation. Reprinted with permission.*

design a solution for a problem of low production. After gathering more data, they determine whether the solution should involve training or, perhaps, changing the environment or attitudes of the workers.

A computer program called *Thinkin' Things* makes use of various problem-solving strategies, such as working backwards, analyzing a process, determining a sequence, and thinking creatively. The software provides the user with a factory that produces creative-looking feathered friends (Figure 5–1). The preschool-aged child selects from a set of options in order to create the next appropriate bird in the sequence.

Games

Instructional **games** provide an appealing environment in which learners follow prescribed rules as they strive to attain a challenging goal. It is a highly motivating approach, especially for tedious and repetitive content. Games often require learners to use problem-solving skills or demonstrate mastery of specific content such as math facts and vocabulary words. Games include elements of competition or challenge wherein players compete against themselves, against other individuals, or against an objective standard (Figure 5–2).

Examples

Where in the World is Carmen Sandiego? is a popular computer game that develops students' understanding

FIGURE 5–2 Instructional games provide a challenging approach to experiencing a variety of activities

of geography and world culture. Students assume the roles of detectives who must track down a thief who has stolen a national treasure from somewhere in the world. By gathering clues and conducting research, players are able to track the thief around the world, learning about geography as they go. See Chapter 8, Figure 8–5 (page 169) which depicts a screen from this scenario.

Spelling bees and speed math facts (e.g., students are given a number of problems to solve during a short time period; points are awarded for accuracy and speed) are common instructional games used in elementary classrooms to teach basic skills.

Role Playing

Role playing is a type of instructional simulation. It is like a drama in which each participant is assigned a character to depict, but must improvise their performance. Examples include learning how to interview for a job, managing a situation in which a hostile student threatens a teacher, discussing a questionable call with an umpire during a championship baseball game, and establishing a personal relationship.

Role playing encourages creativity and allows students to express their feelings and attitudes. It is an effective means to develop and practice social skills, and it can help students learn to organize thoughts and responses instantly while reacting to a situation or question.

Consider the following guidelines when designing and implementing role play in the classroom (see Dallmann-Jones, 1994; McKeachie, 1994):

▶ Design the situation in sufficient detail prior to class.
▶ Define participants' roles in terms of the situation.
▶ Ask for volunteers rather than choosing participants—volunteers are less likely to feel put on the spot.
▶ Allow participants a short time to get their thoughts together.
▶ Brief all students before role play begins. Describe the situation and indicate what nonparticipants should look for.
▶ Don't let the role play "run" too long. Three to six minutes is usually sufficient.
▶ Stop the role play and reverse roles if a "hot" topic is encountered and emotions begin to get out of hand.
▶ Conduct followup discussion to analyze the performance. To avoid defensiveness, allow players to discuss their perceptions and emotional reactions first.

You may easily adapt other games, such as *Trivial Pursuit* and *Jeopardy,* to contain relevant subject-matter content and at the same time retain the benefits of the game structure.

Simulation

Using **simulation,** learners confront realistic approximations of real-life situations. Simulation allows realistic practice without the expense or risk involved in real situations. The simulation may involve participant dialogue, manipulation of materials and equipment, or interaction with a computer. This method can promote cognitive, affective, and interpersonal skills that emphasize response accuracy, speed, self-pacing, and convergent questioning abilities. Simulations also allow students to practice cooperation and teamwork, and can help foster leadership skills. Simulations can promote decision making and build positive values and attitudes by putting students in unfamiliar roles (see "Toolbox Techniques: Role Playing").

Examples

Interpersonal skills and laboratory experiments in the physical sciences are popular subjects for simulations. In some simulations learners manipulate mathematical models to determine the effect of changing certain variables, such as those affecting the control of a nuclear power plant. *Sim City* is a popular computer simulation. The program allows students to simulate the management of a city, including such elements as budget, construction of infrastructure, traffic, pollution, and crime. Students can build their own city from scratch or manage one of several well-known cities around the world.

High school students can pretend that they are operating a household. They have an "income" from which they "pay" for housing, food, transportation, and recreation. Periodically they may draw a "life event" card, which gives them extra income or leads to a financial setback. These simulated experiences give them insight into how they might respond in similar real-life situations.

Discussion

Discussion is a dynamic method that encourages classroom rapport and actively involves students in learning. Students talk together, share information, and work toward a solution or consensus. They are given the opportunity to apply principles and information through verbal discourse. This method introduces students to different beliefs and opinions, encouraging them to evaluate the logic of and evidence for their own and others' opinions. It provides you with immediate feedback on students' understanding of course material. Discussion prior to a media presentation may help guide students' attention during the presentation.

Students learn content and communication skills by participating in discussions.

There are three important skills associated with the discussion method: (1) asking questions, (2) managing the flow of responses to your questions, and (3) responding to students' questions. Discussions teach content as well as processes such as group dynamics, interpersonal skills, and oral communication. Discussion among students or between students and teachers can make significant contributions throughout students' learning. It is a useful way of assessing the knowledge and attitudes of a group of students. Discussion can foster collaborative and cooperative learning. In combination with written forms of evaluation, you also may use discussion to evaluate the effectiveness of your instruction.

Example

A third-grade teacher may lead a discussion on the meaning of Thanksgiving Day when preparing his students to attend a Thanksgiving play presented by high school students. A discussion after the play helps to answer students' questions and ensures that everyone understands the performance.

Drill and Practice

During **drill and practice,** students are led through a series of practice exercises designed to increase fluency in a newly learned skill or to refresh an existing one. Use of this method assumes that students have previously received some instruction on the concept, principle, or procedure in question. To

be effective, drill and practice exercises should include corrective feedback to remediate errors students might make along the way.

Drill and practice is frequently beneficial when students need to memorize and readily recall information. Certain media formats and delivery systems lend themselves particularly well to drill and practice exercises. For example, audiotapes and CD-ROMs are effective for drill and practice in spelling, arithmetic, and language instruction.

Example

To learn math facts to a level of automatic recall, students employ flashcards. On one side of the card is a simple arithmetic problem, on the other the answer. Students attempt to answer the problem and then flip the card and compare their answer to the correct solution. This format can be used to learn states and their capitals, the names of animals and their young (e.g., goose and gosling, kangaroo and joey), foreign words and their translation, and other paired information sets.

Tutorial

A *tutor*—in the form of a person, computer, or special print materials—presents content, poses a question or problem, requests student response, analyzes the response, supplies appropriate feedback, and provides practice until learners demonstrate a predetermined level of competency. Tutoring is most often done one to one and is frequently used to teach basic skills such as reading and arithmetic, although you may use it to teach higher-level skills as well.

Tutorial arrangements include instructor and student (interactive dialogue), student and student (tutoring or programmed tutoring), computer and student (computer-assisted tutorial software), and print and student (programmed instruction). The computer is especially well suited to play the role of tutor because of its ability to quickly deliver a complex menu of responses to different student inputs. Tutorials can be used for learning all types of content. Unlike drill and practice, which simply goes over previously presented information again and again, you can use tutorials to introduce new material to the student.

Example

A sixth-grade math teacher uses a tutorial to teach her class how to calculate the area of a rectangle. First she helps them recall relevant information from previous lessons (e.g., the concepts of rectangle, length, height, and multiplication). Then she introduces and explains the concept of *area* as the product of the length of the rectangle multiplied by its height. She then demonstrates and shows a number of examples of determining the area of different sizes of rectangles. The students then attempt novel problems using the same format. The teacher gives them feedback on their performance, and they continue practicing until all students can successfully calculate a rectangle's area.

Demonstration

Demonstrations show students how to do a task as well as why, when, and where it is done. In this method, students view a real or lifelike example of a skill or procedure. Verbal explanations become more concrete by illustrating ideas, principles, and concepts. In addition, demonstrations can set performance standards for student work; by demonstrating how to properly perform a task, you establish the criteria you expect students to meet. You may use recorded demonstrations played back by means of a videotape or computer; two-way interaction or student practice with feedback require either a live instructor or a computer. The desired outcome may be for the student to imitate a physical performance, such as swinging a golf club or changing the oil in a car, or to adopt the attitudes or values exemplified by a respected model. You may use demonstration to illustrate how something works, to show how to perform a task, or to teach safety procedures. Demonstrations are essential when teaching a psychomotor procedure (such as jumping rope) or an interpersonal skill (such as participating in a discussion).

Students share their knowledge through classroom presentations.

Example

A student in a science class demonstrates the effect of heat on a bimetallic strip. The teacher demonstrates the manipulative skill of bending glass tubing in the chemistry lab. Instructors use demonstrations to show how to follow a recipe to create the perfect German chocolate cake. A band leader shows trumpet players how correct posture can make a difference in the quality and volume of sound they produce.

Presentation

In a **presentation** a source relates, dramatizes, or otherwise disseminates information to learners. This method makes use of verbal information and/or visual symbols to convey material quickly. Presentations typically provide students with essential background information. A presentation can also introduce a new topic, provide an overview, and motivate students to learn. It is a one-way communication method controlled by the source, with no immediate response from, or interaction with, the audience. The source may be a textbook, an audiotape, a videotape, a computer, an instructor, a student, and so on.

Examples

In a senior history class, a small group of students do a mediated presentation on the origin and meaning of the Bill of Rights to summarize the content studied during a lesson.

During a visit to a museum, you check out a cassette tape and player with headphones. The audiotape and accompanying map guide you through the museum and present information about each exhibit and display.

Each instructional method has unique advantages and limitations (Table 5–2). You may use multiple,

TABLE 5–2 *Advantages and Limitations of Instructional Methods*

Instructional Method	Advantages	Limitations
Cooperative Learning	Promotes positive interdependence, individual accountability, collaborative and social skills, and group processing Encourages trust building, communication, and leadership skills Facilitates student learning in academic as well as social areas Involves students in active learning	Requires a compatible group of students (this may be difficult to form) Takes more time to cover the same amount of content than other methods Is less appealing to individuals who prefer to work alone
Discovery	Encourages higher-level thinking; students are required to analyze and synthesize information rather than memorize low-level facts Provides **intrinsic motivation** (where merely participating in the task itself is rewarding) to discover the "answer" Usually results in increased retention of knowledge; students have processed the information and not simply memorized it Develops the skills and attitudes essential for self-directed learning	Allows for the discovery of "incorrect" or unintended information Can be time consuming
Problem Solving	Increases comprehension and retention; students are required to work with everyday problems and to apply theory to practice Involves higher-level learning; students cannot solve problems by simple memorization and regurgitation Provides students with the opportunity to learn from their mistakes Develops responsibility as students learn to think independently	Limits the amount of content covered; can be time consuming Selecting, modifying, and/or designing effective instructional problems can be time consuming Requires teachers to have good management skills to coach students without giving them the "answer"
Games	Actively involves students and encourages social interaction through communication among players Provides the opportunity for practice of skills with immediate feedback Can be incorporated into many instructional situations to increase student motivation Helps students learn to deal with unpredictable circumstances	May involve students with competition more than content Can be impossible to play if pieces are lost or damaged Can be time consuming to set up if games have many components
Simulation	Provides practice and experimentation with skills Provides immediate feedback on actions and decisions Simplifies real-world complexities and focuses on important attributes or characteristics Is appealing, motivates intense effort, and increases learning	Can cause deep emotional involvement (e.g., students in veterinary school get very attached to "sick" animals they diagnose and attempt to "save," even though the animals exist only within the simulation) Both setup and debriefing can be time consuming

TABLE 5–2 *Continued*

Instructional Method	Advantages	Limitations
Discussion	Allows students to actively practice problem-solving, critical-thinking, and higher-level thinking skills Is interesting and stimulating for teachers and students alike Can change attitudes and knowledge level Makes effective use of students' backgrounds and experiences	Students must have a common experience (reading a book, viewing a video, participating in an activity) in order to meaningfully participate and contribute Teacher must prepare and possess discussion-leading skills for the method to be effective
Drill and Practice	Provides repetitive practice in basic skills to enhance learning, build competency, and attain mastery Promotes psychomotor and low-level cognitive skills Helps build speed and accuracy	Students can perceive it as boring Does not teach when and how to apply the facts learned
Tutorial	Provides optimum individualized instruction; all students get the individual attention they need Provides the highest degree of student participation Expands the number of "teachers" in the classroom by using students or computers as tutors Frequently benefits student tutors as much as, or more than, the tutees Introduces new concepts in a sequenced, interactive way	May be impractical in some cases because appropriate tutor or tutorial material may not be available for individual students May encourage student dependency on human tutor; students may become reluctant to work on their own
Demonstration	Utilizes several senses; students can see, hear, and possibly experience an actual event Has dramatic appeal if the presenter uses good showmanship techniques, such as demonstrating an unexpected result or a discrepant event Provides a holistic perspective by showing a complete performance before students learn to do part or all of it Reduces hazards and trial-and-error learning of experiments or procedures involving materials and equipment (as in science labs, shops, home economics classes)	May be difficult for all students to see the demonstration Is time consuming if demonstrations are done live Demonstrations may not go as planned
Presentation	Can be used with groups of all sizes Gives all students the opportunity to see and hear the same information Provides students with an organized perspective of lesson content (i.e., information is structured and relationships among concepts are illustrated) Can be used to efficiently present a large amount of content	Requires little student activity Makes assessment of student's mental involvement difficult Doesn't provide feedback to students; by definition, presentation is a one-way approach

mixed and matched methods within a single lesson. In many instructional situations one method will not do the job, and you may decide to combine methods within a single lesson. For example, you may follow a tutorial with drill and practice exercises to reinforce learning. In another case, the best methods may be a presentation followed by a discussion. Combining methods may be more powerful and result in more learning than using either method alone.

Which Method?

In the blank before each description, write the name of the method described. The methods to choose from are cooperative learning, discovery, problem solving, games, simulation, drill and practice, tutorial, presentation, and demonstration. Our answers appear at the end of the chapter on page 140.

_____ 1. Students apply the scientific method in a study of the evolution of language in a primitive culture.

_____ 2. High school students in an English class go to the elementary school next door and work with primary students one on one to improve the young children's reading ability.

_____ 3. In a physics lab, students manipulate batteries, resistors, and multimeters to determine if there is a relationship among voltage, resistance, and current.

_____ 4. Students practice resolving conflicts on the playground, at the local shopping mall, and on the school bus.

_____ 5. Students in Bible study class at the local Christian school exchange their interpretations of the Samson story in the Old Testament Book of Judges.

_____ 6. Orchestra students individually record their parts of an upcoming musical on audiotape. The conductor listens to the tapes and helps each musician individually. Students then rerecord their tape until the conductor feels the recordings are satisfactory.

_____ 7. Middle school students practice their keyboarding skills by attempting to destroy prehistoric monsters by typing certain letter combinations for each type of monster as it appears on the screen.

_____ 8. Students intensely watch a videodisc that illustrates effective communication skills, knowing that each of them will have to present a speech before their peers in upcoming classes.

_____ 9. Students individually explore various aspects of the history, famous citizens, industries, and contributions of their home state. Following their research, they get together in small groups and prepare a *PowerPoint* presentation for the entire school.

_____ 10. At the beginning of the school year, Mr. Ward encourages each student in his sixth-grade class to bring in an object for "show-and-tell" that represents something exciting that the student did during the summer.

Reflective Questions

1. What different types of instructional methods have you experienced within the last week or so?
2. What worked and what didn't for you? Why do you think some methods worked and some didn't?
3. In any of your recent instructional experiences would a combination of methods have worked better than the one method you experienced?

INSTRUCTIONAL MEDIA

You cannot use instructional methods without also using some form of media for communication. In that sense the two are inseparable. We now examine various types of instructional media, discussing the advantages and limitations of each.

A **medium** (plural, **media**) is a channel of communication. Derived from the Latin word meaning "between" the term refers to that which carries information between a source and a receiver. Examples of media include slides, videotapes, diagrams, printed materials, and computer software. These are considered *instructional media* when they carry messages with an instructional purpose. The purpose of instructional media is to facilitate communication and enhance learning.

Media serve a variety of roles in education. Their primary role is to *facilitate student learning*. One way they do this is by providing a stimulus-rich environment. Media can provide vicarious experiences. Students don't have to go to a foreign country to "see" it. Visuals give added meaning to words. Students can see what a new invention looks like, not just hear or read a verbal description of it. Motion media and sequential still visuals can demonstrate a process. It is better if learners see a skill demonstrated before being asked to practice it. The demonstration can be live, videotaped, or presented through a series of photographs. In addition, color, sound, and motion can increase student interest and motivation to learn.

Students can learn from a variety of sources when using a multimedia kit.

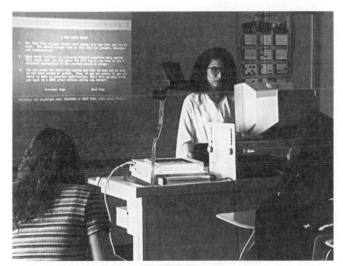

Media can be used to involve students in learning.

Another role of media, often overlooked, is their use in evaluation. You can ask students to identify an object or parts of an object in a photograph, or to describe the movements in a musical composition recorded on audiotape. Videotapes can present the events leading up to a problem situation, and you may have students describe their responses to the problem.

Media commonly used in elementary and secondary schools include multimedia, video, graphics, audio, text, and real objects and models. We discuss each of these, along with examples of classroom applications.

Multimedia

The term **multimedia** conveys the notion of a system in which various media (e.g., text, graphics, video, and audio) are integrated into a single delivery system under computer control. A modern **interactive multimedia** system may weave together text, graphics, animation, data, video, and audio from various sources, including a videodisc, a CD, and the computer itself.

Picture a student in Ms. Moreno's Spanish Conversation class seated in front of a multimedia system. It looks pretty much like a computer system, perhaps with a few additional pieces of equipment connected to it via cables. The student reads the directions on the computer screen and clicks the mouse to get started. The lesson begins with a video clip, originating from a network, CD-ROM, or DVD, which depicts a conversation between two native speakers of Spanish. The video not only allows the student to see and hear two native speakers, but it also provides a cultural backdrop, as it was shot on location overseas. As the lesson progresses, the student makes use of a Spanish dictionary stored on a CD-ROM that provides definitions and translations, as well as the actual aural pronunciation of each word and phrase. The computer facilitates the student's access to all of this information and provides periodic review questions and feedback about her progress. This is just one example of what interactive multimedia can be like.

The computer—with its virtually instantaneous response to student input, its extensive capacity to store and manipulate information, and its unmatched ability to serve many individual students

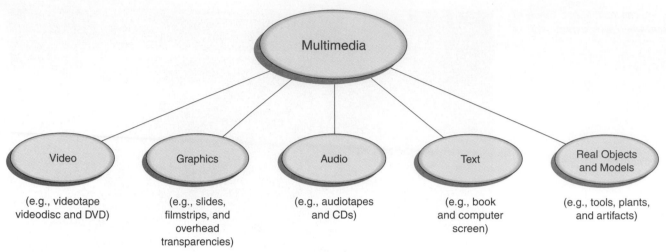

FIGURE 5–3   Multimedia is a combination of different media types

simultaneously—has wide application in instruction. The computer can also record, analyze, and react to student responses typed on a keyboard or input with a mouse. Some display screens react to the touch of a student's finger. **Computer software** is the programs or instructions that tell the computer what to do. As noted, *multimedia* usually refers to the delivery of video, graphics, audio, and text by a computer using instructional software.

Examples

Ninth-grade students use a computer research database to locate books and articles describing the recent Olympics. In addition to the bibliographic citations, summaries of some of the texts are included along with photographs of some of the Olympians, and video of some of them in competition.

Students use a literature program to read a passage and instantaneously receive definitions, explanations, or clarifications for any unknown word, name, or phrase specified. The students are excited to be able to get the needed definitions without interrupting their reading and going to a dictionary.

As indicated, multimedia is a conglomerate of a number of different media formats, including video, graphics, audio, text, and real objects and models (Figure 5–3). These media can be used together as multimedia, and can also be used individually. To select and use them properly, you will need to know what they are, and their advantages, limitations, and possible applications.

Video

Moving images can be recorded on videotape, videodisc, DVD, and computer disk. All these formats offer ways to store and display moving images ac-

companied by sound. As we will see, the formats differ considerably in cost, convenience, and flexibility.

Video is defined as the display of recorded pictures on a television-type screen. Any media format that employs a cathode-ray screen to present a picture can be referred to as video: videotapes, videodiscs, and DVD.

The VHS half-inch **videotape** is the preferred medium for commercial distribution of moving images. VHS is also the current preferred format for amateur video production in education.

A **videodisc** resembles a large compact disc, or CD. Images and sound are recorded optically in a manner similar to that for CD. A typical education videodisc can hold up to 30 minutes of motion video images or up to 54,000 still images, or a combination of both motion and still images. As with the CD, the videodisc can be indexed for rapid location of any part of the material. However, indexing must be incorporated into the disc during production; the user cannot add it. When a videodisc playback unit is connected to a computer, the information on the disc can become an integral part of a computer-assisted instructional program. The computer program makes use of the index on the disc.

A newer type of video medium is **DVD.** Some professionals refer to it as **digital video disc,** others use the term **digital versatile disc.** DVD is a compact disc format for displaying motion video. It offers truly digital, optical recording, storage, and playback of full-motion video and/or computer data (like a CD-ROM). The disc is the same physical size as an audio CD or a CD-ROM. However, one current-generation DVD can hold enough data for a full-length feature film—about two hours. Future DVD discs will be able to hold about four times that amount. Like CDs and CD-ROMs, DVD has instant random access and is highly durable. Recordable DVDs are just beginning

Digital video discs (DVD) allow learners to view full-motion video on a computer.

to appear on the market. They have the potential to do for video what the CD did for music. (See Appendix A for further discussion of these formats.)

Both videotape and videodisc have fastforward and reverse search capabilities. Video formats, particularly videodisc, can be indexed, making it possible to locate specific sections of a program. Certain special effects, such as slow motion and still images, are available during the video presentation. Because the equipment is easy to operate, video lends itself to individual study.

Examples

Physical education students use videodisc's slow-motion and freeze-frame capabilities to practice imitating the grip and swing of a golf professional. Their coach is able to point out the critical parts of the pro's swing. Students can imitate the swing and also get feedback from their peers.

Students write a position paper after viewing videos presenting the opposing positions of the lumber industry and environmentalists on retaining the virgin forests of the northwestern United States. Viewing actual forests on videotape and hearing and seeing representatives of both sides of the issue stimulate the students to investigate the issue and to put their thoughts on paper.

Graphics

Several types of graphics are used in teaching and learning. We look at four here: visuals, slides, overhead transparencies, and display boards.

Visuals

Visuals are two-dimensional materials designed to communicate a message to students. They usually include verbal (text or word) elements as well as graphic (picture or picturelike) elements. Examples include drawings, charts, graphs, posters, and cartoons. Sources of visuals include textbooks, reference materials, newspapers, and periodicals, as well as those created by teacher or students.

We live in a very visual society. From pictures in the morning newspaper, to signs on the roadway, to graphics downloaded from the Internet, we are bombarded with visuals every day. Why are visuals used so prominently? Because they work. Visuals can increase *effectiveness* by highlighting information, which increases viewers' comprehension and memory. For example, visuals can depict real or abstract items, illustrate procedures, provide examples, identify parts and pieces, and draw attention to similarities and differences among various objects. Additionally, visuals can increase *efficiency* by representing, in a single form, what may take hundreds if not thousands of words to explain. Finally, visuals can increase *appeal* by attracting attention, as well as stimulating thought and inquiry.

Visuals have numerous applications. For example, you may use photographs or drawings to illustrate specific lesson topics, especially those involving processes. Visuals are helpful with objectives requiring the identification of people, places, or things. You may use them to stimulate creative expression such as telling or writing stories or composing poetry. They can provide an excellent means to review or

Using Visuals in Instructional Materials

Your selection and use of visuals are important when adapting or creating instructional materials. Just as the proper visual may lead to increased instructional effectiveness, efficiency, and appeal, one that is not appropriate may cause learner difficulties and frustration. Ask yourself the following questions when selecting visuals to use with your instructional materials:

▶ Is the visual relevant to the instructional outcomes?
▶ Is the information depicted accurately?
▶ Is the information current?
▶ Is the information presented clearly and simply?
▶ Will learners comprehend what is depicted?
▶ Will it be big/small enough for the given purpose and size of audience?
▶ Is it aesthetically pleasing?

preview experiences of past or future field trips. Visuals also serve to pique interest and curiosity and provide specific information for testing and evaluation purposes (see "Toolbox Techniques: Using Visuals in Instructional Materials").

Examples Sixth-grade science students sequence the major steps involved in the production of oxygen by plants using a set of drawings. Manipulating the actual visuals stimulates discussion and learning.

High school history students use geography maps to point out the difficulties an army would have if it attempted to invade Switzerland. Using maps the students attempt to find possible routes before the teacher points out the routes actually used by invaders in the past.

Slides

Slides are small, transparent photographs individually mounted for one-at-a-time projection. Like other forms of projected visuals, teachers use slides at all grade levels and for instruction in all curricular areas. Many high-quality slides are available commercially, singly, and in sets. The fine arts, geography, and the sciences are especially well represented with commercially distributed slides. A very similar format is the filmstrip, which is essentially a set of slides on a single strip of film.

Examples Students view a slide show of clothing articles designed, sewn, and modeled by fellow students. The students find it rewarding to see themselves and their garments on the screen. The class also discusses the strengths of each garment and offers suggestions to improve future designs.

Students design and produce a slide show of the history of their community. Using inexpensive cameras, students go into their community to take pictures of older buildings. The media specialist helps

them locate photographs from years ago that they can have converted to slides for the presentation.

Overhead Transparencies

Overhead transparencies are widely used in classrooms because of their many virtues. Basically, the overhead projector is a box with a large "stage" on the top. Light from a powerful lamp inside the box passes through a transparency (approximately 8 inches by 10 inches) placed on the stage. A lens-and-mirror system mounted on a bracket above the box turns the light beam 90 degrees and projects the image onto a screen or blank wall.

Overhead transparencies may be created from clear acetate, photographic film, or any of a number of other transparent materials capable of being imprinted with an image. In addition, you can project a variety of materials, including cutout silhouettes, small opaque objects, and many types of transparent objects. Transparencies may be used individually or made into a series of images. You can explain complex topics step by step by adding a series of overlays one at a time to the base diagram.

The overhead has many group-instruction applications. Commercial distributors of transparencies have made materials available for virtually all curricular areas, from kindergarten through adult education. These materials range from single, simple transparencies to elaborate sets with multiple overlays.

Examples Students illustrate the flow of information between a computer's central processing unit and its random-access and read-only memories by drawing arrows on a transparency. All students will be expected to duplicate the flow on a paper-and-pencil test at the end of the unit.

Kindergarten students classify various items placed on the overhead projector stage as either cir-

It is easy to use the overhead projector to show visuals to a group.

cles, triangles, squares, or rectangles. The students are stimulated by the brightly colored shapes and eagerly await their turn to go to the overhead projector and manipulate the items.

Display Boards

There are many surfaces in the classroom on which to display text and visual materials, including chalkboards, multipurpose boards, and bulletin boards. The most common medium in the classroom is the chalkboard. Once called blackboards, chalkboards, like chalk, now come in a variety of colors. Although the chalkboard is most commonly used as a medium of verbal communication, you also may use it as a surface on which to attach or draw visuals. You can fasten pictures to the upper molding, tape them to the board with masking tape, or place them in the chalk tray to help illustrate instructional concepts and support verbal communication. You also may draw visuals, such as sketches, diagrams, charts, and graphs, on the chalkboard for display to the class.

Some classrooms are equipped with multipurpose boards (also called whiteboards or marker boards) instead of chalkboards. As their name implies, they have more than one purpose. Their smooth, white plastic surface requires a special erasable marker rather than chalk. The surface is also suitable as a screen on which you can project slides and overhead transparencies. Materials cut from thin plastic, such as figures and letters, will ad-

here to the surface when rubbed in place. Some of these boards have a steel backing as well and can be used as a magnetic board for displaying visuals.

A *bulletin board's* surface is made of a material that holds pins, thumbtacks, staples, and other sharp fasteners without damage to the board. In practice, bulletin board displays tend to serve three broad purposes: decorative, motivational, and instructional. The decorative bulletin board is probably the most common in schools. Its function is to lend visual stimulation to the environment. Displaying student work exemplifies the motivational use of bulletin boards. The public recognition offered by such displays can play an important role in classroom life. It fosters pride in achievement, reinforcing students' efforts to do a good job.

The third purpose of bulletin boards is instructional, complementing the educational objectives of the formal curriculum. Rather than merely presenting static informational messages, you can design displays to invite participation. Such displays ask questions and give viewers some means of manipulating parts of the display to verify their answers (e.g., flaps, pockets, dials, or movable parts). Learners can also take part in the actual construction of the display. For example, to introduce a unit on animals, an elementary teacher might ask each student to bring in a picture of a favorite animal. Students would then make a bulletin board incorporating all the pictures.

Students can share audio experiences.

Examples Students classify various types of igneous, metamorphic, and sedimentary rocks displayed on platforms secured to a bulletin board. Then they check their responses against the correct answer provided under a movable flap. Because the display is available in the classroom during the entire unit, they can check and recheck themselves until they are confident that they know all the types of rocks.

Students sing the simple notes of the treble clef displayed on a multipurpose board. As the teacher adds sharps and flats, different colors draw students' attention to these special notes. The notes can be easily moved around the board.

Audio

In addition to the teacher's voice, there are numerous ways to bring sound into the classroom. The most common is the **audiotape.** Audiotape allows both students and teachers to make their own recordings to share with the class. Another medium is the **compact disc (CD).** Both are very durable.

For hands-on learning, you can record a tape from which students can receive procedural instructions. To be efficient and effective in their work, these students must have both hands free and their eyes on their work, not on a textbook or manual. Audiotapes allow students to move at their own pace and leave you free to circulate around the classroom and discuss each student's work individually.

Students with learning difficulties can revisit classroom presentations via audiotape. They can replay more difficult sections as often as necessary. The students practice their listening skills with tapes of recorded stories, poetry, and instructions. After the students have practiced their listening skills under your direction, you can evaluate them using a tape they have not heard before.

Examples

High school students interview local citizens regarding the history of their community. Excerpts are duplicated and edited into oral histories for other students to use. The students enjoy recording and editing the tapes. The local citizens, especially the senior citizens, enjoy sharing their stories.

Students with visual impairments listen to recorded versions of novels being discussed in literature class. Other students also choose to listen to the tapes. All students, whether they read the novel or heard the tapes, then share their interpretations.

Text

The term **text** refers to letters and numbers, usually presented to students in the form of printed materials or on a computer screen. Examples include study guides, manuals, worksheets, textbooks, and computer displays. Textbooks, such as this one, have long been the foundation of the learning process. You can use many of the other media and computer formats discussed in this book in conjunction with, and as supplements to, textbooks.

The most common application of text is to present information. Students read text to learn its content. They are given reading assignments and held accountable for the material during class discussions and on tests. Text can also complement your presentation. Students may use study guides and supplementary worksheets to augment information you present verbally or through other media. Worksheets allow students to practice what they have learned and to receive feedback. Additionally, students may use text references in the library or media center or search computer databases to find information on a specific topic.

Examples

Students complete worksheets about the workings of an artificial heart after having viewed a videotape on the topic. The worksheet serves as viewing notes during the video. Each student practices applying the information presented and receives immediate feedback from the teacher.

Moderately handicapped industrial education students assemble a bicycle by following the directions in its accompanying pamphlet. The purpose of the activity is to promote reading and to encourage students to follow instructions. After assembling the bicycle, they disassemble it so other students can repeat the process.

Real Objects and Models

Often not thought of as multimedia or even as media, real objects and models can require learners to use all their senses—sight, hearing, smell, touch, and even taste! They bring the outside world into the classroom. **Real objects,** such as coins, tools, plants, and animals, are some of the most accessible media available to promote student learning. **Models** are three-dimensional representations of real objects, and may be complete in detail or simplified for instructional purposes. Models of almost everything are available from teacher supply companies and toy stores.

You often can introduce a new topic with a real object or a model. Invite the students to see and handle it. Both elementary and secondary students can learn about objects in their own environment and those from foreign cultures and other times. Real objects and models add relevance for the students and can generate interest and enthusiasm for a topic. If you cannot bring real things into the classrooms, a field trip can take students to them. Another effective use of these materials occurs during evaluation as students classify objects, describe their functions, and identify their components.

Examples

Elementary students create a terrarium to observe the water cycle. All students are excited by the plants and animals as they place them in the terrarium. They work together in teams under the teacher's direction to complete the terrarium.

Students in a multicultural course discuss the impact of various artifacts (tools, dishes, etc.—real or replicas) on the lives of those from another culture.

Objects and models can bring the real world into the classroom.

The artifacts hold the interest and attention of all the students. The real objects and models make the cultures "come alive."

You are now familiar with six types of media: multimedia (interactive media and computer software), video (videotape and videodisc), graphics (visuals, slides, overhead transparencies, and display boards), audio (audiotapes and CD), text, and real objects and models. To make a good decision about the type of medium to select, you must know the advantages and limitations of each. Table 5–3 presents the main advantages and limitations of the media described in this chapter.

Which Medium?

In the blank before each description, write the name of the medium described. The media to choose from are multimedia, video, graphics, audio, text, and real objects and models. Our answers appear at the end of the chapter or page 114.

_____ 1. Marketing students learn how to increase levels of consumer motivation for buying a specific product by combining dramatic music with emotional oral testimonies of the product's effectiveness and value.

_____ 2. Learners study the *Titanic* by using an interactive videodisc program that provides diagrams of the ship's structure, biographies of individuals sailing on the ship, information about rescue operations, and film footage of the exploration and discovery of the wreckage.

_____ 3. Students use photographs of local buildings to illustrate a unit on architectural styles.

_____ 4. High school students research replicas of handwritten court records from the 1800s to discover information about their ancestors.

...ctional Medium	Advantages	Limitations
Multimedia	*Better learning and retention.* Interactive multimedia provides multiple learning modalities and actively involves learners. *Addresses different learning styles and preferences.* The incorporation of multiple modalities provides opportunities for teaching individual learners. For example, those with weak reading skills can use aural and visual skills to process verbal information. *Effectiveness across learning domains.* Interactive multimedia instruction has been shown to be effective in all learning domains. It can be used for psychomotor training, such as learning CPR techniques; to present simulations that provide opportunities for problem-solving and higher-order thinking skills; and even to address affective components of learning. *Realism.* Interactive multimedia provides a high degree of realism. Instead of merely reading about a speech by Dr. Martin Luther King, Jr., students can actually see and hear the speech as he originally gave it. *Motivation.* Learners show consistently positive attitudes toward interactive multimedia. For today's MTV-conscious youth, multimedia instruction represents a natural avenue for exploring the information revolution. *Interactivity.* The key element of computers is interaction with the user. The computer can present information, elicit the learner's response, and evaluate the response. *Individualization.* The computer's branching capabilities allow instruction to be tailored to the individual. The computer can provide immediate feedback and monitor the learner's performance. *Consistency.* Individualization results in different instructional paths for different learners. But it can be equally important to ensure that specific topics are dealt with in the same way for all learners. *Learner control.* Computers can give the user control of both the pace and the sequencing of instruction. Fast learners can speed through the program, while slower learners can take as much time as they need.	*Equipment requirements.* The equipment requirements for multimedia can be an impediment. While basic systems may involve only the computer and its built-in components, more complex systems may involve external videodisc players, CD-ROM players, audio speakers, and so on. These can be difficult to hook up and maintain. *Startup costs.* Startup costs can be high. The computer itself can be expensive. Adding components and software may cost thousands of dollars. *Complexity and lack of standardization.* Interactive multimedia systems can be quite complex. Sometimes it is a challenge just to get the individual components to work together. Novices may become hopelessly lost. This is complicated by the fact that there is currently little standardization today in many facets of multimedia. *Compatibility.* The lack of compatibility among the various brands of personal computers limits multimedia transportability. Developers cannot always create a single package that will work across all types of computers. *Limited intelligence.* Most computer software is limited in its capacity for genuine interaction with the learner, and often relies on simple multiple-choice or true-false questions.
Video videotape	*Motion.* Moving images can effectively portray procedures (such as tying knots or operating a potter's wheel) in which motion is essential. Operations, such as science experiments, in which sequential movement is critical can be shown more effectively by means of videotape.	*Fixed pace.* Videotape programs run at a fixed pace; some viewers are likely to fall behind, while others are waiting impatiently for the next point.

TABLE 5–3 *Continued*

Instructional Medium	Advantages	Limitations
videotape—cont'd	*Real-life experiences.* Video allows learners to observe phenomena that might be dangerous to view directly—an eclipse of the sun, a volcanic eruption, or warfare. *Repetition.* Research indicates that mastery of physical skills requires repeated observation and practice. Video allows repeated viewing of a performance for emulation.	*Scheduling.* Teachers normally must order videos well in advance of their intended use. Arrangements also have to be made for the proper equipment to be available. The complexity of the logistics discourages some teachers.
videodisc	*Storage capacity.* Videodiscs come in two formats: CLV (extended play) and CAV. The former stores up to one hour of video per side, while the latter stores up to 30 minutes of video per side. CAV videodiscs can also intermix short video sequences with still frames. One side of a CAV videodisc can store up to 54,000 still images (the equivalent of hundreds of slide projector carousel trays). *Rapid access.* Videodisc players can rapidly access any still image or video sequence on a disc, usually in no more than a few seconds. Teachers or students can access the images using a remote control or bar code reader, or via computer connection. *Dual audio channels.* Videodiscs can contain two to four audio channels. Many manufacturers include both English and alternate language (often Spanish) audio tracks to make the videodiscs accessible to different audiences. *Durability.* Videodiscs are exceedingly durable. Unlike videotape, videodiscs do not lose quality with repeated playing. There is no physical wear when the videodisc is played, and discs' clear plastic coating prevents damage during handling. *Image quality and cost.* Videodiscs have high image quality, superior to that of most VCRs. Because discs are inexpensive to duplicate, the cost per image can be very low compared to other media such as slides.	*Expense.* Videodisc players are more expensive than VCRs and slide projectors. In addition, while the cost per image can be low, commercially produced videodiscs can be expensive. Some videodiscs cost several hundred dollars each. *Limited play time.* When used strictly for video playback, the playing time of videodiscs is much less than videotape at only 30 to 60 minutes per side, depending upon format. With most videodisc players (there are some exceptions), the videodisc must be manually flipped over to access information on the second side. *Analog format.* Videodiscs, unlike CDs, are not digitally recorded and so are not directly compatible with computers.
DVD	*Storage capacity.* Each disc holds two to eight hours of full-motion video. *High-quality audio.* The audio is high fidelity, comparable to that on a compact disc. *Digital format.* Because DVD is a digital medium, it is directly computer compatible.	*Limited materials.* At this time limited educational materials are available. *Few playback units available.* Many schools have few, if any, DVD players or player-equipped computers.
Graphics visuals	*Realistic format.* Visuals provide a representation of verbal information. *Readily available.* Visuals are readily available in books, magazines, newspapers, catalogs, and calendars. *Easy to use.* Visuals are easy to use because they do not require any equipment. *Relatively inexpensive.* Most visuals can be obtained at little or no cost.	*Size.* Some visuals are simply too small to use with a large group, and enlarging can be expensive. However, a document camera can project an enlarged image before a class. *Two-dimensional.* Visuals lack the three-dimensionality of the real object or scene. However, providing a series of visuals of the same object or scene from several different angles can address this limitation. *Lack of motion.* Visuals are static and cannot show motion. However, a series of sequential still pictures can suggest motion.

TABLE 5–3 *Continued*

Instructional Medium	Advantages	Limitations
Graphics—cont'd slides	*Flexibility.* Because slides can be arranged and rearranged into many different sequences, they are more flexible than filmstrips or other fixed-sequence materials. *Easy to produce.* Cameras with automatic exposure and focusing controls and high-speed color film allow teachers and students to easily produce their own high-quality slides. *Ease of use.* Projectors allow the presenter to remain at the front of the room while advancing the slides via a remote pushbutton unit. *Availability.* The general availability and ease of producing slides allows teachers to easily build permanent collections.	*Lack of sequence.* Because slides come as individual units, they can easily become disorganized. Even when stored in trays, the slides can spill if the locking ring is loosened. *Jamming.* Slides can be mounted in cardboard, plastic, or glass of varying thicknesses. This lack of standardization can lead to jamming in the slide-changing mechanism. Cardboard mounts become dog-eared; plastic mounts swell or warp in the heat of the lamps; thick glass mounts fail to drop into showing position. *Damage.* Slides not enclosed in glass covers are susceptible to accumulation of dust and fingerprints. Careless storage or handling can lead to permanent damage.
overhead transparencies	*Versatility.* The overhead can be used in normal room lighting. The projector is operated from the front of the room, with the presenter facing the audience and maintaining eye contact. All projectors are simple to operate. *Instructor control.* The presenter can manipulate projected materials, pointing to important items, highlighting them and adding details with colored pens or covering part of the message and progressively revealing information. *Instructor preparation.* Teachers can easily prepare their own transparencies in advance for presentation at the proper time.	*Instructor dependent.* The overhead projector cannot be programmed to display information by itself. The overhead system does not lend itself to independent study. The projection system is designed for large-group presentation. *Preparation required.* Printed materials and other nontransparent items, such as magazine illustrations, cannot be projected immediately but must first be made into transparencies. This can be done using color copying machines.
display boards	*Versatile.* Both students and teachers can use display boards for a variety of purposes. *Colorful.* Display boards provide color and add interest to classrooms or hallways. *Involvement.* Students can benefit from designing and using display boards.	*Commonplace.* Instructors often neglect to give display boards the attention and respect they deserve as instructional devices. Displays can quickly lose their effectiveness if left in place too long. *Not portable.* Most display boards are not movable.
Audio audiotapes	*Student and teacher preparation.* Students and teachers can record their own tapes easily and economically, erasing and reusing them. When material becomes outdated or no longer useful.	*Fixed sequence.* Audiotapes fix the sequence of a presentation, even though it is possible to rewind or advance the tape to a desired portion. It is difficult to scan audio materials as you would printed text.

TABLE 5–3 *Continued*

Instructional Medium	Advantages	Limitations
audiotape–*cont'd*	*Familiarity.* Most students and teachers have been using audiocassette recorders since they were very young.	*Lack of attention.* Students' attention may wander while they are listening to audiotapes. They may hear the message but not listen to or comprehend it.
	Verbal message. Students who cannot read can learn from audio media. Audio can provide basic language experiences for students whose native language is not English.	*Pacing.* Presenting information at the appropriate pace can be difficult for students with a range of skills and background experiences.
	Stimulating. Audio media can provide a stimulating alternative to reading and listening to the teacher. Audio can present verbal messages more dramatically than can text.	*Accidental erasure.* Just as audiotapes can be quickly and easily erased when no longer needed, they can be accidentally erased when they should be saved.
	Portable. Audiocassette recorders are very portable and can even be used "in the field" with battery power. Cassette recordings are ideal for home study since many students have their own cassette players.	
CD	*Locating selections.* Students and teachers can quickly locate selections on CDs and can program machines to play any desired sequence. Information can be selectively retrieved by students or programmed by the teacher.	*Cost.* The cost of CD players has limited their acceptance in the education market.
	Resistance to damage. There are no grooves to scratch or tape to tangle and break. Stains can be washed off and ordinary scratches do not affect playback.	*Limited recording capability.* Students and teachers cannot produce their own CDs as cheaply and easily as they can cassettes.
Text	*Readily available.* Printed materials are readily available in a range of topics and formats.	*Reading level of learners.* Many students are nonreaders or poor readers.
	Flexible. Printed materials may be used in any lighted environment. They are portable. Properly designed text organizes the content and is very user friendly.	*Memorization.* Some critics say textbooks promote memorization rather than higher-level thinking skills.
	Economical. Text can be used again and again by many students.	*Passive.* Others contend that text promotes solitary learning rather than cooperative group processes. Textbooks may be used to dictate the curriculum rather than to support it.
Real Objects and Models	*Less abstract and more concrete.* Real objects and models provide hands-on learning experiences and emphasize real-world applications.	*Storage.* Large objects can pose special problems. Caring for living materials such as plants and animals can take a lot of time.
	Readily available. Materials are readily available in the environment, around school, and in the home.	*Possible damage.* Materials are often complex and fragile. Parts may be lost or broken.
	Attract students' attention. Students respond positively to both real objects and their models.	

TABLE 5–4 *Matching Instructional Methods and Instructional Media*
Which methods are commonly used with which media?

	Computer Software	Video	Graphics			Audio	Text	Real Objects & Models
			Visuals	Slides or Overheads	Display Boards			
Presentation		X	X	X	X	X	X	
Demonstration	X	X	X		X			X
Discussion					X			
Cooperative Learning	X		X					X
Discovery	X		X				X	X
Problem Solving	X	X	X		X		X	
Instructional Games	X		X				X	
Simulation	X		X				X	X
Drill & Practice	X						X	
Tutorial	X						X	

_____ 5. Third-grade language arts students visit a museum's dinosaur exhibit to gain inspiration for creative story writing.

_____ 6. Students view and compare short video clips of a typical school day for children from Taiwan, Germany, Ethiopia, Peru, and the United States.

Reflective Questions

1. What instructional media have you used recently in self-study?
2. What instructional media have been used in classes you attended recently?
3. What are your favorite media to learn from? Why?
4. What are your least favorite media to use for learning? Why?

WHICH MEDIA WORK BEST WITH WHICH INSTRUCTIONAL METHODS?

Which media work best with which methods? The answer is subjective at best. It will vary from situation to situation. Table 5–4 expresses our opinion on matching media to method. These are the most obvi-

ous combinations and the easiest for beginners to manage. With experience you will be able to make the "best" decisions for you, your learners, and your lesson content. Until then, you may wish to use the table as a basis for considering the various possibilities. In reality *all* media could be used with *all* methods.

APPLICATIONS IN THE LEARNER-CENTERED CLASSROOM

A key principle to remember as you design, develop, and have your students experience learning is that *students may learn from many different methods and media; a "live teacher" is not always essential for instruction* (Smith & Ragan, 1999). This principle highlights a couple of things. First, individuals' learning needs vary; moreover, those needs can change from day to day. What makes a concept crystal clear for them today, may not tomorrow. Consequently, learners often must experience lessons in a number of different ways to fully comprehend and learn. Second, from a motivational standpoint, variety is necessary. We have learned that by changing and adapting methods and media, learners attend to a greater degree. Here is a simple example. Think back to the last time that you went to a really boring lecture. What was it that made it boring? Perhaps the lecturer spoke in a monotone voice, with little inflection. This lack of change is a known way of putting people to sleep. Third, individuals who understand their needs for learning are in the position to select the type of method and/or media that works best for them. That is, having more than one mode of presentation/experience for students may allow them to learn more effectively. If they perceive that their learning is not complete or is lacking in some way, they then may attempt to learn through a different mode or method. Finally, the content itself will often dictate what method or media you should or should not use. Limiting the number of methods or media to choose from will limit the content students can learn.

From within the classroom setting, knowing various methods and media is essential for effective learning. Likewise, helping students to understand those different means as well as their own style of learning will help them come to select, whenever possible, what they need to effectively and efficiently learn.

ONE TEACHER'S STORY

by Janette Moreno

I remember the way teachers used to use media to teach foreign languages when I was in high school. Language teachers were noted for capitalizing on the strengths of many types of media and methods. Besides using authentic objects from foreign cultures, including foods, jewelry, clothing, and even games and toys, they displayed a variety of visuals around the classroom. I also remember brightly colored posters and maps, as well as wall hangings and brochures. As students' facility with the particular language increased, they began to read and discuss newspapers and magazines, and eventually novels and textbooks written in the language. Teachers also used phonograph records to present popular music from other cultures. I also recall the yearly homemade slide shows that my language teacher would make following her most recent trip overseas!

When I first started teaching, I utilized many of the media and methods I was familiar with (only instead of creating a slide show, I used a video recorder when I traveled overseas). Traditional media and methods still have a lot to offer language students. But I began to experience some frustrations, due, in part, to the widening range of students enrolling in my courses. I really needed to find ways to increase my own capacity to meet individual learners' needs. Initially, I was hesitant and frustrated in trying to use the computer to meet those needs. It was awful—I was so afraid I was going to break something or mess up a program, or lose what I was working on. I knew nothing about the computer; I didn't even know what a disk or a hard drive was. I attended a workshop one summer that covered a lot of basic technical stuff, and I managed to hook up with another language teacher who was just a few steps ahead of me. What saved me? I learned how to learn from my mistakes!

I've grown a lot in both knowledge and confidence since I took that first computer course. I continue to look for new ways to make learning meaningful and exciting for my students, and, as you might expect, many of my recent teaching innovations revolve around some type of computer application. I've even incorporated several multimedia computer programs. My students and I are now very comfortable using these "new" media.

SUMMARY

Just as we identified different types of methods and media in this chapter, you will need to identify appropriate characteristics of methods and media for your students. We presented the ten most widely used instructional methods, gave examples, and listed advantages and limitation of each method. We then described six broad categories of instructional media, giving examples and listing advantages and limitations of each.

REFLECTIVE ACTIVITIES

▶ How could Ms. Moreno use demonstration, discovery, discussion, cooperative learning, problem solving, and instructional games to teach conversational Spanish? If any of these methods are not appropriate, explain why.

▶ Consider a recent personal learning experience. Determine if the instructional method used was appropriate or if you could have learned more if the instructor had used a different or additional method.

▶ Imagine that you are asked to submit a proposal to a school superintendent to teach the four workshops listed below. Divide each workshop into the main topics you would cover and then select the form(s) of media you feel would be most appropriate to present each topic. Briefly explain your choices, in writing.

a. Basic games for the elementary school physical education class

b. Instruction on conflict resolution in the high school classroom

c. Effective study skills for freshmen high school students

d. How to design and carry out a school-sponsored "Family Art Night"

▸ For the next few weeks, keep a media reference notebook. List instructional media you encounter, how effective, efficient, and appealing you found them to be, what problems you encounter, and what alternatives could have been used.

▸ Look at Table 5–4. What observations can you make as to the medium with the most potential for use with a variety of methods? What methods can logically incorporate the widest variety of media? What media and methods combinations have you used (or seen used) successfully? What media and methods combinations have you used (or seen used) *un*successfully?

SUGGESTED RESOURCES

Barell, J. (1995). *Teaching for thoughtfulness: Classroom Strategies to Enhance Intellectual Development.* White Plains, NY: Longman.

Dallmann-Jones, A. S. (1994). *The expert educator: A reference manual of teaching strategies for quality education.* Fond du Lac, WI: Three Blue Herons.

Heinich, R., Molenda, M., Russell, J. D., & Smaldino, S. (1999). *Instructional media and technologies for learning* (6th ed.). Upper Saddle River, NJ: Merrill/Prentice Hall.

McKeachie, W. J. (1994). Why classes should be small, but how to help your students be active learners even in large classes. In W. J. McKrachie (Ed.), *Teaching Tips* (pp. 197–210). Lexington, MA: Heath.

ANSWERS TO CHAPTER QUESTIONS

Which Method?

1. Problem solving
2. Tutorial
3. Discovery
4. Simulation
5. Discussion
6. Drill and practice
7. Games
8. Demonstration
9. Cooperative learning
10. Presentation

Which Medium?

1. Audio
2. Multimedia
3. Graphics
4. Text
5. Real objects and models
6. Video

C H A 6 P T E R

Selecting Methods, Media, and Materials

KEY WORDS AND CONCEPTS

Instructional materials
Repurposing
Formative evaluation
Copyright

OBJECTIVES

After reading and studying this chapter, you will be able to:

▶ Distinguish among the concepts of method, medium, and materials.
▶ Select the most appropriate instructional methods and media for a particular lesson.
▶ Identify sources of existing instructional materials.
▶ Select, modify, and/or design instructional materials for a particular lesson.
▶ Outline a procedure for acquiring computer software.
▶ Acquire instructional materials in a manner consistent with current copyright law.

PLANNING FOR THE CHAPTER CONTENT

Instructional Technology for Teaching and Learning, will show you how to increase learning by designing lessons that use instructional technology including computers and other media.

In Chapter 4 you learned how to develop a plan for increasing your students' learning. Chapter 5 addressed the advantages and limitations of various instructional methods and media. In this chapter, we focus on how to select methods and media and acquire the specific instructional materials you will use to implement your plan. As we will explain, you may acquire instructional materials by selecting existing materials, modifying available materials, or creating new materials.

This chapter expands the PIE model described in Chapter 1, as shown in the following outline:

Plan
    Identifying characteristics of the students
    Specifying objectives
    Describing the learning environment
    Developing instructional activities
    Selecting instructional methods
    Selecting instructional media
    Acquiring instructional materials
Implement
Evaluate

INTRODUCTION

Imagine that you are in charge of a large machine shop that produces various types, sizes, and quantities of metal machine parts to customers' orders, varying from tiny ball bearings to 2-inch brackets, and on up to 24-inch gear mechanisms. You make your parts from precision-made molds (called *dies*). It is your job to make sure your customers receive the parts they order, in the time allotted, made according to the given specifications.

If you were faced with such a task, it would be important to have a clear plan for filling your orders. The plan would allow you to examine specific requirements (e.g., size, tolerance) and the end product's appearance. Then, to be as productive and cost-efficient as possible, you would need to ask the following questions:

1. Do we have the molds in stock for making the needed parts? That is, can we use what we have already made?
2. If the exact mold does not exist, is it possible to adapt an existing mold to meet the specifications for this particular customer?
3. If adaptation is impossible, can we create a new mold to produce the needed parts on time and within budget?

These questions appear in order of increasing cost, both in money and time. The most cost-efficient is to use existing molds. The next-cheapest alternative is to adapt an existing mold. It is most expensive to produce new molds in order to manufacture the necessary parts.

Similarly, designing and delivering instruction involves following a clear plan. You have already begun developing an instructional plan, using information from Chapter 4. You have identified your students' characteristics, specified your lesson objectives, considered the learning environment, and developed instructional activities. Now you are ready to complete your plan by selecting instructional methods and media and acquiring the necessary instructional materials. As in the machine shop example, this may involve creating new materials. However, you first want to see if something already exists or if you can adapt materials to meet your needs.

METHODS, MEDIA, AND MATERIALS

To begin, we redefine the terms *methods, media,* and *materials* as used in this book. In Chapter 5 we defined an instructional *method* as a technique or procedure used to help students learn (e.g., cooperative

Students and their teacher use instructional materials to facilitate learning.

learning, game, presentation, discussion). We defined an instructional *medium* as a means of providing a stimulus-rich environment for learning (e.g., multimedia, video, text, real objects). **Instructional materials** are the specific items used in a lesson and delivered through various media; for example, you may use a videotape titled *The Second Russian Revolution* in a social studies class. Your method may be presentation or discussion, the medium is video. The instructional material is the specific videotape.

You can incorporate instructional materials throughout the activities outlined in your plan, from motivation activities through evaluation activities. For example, if you were designing a physics lesson on the characteristics of light, you may have several activities requiring instructional materials, which you may present via various methods and media:

> *Motivation.* A videotape demonstration with animation could illustrate the behavior of light.
> *Orientation.* Overhead transparencies could present your learning goals for the lesson.
> *Information.* You may use slides to illustrate key points in a discussion you lead.
> *Application.* You may provide real objects (e.g., lenses, mirrors, prisms) to allow students to explore the behavior of light through problem solving or discovery.
> *Evaluation.* You may employ visuals to determine students' level of mastery.

Selecting methods, media, and materials are separate but interrelated decisions that you can make in any order. Sometimes, you choose instructional materials based on the methods or media you are using. Other times it is appropriate or necessary to select instructional materials prior to deciding on the methods and media. The following examples illustrate the possibilities.

Scenario A: Method → Medium → Instructional Materials. Mr. Hughes wants to teach sentence structure to his eighth-grade English class, which meets right before lunch. He decides to use a game to make the topic interesting and to give his students a chance to practice the skills and receive feedback. Not able to find any instructional materials in his school, he decides to design his own board game in which students roll dice, draw a card, and advance if they can correctly identify the part of a sentence highlighted on the card.

Scenario B: Medium → Instructional Materials → Method. The students in Pat Todd's social studies class are studying World War II. Pat decides to incorporate visuals in her lesson. She wants her students to have images from the war to help them remember the factual lesson content. With the help of the school library media specialist, Pat locates a series of slides with an audiotape. There are 80 slides in the set—far more than she wants to use. She selects from the series a dozen slides that will highlight her key points. Because the level of the tape is too elementary for her students, she decides to develop her own narration to accompany the slides.

Scenario C: Instructional Materials → Medium → Method. Ms. Roth, a fifth-grade teacher in the Midwest, wants to increase her students' awareness of the ways in which living things affect each other. She recently discovered software titled *A Field Trip into the Sea* in the school library media center. After previewing it, she decided it matches the characteristics of her students and teaches the content she wants to cover. She is sure the software will motivate her students to develop an awareness of living things they have not seen. The materials she has selected determine the medium (the classroom computer) and the method (discovery).

Regardless of the order in which you choose these elements, you must consider the following factors (Figure 6–1):

> *The students.* What are their general characteristics? Consider their age, grade level, socioeconomic status, previous experience, and any special needs they may have. What specific knowledge or skills do they have? What are their learning styles and preferences? Do they prefer audio materials, visuals, interpersonal

Students play a board game to learn new concepts in English.

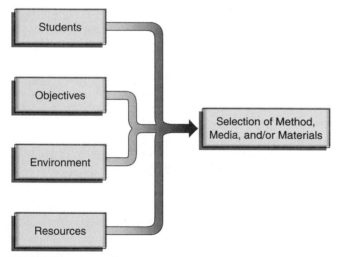

FIGURE 6–1   Factors to consider when selecting instructional methods, media, or materials

experiences, hands-on learning? How many students are there?

▶ *The objectives.* What are the learning objectives? How would you classify those objectives? What types of learning are required? What cognitive demands do they place on the students? In what sequence should you present the content?

▶ *The learning environment.* How large is the space? Will the space allow you to conveniently divide the students into small groups? Will it allow the students to work individually without distractions?

▶ *The available resources.* What resources do you have at your disposal (including materials, equipment, funds)? What constraints are there on what you can do? One important consideration is time: to produce the materials, to prepare for the lesson (gather materials, rehearse your role, etc.), and to complete the activity during the lesson.

SELECTING INSTRUCTIONAL METHODS

You must decide which instructional method(s) you will use in your lesson. In Chapter 5 we described ten different instructional methods—cooperative learning, discovery, problem solving, games, simulation, drill and practice, tutorial, presentation, demonstration, and discussion—and their advantages and limitations. These advantages and limitations provide your foundation for choosing methods for a particular lesson.

We have compiled the advantages of the various instructional methods into a checklist, shown in Figure 6–2, that you may use to select your method(s) for a particular lesson. The checklist will help you remember the factors to consider when selecting instructional methods. Without such a list, it is easy to make choices based only on what you like best or are most comfortable with. The list will remind you that there are other important considerations. It is not meant to replace your professional judgment, but to supplement or support it. We recommend that you use

Which Methods Should I Choose?

The Methods Selection Checklist will help you select the method or methods that will best fit your lesson. Each method has advantages, listed in the first column of the table. There are ten additional columns, one for each instructional method. To use the checklist, place a "√" in all the white spaces that best describe your instructional needs or situation. For example, if you think learning will be enhanced by allowing students to learn on their own, go to item 4 and place a "√" in the five columns that contain a white space. Continue this process for each of the items in the first column. When you have gone through the entire checklist, determine which column has the most "√s."

If most of the "√s" are in:	Select		If most of the "√s" are in:	Select
CL	Cooperative Learning		DP	Drill and Practice
DY	Discovery		T	Tutorial
PS	Problem Solving		P	Presentation
G	Games		DM	Demonstration
S	Simulation		DN	Discussion

It is possible that you will have more than one column with the same number of "√s." In that case you will need to choose which method is best or consider using multiple methods for your lesson.

Student learning will be enhanced by instructional methods that	CL	DY	PS	G	S	DP	T	P	DM	DN
1. Are predominantly student centered										
2. Are predominantly teacher centered										
3. Provide a high level of interactivity										
4. Allow for students to learn on their own										
5. Allow several students (2–5) to be involved simultaneously										
6. Are appropriate for a small group (6–15)										
7. Are group oriented (16 plus)										
8. Provide information and content										
9. Provide practice with feedback										
10. Provide a discovery environment										
11. Present situations requiring strategy										
12. Can be completed in a short time (less than 20 minutes)										
13. Provide more content in a shorter time (are efficient)										
14. Enhance skills in the high-level intellectual skills domain										
15. Enhance skills in the low-level intellectual skills domain										
16. Enhance skills in the psychomotor skills domain										
17. Enhance skills in the attitude domain										
18. Appropriate for a noncompetitive environment										
19. Promote decision making										
20. Provide a realistic context for learning										
21. Are highly motivating										
22. Enhance retention of information										
23. Use the inductive or inquiry approach to learning										

FIGURE 6–2 Method selection checklist

the checklist to narrow your choices and then rely on your experience and judgment to make a final decision. This will, of course, become easier as you gain teaching experience.

It's important to note that you may use multiple or mixed methods within a single lesson. In many instructional situations one method will not do the job. For example, you may follow a tutorial with drill and practice to strengthen the newly learned skills. The combination of methods may be more powerful and result in more learning than either method used alone. The key is to focus on what will work best to help *your* students learn *your* content. Try various methods with actual students to help determine which method or combination of methods is most effective and consider using a variety of methods to keep the instruction interesting.

Reflective Question

Do you think it is better to know a lot about a small number of instructional methods or a little about a large number of methods? Why?

SELECTING INSTRUCTIONAL MEDIA

A second decision you must make is which instructional medium or media to use. In Chapter 5 we introduced six types of instructional media—multimedia, video, graphics, audio, text, and real objects and models—and their advantages and limitations. These advantages and limitations provide your foundation for choosing which medium or media to use in a particular lesson.

As with instructional methods, we have compiled the advantages of the various media into a checklist, shown in Figure 6–3, that you may use to select media for a particular lesson.

As practice, look over each of the following three scenarios. Decide what would be the best method and medium for each situation. Then answer the following questions: What were the reasons you used to make your selections? Did you identify any potential problems with your selections? If so, what were those problems be? What other methods and media could you also have selected? Under what conditions would you switch to those alternatives?

Scenario A: The sixth-grade concert band instructor, Mr. Snyder, has decided that his students need to better discriminate between sharps, flats, and natural notes on the musical scale. He has 56 students currently in his band, and the instruction will take place in the band

room, which is large enough to seat approximately 125 individuals.

Scenario B: The instructor of an advanced survival training course needs to teach the six participants how to recognize edible versus nonedible desert plants found in the southwestern United States. Even though the course involves training for *desert* survival, it is being taught at a small college in Ohio.

Scenario C: Mrs. Spence and her class of 25 tenth-grade students have been studying a unit on developing critical-thinking skills. One section of the content focuses on methods used to solve ill-defined problems and Mrs. Spence has decided that she wants to give the students practice using the different techniques they are studying.

To help you understand how factors such as the students, objectives, and learning environment might affect your choice of method and medium in these scenarios, consider how your selections would change if the following aspects were different:

Scenario A: Instead of being a band director, Mr. Snyder is a private flute teacher with 12 students of different ages who all come at different times during the day for individualized instruction. His goal is still to have the students increase their ability to discriminate between flats, sharps, and natural notes.

Scenario B: The survival course takes place at the University of Nevada, Las Vegas, within minutes from large sections of desert.

Scenario C: The focus of Mrs. Spence's class changes from being able to *apply* the problem-solving techniques to simply understanding them.

Reflective Question

Various authors have expressed different opinions about the impact of media on learning. What do you think? In a particular situation, does the specific medium make a difference or will any medium be just as effective?

SELECTING EXISTING INSTRUCTIONAL MATERIALS

The third decision you must make is which specific instructional materials to use. As we noted at the beginning of the chapter, the simplest, most cost-effective way to incorporate instructional materials into a lesson is to use existing materials. Locating and selecting instructional materials involve the following steps:

1. *Determine needs.* What are you trying to accomplish? What needs might specific instructional materials address?
2. *Check a variety of sources.* There are a number of sources for instructional materials.
   a. Most schools maintain a computer database in the school library or media center. Some school districts also maintain a central collection of instructional materials. In addition, districts sometimes combine their resources to form a regional media center or service center housing a collection of instructional materials.
   b. Commercial producers and distributors of instructional materials publish catalogs listing materials you can buy and, in some cases, rent.
   c. Professional meetings and trade shows held at local, state, and national levels provide opportunities to talk with vendors and other teachers to find out what is available.
   d. Two comprehensive databases are available through which you can locate instructional materials. *A-V Online* is an automated index of commercially available materials. With it, you can locate the distribution sources for thousands of educational, informational, and documentary materials recorded in a variety of media formats. The database covers a range of subject areas at grade levels from preschool to graduate and professional school. *A-V Online* is continually being updated based on information from producer and distributor catalogs, the Library of Congress, media centers, and many other sources. *The Education Software Selector* (*TESS*) is a comprehensive database that includes information about educational software at every level, from preschool to college, in a variety of content areas. Each piece of software is described in terms of subject, learning approach, grade level, computer platform, pricing, and publisher contact. Entries include evaluation citations from educational journals, state evaluation agencies, and technology journals. *TESS* is available on CD-ROM for both Mac OS and Windows platforms through the Education Product Information Exchange (EPIE). The "Suggested Resources" for this chapter include an Internet address you can use to obtain more information about TESS.
   e. As described in Chapter 4 in "Toolbox Tips: Finding Lesson Plans on the Web," the World Wide Web can be a valuable source of instructional materials.
3. *Obtain and preview the materials.* Try to preview all materials before using them to be certain they meet your and your students' needs. See Appendix B for sample preview forms, with which you can evaluate a single set of materials or compare two sets of materials.
4. *Try the materials out with students.* How well do they like the materials? How effectively do the materials help them learn?
5. *Compare any competing materials.* If you have located more than one set of applicable materials, repeat the preview and tryout process to compare their effectiveness and appeal to students.
6. *Make your selection.* Use the information you have gathered to select the instructional materials that you think will work best in your situation.
7. *Keep accurate records.* After you have chosen materials, make sure you follow up on their effectiveness. By keeping records you also can determine how effective the materials could be in other lessons.

If the content of the instructional materials you find doesn't match the objectives of your instructional plan, you have two alternatives: (1) modify the materials so they do meet your objectives, or (2) create new instructional materials. We discuss these options in the next two sections.

MODIFYING AVAILABLE INSTRUCTIONAL MATERIALS

If you cannot locate suitable materials, you may be able to modify what is available. In terms of time and cost, it is more efficient to modify available materials than to create new materials. It is also an opportunity for you to be creative. You can modify almost any type of instructional materials. For example, imagine that, for a piece of equipment being used in a middle school woodworking class, the only available visual is from a repair manual. The picture could be useful, but it contains too much detail and complex terminology for students. One possible solution would be to use the visual but modify the caption and simplify or omit some of the labels.

In another situation, the only videotape available shows a needed video sequence, but the audio is

---

Which Media Should I Choose?

As you begin planning your instruction, it is important to select a medium that will enhance your topic. The Media Selection Checklist will help you in the process.

Each type of media has a set of advantages (e.g., motion, realism) and a set of educational limitations (e.g., room size, group size). These specifications are listed in the first column of the table. There are nine columns next to the specifications. Place a √ in all the white spaces that best describe your instructional needs (or situations).

For Example

If it is important that you draw or write key words during your presentation, go to item #7 on the table and put "√s" in the three columns to the right that are white. Continue the process for each requirement or item that best describes your instructional situation (needs).

When you have gone through the entire table, determine which column has the most "√s" entered in the white spaces in the column.

If most of the "√s" are in:	Select
RO	Real Objects (models)
T	Printed Text (handouts, books, computer screen)
CB	Chalkboard or White Board
OT	Overhead Transparencies
SL	Slides
V	Video (tape, disc, television)
G	Graphics (photos, charts, diagrams)
A	Audio (tape, CD)
CS	Computer Software

It is possible that you will have more than one column with most of the white spaces filled in. In that case you will need to choose which medium is best or consider using multiple media formats in your presentation.

© *Claranne K. English, 1995*

FIGURE 6–3   Media selection checklist

inappropriate because the vocabulary level is either too high or low for your students. In such a case, you could show the videotape with the sound turned off and narrate it yourself. Videotapes can also be shown in segments. You can show a portion of a videotape, stop the VCR, discuss what has been presented, then continue with another short segment, followed by additional discussion.

Often, you can modify the audio portion of foreign-language materials (or English-language materials for a bilingual class). Narration can be changed from one language to another or from a more advanced rendition to a simpler one.

One frequently modified medium is a set of slides with an audiotape. If the visuals are appropriate but the language is not, it is possible to change the narration. It is also possible to change the emphasis of the narration. For example, the original audiotape might emphasize oceans as part of an ecosystem, whereas you may want to use the slides to show various types of fish found in oceans. By rewriting

Selecting the appropriate materials for instruction is an important process.

the narration, you can adapt the material to match your purposes while using the same slides.

Videodiscs, which are produced to teach specific content, lend themselves to a process called repur-

Media Selection Checklist

Student learning will be enhanced by media that	RO	T	CB	OT	SL	V	G	A	CS
1. Enable students to see and/or touch actual objects		■	■	■	■	■	■	■	■
2. Allow materials to be taken from the classroom			■	■	■	■	■	■	■
3. Can be used after the lesson as a reference, guide, or job aid	■		■	■	■	■	■	■	■
4. Allow several participants to respond simultaneously	■			■	■	■	■	■	■
5. Can be easily erased/modified	■				■	■	■	■	■
6. Require minimal expense	■			■	■	■	■	■	■
7. Allow one to draw or write key words during the lesson	■				■	■	■	■	■
8. Are appropriate for a small group (under 25)	■			■	■	■		■	■
9. Can be used in a fully lit room	■			■		■	■	■	■
10. Use visuals that are easy to prepare	■					■	■	■	■
11. Allow advanced preparation of the visuals	■							■	■
12. Present word cues or a lesson outline	■				■	■	■	■	■
13. Provide portability	■		■				■	■	■
14. Offer commercially prepared visuals	■		■			■		■	■
15. Allow the order of the material to be easily changed	■		■			■		■	■
16. Allow the user to control pacing and/or to replay a portion of the presentation	■	■	■					■	■
17. Are appropriate for students who have difficulty reading or understanding English		■	■	■	■	■	■	■	■
18. Reproduce an exact sound	■	■	■	■	■		■		■
19. Are easily used by teachers or students	■	■	■	■		■	■	■	■
20. Present high-quality, realistic images (color/graphics/illustrations/visuals)	■	■	■	■				■	■
21. Can be used independently of the instructor	■		■	■		■	■	■	■
22. Show motion, including sequential motion	■	■	■	■	■		■	■	■
23. Allow observation of dangerous process; real-life reenactments	■	■	■	■	■		■	■	■
24. Provide a discovery learning environment	■	■	■	■	■		■	■	■
25. Present problem-solving situations that lead to group discussions	■	■	■	■	■		■	■	■
26. Shape personal and social attitudes	■	■	■	■	■	■	■		■

FIGURE 6–3 Media selection checklist (continued)

Software Evaluation and Acquisition

We have examined issues related to selecting instructional materials in general and different media in particular. Here we discuss evaluating and selecting computer software.

In most school districts today, hardware decisions are centralized. An individual teacher cannot go out and select just any computer for his classroom. However, individual teachers often make software decisions. There is commonly an approval process that involves the technology coordinator, a technology committee, or an administrator, but software purchasing usually begins with the individual teacher. It is thus important for teachers to know how to evaluate and select software. Following are the steps involved:

1. *Determine needs.* As in any instructional activity, begin by assessing what you need. What needs might you address through the use of computer software?

2. *Specify desired software characteristics.* Your needs assessment should give you a general idea of the type of software you want. For example, if your students are having trouble adding mixed fractions, you may decide that you want a drill and practice program on this topic.

3. *Obtain or construct an evaluation form.* Many useful software evaluation forms are available from a variety of sources (we provide one in Appendix B). Your school may have its own evaluation form. Alternatively, you could design one geared to your specific needs.

4. *Survey available sources of software.* Software is available from a variety of sources. Look through publishers' catalogs. Read software evaluations published in journals and magazines. Talk to your colleagues. Visit vendors' booths at professional meetings. Check collections of shareware.

5. *Obtain software for preview.* Many software companies now provide special demonstration disks for preview. Some are also providing demonstrations on CD-ROM. With these, if you like the software and buy it, the company provides you with a password that unlocks full access to the CD-ROM. Alternatively, you can often preview software via delayed-purchase-order billing. In this case, a purchase order for the product is submitted with the specification that it is for preview purposes. The vendor delays billing for a set period, usually 30 days. If you decide against purchase, simply return the software within the grace period, and the purchase order is canceled. Otherwise, keep the software, and the vendor processes the purchase order at the end of the grace period.

6. *Read the documentation.* While there is a temptation to simply jump into a software program, you should always read the documentation first. It should indicate the recommended audience for the program, and it will provide directions for how to properly use the software.

7. *Run through the software several times.* The first time you go through the software, simply concentrate on using the program correctly. How does it work? For a second pass, make certain that the software is "bombproof"; that is, make certain it doesn't fail when something unexpected happens. Purposely test for problems; if the program indicates, "Enter a number between 1 and 4," see what happens if you enter 5. Finally, run through the program with a pedagogical eye. Is the educational approach sound? Is it appealing? How does the software rate on the criteria given on the evaluation form you are using?

8. *Have students try out the program.* How do they like it? Do they learn from it?

9. *Complete the evaluation form.* Using the information gained from your review of the software, complete the evaluation form.

10. *Repeat the process for any competing products.* If you have more than one possible purchase, look at each competing product in the same way.

11. *Make your selection.* Select the desired software package. File your evaluation with the school, and be sure to enclose a copy of your evaluation with any product that is returned to the publisher.

posing. **Repurposing** refers to creating a new computer program to control the videodisc. For example, *The National Gallery of Art* videodisc contains images of all the paintings in the National Gallery in Washington, DC. An art teacher can design software that will direct students to specific paintings, ask questions about the art, and move to another piece when the student answers the questions correctly.

If you try out modified materials while they are still in more or less rough form, you can then make further modifications in response to student reactions until your materials meet their exact needs. A word of caution about modifying commercially produced materials: be sure your handling and use of such materials does not violate copyright laws and restrictions. If you are in doubt, check with your school media specialist.

CREATING NEW INSTRUCTIONAL MATERIALS

Teachers have long been known for their creative use of available tools and resources to produce instructional materials. Classrooms are usually filled with a variety of teaching materials, from concrete objects to posters, bulletin boards, and printed material of every kind. For several decades the tools for producing instructional materials changed relatively little, with typewriters and ditto machines doing the bulk of the work. But times have changed.

Photocopying machines, long commonplace in society at large, are now standard equipment in schools. Compared to a mimeograph or ditto machine, preparing copies with a photocopier is much simpler. In addition, the tools for creating the master copies of instructional materials have improved by leaps and bounds. The reason, of course, is the computer. Computer-based tools make it much easier to produce high-quality, professional-looking materials.

Figure 6–4 presents guidelines for creating instructional materials. We list important factors you should consider whenever you attempt to create materials in a variety of media formats.

Reflective Question

The preview forms in Appendix B indicate the features or qualities we believe instructional materials should have. What features or qualities do you think are particularly important to have in a set of instructional materials?

How Do I Create Effective Materials?

For many teachers, creating ways to impact student learning is a key reason why they chose their profession. Creating materials allows you opportunity to reflect on what is needed, use experiences from the past, synthesize new materials, and creatively bring together an effective learning experience. Is there a single recipe to creating effective instruction? Of course not. Just as there are different styles of learning, there are different ways to create learning experiences. Here is a general procedure that may help you in this process. It is a guideline only, and certainly not the *only* way to successfully construct instructional materials.

▶ Refer repeatedly to your instructional plan. The plan contains the direction and activities that you have determined your students need (see Chapter 4). Just as the general contractor of a great office building would not dream of beginning construction without the blueprints of the building, you should closely review your instructional plans.

▶ Within the plan, look closely at the overall learning objectives and the key activities that need to occur so that students meet them. Ask yourself, "What needs to be constructed so that the activities are successful?" For example, will the students need explanations, directions, examples, nonexamples, or guided practice? Will feedback be needed and if so, how quickly should you deliver it? (See "Toolbox Techniques: Using Questioning, Examples, and Feedback Effectively within Instructional Materials" on page 131.)

▶ Reflect on what you already know or have seen. If you determined that materials did not already exist, did you see pieces of different sets of materials that might give you insight into to construct what you need? Can you talk with anyone who has taught these or similar concepts before?

▶ Put yourself in the "learner's shoes." What would you want to experience in order to effectively learn this material? Look for means to make materials relevant to students.

▶ Select the appropriate methods and media, as discussed earlier in this chapter, by which students should experience your activities.

▶ Outline your activities. Have students review what you have thought through and determine what major changes need to occur.

▶ Construct a draft set of the materials. Incorporate the use of tools (e.g., copy machines, computers, clip art) to extend your creative development abilities.

▶ Review the materials to ensure that you make all needed changes. In most cases, you will not create perfect materials on the first attempt.

How One Teacher Created Instructional Materials

Nancy Piggot has taught school at Glen Acres Elementary School for 19 years. For the last seven she has taught the fifth grade. Increasingly, Nancy has felt the need to enhance her students' learning experiences as

Multimedia

The development of computer-based multimedia materials is complex and time consuming. The specifics of this process are beyond the scope of this book, but here are some guidelines to assist you if you decide to try your hand at the process.

▶ Follow the guidelines given below for computer software.
▶ Select the best media for addressing particular learning objectives. Whenever possible, provide for different learning preferences; that is, provide the same content via text, audio, and visual modalities.
▶ Ensure that different media are properly synchronized with one another.
▶ Keep navigation as simple and transparent as possible. Learners can become lost and confused in complex multimedia environments. Provide navigational aids such as maps and position markers.
▶ Use embedded cues to assist learners in locating and using information.

Computer Software

The development of computer software may be too time consuming for most teachers. However, the most recent authoring systems make it possible for teachers to develop their own computer software without knowledge of computer programming. Following are basic guidelines for developing computer software.

▶ Make good use of the computer's capabilities and employ a high level of interactivity.
▶ Allow for individualization through learner control, branching, and other appropriate techniques.
▶ Provide informative feedback to learners. Tell learners why particular responses are correct or incorrect.
▶ Keep screen displays simple. Usually, present only one major concept per screen.
▶ Follow the guidelines for textual material (see Chapter 7) when presenting text via the computer.
▶ Use graphics where visual presentation is appropriate. Follow the guidelines for visuals (see Chapter 7).
▶ Keep learners informed of their progress and performance.

Video

Both students and teachers can produce effective videotapes for instructional purposes. All that is required is a camera, a microphone (often built into the camera), and a videotape.

Camera

▶ Use a zoom lens rather than a fixed-focal-length lens to allow flexibility in selecting a view from a range of magnifications without having to move the camera closer to or farther from the subject.
▶ Do not aim the camera at the sun or other bright light, since that can damage the videotube.
▶ Turn the camera off when it will not be used for a period of time.
▶ Cap the lens when the camera is not in use.
▶ Keep the lens clean by dusting with a soft camel's-hair brush.

Microphone

▶ Handheld cameras usually come with a microphone built into the front of the camera. This microphone has automatic level control, which automatically adjusts the recording volume to keep the sound at an audible level. At times this may cause problems.

Videotape

▶ Use high-quality, brand-name videotape. Other tapes may be manufacturer's seconds or tapes that were improperly stored.
▶ Your video production may be preplanned or live action. If you are recording local landmarks for presentation in your classroom, determine what shots you will take before you go. If you are recording an event, simply videotape it as it happens.
▶ Planning a videotape recording is similar to planning other instructional materials. Organize the content and plan the method of visualizing the subject to be videotaped. Pay special attention to the *motion* involved. Movement is basic to successful videotape recordings—otherwise, use slides or overhead transparencies.
▶ When taping people, use a full-body shot for motion (e.g., athletics, dancing, etc.) and a head-and-shoulder shot for speaking.

Visuals

Visuals include photographs, diagrams, posters, charts, and drawings. The following guidelines apply to visuals for printed material, slides, overhead transparencies, and artwork for videotapes. They apply whether you are producing the visuals by hand or with the aid of a computer.

General

▶ Keep visuals simple (avoid too much realism in visuals).

FIGURE 6–4   Guidelines for designing instructional materials

- Place visuals as near the related text as possible.
- Use larger visuals if more detail is required.

Informational/Instructional Purposes

- Use drawings and diagrams whenever possible to illustrate ideas.
- Use graphs to present data.
- Present a single concept in each visual.
- Break down complex visuals into simpler ones or build them up step by step.

Graphic/Picture Elements

- Use visuals that are neither too abstract nor too realistic.
- Eliminate distracting backgrounds.
- If feeling of depth is important, use another object to create the foreground.

Text/Lettering Elements

- Center title at top of visual.
- Use short, concise, meaningful, descriptive titles that contain key words.
- Eliminate unnecessary words.
- Use italics, boldface, underlining, color, or a change in lettering style for emphasis.
- Minimize text on each visual; use a maximum of six words per line and six lines per visual.
- Spacing between lines should be 1½ times word height.

Color

- Use brightest and lightest colors to focus attention on important elements.
- Use lettering and visuals that contrast with background color.
- Select colors that are harmonious.
- Use consistent background colors in a series of visuals.
- Limit the number of colors in a visual to five.

Layout

- Make visuals as simple as possible; avoid excessive detail.
- Use size, relationships, perspective, and such visual tools as color and space to emphasize important elements.
- Use a horizontal format for overhead transparencies and slides.
- Use a pleasing layout that appears balanced and orderly.

Slides

You can produce your own slides, but producing your own filmstrips is impractical and unnecessary. Although principles of photography are beyond the scope of this book, we will describe some general guidelines for designing slides.

General

- Determine the topic for your slides.
- Prepare a list of the slides you need.
- Take several shots of the same scene at different angles and distances. It is cheaper to take several shots originally than to return to the location if none of the original slides meets your needs. If it is a special event that occurs only once, take extra shots in order to have enough slides for your instructional program.
- When your slides are returned, compare the multiple shots by projecting them or by viewing them with a light box.
- Select the specific slides you want to use, and put them in sequence.
- Prepare your narration on note cards (one card for each slide).
- Deliver the narration live by talking through the slides with your note cards. Don't read directly from the cards; make it conversational.
- As an alternative, record your narration on audiotape. Slide-and-audiotape combinations are great for self-instruction.

Overhead Transparencies

When preparing your transparencies, keep in mind these guidelines based on research and practical experience.

General

- Present a single concept on each transparency. A complex transparency may be confusing and unreadable for the viewer. Design a series of transparencies rather than a crowded single transparency.

FIGURE 6–4 *Continued*

- Use transparencies to present visual ideas through the use of diagrams, graphs, and charts.
- Include minimum verbiage, with no more than six words per line and six or fewer lines per transparency.
- Avoid preparing a transparency directly from a paragraph of printed material. Select key points or concepts to summarize the information, and then elaborate on them verbally.
- Use key words to help the audience remember each point.
- Use letters at least ¼ inch high to ensure legibility. One quick way to check it is to lay the transparency on the floor over a piece of white paper. If you can read it from a standing position, your students should be able to read it when projected.
- Use a horizontal format to better fit the rectangular screen. Avoid mixing horizontal and vertical transparencies in a presentation, as this can be annoying to the students and bothersome to you.
- Simplify a complex diagram by dividing it into segments for separate transparencies or by using masking or overlay techniques. Overlays can explain complex ideas by adding information sequentially to the base transparency.

Display Boards

Displays may be created by students or the teacher. The following guidelines apply to chalkboards and especially bulletin board displays, since they are prepared in advance and kept in place for days or weeks. Do not leave these displays in place too long, or they will lose their effectiveness.

General

- Limit the display to one topic.
- Generate a theme and incorporate it into a headline. It is a challenge to work out a catchy theme that will entice the viewer into further examination of the display. Wording should be simple, couched in the students' language, and visually integrated into the arrangement of the display.
- Work out a rough layout. The blueprint you develop should reflect these guidelines:

> Emphatic—conveys message quickly and clearly
> Attractive—color and arrangement catch and hold interest
> Balanced—objects arranged so stability is perceived
> Unified—repeated shapes or colors or use of borders holds display together visually
> Interactive—involves students
> Legible—lettering and visuals can be read from across the room
> Lettered properly—spelled correctly, plain typeface, use of lowercase except where capitals are required
> Durable—well-constructed physically, items securely attached

Audio

A major advantage of audiotapes is the ease with which both teachers and students can prepare them. All that is needed is a blank audiotape, a tape recorder, and a bit of know-how.

Physical Environment

- Record in an area that is as free as possible from noise and sound reverberations. A small room such as an office is preferable to a normal-size classroom.
- Place the recording setup at least six feet from the chalkboard, windows, or hard walls.
- Have a glass of water nearby to "lubricate" your throat if necessary.

Tape Recorder

- Familiarize yourself with the operation of the tape recorder you intend to use.
- Advance the tape beyond the leader before recording (about ten seconds). You cannot record on the clear plastic, nonmagnetic leader of the tape.
- Record an excerpt of about a minute and play it back to make sure the recorder and microphone are operating properly.
- If you make an error while recording, stop the tape recorder, rewind to a segment of tape containing a natural pause, engage the record mode, and continue recording. It is unusual to make an entire tape without making mistakes or mispronunciations.
- Once recording has been completed, play back the entire recording. Listen carefully for any errors. It is better to catch imperfections and correct them immediately than to redo the tape later.

Microphone

- Place the microphone on a desk or table with a sound-absorbing towel or other soft cloth under the microphone.
- Turn off fans and other sources of noise that the microphone may pick up.
- Handle note cards and pages quietly to avoid possible paper rustle.

FIGURE 6–4 *Continued*

- Maintain a constant distance from the microphone. As a rule of thumb, your mouth should be about a foot from the microphone.
- Speak over the top of the microphone, not directly into it.

Text

As we saw in Chapter 3, the word processor is one of the most valuable tools a teacher can have. Word processors make it easy to produce printed materials and to revise them to meet the changing needs of your students. We examined the features and uses of word processors, and graphic tools and desktop publishing programs that can facilitate the production of high-quality printed materials.

Headings

- Headings and subheadings should be used to separate and identify sections and to show the organization of content. Introductions may have to be written in order to relate a series of key ideas so there is a smooth transition from one section to the next one.
- Headings should be briefly worded and explicit so they communicate quickly and effectively. By glancing at a set of sequential headings, the student should gain a clear overview of the topic.
- Use side heads (e.g., words in left margin) to call attention to important concepts.

Writing Style

- State the main ideas or theme at the beginning of the text.
- Put topic sentences at the beginning of each paragraph.
- Use simple sentences and a clear writing style.
- Use active voice where possible.
- Include definitions with technical terms so they won't be misconstrued.

Page Layout

- Be clear and consistent in page layout (use the same type of text in the same typeface, size, and layout from page to page).
- Provide ample white space (use wide margins and uncluttered format) to facilitate reading, note taking, and location of information for review. White space can separate elements and create a feeling of openness.
- Increase the space between lines in handouts to allow room for student notes.
- Use unjustified or ragged right margins. By justifying both margins, extra space is created between words, which makes text more difficult to read.

Type Style/Mechanics

- Choose typeface styles with simple designs.
- Use upper- and lowercase letters for ease and speed in reading. Use uppercase words only for emphasis and to attract attention.
- Use 9- to 12-point type for most text.
- If the material is typed, use a space and a half between lines for ease of reading.
- Avoid breaking words (hyphenating) at the end of lines.

Highlighting

- Highlighting techniques for printed materials include color, size of type, italics, and boldfacing. Do not use capitals, because they are difficult to read within text. Capitals are okay for short headings.
- Highlight important ideas to help students locate key points.
- Use bullets (•) to present ideas in a list (as used in this figure).
- Avoid underlining except to point out negatives (e.g., not and except), as it has little or no effect on retention of content.

Real Objects and Models

Real objects do not lend themselves to design by teachers. However, there are some models available for purchase that teachers can assemble. There are plastic model kits of various animals, including dinosaurs, and of parts of the human body, such as the eye, ear, nose, and skull. These models can be modified and colored with paint to meet your needs.

Teachers can also make models for instruction from readily available materials. For example, small buildings can be used to make model cities. Various materials, such as athletic balls, can be used to model the solar system.

FIGURE 6–4 *Continued*

Guidelines for Designing Graphics

Graphics are communication tools designed to convey a message through a combination of visual elements (pictures, color, etc.) and verbal elements (words, etc.) (Kearny, 1996). You can apply the following guidelines to the production of a variety instructional materials, including printed handouts, overhead transparencies, *PowerPoint* slides, computer screens, and bulletin boards (see also Figure 6–4).

VISUAL ELEMENTS

▶ Present visual elements in close proximity to related verbal elements.
▶ Avoid excessive detail or realism. Remember *KISS*—Keep It Simple for Students.
▶ Break complex visuals into multiple simpler visuals.
▶ Incorporate an ample supply of "white space" (open space).
▶ Use color (if possible) to attract attention and to illustrate key components of the graphic.
▶ Provide contrast between visual elements and the background.
▶ Provide balance with visual and/or verbal elements so they are equally distributed horizontally and vertically.

VERBAL ELEMENTS

▶ Be sure words can be easily read at the intended viewing distance.
▶ Follow the "6 by 6 Rule" by limiting text to about six lines with approximately six words per line.
▶ Use lowercase lettering with capitals only where normally required.
▶ Use a san serif (without serifs) font.
▶ Use left justification only.
▶ Use short, meaningful titles.
▶ Use active, not passive voice.
▶ Avoid highly technical terms and abbreviations.
▶ Use highlighting to draw attention to key words.

they study their science unit, "Insects." She has located a number of great sources of visuals and textual materials, but in most cases they are above her students' level of understanding.

In reviewing and reflecting on her past "Insect" lesson plans, she noted that the different parts of the insect body consistently created problems for her students when it came to identification and descriptions. She determined that to facilitate learning she would assign her students live insects (large cockroaches from the local pet store) to care for. Students would observe their "pets" for a short time each day during the duration of the insect unit. Students could name their pets and draw various pictures of them during the observation periods. In addition, her plan was to design and create a short multimedia *HyperStudio* program that would introduce students to their "pets" and show them things that they should observe and watch for. In particular, she planned for various pictures and drawings to explain how to identify the specific parts of the insect, highlight the body parts, and describe their functions.

During the development phase of the *HyperStudio* program, Nancy completed a number of in-teresting steps. First, she reviewed closely her overall lesson plan for the unit. She noted the weaknesses and the areas that she felt she could add to the instructional effectiveness. Through past experience she knew that within the program she would need to focus student attention via questioning, examples, practice, and feedback. Likewise, she knew it would be critical to use audio and visual stimulation techniques to effectively highlight key features. The *HyperStudio* multimedia software allowed her to include such features within a tutorial that students could review on their own. Nancy did one additional thing to ensure the success of the program: She began by drawing out all of the key concepts on 3 by 5 inch cards. She used rough sketches of what the actual program would look like. After developing several of these cards, she asked several of her students to tell her what they liked and did not like about them. Her students actually helped her determine when more explanation was needed and when she was giving too much. By the time she actually sat at the computer, she had a good idea of the length of the program and that it would

TOOLBOX TECHNIQUES

Using Questioning, Examples, and Feedback Effectively within Instructional Materials

You can use a variety of techniques to enhance the effectiveness of instructional materials. In particular, materials should incorporate questions, examples, and feedback. Listed below are several suggestions and guidelines for incorporating these techniques within materials.

QUESTIONING

You can use questions to gain attention, maintain focus, pique interest, probe for depth of understanding, increase relevance for a topic of focus, or evaluate the quality of the instructional materials. Questions may be generated by the teacher or student, and answers can range from simple, to difficult, to unknown.

Several guidelines can help you incorporate productive questions into your instructional lessons (Dallmann-Jones, 1994; Wasserman, 1992).

When planning and developing questions:

▶ Determine why you will ask the question. Make sure each serves an important purpose.
▶ Use "who," "what," "when," and "where" questions to check information for review purposes. "Why" and "how" questions encourage higher levels of thought. Ask students to provide in-depth explanations or additional examples.
▶ Frame questions to invite, rather than intimidate. Help students feel safe to express their thoughts. Questions and responses should be respectful, nonthreatening, and productive.

When using questions:

▶ Sample class responses randomly; that is, ask questions of all students equally.
▶ Take time to pause after asking a question; provide students with time to think.
▶ Listen to students' responses before formulating your own so you can accurately reflect their ideas.
▶ Respond positively to appropriate responses, but never belittle incorrect answers.
▶ Allow students the chance to formulate questions in response to comments from you or from other students.
▶ When a student repeatedly provides incorrect answers, coach that individual during one-on-one sessions. Provide the student with opportunities to answer questions that you have previously discussed during your session.

EXAMPLES

Research has shown that examples are very effective in helping learners understand concepts and applications. Examples can highlight key characteristics and information about concepts, make ready comparisons, and illustrate how things are applied and generalized across different situations. Guidelines for using examples include the following:

▶ Begin with simple examples so students can readily identify their critical attributes. Simple examples can also increase your learners' confidence.
▶ Present examples in different formats, such as flowcharts, pictures, live demonstrations, and real objects.
▶ Use nonexamples (negative examples) to help highlight examples' critical attributes. Nonexamples may have some of the same attributes of the examples but vary on those features that make the critical difference. For example, to teach the concept "red" you may present learners with an example of a red ball. To make sure they understand the critical attribute of color, introduce nonexamples such as a blue ball and an orange ball. All of the attributes in the examples and nonexamples are the same, *except* for the critical attribute of color. The nonexample helps to identify the critical attribute.
▶ Gradually increase the difficulty level of the examples until you end with more difficult ones that approximate the real-world cases that students will encounter.

FEEDBACK

We are all familiar with the phrase "practice makes perfect," but is it true? With a short addition we can capture a more accurate picture—"Practice makes perfect, *as long as feedback is provided.*"

TOOLBOX TECHNIQUES
(continued)

Feedback, according to Rothwell and Kazanas (1992, p. 13), is "a continuous process of providing information about an activity, sometimes during the activity itself." Feedback can serve two functions: (1) it can inform students about *how much* of the task they have completed, thus encouraging them to continue working; and (2) it can inform students *how well* they are performing and indicate what they can do to improve their performance.

As you design and implement instruction, it is important to make provisions for delivering feedback to students. Without timely, reliable feedback, students may not know if their work is correct. Without some form of feedback, students could potentially continue practicing errors over and over. Use the following guidelines when designing practice and feedback exercises (adapted from Leshin, Pollock, & Reigeluth, 1992):

- Effective feedback should be delivered immediately (or as soon as reasonably feasible) after practice is completed.
- Well-designed feedback can motivate students to greater levels of performance.
- Informative feedback should function like a good example.
- Corrective feedback should require learners to think. Give hints but do not provide the correct answer immediately.

be effective. Figure 6–5 contains examples of some of the screens that students viewed as they worked through this program.

From start to finish this project took Nancy a number of hours to complete. In fact, every year when she gets to the insect unit she finds herself adding new things based on her students' suggestions and new information she uncovers. She has found that this unit has really helped to increase her students' knowledge of insects and also has piqued their interest and motivation.

FORMATIVE EVALUATION OF INSTRUCTIONAL MATERIALS

Any time you modify or create instructional materials, you should assess how effective they are in helping students learn *before* you put the materials to use. This is done via the process of formative evaluation. **Formative evaluation** is evaluation done during the planning or production of instructional materials to determine what, if any, revisions should be made to make them more useful. Formative evaluation can help identify aspects of the materials that

FIGURE 6–5 Instructional cards from Nancy's *HyperStudio* "Insect" stack *Contributed by Nancy Piggott, Glen Acres Elementary, Lafayette, Indiana.*

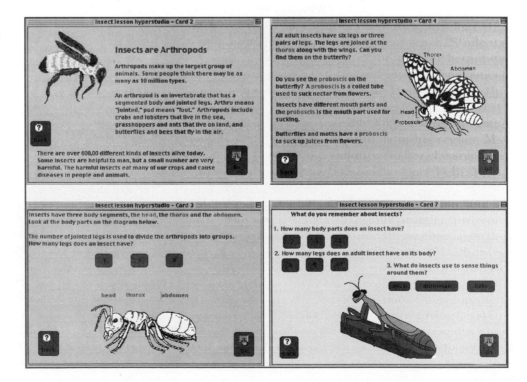

Authoring Tools for Computer-Based Instruction

Options for developing computer-based instruction (CBI) range along a continuum from authoring systems to general-purpose programming languages. **Authoring systems** are computer programs that permit the development of interactive computer-based applications without a need for programming knowledge. While easy to use, they can have limitations that may restrict their utility in some cases. In addition, high-quality authoring systems can be quite expensive. Examples are *Authorware, Macromedia Director, IconAuthor, Quest,* and *TenCORE.*

On the other end of the continuum are general-purpose programming languages such as BASIC, Pascal, and C++. In the past, all development of CBI was done using programming languages. They offer the greatest power and flexibility. But programming languages can be difficult to use and time consuming to learn. While programming languages are used by professionals or designers to develop commercial applications, most teachers avoid pure programming languages.

Between authoring systems and programming languages are hypermedia packages like *HyperStudio, HyperCard,* and *Toolbook.* These hypermedia programs are built for developing multimedia applications. They are easier to use than general-purpose programming languages, and much of their flexibility comes from the fact that scripting (programming) languages are available as part of the program. They also tend to be reasonably priced. As a result, these programs have become very popular platforms for development in schools.

USING AUTHORING TOOLS IN THE CLASSROOM

Teachers can make use of authoring tools to develop CBI for student use. A major justification for such an activity would be to meet a specific local need that cannot be met with existing commercial software. In some cases it might be more economical to develop something locally than to purchase a commercial application. Of course, there are also some teachers who simply enjoy developing their own CBI applications.

It is important to recognize, however, that authoring tools are valuable for students as well as for teachers. Using authoring tools, students can produce computer-based reports, portfolio presentations, projects, and lessons. As a way of "killing two birds with one stone," students in programming classes at the secondary level can be encouraged to develop educational projects for use in other classes in the school. Students developing multimedia projects must learn the content, locate and incorporate appropriate multimedia examples, and organize and present the material in a coherent way. Many educators believe that this is a very powerful learning experience for students. See Chapter 8 for more about this approach.

---

are unclear, confusing, inconsistent, obsolete, or otherwise not helpful to students. Chapter 10 provides guidelines for a number of techniques that you can use to carry out formative evaluation of instructional materials. The point we make here is that formative evaluation is a critical step in either modifying existing materials or creating new materials.

As an example, we noted earlier that one common way to modify existing materials is to show a videotape with the sound turned off, providing separate narration that better matches your students' vocabulary level. In this situation, formative evaluation would involve checking the narration to make sure it is, in fact, consistent with students' vocabularies and to identify any further revisions you might make to make it more useful.

We also noted earlier that teachers commonly produce their own instructional materials. They may, for example, produce their own instructional game for a particular lesson. In this situation, for-

mative evaluation would involve checking the game against students' needs and interests and against the lesson objectives. If the game matches both students and objectives, then it is ready for use. If, on the other hand, it doesn't match the students or objectives in some way, then it will be important to revise the game before using it.

COPYRIGHT ISSUES

One of the most important issues related to the acquisition or creation of instructional materials, especially in this age of computers and digital reproduction, is copyright. **Copyright** refers to the legal rights to an original work. Schools have an obligation, both under the law and from an ethical standpoint, to adhere to the law themselves and to instruct students in proper behavior. The penalties for violation of copyright law can be severe, and, as a number of schools and businesses have found, publishers' groups are willing to take action against organizations that are in violation. To avoid problems, schools should establish clear copyright policies and make those policies known to both teachers and students.

The origin of copyright can be found in the U.S. Constitution. Article I, section 8 specifies: "[Congress shall have power] to promote the progress of science and useful arts, by securing for limited times to authors and inventors the exclusive right to their respective writings and discoveries." Current law governing copyright can be found in Title 17 of the U.S. Code (available online at: http://www.law.cornell.edu/uscode/17/). Although a complete discussion of copyright law is beyond the scope of this book, in this section we provide some basic guidelines. For more information, contact your school's library or media specialist or consult references on the subject.

In the following questions and answers, we cover some of the most important points of copyright law.

What are copyrighted materials? Copyrighted materials are original works of authorship that are fixed in any tangible medium of expression. This includes such things as written works, works of art, music, photographs, and computer software. Basically, any tangible authored work qualifies. A work does not have to be registered to be protected under copyright law; such protection is automatically granted to the creator of the work when it is produced. Ideas, concepts, and procedures cannot be copyrighted.

How long does copyright last? Under current law, copyrighted works are protected for the life of the author plus 70 years. Works for hire are protected for 95 years from the date of publication or 120 years from the date of creation, whichever comes first. Similar rules apply to works created before 1978.

What rights does the law give copyright owners? The copyright owner is the person or entity that holds the copyright to a work. Usually, this is the creator of the work, except in the case of work for hire or when copyright is transferred (e.g., to a publisher). The owner of the copyright to a work has *exclusive* rights to: reproduce (copy) the work, create derivative works, sell or distribute the work, and perform or display the work in public.

Are there any limitations or exceptions to copyright owners' rights? The law spells out several specific exceptions to the exclusive rights of copyright owners. For example, libraries are allowed to make copies under certain circumstances, which allow us to enjoy things like interlibrary loans of materials. Also, works produced by the U.S. government cannot be copyrighted; they are in the public domain. This means that students or teachers can use things like NASA photographs in their multimedia projects without special permission. (For more details about using NASA materials, visit their Website at http://www.nasa.gov/gallery/photo/guideline.html). There are also important exceptions related to software backup, face-to-face teaching, and fair use of materials. Because these are so relevant to teachers and schools, we discuss them here in more depth.

Software Backup

Under copyright law, computer software may be duplicated when such duplication is essential to the use of the software on a particular computer or to create an archival backup copy of the software to be used if the original fails. Other copying of computer software, except as may be allowed by the license for a particular software product, is illegal. This applies to networks as well as to stand alone computers. While a network file server actually holds only one copy of a particular program, multiple copies can be operated on the network. This is illegal if only a single copy of that software was purchased. Schools must purchase network licenses or multiple copies of the software to run multiple copies on a network, and the network must monitor use to prevent violations if the license is restricted to a specific number of copies.

Face-to-Face Teaching

Educators are given some latitude under copyright law to publicly display copyrighted works for the purpose of face-to-face teaching. For example, a teacher may show a videotape in the classroom, even one labeled FOR HOME USE ONLY, as long as the tape was legally purchased, is materially relevant to the subject being taught, and is used in face-to-face teaching at a nonprofit educational institution.

This particular exception in copyright law, while clearly of help to teachers, can be a stumbling block for those who teach at a distance (we discuss distance education in Chapter 9). The exception for face-to-face teaching does not extend fully to those who teach at a distance (e.g., via one-way or two-way video). In distance education, some display of works is permitted, but only when the transmission is into classrooms or similar educational facilities (not homes, for example), and certain works, notably audiovisual materials, are not included. So, distance educators face some significant limitations. Congress is considering legislation that would extend the face-to-face teaching exception to distance education.

A teacher contemplates making copies of a textbook illustration for her students.

Fair Use

Fair use applies to situations involving criticism, comment, news reporting, educational use, and research associated with copyrighted material. Researchers, for example, can make single copies of articles from library journals as part of their research. A critic can excerpt dialogue from a book as part of a published review of the work. Fair use can also apply to education, and it is one of the most important exceptions for teachers and students. There are no absolute guidelines for determining what constitutes fair use in an education setting. Instead, four factors must be weighed:

- The purpose and character of the use (e.g., using a copyrighted work for an educational objective is more likely to be considered fair use than using it for commercial gain)
- The nature of the copyrighted work (e.g., if the work itself is educational in character, this would tend to support a judgment of fair use)
- The amount of the work used in relation to the whole (e.g., using a smaller amount of a total work is more likely to be fair use than using a larger amount)
- The effect of the use on the potential market for the work (e.g., if the use negatively impacts potential sales of the original work, this weighs against fair use)

Fair use guidelines must be applied case by case. However, guidelines on the subject suggest that educational use of a copyrighted work can meet fair use guidelines if: (1) only a brief excerpt is used (e.g., an excerpt of less than 1,000 words or less than 10% of the whole written work), (2) it is a spontaneous use (e.g., a teacher could copy an article for a class if the decision to use it was on the spur of the moment, occurring too late to reasonably seek permission), and (3) there is no cumulative effect (e.g., the use doesn't occur in more than one course, it isn't repeated, and it doesn't serve as a substitute for purchase). Other rules govern the use of specific media, such as taped television broadcasts. Consult with your media specialist for specific guidelines.

With the advent of digital media and the Internet, copyright issues have become even more important, and more difficult to sort out. While it is possible to scan images or digitize audio and video and incorporate the digital representations into multimedia presentations or World Wide Web pages, is it legal? In most cases, the answer to that question is, "Probably not," although matters are not altogether clear today. A number of groups around the country are working on revisions to copyright law, or interpretation guidelines for specific situations, that would clarify issues related to digital media and other new technologies. But, as of this writing, nothing has been settled.

The best advice is probably for teachers and students to treat digital media according to established fair use guidelines. That is, use of copyrighted material in digital format (text, graphics, audio, or video) is likely to be considered fair use when (1) the use is of an educational nature (e.g., part of classroom

TABLE 6–1   *Websites Related to Copyright and Fair Use*

Website	URL
Title 17 of the U.S. Code—copyright law	http://www.law.cornell.edu/uscode/17/
U.S. Copyright Office	http://lcweb.loc.gov/copyright/
U.S. Office of Patents and Trademarks	http://www.uspto.gov/
Guidelines for use of NASA images	http://www.nasa.gov/gallery/photo/guideline.html
Stanford University fair use site	http://fairuse.stanford.edu/
Multimedia fair use guidelines	http://www.libraries.psu.edu/mtss/fairuse/default.html

instruction, probably including student-created projects), (2) the material itself is educational in nature, (3) relatively little of the original material is used (and credit is given to the source of the materials), and (4) it is unlikely to detrimentally affect the market for the original materials. However, use or distribution beyond the classroom is a problem. So, for example, putting copyrighted materials on the Web without permission is almost certainly contrary to copyright law.

There are several ways teachers and students can avoid problems with copyrighted material. One solution is to request permission to use them. Publishers are often willing to permit copyrighted material to be used free of charge for nonprofit educational purposes in the classroom. Another solution is to obtain "royalty free" collections of media. Many vendors now sell CD-ROMs that contain collections of images and sounds that can be used in presentations or other products without payment of royalties. Be sure to read the fine print, however. What is meant by "royalty free" varies from one collection to the next. In some cases, there are almost no restrictions on the use of materials; in others, you may not be allowed to use the materials in any kind of electronic product.

There are also many collections of images and other materials on the World Wide Web. While images available on the Web are often described as "public domain," they may not be. Use caution when acquiring materials this way. Some Websites permit you to use materials from the site as long as you give proper attribution and create a link to the site on your Web page. This can be a small price to pay for good material. Another way to "get" images or other materials on the Web is to create a link on your site to the original source. In this way your site provides access to the information without actually copying it. If you adopt this approach, it is considered polite to request permission from the source site to create a link, and you need to be alert to the possibility that

your link may be broken if something changes on the source site.

For more information about copyright, or to track the latest developments in the debate about copyright law and new technologies, visit the Websites shown in Table 6–1.

APPLICATIONS IN THE LEARNER-CENTERED CLASSROOM

A key concept within this chapter is for you to learn about the use of selection criteria. What is it that allows individuals to know what they need for a learning experience to be effective? What are the key elements, the key methods, and the key media that should be involved? How should it be presented for learning to be as effective and efficient as possible? These are important skills for any individual who will be attempting to develop some instructional materials. However, we frequently only think about it from the teacher's point of view. That is, "What can the teacher do to effectively select materials, methods, and media?" Perhaps the question that should be asked is, "What can the teacher do to help students learn to develop and use selection criteria of their own?"

Learning higher-order thinking skills is an important element of the learner-centered classroom (McCoombs & Whistler, 1997; Wagner & McCombs, 1995). Such metacognitive skills include learning how to think about one's own thinking and learning. It is important for individual learners to be able to analyze what is being offered within a learning situation, to identify what they need to be able to effectively learn, and to reflect and determine if they need additional information (Ertmer & Newby, 1995).

What can you do within your classroom to help learners gain experience with selecting methods, media, and materials? First, help students understand that criteria are frequently used in their lives to make all sorts of selections. They use criteria each day as they switch from one television program to another, when they select "Value Meal" 1, 2, or 3 at a fast-food restaurant, or when they choose who they will hang around with at school. Second, within the classroom setting, you can explain and model why you used specific selection criterion. What was the thought process used to select one criteria over another? At times it would be important to highlight the key selection criteria and model the process to make the final selection. Students need to know that obstacles (e.g., money, time) sometimes interfere with selecting the best alternative. Finally, students need to know that they should reflect on their selection process. Did it work?; What was successful?; What could have been improved?; What additional things were needed? are all important questions students should ask themselves about their selected criteria.

The goal of developing higher-order thinking skills is to help learners understand their own learning process. Within the learner-centered classroom, you can further this goal by helping students understand criteria for selecting and evaluating instructional materials, methods, and media.

ONE TEACHER'S STORY

by Janette Moreno

I've spent a lot of time discussing my concern for helping my students increase their oral communication skills. This was not an isolated goal in my Spanish Conversation course; this goal was situated within the larger context of improving students' understanding of Spanish culture, including knowledge of Spain's unique geographical features and an appreciation for its special customs, beliefs, and folklore.

As students' communication skills increased, I decided that it might be interesting to have my students work in cooperative groups and "own" their own travel agencies. Each group would be responsible for persuading travelers from northern Spain to visit towns and cities in the southern part of the country. Students were told to select, adapt, and create any materials they needed to introduce potential tourists to the people, culture, and attractions of the southern region.

This was a very interesting assignment. The students worked well together, and for the most part they divided up the work load and got right to work. Some immediately focused on gathering information about the geographical area, others looked for audio and visual materials that would help their potential customers visualize what the area would be like, others worked on what types of media

would be the best to convey their message. Some groups ended up producing short seminars and written materials, others adapted professional videos of the region, and others developed brochures.

One thing that I really think helped all of the students was the debriefing that we went through. After all of the groups presented their information, we spent some time discussing how they came to the conclusion of what they would use to "sell their clients" on the tour packages. Some determined that their people needed to see and hear about the location, and so selected a video. Others felt that the emphasis should be on something their customers could read and ponder thus developed a brochure with pictures and critical information. But the interesting thing was the discussion on their selection of criteria. They had to first discuss what their goal was, who they were trying to get to buy their product, what materials were available and cost effective, possible cultural differences in the way they would make the pitch and how it might be received, and the time limits that they had to deal with. As they dealt with all of these issues, they were also using their Spanish in new and different ways.

We also had a few other interesting questions come up during our discussions. Some of the students used pictures from different brochures that they got from a local travel agency. Others got pictures from various Internet sources. All of the students wanted to know whether, if they had really produced their project as a commercial project, they would have violated copyright laws. It led to some very interesting discussions.

SUMMARY

In this chapter you learned to complete an instructional plan by selecting instructional methods, media, and materials that will match your students, objectives, learning environment, and instructional activities. You can choose your instructional methods, media, and materials in any sequence, and deciding on one may affect the other two. In acquiring instructional materials, select existing materials whenever possible. If appropriate materials are not available, try to modify existing materials to meet your students' needs. Only as a last resort should you attempt to create new materials. In all cases, whether selecting, modifying, and creating, you should follow established copyright guidelines.

REFLECTIVE ACTIVITIES

▶ Think back to the last time you were given the opportunity to teach. It may have been for a formal in-class setting (e.g., at school or church), or it may have been very informal (such as showing a friend how to program a VCR). Consider the method, media, and instructional materials you used. Describe how that teaching/learning situation would have changed if the students or learning environment had been different. Explain why the selection of media is affected by the method used and why the selection of a method can be constrained if a specific medium is required.

▶ Using the preview forms found in Appendix B, preview a number of sets of instructional materials that use the same medium. Select the best of those you preview and explain why you rated it the highest.

▶ Locate a textbook—other than this one—that you are currently using (or used recently). Select a chapter and compare the text design principles listed in Figure 6–4 with the layout of the chapter. If you were the editor of the text, what suggestions would you make to the author for improvements in the text design before the next edition is printed?

▶ Go to a school or university library media center and check out a number of different sets of instructional materials that cover the same topic but involve different media formats. Using the preview forms found in Appendix B, review the different materials. Describe the major differences among them. If you were a student using these materials, which ones would be most effective for learning?

SUGGESTED RESOURCES

Fleming, M., & Levie, W. H. (Eds.) (1993). *Instructional message design: Principles from the behavioral and cognitive sciences* (2nd ed.). Englewood Cliffs, NJ: Educational Technology Publications.

Heinich, R., Molenda, M., Russell, J. D., & Smaldino, S. (1999). *Instructional media and technologies for learning* (6th ed.). Upper Saddle River, NJ: Merrill/Prentice Hall.

Kearny, L. (1996). *Graphics for presenters: Getting your ideas across.* Menlo Park, CA: Crisp.

Leshin, C. B., Pollock, J., & Reigeluth, C. M. (1992). *Instructional design strategies and tactics.* Englewood Cliffs, NJ: Educational Technology.

McCombs, B. L., & Whistler, J. S. (1997). The learner-centered classroom and school: Strategies for increasing student motivation and achievement. San Francisco: Jossey-Bass.

Moore, D. M., & Dwyer, F. M. (Eds.) (1994). *Visual literacy: A spectrum of visual learning.* Englewood Cliffs, NJ: Educational Technology Publications.

Rothwell, W. J., & Kazanas, H. C. (1992). *Mastering the instructional design process: A systematic approach.* San Francisco: Jossey-Bass.

Wagner, E. D., & McCombs, B. L. (1995). Learner centered psychological principles in practice: Designs for distance education. *Education Technology, 35*(2), 32–35.

Wasserman, S. (1992). *Asking the right question: The essence of teaching.* Bloomington, IN: Phi Delta Kappa.

WEBSITES

http://www.interhelp.com/epie_tess.htm

SECTION

III

IMPLEMENTATION

Although we have covered a lot of ground to this point, our question now is, "If your students interact with your instructional materials, will they learn?" The answer is, "It depends." Moving to the "I" in the PIE model, in the next section of this textbook we concentrate on how instructional materials are best *implemented*. We will illustrate how you *must* couple an excellent plan and set of instructional materials with good implementation strategies for your students to achieve the highest-level learning. Consider the last few times you experienced *poor* results from instruction. Was your learning inhibited by poorly planned materials, by the manner in which the materials were implemented, or by some of both? Were there, for example, distractions because of a poor-quality video, uninterpretable audio, or visuals that weren't relevant to the information being presented? What about discussions that were dominated by a single individual, groupwork that turned divisive instead of cooperative, or a game that had no perceivable instructional value or purpose? The point is, you may have the best instructional plan ever developed and a wonderful set of instructional materials, but if you do not properly implement them, your students will not learn as they should.

In this section we emphasize that learning is a function of both instructional content and the manner in which students interact with the content. There are principles of utilization that can help to ensure that learning occurs. These principles apply to both the specific media format (e.g., audio, projected visuals, video, computer software) and the particular instructional method (e.g., discussion, cooperative learning) you use with your instructional materials. It is not enough to know the different types of media and methods that exist and the situations in which to use them; you must also know *how* to use them effectively.

To begin this section, Chapter 7 explores general principles of preparation that ensure that all is in readiness before instruction begins. It includes a description of utilization principles for a variety of methods and media formats. In Chapter 8, we explore the computer specifically as a means to invoke student learning. The section concludes with Chapter 9, in which we focus on the Internet and various forms of distance education. This section's subject is *using* the tools for learning. In some cases, those tools will be in the form of high-tech hardware, in others they are powerful process technologies. To be effective however, you must use these technologies at the right time, with the right audience, and in the correct manner. Otherwise your students will not learn as you wish them to.

CHAPTER 7

Using Methods and Media

OUTLINE

KEY WORDS AND CONCEPTS

advance organizer

OBJECTIVES

After reading and studying this chapter, you will be able to:

▶ Generate examples of the four basic steps in preparing for and presenting instruction.
▶ Demonstrate the correct procedures for using cooperative learning, discovery, problem solving, games, simulations, drill and practice, tutorial, presentation, demonstration, and discussion.
▶ Demonstrate the correct procedures for using multimedia, computer software, video, audio, text, real objects and models, graphics, slides and filmstrips, overhead transparencies, and display boards.
▶ Discuss ways you can integrate methods and media.

PLANNING FOR THE CHAPTER CONTENT

Instructional Technology for Teaching and Learning, will show you how to increase learning by designing lessons that use instructional technology, including computers and other media.

This chapter will focus on *using* technology, including computers and other media. Some of the tools of technology include the methods and media discussed in Chapter 5. In Chapter 4 you learned how to develop a plan for increasing your students' level of learning. Chapter 5 identified the methods and types of media to use in your plan. Chapter 6 focused on acquiring the specific instructional materials that will increase student learning. Now that you have chosen the methods and media for your plan, this chapter will focus on using these methods and media to maximize learning. Remember, the best tools will not give you the best possible outcome if you do not use them properly.

INTRODUCTION

Remember in our story of the cabinetmaker in Chapter 1, before ever touching a tool, the woodworking expert spends time planning and preparing his creation, just as a teacher plans a lesson. The expert, whether cabinetmaker or teacher, visualizes not just the end result but the process of creation as well—

Preparation is an important part of classroom success.

what techniques or methods to incorporate, which tools or media will be most useful, how and when to use those tools or media, and even what to do if certain problems are encountered. In this chapter, you, as an instructional expert, will learn how to use the methods and media described in chapters 5 and 6 so your students will learn to the best of their ability.

PREPARING FOR LEARNING EXPERIENCES

In learning as in cabinetmaking, you must prepare the materials, prepare the environment, and prepare your learners before you proceed with the lesson. These four P's are summarized in Table 7–1 (page 144). As a teacher, preparation is critical.

Prepare Instructional Materials

You and your learners have already selected, modified, and/or developed the materials for the lesson. This may have been done some time ago. Now gather all the materials you and your students will use during the lesson. Make sure everything is available. Some teachers store a list of necessary materials for each lesson in their computer, updating it as needed. Some materials, like audio- and videotapes, will need to be "cued up" prior to beginning the lesson. Other materials, like bulletin boards and displays, will need to be assembled and/or put up. Learners may also be responsible for locating learning materials (see "Toolbox Tips: General Use Guidelines for Media and Methods").

Prepare the Learning Environment

The instructional expert (you) sets up the learning environment so learners can have an effective learning experience. Wherever the instruction is to take

TOOLBOX TIPS

General Use Guidelines for Media and Methods

BEFORE THE LESSON

▶ The person (you or your student) using the methods or media must be familiar with the materials and how to operate any associated equipment.
▶ Check that all equipment is working properly.
▶ Keep materials as simple as possible.
▶ Check that all materials are readily available.
▶ Cue any audio or video materials so they are ready to play.
▶ Be sure that everyone can see and hear the materials.

DURING THE LESSON

▶ Highlight major points on chalkboard or overhead projector.

AFTER THE LESSON

▶ Follow up lesson with discussion, projects, or activities.

---

place—classroom, laboratory, or playground—the facilities will have to be prepared. Certain factors are taken for granted for any instructional situation: comfortable seating, adequate ventilation, climate control, suitable lighting, and the like. Some media require a darkened room, a readily accessible power supply, and access to light switches. You should verify that all equipment is in working order and arrange the facilities so that all students can see and hear properly.

Prepare Learners

As you begin the lesson, the first step is to prepare your students. Research on learning tells us very clearly that what students learn from a lesson depends on how well they are prepared. You have probably noticed that entertainers are obsessed with having their audiences properly warmed up. Preparing students is just as important when they are involved in a lesson.

Preparation is often accomplished by providing an **advance organizer.** It may be an outline of the content, a preview of the activities, or other such preinstructional information used to promote retention of the knowledge, skills, and attitudes presented (Ausubel, 1968). The purpose is to gain student attention and to create a need to know the material.

As discussed in Chapter 4, as part of instructional activities, motivation and orientation are very important at the beginning of a lesson. A proper warmup, from an instructional point of view, gives a broad overview of the lesson, arouses interest, motivates students to learn, creates a need to know by telling learners how they will profit from learning, and explains how the lesson relates to previous and future topics. You may serve several of these functions—directing attention, arousing motivation, and providing a rationale—by informing students of your desired learning objectives. In other cases, learners may prepare themselves, such as by looking through a reading assignment to see what interests them. Or, they may already be excited about exploring the topic.

Proceed with the Lesson

You can keep learners on task and keep the classroom running smoothly by doing the following:

▶ *Giving clear instructions.* Students who don't know what to do are apt to get off task. You can minimize problems by providing precise instructions and then checking for student understanding of those instructions.
▶ *Setting the stage for learning.* At the outset of a learning activity, establish an atmosphere for learning. This can be accomplished by removing potential distractions, presenting the goals of the activity, relating it to previous work, or presenting a puzzle or story designed to stimulate students' thinking.
▶ *Maintaining attention.* In order to learn, students must attend to the task at hand. You can maintain students' attention by varying tasks and classroom activities, encouraging student interaction and involvement, varying pacing, and calling on students.
▶ *Questioning.* Frequent questioning is a technique that you can use to maintain students' involvement, promote students' thinking, assess students' learning, and verify that students understand what they are to do.

TABLE 7–1   The Four Ps of Preparation and Presentation

Prepare Instructional Materials

Check list of materials needed

Gather media and materials

Check equipment

Cue media and put up materials

Prepare Learning Environment

Provide comfortable seating

Provide adequate ventilation

Control temperature

Provide suitable lighting

Arrange seating so all can see and hear

Prepare Learners

Arouse interest and motivate

State purpose

Present overview of content

Relate content to previous and future topics

Explain unfamiliar vocabulary

Proceed with the Lesson

Give clear instructions

Set a learning tone

Maintain attention

Question

Provide feedback

Make smooth transitions

▸ *Providing feedback.* Timely feedback is essential to students' learning. Provide frequent feedback about student performance. This includes feedback on learning processes—not just learning outcomes. Discuss your instructional activity with your students—ask them what they are doing and why.

▸ *Making smooth transitions.* Classroom activities are constantly changing. A skillful teacher makes the transitions from one activity to another as smoothly as possible. You can accomplish this by using posted agendas, giving clear directions, arranging the classroom appropriately, and by orchestrating students' interactions.

In this chapter we will look at three very different scenarios. In each scenario, you are to identify the *methods* and *media* used. You may want to refer back to Chapter 5 to refresh your memory about the various types of methods and media. Also note the *utilization/implementation* procedures used with each method and medium.

SCENARIO: *RAINFOREST RESEARCHERS*

Lauren Henry, a middle school science teacher, wants her students to learn about research methods and to learn some science at the same time. She remembers her "junior high" days when Mr. Morgan lectured on the facts of biology while the students recorded all the details in their notebooks to regurgitate them on the six-weeks test. Lauren wants science to be different, and more meaningful, for her students. One day after school, she stops by the media center and looks through the myriad catalogs from media producers. A new package called *Rainforest Researchers* by Tom Snyder Productions catches her attention. She notes that in 1997 it had been selected as "Best Curriculum Software for Middle Schools" by the Software Publishers Association.

Lauren asks the media librarian to order the multimedia package for preview. When it arrives, she reviews it carefully and decides to try it with her students. The package includes a CD-ROM, videotape, and printed materials for both students and teacher. She can use it with the one computer in her classroom.

Her students begin by viewing the "Introduction" on the videotape. Lauren then divides the class into teams of four, with each student taking the role of chemist, ethnobotanist, taxonomist, or ecologist. Each student has a printed booklet for his/her role. To explore "The Case of the Disappearing Durians" (a tree known for its fruit), the students read the Case Background, learn about their individual jobs, share information, and answer a quiz on the Field Worksheet to be sure they are ready to begin. Each book has only some of the answers to the quiz, so students have to work together.

A "Random Expert Picker" on the classroom computer selects a leader for each team's turn. The first leader types in the name of the team and the names of each team member, then types in the team's consensus answers to the quiz. The class period ends just as the students are getting excited about their new adventure.

The next class period, each team prepares for its trip to Java. As a team they select seven supplies from a list of fourteen. (All of the available supplies could be useful depending on which hazards they en-

A screen from the program,
Rainforest Researchers. *Source:*
Rainforest Researcher, *Tom Snyder*
Productions.

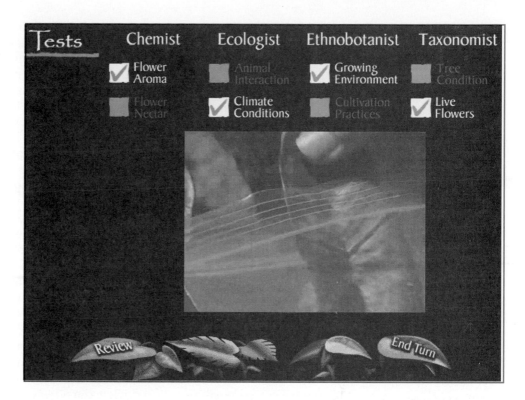

counter.) They have a budget, and charge supplies against it. After choosing their supplies, the team views a "trip video" on the computer which describes the problem they face—finding out why the durian tree is not producing as much fruit as before.

With the problem identified, each team member reads two pages of background information that is the same for each team member and then a page specific for each role. Each team member selects one of two tests to conduct for his area of expertise. The team enters its test choices into the computer and gets results. There are no strictly right or wrong choices. Each test provides the team with a piece of information. A short video plays on the computer, illustrating the testing process. The test results appear on the screen and can be printed out. The results are recorded on each team member's worksheet before the class period ends.

Test results in hand, each team reconvenes the next day as a group, analyzes the results, and refers to information in the individual booklets. Team members share information about possible solutions to the problem. No one student can determine the answer from his/her individual test results. The team must work together to come up with the best analysis. Possible causes are faulty flowers, no pollinator, fungus, and low rainfall. Each team then ranks the possible causes according to three categories: definitely, maybe, or no way.

Teams enter their choices into the computer. To keep the suspense alive, the teams get a response only when the last team has entered its choices.

Periodically the team encounters a "Supply Event," random occurrences based on the reality of conducting scientific research in remote places (such as passports not in order, running out of gasoline in the all-terrain vehicle, not having foul weather gear, or lacking insect repellent). The students think they are fun and provide an unpredictable element. The program randomly selects an event, then checks the team's supply list to see if the team has previously selected the right item to overcome the problem. If the team has the relevant supply, they proceed smoothly. If not, they are charged to overcome the problem.

The rainforest researchers continue their learning adventure for several additional class periods, collecting information from the computer and their booklets. As teams, they consider how ecosystems change and what caused the changes. To close the activity, each team receives a final rating based on the amount of money remaining in its budget and a researcher rating.

Lauren chooses to evaluate her students by their individual worksheets and the team history compiled by the computer software. She also has an observational checklist, which includes such items as understanding cause and effect relationships, ability to read and interpret graphic information, and the ability to draw conclusions and make judgments. Lauren checks off each characteristic as she observes each student demonstrate it. She also conducts a group discussion of the content using questions such as, "What is biodiversity?"; "What's happening to the world's rainforests?"; and "What can cause ecosystems to change?" Rather than testing students' retention of specific bits of content, Lauren decides to have the students complete research reports and presentations.

Reflective Questions

▶ Which types of *methods* did the students experience in this scenario? How were they *implemented?*

▶ What types of *media* were used? How were they *used?*

▶ What experiences did the learners have? How could they have been improved?

Our Observations

Rainforest Researchers utilized cooperative learning, discovery, and problem-solving methods. While Lauren Henry used a variety of media, we focus here on multimedia (computer software) and video. In this section, we explore both Lauren's use of and general guidelines for each of these methods and media. You can decide if she used them effectively. (Refer again as needed to Chapter 5 for discussions of the different methods and media.)

Using Methods: Cooperative Learning

Cooperative learning refers to a small group of students working toward a common goal or task. This method is specifically designed to encourage students to work together, drawing on their individual experiences, skills, and levels of motivation to help each other achieve the desired result. The central idea is that cooperation and interaction allow students to learn from several sources, not just the teacher, while also providing each student opportunities to share their own abilities and knowledge. (See page 92 of Chapter 5 for characteristics of the cooperative learning method.)

In the *Rainforest Researchers* scenario, students worked in groups of four, with each student performing a different role. They had to work together cooperatively as a team to solve the problem.

Utilization Guidelines: Cooperative Learning

▶ Build an atmosphere that encourages participation and cooperation. Help students realize the advantages of working together as a team. This can be facilitated by requiring that all members of the group have roles to fill that are necessary for the group's success.

▶ Teach group processes to the students. Effective group cooperative efforts do not happen by chance.

▶ Learn to facilitate, not dominate. It is important for you to take on the role of monitor, facilitator, and guide instead of director.

Cooperative Learning Examples

Recently the four members of the fifth-grade Elementary Ecology Club and their advisor went on a field trip to view a creek near their school. Upon close observation of the creek, the students noticed patches of oil floating in the slow-moving water. After further investigation, the club advisor decided it would be a good project for the club to research what was occurring and to determine what could be done about it, and divided the students into four-person teams. Each team member was given a specific task. One student was to determine who should be contacted at the public health department. Another was to find out what the oily substance was and determine how it could have been introduced to the creek. Still another was in charge of identifying potential ways of publicizing what was occurring and determining the potential impact on the animals and community. The fourth was to review what the club could do to raise public awareness.

In a high school art appreciation class, groups of students were assembled to learn about the different forms of creative art. Each group was composed of three students: one who was accomplished at a musical instrument, another who had the ability to paint, and a third who had the ability to sculpt. The group's task was to learn about the different art forms and their relationships.

Using Methods: Discovery

Implementing a discovery method places students in the "actual" situation so that they can learn through personal experience. Such experiences generally require learners to develop and use observation and comparison skills. Moreover, like detectives, students must learn to follow leads and clues and record findings in order to explain what they experience. (See page 93 of Chapter 5 for characteristics of the discovery method.)

In the *Rainforest Researchers* scenario, students were not told the content and asked to memorize it. Instead they were given information and had to construct meaning from the data and "discover" the relationships.

Utilization Guidelines: Discovery

▸ Be prepared for all types of "discoveries." Combining unique students with unique learning environments often leads to unique results. Be prepared for all types of standard and not-so-standard findings when students are allowed to make their own observations and draw their own conclusions.

▸ Encourage students to share their discoveries. Through the experience of discovery, students often gain both great insights into their subject and great enthusiasm for what they have learned. These important insights and feelings should be shared with other individuals.

▸ Make sure students understand that "one right answer" may not exist. They may need instruction and examples on how to observe, compare, and evaluate phenomena.

▸ Constantly encourage and reward students for being inquisitive, for asking questions, and for trying new approaches.

Discovery Examples

To have her students discover the relation between current, voltage, and resistance (Ohm's Law), Linda Harrison has them "experiment" with different resistors and different voltages while measuring the current. Linda has the laboratory lesson carefully planned, but does not tell students what the result "should be." The students work in pairs and each lab pair manipulates the data with the aid of a computer, which constructs graphs of the data. Each pair shares its results with the entire class. Often, individual pairs' data does not show that current equals voltage divided by resistance. However, when the class pools the data, the relationship among the three variables becomes evident to everyone.

Judy Lewis gives her first graders a variety of water colors and encourages them to mix any two colors together and see what color is produced. Judy uses the activity to teach color names. She has printed the color names on large cards along with a sample of the color. She also used cards with plus signs and equal signs to form equations such as "Blue + Yellow = Green." The activity allows students to "discover" the results of various combinations of colors. In addition, they learn to read the names of colors and are introduced to the basics of the mathematics of addition.

Using Methods: Problem Solving

The real world is filled with problems that need resolution. Some problems may be very well defined (e.g., determining if purchasing a new outfit is within one's current monetary means; finding the best route to travel to a nearby art museum), while others may be somewhat ill defined (e.g., determining how to increase neighborhood safety; finding the "best" postsecondary education). To fully participate in this world, students need to be able to analyze problems, form tentative hypotheses, collect and interpret data, and develop some type of logical approach to solving the problem. (See page 93 of Chapter 5 for characteristics of the problem solving method.)

In the *Rainforest Researchers* scenario, students had to work together as a team to solve the "real-world" problem related to the disappearing Durians.

Utilization Guidelines: Problem Solving

▸ Clarify the problem when necessary. Especially with less mature students, one of the most difficult parts of problem solving is getting a true, accurate picture of the problem itself. In the initial stages of problem solving, your role often involves helping students in identifying and outlining the specific problem. Be careful, however, to not overdo the clarification. If you explain the problem too thoroughly, the students won't have to work for the answer.

▸ Use additional resources and materials when necessary. It is important that students have access to additional resources, as well as instruction on how to use those resources most effectively.

▸ Keep groups small. Because of the uniqueness of the potential solution paths to the problems and the time required to complete the various steps, a smaller number of students is often essential.

▸ Help students understand the need for generalization. Students must recognize that problem solutions are generally unique and that no single answer works for all problems. This connotes an emphasis on learning general problem-solving strategies and procedures and adapting them as each new situation dictates.

Problem-Solving Example

Sister Anne is a sixth-grade science teacher at St. John's Catholic School. During a recent unit in science, she wanted her students to directly experience the impact of human population on the environment. She posed the following problem: "Does acid rain have an impact on the environment?" She quickly felt the need to clarify and redefine the question at her students' level, so she revised her question to, "In what ways does acid rain affect the growth patterns of common outdoor plants?" She asked her students to design an experiment that would provide an answer to that question.

Using Media: Multimedia, Including Computer Software

When you use multimedia materials, you should assemble and test all of the components of the multimedia system well in advance of your lesson. Make sure you have all adjunct materials, such as printed materials, for all students. Multimedia systems can be difficult to operate, and you want to make certain that everything will work when you are ready to use it.

In the *Rainforest Researchers* scenario, students used a variety of media. The lesson's centerpiece was the computer software on the CD-ROM. Students used the software to manage almost every aspect of their learning experience. The CD-ROM and computer system allowed them to work both collaboratively and independently, and provided the means for them to discover new information and solve challenging problems.

Utilization Guidelines: Multimedia, Including Computer Software

▶ Use a display technology (computer monitors and/or projection systems) that is appropriate for the number of students. Be sure that all students can see projected computer images.
▶ Install and test all software in advance of presentation.
▶ Run the software from the hard drive rather than from floppy disk, if possible. The computer program will respond more quickly.
▶ Encourage student participation through questioning and having students decide next steps.

Multimedia Example

Nancy Matson is presenting a unit on television violence, free speech, censorship, and the television industry in her eighth-grade social studies class. She has selected a multimedia program from Tom Snyder Productions titled *Violence in the Media* as the core of the unit (see Chapter 5 page 101). The program provides introductory material for both Nancy and her students. A teacher's guide and student booklets direct lesson activity. Followup discussions and other activities included with the materials promote student learning as students form their own opinions on the controversial issues of free speech vs. censorship and television violence.

Computer Software Example

Students in George Morgan's middle school mathematics class are using the computer simulation *Hot*

Dog Stand to develop a variety of mathematical and practical skills. The simulation requires planning and record keeping, as well as judgments based on computational skills, to make as much money as possible while managing a hot dog stand during a season of high school football games. Random generation of variables assures that the same students can use the program again and again. Participating students are gathered around a computer in the corner of the classroom while other students are engaged in different activities. Mr. Morgan has checked to be sure that all can see the screen and interact without disturbing other students. The students record data, enter the data into spreadsheets, and generate graphs. There is friendly competition to see which group of students can "earn" the most money from its hot dog stand.

Using Media: Video

Video, regardless of its format, provides motion, color, and sound. Students are accustomed to viewing television passively at home. Therefore, you must prepare students for active viewing of video in the classroom.

In the *Rainforest Researchers* scenario, Lauren Henry used a videotape to "set the stage" and provide an introduction to the jungle adventure the students were about to embark upon (see Chapter 5, page 102).

Utilization Guidelines: Video

▶ Check lighting, seating, and volume controls before the showing.
▶ Prepare students by reviewing previously learned content and by asking new questions.
▶ Stop the videotape at appropriate points for discussion.
▶ Highlight major points by writing them on the chalkboard or overhead.

Video Example

Paige Ertmer's preservice teachers are viewing the acclaimed videotape *Good Morning Miss Tolliver* in their mathematics methods course. The program was awarded the 1993 George Peabody Award, broadcast television's highest honor. Originally shown on public television, the video is a captivating look at how Kay Tolliver, an East Harlem math teacher, combines math and communication arts skills to inspire and motivate her students. Dr. Ertmer is hoping this videotape will inspire and motivate her students, who will be doing their student teaching next semester. She has distributed a set of questions to direct students' viewing of the videotape, asking them to look over the questions prior to seeing the tape and to take notes during the viewing.

Proper showmanship increases the effectiveness of media in the classroom.

These questions will form the basis of a whole-class discussion following the video.

Your Investigation

Now it is time for your investigation. Your job is to review the scenario and suggest ways to improve or change the teacher's use of methods and media, and determine how to improve both the lesson and the resulting student learning. Record your answers to the following questions and then compare them with ours at the end of the chapter on page 161.

1. What media did the package contain?
2. For what purpose did she use the videotape?
3. For what purpose did she use the printed materials?
4. For what purpose did she use the computer software?
5. What additional methods and media would you have used?
6. What should Lauren have done to properly use the videotape, the print materials, and the computer software?

As we wrap up our discussion of the Rainforest Researchers, let's review what we have discussed. We pointed out uses of several methods and media. You probably noted some things that we didn't point out. We saw cooperative learning, discovery, and problem solving as the key methods. The media we discussed were multimedia and video, even though others such as printed materials were used.

Now we explore another scenario. This one deals with translating numbers in first-year Spanish. See if you can identify the *methods* and *media* used. You may want to refer back to Chapter 5 to refresh your memory about the various types of methods and media. Note the *utilization/implementation* procedures used with each method and medium.

SCENARIO: SPANISH NUMBER TRANSLATIONS

To introduce his first-year Spanish class to number translations, Lance Thomas develops a tutorial booklet. The booklet teaches students the Spanish equivalent of numbers from one to twenty and then provides practice for visual recognition of these numbers (reading skills). A short quiz at the end of the booklet allows each student to check his/her mastery of the topic.

To develop oral language skills the students listen to an audiotape, on which the speaker pronounces the numbers in Spanish and asks the student to repeat the number. The speaker later says the numbers in random order, asks the student to say the English equivalent, then gives the correct answer.

To provide variety in the classroom activities, the students enjoy playing the game "Ay Caramba" ("Oh, my goodness!"). The game begins with each student standing beside his desk. Mr. Thomas randomly picks a student to begin with "uno." The students then go in order pronouncing the Spanish numbers in sequence. To make the game interesting, when a number has a "3" in it, the student must say "Ay Caramba." A student who makes a mistake must sit down. The game continues until only one student is left standing. The students enjoy the fast-moving game and want to play it anytime there are a few extra minutes in the class. The game provides drill and practice with Spanish numbers. The students suggest modifications in

Students enjoy and learn from role playing in a mock store setting.

the game to continue to make it interesting, such as saying "Ay Caramba" for numbers other than "3" or for either of two numbers such as "5" or "7."

An application of Spanish numbers in a later lesson takes students to a Spanish market. The lesson begins with a videotape Mr. Thomas shot in Spain to show his students an actual market ("el mercado"). In the classroom is a simulated market with boxes, packages, and other food containers labeled in Spanish Mr. Thomas collected during his visit to Spain and which friends in Mexico have sent to him. Mr. Thomas has supplemented the packages with plastic food items (meat, fruit, vegetables, etc.) from a local toy store.

In pairs, students role play a clerk and a customer. The "customer" must read from a grocery list the number of items (e.g., how many eggs, cereal boxes). The "customer" says the number to the "store clerk." The "clerk" may or may not (deliberately or accidentally) give the "customer" the correct number of items. The "customer" accepts or rejects the number of items. As a variation, students record the transaction on videotape and play them back later in small-group sessions, where they stop the tape after each transaction to discuss whether the "clerk" gave correct number of items to the various "customers."

Reflective Questions

▶ Which types of *methods* did the students experience in this scenario? How were they *implemented?*

▶ What types of *media* were used? How were they *used?*

▶ What experiences did the learners have? How could they have been improved?

Our Observations

We saw that Lance Thomas utilized games, simulations, drill and practice, and tutorial methods. You can decide if he used these methods effectively. He also used a variety of media, primarily audio, text, and real objects and models. In this section, we explore both Lance's use of and general guidelines for each of these methods and media. You can decide if he used them effectively. (Refer again as needed to Chapter 5 for discussions of the different methods and media.)

Using Methods: Games

Games have two key attributes: first, a clearly defined set of rules that outline how the game will be played, what actions are and are not allowed, what constitutes winning the game, and what the end result will be for a winning performance; and second, elements of competition or challenge wherein players compete against themselves, against other individuals, or against a standard of some type.

In this scenario, Lance Thomas used a game, "Ay Caramba" ("Oh, my goodness!"), to let his students practice their numbers in Spanish. The game provides drill and practice (discussed later) while students learn their numbers.

Utilization Guidelines: Games

▶ Students must have a clear concept of the instructional goal of the game. Ask yourself, "What do students need to learn, and how will a game help accomplish that?" Make sure to communicate the answer to these questions to your learners.

▶ Students must understand the procedures and rules for how the game should proceed and how all scoring should occur. With a new game it always helps to have written rules.

▶ Make sure the game is structured so active involvement is maintained at the highest possible level for all participants. If groups are too large and long waits occur between "turns," the effectiveness of the game will wane. Allow enough time to play but not so much that students grow tired of the game.

▶ Include a debriefing or discussion following the game's conclusion. This should focus on the instructional content and value of the game and why it was played. Make sure the students understand that their participation in the game had an instructional purpose, and summarize what they should have learned from it.

Game Examples

A group of high school chemistry students is given the assignment to memorize 15 element names and their associated numbers and symbols from the periodic table. The teacher has designed a board game in which four teams of two students each compete to complete the "experiment" by answering questions related to the 15 elements.

The religious education students in Reverend McCullan's class of middle school students enjoy playing "Jeopardy." Rev. McCullan generates answers each week based on the reading assignment. The student teams actively participate to come up with the correct questions.

Using Methods: Simulations

Simulations approximate real-life situations or phenomena. They give learners the opportunity to interact with these situations or phenomena without the danger, expense, or difficulty associated with the reality.

Mr. Thomas used a simulated market or "el mercado" to allow students to practice reading and talking in Spanish. To make the activity as realistic as possible he stocked the "mercado" with boxes, packages, and other food containers labeled in Spanish.

Utilization Guidelines: Simulations

▶ Explain the purpose, procedures, and/or rules for the simulation. Make students aware of oversimplifications implicit in the simulation. Explain the goal to be achieved and, where appropriate, the role of each student.

▶ Simulations can be confusing, and students may need guidance or direction in order to benefit from them. Questions, activities, and scenarios can fill this guidance role.

▶ Allow participants to play out their roles with minimum input from you.

▶ Conduct followup discussions or debriefing with students to maximize the benefit from the simulation. Provide feedback following the simulation (some commercial simulations provide feedback during their use).

Simulation Examples

Students in John Morales's social studies class learn about the operations of government by participating in a role-playing simulation about creating and passing new legislation. John sits in the back of the room and lets the simulation progress at the students' pace. He takes extensive notes for a debriefing at the conclusion of the "legislative session."

The sixth graders in Judy Krajcik's class learn about surviving in the inner city by playing a computer simulation about life downtown in a large city. She introduces the simulation to the entire class, then lets groups of four at a time participate on each class computer. She moves among the groups to answer questions, to monitor the progress of each group, and to discuss students' feelings about the conditions in the inner city.

Using Methods: Drill and Practice

Drill and practice is a common classroom technique for helping individual learners master basic skills or knowledge through repetitive work. Drill and practice is not designed to introduce new content. It is assumed that the skill or knowledge has already been introduced, and thus its purpose is to give learners the opportunity to master the material at their own pace. (See page 96 of Chapter 5 for characteristics of the drill & practice method.)

Lance Thomas used a game, "Ay Caramba" ("Oh, my goodness!"), to let his students practice their numbers in Spanish and a simulation to let his students practice reading and talking in Spanish. Both of these activities provided drill and practice of the skills students were learning.

Utilization Guidelines: Drill and Practice

▶ Introduce content prior to the drill and practice session.

▶ Use many short drill and practice sessions instead of a few longer ones. Use both individual and group activities. Use competition (against self or others) to make drill more interesting.

▶ Make sure students are practicing the correct information or procedures. Only correct practice makes perfect!

▶ Provide opportunities for students to apply what they master through drill and practice.

Drill and Practice Examples

Mary Owens uses arithmetic flash cards to work individually with her first graders on basic addition skills. She limits the time with each student to three to five minutes.

Students in Wilber Groves's seventh-grade geography class work on their map-recognition skills using printed worksheets. He circulates throughout the classroom to monitor each student's progress and to make sure they all are getting the correct answers.

Using Methods: Tutorial

Tutorials introduce content to the learner and assess the learner's progress. The typical tutorial introduces a well-defined body of content, usually broken up into blocks that may be delivered via almost any medium, although most tutorials involve text and graphic information. (See page 96 of Chapter 5 for characteristics of the tutorial method.)

In our scenario, Lance Thomas used a booklet to teach his students the Spanish equivalent of numbers. The booklet "tutors" the students in the numbers from one to twenty and then tests them on what they have learned. Students who have not mastered all the numbers can go through the booklet a second time.

Utilization Guidelines: Tutorial

▶ Present an overview of the material. Prompt students through content or skills, then release them to demonstrate content or skills on their own. Provide opportunities for students to apply what they have learned.

▶ Present content or skills one step at a time.

▶ Ask questions of the student, and encourage the student to ask questions.

▶ Plan for varying rates of completion. Monitor students' progress regularly to ensure that they are on task and learning.

Tutorial Examples

Jill Day, an industrial arts teacher, uses a video-based tutorial on shop safety as a prelude to having her students work with power equipment. The video shows each step of shop safety procedures and poses questions for students to answer.

John Johnson uses a tutorial, in the form of an illustrated storybook on local history, as a makeup activity for his fourth-grade students who were absent when the topic was covered in class. He monitors their progress to check their understanding and learning.

Using Media: Audio

In formal education, a lot of attention is given to reading and writing, a little to speaking, and essentially none to listening. Like all skills, listening and learning from audio can be improved with practice. (See page 106 of Chapter 5 for the characteristics of audio.)

Lance Thomas used audiotapes to develop his students' oral language skills. The tapes were used in a tutorial mode. The Spanish numbers were pronounced on the tape, the student was expected to repeat the equivalent in English, then the tape gave the correct equivalent.

Utilization Guidelines: Audio

▶ Cue the audio material before you and your students use it.

▶ Make sure that all students involved can hear and that other students aren't distracted.

▶ Use a handout or worksheet to maximize learning from audio media.

▶ Use a followup activity after each audio lesson.

Audio Example

The eighth-grade students at Fairfield Middle School are using cassette tape recorders to gather an oral history of their community. The project is a cooperative effort by all eighth-grade social studies teachers and their students. The teachers each chose to focus on an aspect of the community's history, such as transportation, government, business, industry, and recreation. Students spent many weeks deciding on important topics in the area assigned to their class, then worked together to develop a set of questions to ask each individual they would interview. Armed with tape recorders, students interview people from the community. Some of the citizens come to the school; the students visit others. Students edit the individual tapes into one tape that highlights important aspects of the community's history. The finalized copy is available for use by community groups and organizations. Copies are also available in the school and community libraries.

Using Media: Text

Textbooks and other text-based materials, such as those found on the Internet, should meet your students' needs rather than dictate what they do. As indicated in the PIE model, you should determine learning objectives and then select materials that will facilitate your students achieving them. Too often text is selected first, and then what the students learn and do are determined by what is in the text. (See page 106 of Chapter 5 for the characteristics of text.)

Mr. Thomas used text to present his tutorial in booklet form using English. Text also appeared on the boxes and packages of food, this time in Spanish.

Utilization Guidelines: Text

▶ Direct student reading with objectives and/or questions.
▶ Emphasize the use of visuals with text-based materials.
▶ Check the teacher's guide for additional materials and activities.
▶ Supplement text with other media.

Text Example

Jean Montgomery's fourth graders are reading in their textbooks about the countries of Africa. Ms. Montgomery has taught them that reading is especially fun if you can share with others who are reading the same material. Students are working together in small groups, with each group studying a different country. Each student in turn leads a discussion after all students have read a section of the text. Some students also refer to the encyclopedia on CD-ROM in the classroom to get additional information.

Using Media: Real Objects and Models

There are countless things in the environment that you and your students can use to learn from—leaves, globes, dolls, manipulatives (objects designed for educational use, such as letter blocks and counting rods), tools, and so on. However, real objects and models will be effective only if they are used properly.

The real objects Mr. Thomas used in this scenario were the actual packages and boxes that originally contained food products, as well as the plastic models of meats, fruits, vegetables, and other perishable foods.

Utilization Guidelines: Real Objects and Models

▶ Familiarize yourself with the object or model.
▶ Make sure objects are large enough to be seen.
▶ Indicate actual size, shape, and color of objects represented by models.
▶ Avoid passing a single object around class. It can be distracting and student may play with it while you are trying to move on in the lesson.

Real Objects and Models Example

Nancy Foust, an instructor in the high school vocational-technical program, is demonstrating how automobile carburetors work so her students can adjust and repair them. She brings several different carburetors into the classroom to arouse interest at the beginning of the class. The students can handle and look at them before the class begins, then she puts the car-

buretors away. Nancy uses a larger-than-life model of a carburetor to show how the internal parts operate. Some of the parts are made of clear plastic, and many are color coded for easy identification. Having seen and manipulated the actual carburetors, Nancy's students know how big they are and what they look like. The enlarged model allows all of her students to see the various parts as she describes their functions.

Your Investigation

It is again your turn to review the scenario and suggest ways to improve or change the teacher's use of methods and media, and determine how to improve both the lesson and the resulting student learning. Record your answers to the following questions and then compare them with ours at the end of the chapter on page 161.

1. What media did Mr. Thomas use in his lessons?
2. For what purpose did he use printed text?
3. For what purpose did he use audiotape?
4. For what purpose did he use videotape?
5. For what purpose did he use real objects and models?
6. What tips would you give Mr. Thomas on proper use of printed materials, audiotape, videotape, and real objects and models?

Now we explore another scenario. This one deals with the history of railroads in the United States. See if you can identify the *methods* and *media* used. You may want to refer back to Chapter 5 to refresh your memory about the various types of methods and media. Note the *utilization/implementation* procedures used with each method and medium.

SCENARIO: RAILROADS IN THE UNITED STATES

As part of a social studies unit on transportation, Jennifer Jacobs is presenting a series of two lessons on railroads in the United States to her fourth-grade class. The day before the first lesson she puts up a colorful bulletin board showing photographs and artists' sketches of historical events in American railroading, such as President Lincoln's funeral train and the driving of the golden spike joining the rails of the Union Pacific and the Central Pacific at Promontory Point, Utah. These visuals tie railroads to other events of history her students have studied.

She begins the first lesson with a 4-minute segment from a commercial filmstrip with audiotape. The entire 20-minute audio filmstrip is devoted to transportation in the United States covering horses, the railroad, the automobile, and the airplane. She has already used the first portion of the filmstrip, on horse-drawn vehicles, and will use the other segments later.

She follows the historical perspective of the filmstrip presentation with a discussion of the types of railroad equipment and the purposes each serve. Ms. Jacobs has borrowed from her son HO-scale examples of various locomotives and railroad cars. She shows her students a steam locomotive and a diesel engine, then leads a discussion of the advantages and disadvantages of each type. She lists on the chalkboard the advantages and limitations generated by the discussion. She is surprised how much her students know about trains even though a railroad no longer runs through their town.

The following day Ms. Jacobs reviews the first day's lesson and shows various types of train cars from her son's HO-scale train layout. As a class they discuss the differences between freight cars and passenger cars. As a class they classify the various cars as freight or passenger.

To supplement the model train cars, Ms. Jacobs locates a set of commercial overhead transparencies in the media center. Included in the set are overheads showing line drawings of various types of freight cars. She uses them to orally quiz the students on the types of cars and their purposes.

Ms. Jacobs had noted when planning the lesson that the commercial set had no overhead transparencies showing passenger cars. Before presenting the lesson, she took her camera to a nearby large city served by Amtrak passenger service. She called and checked the schedule and was at the station to take

Ms. Jacobs shows students scale models of railroad cars.

slides of a baggage car, coaches, a diner, sleeper cars, and even a domed lounge car. During the lesson, she shows her slides to the class. The students are surprised by her picture-taking ability, enjoy hearing about her trip to the city, and eagerly learn about the many types of passenger cars and their purposes.

To wrap up the lesson, each student draws and colors a picture of their favorite train engine or car, and shares the drawing with the class. Ms. Jacobs then puts all the students' drawings around the classroom to remind the students of the lesson and to tie in with her bulletin board.

Reflecting on the lesson, Ms. Jacobs is very pleased that her students seemed to enjoy learning the role of railroads in U.S. history. They could identify types of locomotives and freight and passenger cars and discuss the purpose of each. She feels she has provided an important awareness about a "vanishing" type of transportation in the United States.

Reflective Questions

▶ Which *methods* did the students experience in this scenario? How were they *implemented*?

▶ What *media* were used? How were they *used*?

▶ What experiences did the learners have? How could they have been improved?

Our Observations

Jennifer Jacobs utilized presentation, demonstration, and discussion methods in her lesson. She also used a variety of media, primarily graphics, slides, overhead transparencies, and display boards. In this section, we explore both Jennifer's use of and general guidelines for each of these methods and media. You can decide if she used them effectively. (Refer as needed to Chapter 5 for discussions of the different methods and media.)

Using Methods: Presentation

In a presentation, the content is presented verbally by the teacher or a student and the "audience" listens and takes notes. Video- and audiotaped presentations can also be used, either as the main way of presenting new material or as an ancillary approach for covering a specific topic in more detail.

In her lesson, Jennifer Jacobs used the presentation method with several media: a filmstrip to present the railroad as part of transportation in America, overhead transparencies to show various types of freight cars, and slides to illustrate the various types of passenger cars.

Utilization Guidelines: Presentation

▶ Inform students of the purpose of the presentation by providing them with an agenda or outline.

▶ Highlight the critical points of the presentation by showing a visual that illustrates a key point, by repeating the key points several times, by using voice inflection to emphasize important points, and by simply declaring a point as one of central importance.

▶ Make the presentation relevant. Learners need to be able to relate the information from the presentation to their own experiences. You can accomplish this by asking questions such as the following: How does this relate to you? Have you ever had a similar kind of experience? How could you use this information now or in the future?

▶ Use variety to maintain attention. Add variety by introducing graphics or other forms of media, by asking questions, by incorporating relevant personal experiences, or even by making a simple change in your volume or rate of speech.

Presentation Examples

A videotape presents Ralph Watson's social studies class the television news coverage of the same story from four different cultures (United States, United Kingdom, Spain, and Israel). Ralph shows the videotape and asks, "What do you learn or gain from watching this video?" Students then compare and contrast the nature of coverage, length of coverage, content, and depth of coverage of the same news story from four different perspectives.

The Website from a major food company lists the nutritional information for all its products. Wanda Elliott's food and nutrition class then discusses the pros and cons of eating each of the products.

Using Methods: Demonstration

In a demonstration an individual performs a procedure in order to highlight an important principle or process. Demonstrations may be done live or recorded on a media format, such as videotape or CD-ROM. (See page 97 of Chapter 5 for characteristics of the demonstration method.)

In the scenario, Ms. Jacobs used models of railroad equipment to demonstrate the different types of cars on a train.

Utilization Guidelines: Demonstration

▶ While planning, preparation, and practice are important for all instructional methods, they are especially critical for demonstrations if you are going to be manipulating materials and equipment that you do not use regularly.

▶ Ensure that all can see and hear.

▶ Present the demonstration in small, sequential steps.

▶ Allow the audience to practice. It is often motivational for learners to watch a demonstration and then attempt to complete it themselves.

Demonstration Examples

Jason LaJoy, the physical education teacher, demonstrates how to perform a forward flip on the trampoline as students watch. He describes each step and then demonstrates them in sequence. Next, each student is given an opportunity to practice the forward flip with feedback from Mr. LaJoy.

A CD-ROM program demonstrates how to deal with sexual harassment between students. The program dramatizes a variety of ways to deal with sexual harassment. Following the demonstration, students role play how to deal with unwanted sexual advances.

Using Methods: Discussion

Discussion involves a group of individuals sharing information about a topic or problem. A major benefit of the discussion method is the amount of interaction that occurs and the learning that results from that interaction. (See page 95 of Chapter 5 for characteristics of the discussion method.)

Ms. Jacobs used discussion to help her students understand the advantages and limitations of steam engines and diesel locomotives.

Utilization Guidelines: Discussion

▶ Provide inspiration/motivation before beginning a discussion by using a still picture, an audio recording, or a short video to secure the interest and attention of the participants.

▶ Encourage active participation from each group member. The exchange of ideas among group members is a critical factor in learning from discussion.

▶ Questions are needed to stimulate discussion, and should be prepared beforehand. Either you or your students may prepare questions.

▶ Summarize and/or synthesize the different viewpoints of various small groups discussing aspects of a specific topic.

Discussion Examples

Officer Richardson from the local police department shows a picture of a mangled car resulting from an

Visuals help to clarify information for many students.

auto accident involving a drunken driver to gain a student group's attention before discussing the problems of drug and alcohol abuse.

Jolene Moller's social studies students gather points of view from several small-group discussion sessions and assemble them into a single paper. The text is distributed to all class members as a summary of the discussion.

Using Media: Graphics

A variety of pictures, drawings, charts, and other visuals are available or can be prepared for classroom use. Graphics are available in textbooks and other printed materials, in computer software and multimedia programs, and as separate paper-based visuals. (See page 103 of Chapter 5 for the characteristics of graphics.)

While teaching about railroads, Jennifer Jacobs used a variety of graphics, including a bulletin board containing photographs and sketches, a filmstrip with pictures and drawings, overhead transparencies with line drawings, slides, and student drawings.

Utilization Guidelines: Graphics

▶ Use simple materials that everyone can see.
▶ Provide written or verbal cues to highlight important aspects of visuals.
▶ Use one visual at a time except for comparison.
▶ Hold visuals steady.

Graphics Example

Tom Keller selects one of his students' favorite books, *Alexander and the Terrible, Horrible, No Good, Very Bad Day,* to read to a small group of sec-

ond graders. Before beginning the story, he asks questions that the students should be able to answer after listening to the story. To enhance the students' interest and understanding, Tom uses study prints (large visuals) depicting parts of the story. He asks his students to discuss the characters shown in the study prints. After reading and discussing the questions related to the story, Tom has the students create their own visuals based on one of the study prints.

Jean Montgomery's fourth graders are carefully studying the photographs in their textbooks as they read about the countries of Africa. Ms. Montgomery has taught them that photographs are an important part of all books and printed materials. Students are working together in small groups, with each group studying a different country. Some students are referring to the encyclopedia on CD-ROM in the classroom to get additional information. Ms. Montgomery reminds them that the CD-ROM is like a "book" with unique features, such as the addition of moving images with sound, and should be used accordingly.

Using Media: Slides

Slides provide a way to bring the outside world into the classroom in full color. Slides can also show anything from microscopic views of cells to representations of outer space. Even though filmstrips are a different media format, you can think of a filmstrip as a series of slides connected on a roll of film.

Ms. Jacobs used slides to show visuals of passenger cars that she could not find in materials at her school. She also showed a commercial filmstrip to introduce the lesson.

Utilization Guidelines: Slides

▶ Make sure slides are in the correct order and right side up.

▶ Darken the room so all can see.

▶ Stand facing your class and use a remote control to advance the slides.

▶ Break up long presentations with a gray slide or turn off the projector and turn the classroom lights on.

Slides Examples

Instead of taking a field trip to the local food-processing plant, Ned Quinn's consumer science students view a set of slides showing various operations within the plant. Students view the slides as Mr. Quinn provides the narration from his notes and distributes literature provided by the plant. Students learn the processes and see the operations without actually leaving the classroom.

Individual fifth- and sixth-grade students in Jim Crawford's bilevel Spanish class sit at a learning carrel and view slides that their teacher took during his trip to Spain last summer. Jim decided to use an audiotape to narrate the slides, which show various people, animals, and buildings in Spain. He recorded native Spanish speakers describing the scenes and objects shown in the slides, and he added Spanish music to set a mood before the recorded narration and during scenes showing folk dances. The purpose of the slide-tape show is to visually and aurally present basic vocabulary (the key vocabulary words are contained in a handout). Jim has checked to make sure his slides are in the correct order and right side up. The slide-tape presentation begins and ends with a black slide. He cues the slides and tape before his students use them. The students use headphones to not distract others in the classroom.

Using Media: Overhead Transparencies

The overhead projector is one of the easiest devices to use. With a little practice, anyone—including your students—can make a professional presentation using overhead transparencies.

Ms. Jacobs used overhead transparencies to illustrate different types of freight cars, and to orally quiz her students on the types of cars and their uses.

Utilization Guidelines: Overhead Transparencies

▶ Focus the image so it fills the screen.

▶ Place notes (key words) on the frame of the transparency.

▶ Direct viewers' attention to important parts of the transparency.

▶ Shift viewers' attention back to your presentation by switching off the projector.

Overhead Transparencies Example

The chalkboard and overhead projector make a good team for teaching problem solving in Dianna Williams's physics class. After she demonstrates how to solve acceleration problems, Dianna projects similar problems with the overhead projector. Prior to class time she had prepared the problems on transparencies, using an 18-point font so all students would be able to see and read the problems. The screen is in the front corner of the room so it won't block the chalkboard. She randomly selects several students to do a problem on the chalkboard, telling them to print large enough so that everyone in the room can see their work. The other students work on the same problem at their desks. When all students are finished, Dianna leads a discussion on the various ways to approach the problem. Students indicate errors they find in the methods and the calculations of each other's problems.

Using Media: Display Boards

In the classroom, the most widely used (and misused) tool is the chalkboard. Although chalkboards have been replaced by dustless multipurpose boards in some classrooms, the same simple techniques can increase the effectiveness of both.

Jennifer Jacobs used a bulletin board to generate interest (motivation) in her lesson on railroads. Later in the lesson she used the chalkboard to list the advantages and disadvantages of two types of locomotives. As a concluding activity she displayed students' drawings around the classroom.

Utilization Guidelines: Display Boards

▶ Check the visibility of the board from several positions around the room.

▶ Decide in advance how you plan to use the board.

▶ Print using upper- and lowercase, not all caps or in script.

▶ Face your audience, do not talk to the board with your back to the class.

Display Boards Examples

Three of Carl Shedd's fifth-grade students print an outline on the chalkboard for their class presentation on the characteristics of gorillas. After describing each characteristic one student puts a check mark at the appropriate place on the outline so the students in the class can easily follow the presentation.

Bonnie Johnson uses a marker board and a variety of colored markers to diagram the relationships among the various components of several computer software applications. She leaves these diagrams on

Chalkboards or markerboards are available in most classrooms.

the marker board during class so students can refer to them. She also puts key commands on the board for her students' easy reference.

Your Investigation

Again, your task is to review the scenario and suggest ways to improve or change the teacher's use of methods and media, and determine how to improve both the lesson and the resulting student learning. Record your answers to the following questions and then compare them with ours on page 161.

1. What display materials did Ms. Jacobs use?
2. How were they used?
3. How and why were slides and filmstrips used?
4. How and why were real objects and models used?
5. How and why were overhead transparencies used?
6. How were graphics used?

As we wrap up our discussion of the lesson on railroads, let's review what methods and media were used. We saw presentation, demonstration, and discussion as the key methods. The media we saw were graphics (including slides, filmstrips, and overhead transparencies) and display boards (including the chalkboard and bulletin boards). What methods or media did you notice that we didn't mention?

INTEGRATING METHODS AND MEDIA

At this point we would like to reemphasize the complexity of learning. As we stated in the initial chapters, learning is not easily identified, mea-

sured, or produced. Because of the variations one encounters with different individual learners, with different settings, and with different types of content, it is important to realize that implementing any one instructional method doesn't exclude other methods. That is, choosing one method doesn't mean that another method may not be equally effective, and it also doesn't mean that you cannot combine the methods. Some of the most powerful instruction is that which accounts for the various needs of learners and incorporates a number of methods within the same materials. For example, imagine placing students within cooperative learning groups with the task of researching and collecting data on a specific problem (i.e., combining cooperative groups and problem solving). Then expand this experience by having the different groups discuss and/or debate their findings with other groups that have carried out their own investigations. In another situation, you might expand your presentation to a large group by demonstrating a specific procedure and then dividing students into smaller groups to play a game that requires use of the new concepts and procedures introduced during your presentation and demonstration. Again, combining the methods can lead to a more powerful learning experience for students.

Just as you can use different methods in combination, so can you use different media simultaneously. The best example in the scenarios was the *Rainforest Researchers* multimedia package Lauren

TABLE 7–2   *Examples of Combining Instructional Methods and Media*

Method	Example of combining media with method
Presentation	▶ Audiotape of John F. Kennedy's inaugural address for a high school history course
	▶ Taped video presentation on the topic of weightlessness given by shuttle astronauts while on a shuttle mission
Demonstration	▶ Video of steps involved in making a model rocket
	▶ Slides of finished products that show the end result of a woodcarving demonstration
	▶ Use of a cadaver to demonstrate how leg muscles are attached to bone
Discussion	▶ Review of a television documentary on the problems created by illegal immigration, followed by a debate on the issues involved
	▶ Use of a visual depicting an abused child to stimulate buzz group discussions on ways to eliminate child abuse
Cooperative learning	▶ Small-group development and demonstration of a series of drawings showing how balloons are manufactured
	▶ Use of overhead transparencies to present results of a group research project involving how to feed and care for exotic zoo animals
Discovery	▶ Use of an interactive video multimedia program investigating all aspects of the *Titanic*— its voyage, crew, and passengers
	▶ Dissection of a sheep brain to locate and identify the different lobes and fissures
Problem solving	▶ Use of a software package to present logic problems and then provide specialized feedback as each section is attempted
	▶ Display of math story problems and possible solution techniques on a classroom bulletin board
Instructional games	▶ Use of audiotaped instructions on how to play a game involving the rescue of members of a disabled space station
	▶ Use of a computer game that tracks a criminal across several countries and cultures of the world

Henry used. Students can use text while learning about real objects. They can create drawings (graphics) to illustrate new ideas learned from a videotape. Students can produce audiotapes in their own words to summarize their learning from a reading. A similar example is an oral book report.

Just as it is important to combine different instructional methods and to combine different media, it is also important to consider how you might combine media with the various instructional methods. Across the different methods, one or more different media may be needed. Table 7–2 lists the methods discussed in this chapter and gives examples of how to incorporate media with each. Refer back to Table 5–4 in Chapter 5 for common method and media combinations. Next refer back to each of the scenarios and identify which methods and media combinations were used. Under the right circumstances, you can use *any* method with *any* media!

APPLICATIONS IN THE LEARNER-CENTERED CLASSROOM

Another key principle to consider within the learner-centered classroom is *the relationship among practice, confidence, and motivation.* As we explain in this chapter, each different instructional medium and method represents a different means by which learners can go through an experience. If the learning experience is well designed and practiced, students' learning can be measurable and reliable. However, problems occur when preparation is not completed, questions go unanswered, media create a distraction instead of insight, and confusion, frustration, and discouragement develop.

Learners need to experience in order to learn. Likewise, one of the important things that they need to experience is the direct and indirect results of preparation. Opportunities to prepare within the classroom, to use new hardware technologies, to practice for presentations, and so on allow learners to also experience the confidence that comes with such preparation. As students' confidence increases, their level of motivation also increases.

ONE TEACHER'S STORY
by Janette Moreno

There is something about gaining confidence in one's own ability that I know is important for me and I know my students also find important, whether it is confidently carrying on a conversation in Spanish, presenting a discussion topic in a small-group setting, or demonstrating a procedure using new computer hardware and software. Every time I approach the task, something I have practiced and feel comfortable with, I know that my motivation for doing that task increases. I think that this is also true for my students. So whenever I get the chance I have them practice and practice, until their confidence is built up so they know that they can succeed. Sometimes this takes the form of working on a drill and practice vocabulary development software program. At other times students may role play with one another to develop conversational skills. In still other situations, practice means working on the computer hardware that we use in class so a presentation can be carried off flawlessly. In each case, as the students' confidence level has increased, so has their motivation for learning.

In my class, students often give oral presentations. For part of the presentation, some students have begun incorporating videotapes of themselves and others conducting panel discussions, interviews, completing demonstrations, or even trying to introduce certain problems that the class must try to solve. This allows them to work on their Spanish, go over it enough times to make it almost perfect, and then to use it in class to illustrate some critical part of their speech. For the most part, it really builds their confidence in their presentation skills. I remember one instance, however, in which one student forgot to preview the tape that he used in his presentation. He had accidentally picked up his sister's audition tape for an upcoming musical at Civic Theatre. He was all excited to show us what his group had done to demonstrate the concepts we were discussing, instead we got his sister singing a verse of "My Country 'Tis of Thee." He was embarrassed, and the rest of us had a good laugh. I know that his experience really reinforced the idea of preparation for everyone.

SUMMARY

Preparation plays a key role in the learning process. Preparation of yourself, your materials, the environment, and the students can all affect the effective-

ness of your instruction. Additionally, this preparation is important not only for traditional teacher-dependent instruction (e.g., lectures or demonstrations) but also for those methods and media used in the learner-centered classroom.

There are a number of ways in which you may implement different media formats within the instructional setting; however, general principles for the correct utilization of all media do exist. These include (1) becoming familiar and comfortable with the media format (e.g., previewing the materials, making sure you understand how to run the necessary machines); (2) making sure all in the audience can see and hear; and (3) emphasizing the relevance of the media and, (4) most importantly, highlighting what students should expect to gain from their experience.

We discussed specific and general utilization principles for all of the different media formats. We then provided examples to illustrate how the principles could be put into practice and what problems may be encountered during utilization.

REFLECTIVE ACTIVITIES

▶ Reflect on a classroom experience you were involved in planning and implementing. How did you prepare yourself, your materials, your environment, and your students for the experience? If you were to do it again, would you modify your preparation in any way? Why or why not?

▶ Consider some of your own experiences with different types and qualities of presentations. First, recall a specific presentation that was a positive learning experience, and then think of one that wasn't. Compare the two and try to identify basic differences in the manner in which they were presented. What helped you learn from one presentation; what impeded learning from the other? Was one easier to follow, to attend to, or to comprehend?

▶ Imagine you are a media specialist for Franklin Middle School. One of the eighth-grade students at the school, Joey Miller, has come to you and asked for help on an assignment that includes giving a seven-minute oral presentation on a famous person or event of the twentieth century. Joey has selected the 1969 moon landing as his subject matter. He has asked for your ideas on how he can combine different forms of media within his oral report to enhance his presentation. What would you suggest?

▶ Prepare and deliver a presentation or demonstration that involves the use of media and have it videotaped (or videotape someone else's presentation). With a group of two or three individuals, review the video and discuss the following:

   a. What did you gain or learn from this presentation or demonstration?

   b. How did the media enhance or detract from the presentation?

   c. Was the media effectively utilized? Could it have been improved? In what ways?

   d. What additional media could have been used to facilitate learning?

   e. Could another medium have done the job better?

SUGGESTED RESOURCES

Ausubel, D. (1968). *Educational Psychology.* New York: Holt, Rinehart, & Winston.

Heinich, R., Molenda, M., Russell, J. D., & Smaldino, S. (1999). *Instructional media and technologies for learning* (6th ed.). Upper Saddle River, NJ: Merrill/Prentice Hall.

Satterthwaite, L. (1990). *Instructional media.* Dubuque, IA: Kendall/Hunt.

Teague, F. A., Roger, D. W., & Tipling, R. N. (1994). *Technology and media: Instructional applications.* Dubuque, IA: Kendall/Hunt.

Volker, R., & Simonson, M. (1995). *Technology for teachers.* Dubuque, IA: Kendall/Hunt.

ANSWERS TO CHAPTER QUESTIONS

Rainforest Researchers

1. CD-ROM, videotape, text
2. To introduce the unit, to show the planned trip, to describe the problem, to illustrate the testing processes
3. To describe the scientists' roles, to provide background information, to question
4. To select leaders for the teams, to record answers and data such as supplies and budget, to receive test results, to present random occurrences
5. Answers will vary
6. Answers will vary

Spanish Number Translations

1. Printed text, audiotape, videotape, real objects and models
2. To provide a tutorial
3. To demonstrate pronunciation, to provide practice
4. To show a market in Spain, to provide student practice, to record student activities
5. As merchandise in the classroom "market"
6. Answers will vary

Railroads in the United States

1. Bulletin board and chalkboard
2. Bulletin board to generate interest and to relate new topic to history, chalkboard to list advantages and limitations of various types of railroad equipment
3. Four minutes of audio filmstrip to introduce lesson, slides taken by teacher to show various types of passenger cars
4. To stimulate discussion, to review previous day's lesson
5. To show various examples of freight cars
6. Students drew and colored pictures as a summary activity and pictures were put on bulletin board

CHAPTER 8

Using Computers

KEY WORDS AND CONCEPTS

One-computer classroom
Logo
Programming language
Hypermedia
Event driven

OBJECTIVES

After reading and studying this chapter, you will be able to

▶ Describe the characteristics and give at least one example of each of the common categories of computer-assisted instruction.
▶ Discuss a rationale for having students learn through programming or by developing their own hypermedia materials.
▶ Discuss ways that students can learn by using the computer as a teacher, as an assistant, and as a "learner."

PLANNING FOR THE CHAPTER CONTENT

Instructional Technology for Teaching and Learning, will show you how to increase learning by designing lessons that use instructional technology, including computers and other media.

In Chapter 7, we presented the basics of using various methods and media in the classroom. In this chapter, we focus specifically on the computer and how you can use it in the classroom to promote student learning. Recall that in introducing the computer and its uses in education in Chapter 3, we briefly explained three ways of using it: as a teacher, as an assistant, and as a learner. We revisit and expand that classification scheme in this chapter with a special focus on using the computer to promote student learning. In Chapter 9, we look specifically at the Internet and ways that you can use it in the classroom.

INTRODUCTION

Have you ever played chess? If you have (and probably even if you have not), you know that it is a game of strategy in which players maneuver their playing pieces against those of an opponent (Figure 8–1). The goal of the game is to checkmate the opposing player's king. This goal can be accomplished in millions of different ways.

Each of the playing pieces in chess has its own characteristic ways of moving and hence strengths in different situations. Bishops, for example, move along diagonals and can exert an influence far across the board. Rooks can also exert influence from far away, but move straight along rows or columns only. Knights move in an L-shaped pattern that allows them to slip into spots that other pieces cannot. Good players understand the different strengths of each piece, from the lowly pawn to the powerful queen, and as a result they are able to successfully use these pieces to achieve the goal of the game.

FIGURE 8–1 Instructional technology tools, similar to chess pieces, have different strengths.

What does the game of chess have to do with using computers in education? Education, of course, is about learning, not about beating an opponent. But, when using computers in the classroom, as when playing chess, there is more than one way to achieve your learning goal. In chess, players must understand each piece's strength to find ways to checkmate their opponent's king. In the classroom, as we pointed out in Chapter 3, there are multiple ways to use computers and related technologies. To teach with them effectively, you must understand the strengths of different computer applications so that you can use them to achieve your ultimate goal in the classroom—enhancing student learning.

In Chapter 3, we introduced you to Taylor's (1980) simple but useful categorization scheme for educational applications of computers: computer as teacher, computer as assistant, and computer as learner. In the first category, the computer presents instruction to the learner much as a teacher or tutor might. In the second category, the computer assists the learner in performing routine tasks such as writing, calculating, or presenting information. In the final category, the computer functions like a learner as the student tries to determine how to make it do something. Like chess pieces, each way of using computers in education has its strengths that make it suitable for different classroom learning situations. In this chapter, we revisit this organizational scheme to help you better understand how to use computers to promote student learning.

COMPUTER AS TEACHER

The oldest use of the computer in education, dating back to the early 1960s, is as a tool that presents instruction directly to students. As we indicated in Chapter 3, such use is usually termed *computer-assisted instruction (CAI), computer-based instruction (CBI),* or *computer-assisted learning (CAL).* In this mode, the computer can present instruction, provide instructional activities or situations, quiz or otherwise require interaction from learners, evaluate learner responses, provide feedback, and determine appropriate followup activities.

The chief advantage of the computer is its interactivity. Whereas a printed worksheet may leave space for a student's answer or an instructional video may pose a question for the viewer, there is no guarantee that the student will in fact respond. The computer can require a response; it can demand the learner's active involvement. When used as a teaching machine, the computer can be highly interactive, individualized, engaging, and infinitely patient. Research analyses of studies comparing computer-assisted instruction with traditional methods suggest that it produces slightly superior achievement, usually requires less time, and may produce improved attitudes toward computers and sometimes toward the subject matter itself (Kulik & Kulik, 1991; Niemiec & Walberg, 1987). The positive effects are somewhat greater in the lower grades.

CAI has a long history of use, and it remains a popular option in classrooms today. Consider the scenario that follows. As you read, identify how Ms. Stanley uses the computer as a teacher.

Scenario: States and Capitals

Sue Stanley is a fifth-grade teacher at Riverside Elementary School. The school district's social studies curriculum guide calls for all students in the fifth grade to be able to name and correctly spell all of the 50 U.S. states and capitals from memory. To help her students meet this requirement, Ms. Stanley set up a series of activities stretching over several weeks.

At the beginning of the unit on U.S. geography, Ms. Stanley handed out a labeled U.S. map and a printed list of all fifty states and capitals to her students, and explained that each student would be responsible for learning the names and correct spellings of all 50 states and capitals. Realizing that this task can be daunting to fifth graders, she looked for ways to make it easier and to give her students plenty of opportunities for practice.

First, she broke up the task into more manageable pieces. She divided her class of twenty-four students into four groups of six students each. Students in each group were assigned the task of becoming class "experts" on the states and capitals from one of four geographical regions of the United States: the Northeast, the South, the Midwest, and the West. Each student was responsible for learning information about the states and capitals in his region. Ms. Stanley set up the two computers in her classroom as learning stations. One station had a CD-ROM almanac that students could use to research each state, its major points of interest, population, and so forth. The other had a drill and practice program that allowed individuals to quiz themselves over the states and capitals. As students worked, Ms. Stanley circulated throughout the classroom, helping those students who needed assistance.

After giving the students time to develop their expertise, Ms. Stanley set up a rotating system where a student from one group was paired with a student from another group. The students took turns peer tutoring and drilling each other over the states and capitals in their respective regions, and, through the rotation schedule, they were able to practice all 50 states and capitals by the end of the week. Each week, Ms. Stanley gave each student a worksheet on a subset of states and capitals to complete, and gave a quiz over the subset each Friday.

To help students with particular learning difficulties, Ms. Stanley worked closely with Ms. Epstein, the school's special education teacher. Some special practice activities were arranged and assignments were adjusted for students with special needs. She also talked to Ms. McHenry, the music teacher, who was able to help by using music time to teach the class a song that helped everyone learn the names of the fifty states.

Ms. Stanley also scheduled the computer lab several times during the unit. On computer lab days, students played the educational game, *Where in the USA is Carmen Sandiego?* In this game, students must use geographic clues about the United States to track a criminal who has stolen a national treasure. The first few lab days, Ms. Stanley had students work in pairs on the game. She found that students working in pairs more quickly grasped how the game worked and were able to get through any problems that arose. In later sessions, she had students work alone, so that she could get a sense of how well individual students were progressing.

After several weeks, most of the students became fairly proficient at writing the names of U.S. states and capitals from memory. Ms. Stanley was pleased with their progress, and gratified that her unit had been successful in meeting the district objective. As a culminating activity, the class put on a "United States Day." Each student took one of the states and prepared a short oral presentation about it. Ms. Hopper, the art teacher, helped them create illustrations for their presentations. Many drew maps of their state, but some did other projects; one student even made a papier mâché model of Mount Rushmore for her presentation about South Dakota. Parents were invited, and everyone made their presentations, then sang the song they had learned to end the program. The day was a big hit with the kids and their parents, and it was a great way to wrap up the unit.

What can this scenario tell us about using the computer as a teacher? We can note the following:

▶ *CAI is usually used in a supporting or adjunct role.* In this example, educational software was only one part of a broader strategy of classroom activities. Since the earliest uses of CAI, there has been an enduring myth that computers will become perfect teaching machines and one day replace human teachers. This has not happened, and does not seem likely anytime in the near future. Few computer programs approach the capabilities of a human tutor. We see little evidence to suggest that computers will ever replace teachers. CAI is merely one more tool at your disposal for helping students learn.

▶ *Certain types of CAI are appropriate for certain learning goals.* In this example, the specific learning goal of the school district was to have every student learn the 50 U.S. states and capitals. Sue Stanley wanted to make certain that each child had the opportunity to master this rote task. The CAI she used, a drill and practice program and an educational game, was appropriate to this learning goal. These programs were able to engage students' interest while providing opportunities for practice and repetition. Other forms of CAI may be appropriate to higher-level learning goals. (See the next subsection, "Categories of Computer-Assisted Instruction.")

▶ *CAI can help students and free time for the teacher.* Not only were students able to benefit from the software, but it gave the teacher the opportunity to address individual learners' needs. When the learning stations were operating, Ms. Stanley could help those students who needed the most help. Later, when all of the students were playing the game, she could take time to assess the progress of individual students.

In Chapter 5, we introduced you to various instructional methods including the two employed here: drill and practice and instructional game. Other common methods that are embodied in instructional software include tutorial, simulation, and problem solving. Keep in mind, also, that you can use the computer as a teacher in many other ways that do not neatly fit these categories, such as with demonstrations, content review or testing programs, dialogues, context-sensitive help systems, and others. It is important to recognize that categories are a useful place to begin discussions, but they should never be allowed to restrict your thinking about computer applications in education. There are many forms of CAI and many ways to view the role of the computer in education. As software and our knowledge of human learning evolve, we may invent new categories or change old ones to better reflect the reality in the classroom. We next look at the most common current categories of CAI,

FIGURE 8–2   A screen from *Stickybear Math Splash,* a popular drill and practice computer program *Source: Stickybear's Math Splash, Optimum Resources, Inc.*

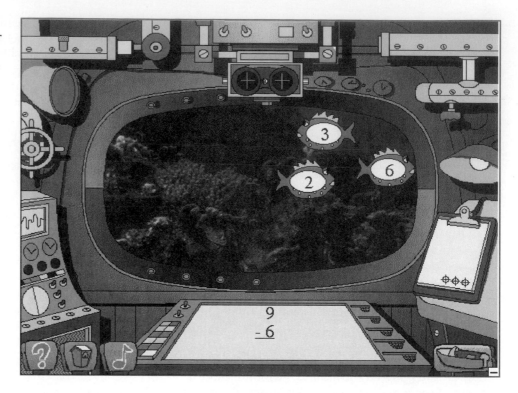

Categories of Computer-Assisted Instruction

Drill and Practice

As you learned in Chapter 5, a drill and practice application is designed to help learners master already introduced basic skills or knowledge through repetitive work. Compared with noncomputer drill and practice, the computer offers significant advantages:

▶ *Interactivity.* The computer can present many problems and require student responses.

▶ *Immediate feedback.* The computer can immediately inform the learner if an answer is right or wrong, and, in a well-designed program, tell the learner why. Many drill and practice programs automatically recycle missed items until they are mastered.

▶ *Infinite patience.* A computer drill and practice program can go all day without getting tired or irritable.

▶ *Variable level of difficulty.* The computer can adjust the level of difficulty. This might be set by the teacher or by the learner, or the program may adjust automatically based on the student's performance.

▶ *Motivation.* Through the use of challenge and gaming elements, or just because it is on the computer, a computer drill and practice program may be more motivating to students than similar paper-and-pencil exercises.

These characteristics make the computer an excellent tool for drill and practice applications and explain why they are among the most popular of all computer applications in education, especially in the elementary grades. In the previous scenario, Ms. Stanley used a drill and practice program on the states and capitals as a learning station in the classroom. Drill and practice programs tend to be used for basic information and skills in a variety of subject areas. They are most effective for rote learning or where automatic student responses are desired. *Stickybear Math Splash* and *Reader Rabbit* are examples of computer drill and practice programs (in the content areas of arithmetic computation and beginning reading skills, respectively) that are popular in the elementary school. *Reader Rabbit* helps students practice beginning word-recognition and word-construction skills. In *Stickybear Math Splash,* students are drilled on basic arithmetic facts (e.g., 3 + 1 = ?). As the student answers each question, the program provides reinforcement, and after accumulating a number of correct answers the student is able to help Stickybear (a cartoon bear) get out of some kind of jam. Figure 8–2 shows a sample screen from *Stickybear Math Splash.*

Students can usually gain some benefit from drill and practice programs even with relatively lit-

FIGURE 8–3   A screen from *Science Smart,* a popular tutorial program *Source: The Princeton Review "Science Smart".*

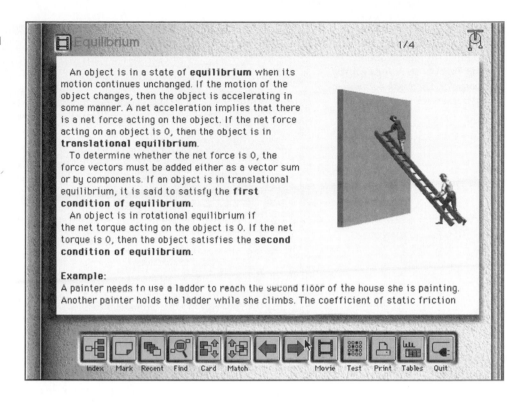

tle exposure per session. As a result, such programs are a popular option when computer hardware is scarce. A common strategy is to rotate individual students through the program so that each student is able to get 10 or 20 minutes of practice at a time. Over time, many short practice sessions can build skills. Refer to the utilization guidelines in Chapter 7 for more tips about using drill and practice and the other methods discussed in this chapter.

Tutorial

In a tutorial application, the computer assumes the primary instructional role of teacher or tutor. It presents new content and assesses learning. A tutorial typically contains an organized body of knowledge, one or more pathways through that knowledge, specific learning objectives, and built-in tests of student learning. Computer-based tutorials offer a number of advantages:

▶ *Embedded questions.* Like computer drills, tutorials on the computer have the advantage of being interactive. Students must take an active role by answering embedded questions. As with drills, immediate feedback is provided.

▶ *Branching.* Computer tutorials can automatically branch, that is, adjust content presentation order, according to the learner's responses to embedded questions. Remediation or advancement can be built in to meet the needs of individual learners.

▶ *Dynamic presentation.* The computer can present information dynamically, such as by highlighting important text on the screen to capture learners' attention, or by depicting processes using animated graphics. A multimedia computer system, may also employ audio and video.

▶ *Record keeping.* Computer tutorials can automatically maintain student records, which you can use to inform them of their progress. In addition, you can check the records to ensure students are progressing satisfactorily.

While a poorly designed tutorial may be little more than an electronic page-turner, a well-designed one can be a highly interactive and effective form of instruction that responds to the needs or wants of individual learners. They are often used to address verbal and conceptual learning. Tutorials are available for a range of subject matter and at all grade levels. *Science Smart* from The Princeton Review, is an example of a tutorial program designed to teach key science concepts in schools (Figure 8–3). Also, most popular computer productivity packages (e.g., Microsoft *Word,* a word processor) come with associated tutorials that provide instruction on how to use the package.

In many cases, computer tutorials are used in schools to supplement regular instruction rather than to replace it. Because tutorials often require a significant time commitment (a student may require

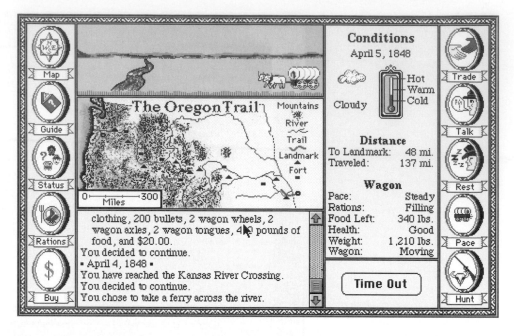

hours to complete an extensive one), it is difficult to use tutorials effectively with large numbers of students without access to a computer laboratory. Where computer hardware is limited, you may use computer tutorials with selected students for remediation, enrichment, or makeup work.

Simulation

A *simulation* is a representation or model of a real (or sometimes imaginary) system, situation, or phenomenon. In most cases, this representation is simplified to make learning easier. Simulations make excellent use of the computer's capabilities:

▶ *Control of multiple variables.* Computers can manage multiple variables simultaneously. As a result, they can realistically depict complex phenomena, such as the growth and change of a city or the physics of bodies in motion. Learners can manipulate these variables to observe their effects on the system being modeled.

▶ *Dynamic presentation.* As with tutorials, the computer's ability to dynamically present information is important in simulation. Simulated instrumentation can change like the real thing, and processes such as plant growth can be graphically depicted.

▶ *Time control.* The computer can contract or expand time to allow study of phenomena that are too slow (e.g., population growth) or too fast (e.g., chemical reaction) for normal classroom observation. The computer can also depict historical situations (e.g., a nineteenth-century wagon train).

▶ *Effects of chance.* Many simulations include an element of chance or randomness that makes them even more realistic, allowing students to interact with them differently on different occasions.

Simulations have found their greatest use in the natural and social sciences. There are many good examples of educational simulations, including *SimCity* (management of a growing city), *CatLab* (simulated cat breeding), *Decisions, Decisions* (social studies role-playing simulation series), and *The Oregon Trail* (travel by covered wagon). Most simulations are designed to promote application of information, thinking, and problem-solving skills. Most tend not to teach basic concepts. As a result, it is usually important for students to be well grounded in the underlying concepts of the simulation before use, and guidance is often needed during use. For example, *The Oregon Trail* simulates pioneers crossing the United States by covered wagon in the nineteenth century. Students must make decisions about the amount of food and ammunition to take at the start, and they must decide what to do when they encounter various problems and opportunities along the trail. But, to make the experience meaningful as an historical exercise, students may need background about the westward expansion, the factors that promoted it, and nineteenth-century life in general. Figure 8–4 shows a sample screen from *The Oregon Trail.*

Simulations vary in the degree to which they accurately depict what they are modeling. Educational simulations are simplified, and students should

FIGURE 8-5 A screen from *Where in the World is Carmen Sandiego?*, a popular educational computer game *Source: Where in the World is Carmen Sandiego?* ®, ©1999 The Learning Company, Inc.

be made aware of this. Simulations also vary in the time required for use. Simple simulations of some processes may require only a few minutes of student time; others may demand hours. So, you must plan accordingly. You may effectively use computer simulations with both individuals and small groups of students.

Instructional Game

Instructional games add an element of fun to CAI. In most cases, games are simply modified versions of other types of CAI, such as drill and practice or simulation, but are distinguished by having the following characteristics:

- *Motivation.* The chief advantage of computer games is the variety of motivational elements they may employ, including competition, cooperation, challenge, fantasy, recognition, and reward.
- *Game structure.* The game structure means that there are rules of play and an end goal.
- *Sensory appeal.* Games on the computer often appeal through the use of graphics, animation, sound, and other sensory enhancements.

Computer games, as noted, are usually modified forms of other types of CAI. A game may have begun as a drill and practice, problem-solving, or simulation program to which gaming elements were

added. One of the most popular CAI programs is the geography computer game, *Where in the World is Carmen Sandiego?* In this simulation game, a student assumes the role of a detective who must use geography clues to track a thief around the world. In this role, the student experiences an element of fantasy. There is challenge in that the player must locate the thief within a set amount of time by using clues embedded in the game. Students may compete against one another for the best times, or cooperate with one another to help catch the villain. All of these elements make the program a terrific game. It has proven so popular that it has spawned a series of other similar games (including *Where in the USA is Carmen Sandiego?* mentioned in the previous scenario), a line of merchandise, and a television series. Figure 8-5 shows a sample screen from *Where in the World is Carmen Sandiego?*

Computer games vary in their time requirements. Some may require only a few minutes. More complex games may extend over hours or even days. Probably the biggest concern about educational computer games is that the education should not take a backseat to the game. You must take care to carefully integrate these games into your curriculum.

Problem Solving

Some CAI applications are designed to foster students' problem-solving skills but don't fit into any of the previous categories. Computer problem-solving applications have certain advantages:

▸ *Focus on specific problem types.* Specific problem-solving programs often focus on specific skills (e.g., spatial ability, logic).
▸ *Quantity.* The computer can provide students with practice over a large number of problems in a short period of time, requiring interaction and providing feedback as in other forms of CAI.
▸ *Variety.* The computer is capable of presenting a variety of problems. This helps students to generalize their problem-solving skills.

Problem-solving applications are designed to promote students' higher-order thinking skills, such as logic, reasoning, pattern recognition, and strategies. Problem-solving software often helps students by providing concrete representations of abstractions. Examples of problem solving programs include *The King's Rule* (mathematical patterns), *The Factory Deluxe* (spatial orientation, strategies, and reasoning), and *Geometric Supposer* (geometry). Some teachers use this software to enhance students' problem-solving skills for their own sake. Others link it to relevant curricular areas such as mathematics.

Most problem-solving programs, like drill and practice, require relatively short stretches of time for use. As a result, programs can often be used by individuals or small groups of students in rotation when computer hardware is limited.

Integrated Learning Systems

Integrated learning systems (ILSs) are the most complex and sophisticated computer systems that function as a teacher. They combine comprehensive computer-assisted instruction (CAI), any or all of the categories mentioned previously, and computer management features into a single networked computer delivery system. They are designed to provide a cycle of instruction, assessment, and prescription for a particular subject matter—all on the computer.

ILSs are usually supplied by a single vendor that provides all of the hardware and software. The leading ILS producers today are Jostens Learning Corporation, Computer Curriculum Corporation, and Wasatch Educational Systems. While ILSs are expensive, they provide a lot for the money. The hardware consists of a local area network (LAN) of computers linked to a large file server that contains all of the software. The software includes a fully articulated curriculum in a particular subject area, such as mathematics or language arts, as well as software that tracks students and manages their progress.

Students in schools that have ILSs typically use the system regularly, from daily to once or twice per week. The computer delivers instruction, most often tutorials and drill and practice exercises, and tests students. Instruction, testing, and test scoring are all managed by the system. Because the curriculum is well integrated and spans a number of grade levels, students may work on the ILS over a period of years and progress at their own rate. Teachers like the fact that the instruction is individualized. In addition, because the computer handles both the instruction and the assessment, the teacher is freed to provide individualized assistance, plan ancillary learning activities, and guide the learning process. Administrators like ILSs because they provide detailed information about the levels of mastery of the student body. A study by the Educational Products Information Exchange (1990) found a high level of satisfaction among adopters of ILSs, and Becker (1992) reports that students tend to do somewhat better in ILS programs than with competing approaches. However, some teachers and schools believe that ILSs are too focused on basic skills, and there is concern that the ILS curriculum may drive the school's curriculum rather than the reverse. So, the ILS approach is not right for everyone.

Problems and Pitfalls

We have emphasized the many advantages of using the computer as teacher, and rightly so. CAI has much to offer. However, there are concerns that we must consider, as well. Critics charge that CAI is a low-level use of the computer that simply puts a new face on old busywork and that is not consistent with a view of learning as knowledge construction. In some cases this charge is surely justified. Some drill and practice programs are little more than electronic worksheets. Some tutorials are mere electronic page-turners. There is a tendency for the first uses of a new technology to be simply re-creations of older forms. For example, many early films and television programs were just stage plays performed in front of a camera; it took a while for these media to develop their own unique forms. In similar fashion, many early CAI programs were simply adaptations of older instructional forms such as paper-and-pencil worksheets. But that is changing. Newer software releases tend to make better use of the computer. However, it remains your responsibility to see that CAI is used productively in the classroom to help students learn and not simply as busywork.

Classroom management is also an important consideration in the use of CAI. Effective use often

TOOLBOX

TIPS

One-Computer Classroom

Classrooms with a single computer are common in schools across the country. In fact, despite the fact that millions of computers are now installed in U.S. schools, the **one-computer classroom** remains a fixture of the educational landscape. What can be done with a single computer in the classroom? The answer is, a lot!

All of the methods of using computers in the classroom discussed in this chapter can apply to the one-computer classroom. Students can work on computer-assisted instruction, either individually or in small groups. The computer can be used as a productivity tool, for example, to graph data from a science experiment or make an in-class multimedia presentation. One computer can even be used, with appropriate management, for "computer-as-learner" activities.

One simple but useful approach to utilizing limited hardware is to provide individual students access in rotation. This model is especially popular at the elementary level, where the computer is often established as one of a number of learning centers through which students rotate. For example, primary-age learners working on basic arithmetic skills might rotate through several related learning stations featuring concrete manipulatives, traditional flash cards, and a computer drill and practice game. While time on the computer is necessarily limited in this approach, it does give an entire class at least some access. You, the teacher, must effectively manage students' access to the computer to avoid conflicts and to keep those students who are not working on the computer productively engaged in other activities. Sign-up sheets, schedules, fixed time intervals, and other similar techniques can help with the management challenge.

Students can also use the computer in small groups. Research suggests that for many types of computer-assisted instruction there are benefits to having small groups as opposed to individuals work on CAI programs (Johnson, Johnson, & Stanne, 1985). Cooperating students can learn from and help one another, where a single student might become confused or stuck. Small groups can also use the computer to do such things as create presentations or develop hypermedia projects. Even whole-class use of a single computer is possible. Using an appropriate large-group display (see "Toolbox Tools: Presentation Hardware," later in this chapter), you might lead a whole class through a session with a program such as *The Oregon Trail,* calling on different students to make decisions along the trail. Some CAI programs are even designed to support whole-class use with a single computer. A notable example is Tom Snyder Productions's *Decisions Decisions* software line. The activities in these role-playing simulations are orchestrated by a single computer.

Finally, although the emphasis in this chapter is on students' learning, one should not overlook the single classroom computer as a tool for you, the teacher. Word processing is a great tool for producing printed material. With a single computer equipped with word processing software and attached to a printer, you can produce printed instructional materials you can then copy for the whole class to use. Many textbooks today come with computerized question banks; you can make copies of selected questions to help guide review activities. You may use a database to keep student records, a spreadsheet to maintain student grades, and so on. As some experts have argued, if you only have one computer in a classroom, the most useful place for it is on your own desk!

---

requires special classroom management strategies. If you have only one or perhaps two computers in the classroom, you must devise mechanisms to ensure that each student gets access (see "Toolbox Tips: One-Computer Classroom"). If a computer laboratory is available, you must plan computer activities well in advance in consultation with the school's technology or media coordinator. Laboratory settings, too, have the potential to become chaotic as many students forge off in their own directions. You often will need careful planning and structured activities to provide the direction required to keep students productively on task.

Reflective Questions

▶ Critics argue that CAI is a low-level use of the computer that should be discouraged. Do you agree? Why or why not?

▶ What examples can you identify of ways to use CAI software in the classroom in addition to those mentioned in this section?

COMPUTER AS ASSISTANT

In the role of assistant, the computer aids the learner in performing routine work tasks. In Chapter 3, we stated that important computer applications that fall into this category include word processors, graphics packages, presentation software, databases, spreadsheets, and telecommunication/Internet tools. Both teachers and students can use these programs in a variety of ways.

In this chapter, we focus on the use of computer productivity tools that can assist the learner. This use of computers in the classroom is one of the most important, and it is one of the most common as well. In many ways, this is only natural. When computers are used in the workplace, they are most often used as a tool to assist the worker. Secretaries prepare documents using word processors, businesspeople store customer records in databases, accountants use spreadsheets to calculate, graphic artists use drawing programs, and so on. So, it makes sense that students should learn to use computers in schools in the same ways that they are used in the workplace.

In this section, we will revisit the popular computer applications that we introduced in Chapter 3. To begin, read the following scenario, looking for examples where students use the computer as an assistant.

Scenario: Stock Market Game

Bob Goins is an economics and social studies teacher at George Washington Carver High School. For the past several years, he has used a popular unit as part of his economics class. In this unit, students "play" the stock market by creating and tracking a portfolio of investments. Bob uses the unit as a synthesizing activity in which students learn and apply information about investing, the market, and financial tracking. Here's how it went last year.

To ensure that his students were adequately prepared, Mr. Goins waited until the start of the second semester of his economics class to begin the game. Once started, however, the activity spanned the entire semester. At the beginning of the unit, the class was divided into teams of three or four students each. Each team was given an initial investment of $100,000 of play money. Teams were allowed to invest in the stock market in any way that they wanted, and they could change their investments during the game by buying or selling stocks (taking sales commissions into account). Each teams' goal was to have their initial investment grow as much as possible by the end of the game. The teams competed against one another to achieve the best overall performance, and Mr. Goins added an extra incentive by offering to treat the winning team to pizza at the end of the semester.

Before the teams actually made their first investments, Mr. Goins set aside two weeks for research. During this period, each team investigated stocks that it might want to purchase. Using computers available in the Business Department's lab, students used the Internet to do online research of various companies and mutual funds. Mr. Goins provided the class with the URLs of online brokerage houses and other sources of investment information on the Web. When teams identified promising investments, they requested more information online or used the lab's word processor to compose a letter requesting more information. Mr. Goins also invited a local stockbroker in to talk to the students about investing and to provide some tips about possible investment selections. At the end of the two-week research period, each team made its mock purchases, and the game was underway!

To keep track of their investments, Mr. Goins had each team maintain an investment spreadsheet. To help the students learn to use the software, Mr. Goins briefly demonstrated it during class, and provided a handout that covered the basics. But, he let the students figure out the details, and they seemed to do just fine. Mr. Goins required the students to design the team spreadsheet so that it listed each individual investment and calculated the total value of the portfolio. He required that each team update its spreadsheet weekly, though most teams were so engaged in the game that they checked their stocks daily. Each team created a graph from the spreadsheet to show the overall performance from the beginning of the game to the current week. These graphs were posted on the classroom bulletin board every Monday, so all of the teams knew where they stood. A few of the teams went further and used their spreadsheets to do projections—calculating what would happen if market conditions changed in certain ways. They used their projections to decide whether to buy or sell certain stocks.

As a final activity at the end of the semester, each team prepared a presentation to summarize their investments, the strategies they used during the game, and their results. The students developed their presentations in the computer lab using *PowerPoint* software (Figure 8–6). With the presentation software, the students were able to import graphs and data from their spreadsheet. Finally, each team presented its report using the classroom computer and a portable LCD projector that Mr. Goins checked out from Mr. Habib, the technology coordinator. The unit went well, it was a favorite of the students, and Mr. Goins expects that it will be a part of the curriculum in his economics class for many years to come.

What can we learn about the use of the computer as an assistant from this scenario? Consider the following points:

FIGURE 8–6   Students using computers as productivity tools

▶ *Content comes first.* When the computer is used as an assistant, the computer and its software play a secondary role to the subject matter itself. In this example, the goal of the activity was for students to learn economics. The computer simply helped them achieve this goal.

▶ *The computer as assistant offers benefits over traditional tools.* The students in this example were able to easily create a graph of their investment history each week because they had the data in a spreadsheet. They could have done this by hand, but the computer made the job much quicker and easier, and the computer-generated graph was neater and more accurate than one created by hand. However, it is important to point out that initial time and effort is needed, often *more* than is required with conventional tools. The students had to create the spreadsheet before they could realize the advantages it provided.

▶ *The computer as assistant can help students achieve various learning goals.* While some applications are relatively basic (e.g., totaling the value of the stock portfolio), others can foster more high-level learning (e.g., using a spreadsheet to do projections based on market changes, communicating information to an audience). See the discussion in the next subsection for ways to use the various computer tools.

▶ *Extensive software instruction is not necessarily required.* Some teachers are reluctant to have students use the computer as an assistant unless the students (and the teacher too) have extensive knowledge of the software. But, as with Mr. Goins in the scenario, many teachers find that students are able to function adequately when they have just the basics, whether from prior exposure (e.g., a computer application class) or, as in this example, from instruction such as a handout or in-class demonstration. Students tend to learn computer applications rapidly, and can often learn what they need to know while using them.

In Chapter 3, we introduced you to a number of the most popular computer productivity tools. Refer to the information there for their features and advantages. Here, we examine these tools—word processors, graphics tools, presentation software, databases, and spreadsheets—to see how students can use them as assistants. We consider the Internet in Chapter 9.

Common Computer Assistant Tools

Word Processors

As we indicated in Chapter 3, word processors take much of the drudgery out of creating and editing written work. As a result, they are useful for a variety of student learning activities that involve literacy. Students can use word processors to do the following:

> *Write papers, stories, poems, and other in-class work.* The major emphasis today is on the process of writing. With almost any written work, students can use the word processor to practice creating a draft, editing the work, and producing a new draft. The ease with which they can do this encourages students to write more and do more revising.
>
> *Write letters.* In the stock market game, students wrote letters to obtain information during their initial research. This is one way to encourage students to reach out beyond the classroom. Many teachers have students write to other students through pen-pal projects. Writing to another student seems to provide an extra motivation for students to do their best.
>
> *Do writing-related activities.* The word processor can be useful for any type of writing-related activity. Students can use it singly or in groups to take notes, to record an experiment's or project's progress, or to collect ideas from a brainstorming session.
>
> *Do individual language arts exercises.* Students can use the word processor, for example, to type spelling words, science vocabulary words, or other language exercises as a way of practicing these skills.
>
> *Type handwritten notes as a way to study.* By typing their own handwritten notes on a word processor, students can reinforce learning or study for an exam.

Research on the effectiveness of word processors in writing instruction, while not unequivocal, suggests that they can be beneficial if used appropriately. In a statistical review of 32 studies, Bangert-Drowns (1993) concluded that using word processors in writing instruction results on average in both longer documents and better-quality writing. However, much of the research is mixed, and you should not assume that any use of word processors in a classroom automatically results in better student performance. The effects of word processors in instruction derive from the teacher's methods and the classroom organization (Cochran-Smith, 1991). As a result, it is important to integrate word processors into a well-conceived process approach to writing, provide students with adequate opportunity to learn to use the software, and take into account the particular classroom environment where the word processors are used.

Graphics and Desktop Publishing Tools

Graphics tools provide students with the capability to work with images of all types (e.g., photographs, clip art, charts, graphs), and desktop publishing software gives them control over the layout of text and graphics on a printed page to produce professional-looking printed material. See Chapter 3 for basic information about these tools. Students can learn by using these tools for the following:

> *Creative drawing.* Students can use drawing or painting programs to produce original artwork.
>
> *Illustration of work.* Students can use drawing or painting programs and clip art to illustrate written stories, reports, or hypermedia projects.
>
> *Charting or graphing.* As in the stock market game scenario, students can chart or graph data. This is especially applicable in data-rich subjects such as mathematics, science, and economics.
>
> *Production of school newspaper and yearbook.* Desktop publishing software now is widely used in the production of school publications.

While graphics tools reduce the effort it takes for students to produce visual materials, they still rely on users' abilities to effectively communicate ideas. You need to help your students find the best ways to visually present information. Refer to "Toolbox Tips: Guidelines for Designing Graphics" in Chapter 6 for tips about good visual design.

Presentation Software

As we pointed out in Chapter 3, presentation software is designed for the production and display of computer text and images, usually for presentation to a group. Appropriate presentation hardware is needed for group display; see "Toolbox Tools: Presentation Hardware" for more information. While presentation applications are often seen as tools for the teacher to enhance lectures and other presentations, students can use them as well. These packages are in general quite similar to hypermedia authoring tools, discussed later in this chapter. Students can use presentation software to do the following:

> *Make in-class presentations or reports.* Presentation packages make it easy for students to create professional-looking electronic reports complete with multimedia elements.
>
> *Store and display electronic portfolios.* Because presentation packages are capable of handling multimedia elements, students can use them to assemble a portfolio of work including text, graphics, and even digital audio and video.
>
> *Transfer work to other media.* Many presentation packages provide a simple

mechanism for converting electronic slides to print, photographic slides, or Web pages. As a result, they can be used as authoring tools.

Presentation software, because of its multimedia capability, shares usage characteristics with graphics software as well as hypermedia authoring software. For all of these programs, it is important that students avoid becoming caught in the trap of form over substance. You must emphasize to your students that *what* they are presenting is as or more important than *how* they are presenting it. You and your students also need to be aware of copyright regulations to avoid making improper use of copyrighted material in presentations or other multimedia products. See the information on copyright in chapter 6 for more information.

Databases

As you have already learned, computer database software provides the capability for creating, editing, and manipulating organized collections of information. Students can use databases and database management software to do the following:

▶ *Locate information in prepared databases.* Given the widespread use of computer databases today, at a minimum, students should be able to use database software to find information (e.g., locate a book in the school library's electronic card catalog or find the name of the nineteenth president in a database of U.S. presidents). As students progress, they should learn to apply the Boolean (logical) operators AND and OR to narrow or expand searches, respectively.

▶ *Develop problem-solving and higher-order thinking skills.* Databases make excellent tools for the development of problem-solving and higher-order thinking skills. Using a database of U.S. presidents, for example, students might explore questions such as: "How does war impact presidential elections?" or "Is there a relationship between the rate of increase in federal spending and the political party of the president?"

▶ *Develop original databases.* Students can learn a great deal about research, information organization, and a particular content area by developing their own databases. For example, as a social studies class project, students might develop a database of historical sites within their community.

Research into the use of databases in the classroom suggests that students can acquire information from databases and can learn from them but that they often need assistance to do so effectively (Collis, 1990; Ehrman, Glenn, Johnson, & White, 1992; Maor & Taylor, 1995). Just because students have access to databases does not ensure that they will learn. Students often exhibit poor inquiry skills. They may have difficulty formulating appropriate questions and corresponding searches, and they have difficulty interpreting results. You should help students understand the structure and organization of the database, and guide them through the process of using it.

Spreadsheets

Spreadsheets, as we noted in Chapter 3, are tools for calculating. In many cases, they include enhancements such as database elements and the capability to graphically depict data. Students can use these versatile tools to do the following:

▶ *Track financial information.* Spreadsheets first became popular tools for helping businesses track finances. Students, likewise, can use them for tracking financial information ranging from personal budgets to the finances of student clubs and organizations to class projects such as the stock market game in the previous scenario.

▶ *Keep records.* Although primarily calculating tools, spreadsheets can be used for simple record keeping, such as maintaining lists of information you may need to quickly sort or otherwise manipulate.

▶ *Create charts and graphs.* In addition to the previously mentioned graphing software, spreadsheets are excellent tools for quickly producing a chart or graph from data. In the stock market game scenario, students graphed their investment data using a spreadsheet.

▶ *Perform complex calculations.* Spreadsheets can quickly produce results involving complex calculations. For example, students in an economics or business class might generate loan amortization tables, while students in a trigonometry class could calculate trigonometric functions of various triangles.

▶ *Perform "what-if?" simulation or hypothesis-testing activities.* Because of their rapid recalculation, spreadsheets are well suited to having students investigate how changes in one factor impact other factors—"What will happen if I change . . ." Using a spreadsheet, students in a high school business class, for example, might examine the effects of changing insurance rates on the cost of owning and operating a car. Students in a biology class could explore the effects of changing birth and death rates on the growth of populations. Students in a geometry

TOOLBOX

TOOLS

Presentation Hardware

To make the computer's display visible to a group, you must choose one of several hardware options. The most common choices include: a large television or video monitor with special computer-to-video conversion hardware, a video projector, and a liquid crystal display (LCD) projector or panel. We look at each of these options.

LARGE TELEVISIONS OR VIDEO MONITORS

Most schools possess large televisions or video monitors, often mounted in classrooms or available on carts, for use with VCRs or other video programming. For classroom use, sizes ranging from 21 inches to 35 inches are common. Large-screen televisions, although less common, can also be used for group presentations.

Today most personal computers are incapable of working with standard video monitors or televisions without special hardware. However, a number of vendors are now supplying the special hardware needed to convert the computer's output to standard video. These devices, which can be plug-in boards for the computer or external boxes that connect to the computer and its regular monitor, convert the computer's display output into standard video (often referred to as NSTC, the U.S. video standard). Most of these products, which typically cost a few hundred dollars, provide composite video output (the standard used by most VCRs), and some also support S-video output (super VHS video, a better quality). This output can be directed to a large video monitor or video projector for group presentations.

Computer-to-video conversion devices provide one convenient option for displaying computer images in the classroom. However, they have a disadvantage. Standard video cannot reproduce the high resolutions found on most personal computers today. As a result, when the computer image is converted to video there is some degradation of the image. The output may become somewhat fuzzy, and small text fonts are likely to become completely unreadable. To compensate for this loss of resolution, select larger text fonts (at least 18 point) when using the computer with a video monitor.

VIDEO PROJECTORS

Video projectors provide the capability to project a video image onto a screen, much like a motion picture projector projects an image onto a screen. Because video projectors are capable of producing very large images—in some cases 20 feet or more across—these devices provide an option for very large groups. Indeed, they are popular in university lecture halls, auditoriums, and other facilities that seat large numbers of people.

The capabilities and costs of video projectors vary considerably. Better video projectors are capable of faithfully reproducing the computer's output on a large screen. As such, they are a good option when computer projection is needed with very large groups. As with televisions and video monitors, an adapter is needed to convert the computer's output into a form that these projectors can display. A disadvantage of these devices is that they can be very expensive (thousands of dollars), and may need frequent maintenance to keep the image well focused. In addition, some lack portability and may be permanently mounted in one room. All video projectors function best in darkened rooms, although many are sufficiently bright for use in subdued lighting.

LIQUID CRYSTAL DISPLAY (LCD) PANELS AND PROJECTORS

Liquid crystal display (LCD) technology is used in the screen displays of laptop computers. This same technology has been adapted to produce large-group display devices: LCD panels and LCD projectors. LCD panels are compact, flat units that mount on top of overhead projectors. LCD projectors use the same basic technology but include a built-in light source. These are the newest, and in many ways the most desirable, of the hardware options for large-group presentations in schools.

A variety of LCD panels and projectors is now available. Different units are distinguished by such features as the maximum screen resolution supported, the number of colors simultaneously displayed, and how rapidly the display is "refreshed" or renewed, an important consideration when tracking rapid motion such as the movement of a mouse cursor on the computer screen. LCD displays are portable and easily hooked up to the computer. Most LCD units today can display video (e.g., from a VCR) as well as computer output from either *Windows*-based or *Mac OS*–based computers, usually with only an appropriate cable connection. Costs vary but typical full-color units run in the thousands of dollars.

TOOLBOX TOOLS
(continued)

LCD panels are made to work with overhead projectors, one of the most common of all educational tools. The image from an LCD panel can be projected to any size that the overhead projector will support, so, in image size, LCD panels rival projection systems. However, most LCD panels have problems with image brightness. Even when used with the recommended extra-bright overhead projectors, they require mostly darkened rooms for optimal viewing. In addition, LCD panels often suffer from thermal sensitivity. On a hot overhead projector, the image can become "washed out" or the panel damaged with extended exposure to heat. LCD panels often use fans and/or specially treated glass to minimize the effects of heat. Their portability, while usually an advantage, can create problems. Because LCD panels are handled, there is a greater likelihood that one may be dropped and damaged, and their portability makes them a ready target for theft.

LCD projectors remedy a number of the shortcoming of LCD panels (Figure A). With their built-in light sources, they are brighter. Some LCD projectors are so bright that they can function effectively in fully lighted rooms; no other common presentation device can accomplish this feat. Like panels, LCD projectors are portable; most weigh under 20 pounds and are equipped with a carrying handle or come in a transportable case. Many come with their own speakers to support audio as well as video. Because they include the light source, LCD projectors are somewhat more expensive than comparable LCD panels. However, because of their advantages they are an especially attractive option for classroom display of computer images.

FIGURE A An LCD projector (Photo courtesy of View Sonic Corporation.)

class could examine the relationship between perimeter and area in various geometric shapes.

Spreadsheets allow students to concentrate on real-world problems without becoming bogged down in the calculations. However, you need to make certain your students understand that the results from spreadsheets are only as good as the data and formulas entered in them. An incorrect formula or bad data can lead to erroneous results. The relevant old expression in the computer world is "garbage in, garbage out." If what you start with is not correct, the computer cannot magically fix it. Spreadsheets are great tools, but like any other computer tool, they must be used properly.

Problems and Pitfalls

There are problems and pitfalls associated with each of the computer-as-assistant productivity tools dis-cussed here. Refer to the discussion in Chapter 3 in addition to this chapter for specific concerns associated with each type of software. As with any instructional tool, the important thing to remember is that computer use should be appropriate to the specific instructional goals, the educational context, and the students. Keep in mind that you may need special hardware and/or software to meet students' special needs. See "Toolbox Tools: Assistive Technology" for more information.

Reflective Questions

▶ In the stock market game scenario, what other ways might Mr. Goins and his students have used computer tools? How might the game have been conducted without the computer, using only traditional classroom tools?

Assistive Technology

When planning instruction for students with special needs, it is important to make available appropriate assistive technology. Computers can empower students with special needs, and access to the technology can be provided in various ways. For example, you may easily accommodate a student in a wheelchair by using an adjustable-height computer table in a laboratory. Various forms of adaptive technology are available to assist students with particular disabilities.

For visually impaired learners, for example, there are numerous solutions available. With mild visual impairment, simply enlarging fonts on the computer can provide a simple solution. You can use special software to magnify on-screen text even further. Optical character recognition (OCR) systems can convert print materials into electronic form for computer accessibility. For individuals with significant visual impairment, speech synthesizers can convert text on the computer screen into spoken language. In addition, Braille printers are available for personal computers. There are even special software packages that allow visually impaired individuals to access the often nonlinear and graphically oriented World Wide Web (although they work best when Web page developers design their pages to be easily accessible).

A variety of special computer input solutions are available for physically challenged learners. Alternative keyboards, for example with oversize keys, are available for individuals who lack fine motor control. Accessibility options are built into modern computer operating systems; for example, *Windows 95* has a feature called StickyKeys that makes it possible for a user with motor difficulty to more easily use shift and control keys. When StickyKeys are activated, pressing the shift key twice activates it, so that the user does not have to be able to simultaneously depress shift and another key to type a capital letter, for example. Also, the keyboard can be used as an alternative to the mouse for selecting information. In addition, speech recognition systems allow spoken input of text as well as voice control of the computer. For individuals with significant motor impairment, there are adaptive hardware and software systems that provide computer input through any kind of simple switch (e.g., finger movement, head movement, puff switch). Depending upon the particular system, the switch can be used to do such things as select an option within the computer operating system (e.g., pick an application to open), select options from within an application program, and select letters or even whole words for input. Figure B shows a student using computer adaptive hardware.

Many assistive technologies are available today that offer a range of options to meet specific students' needs. If you have a student who might benefit from assistive technologies, talk to your school's special education teacher. Availability of these technologies can make a world of difference to a student with special needs!

FIGURE B Student using adaptive hardware to work with a computer

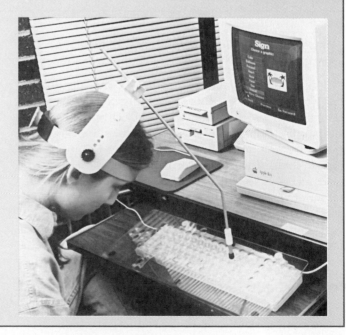

▶ Some teachers feel that students must have instruction in the use of each computer productivity tool (e.g., word processor, spreadsheet) before using that tool for content work in the classroom. Other teachers think students can learn to use the computer in the context of using it for content work in the classroom. What do you think? Why?

COMPUTER AS LEARNER

When the computer functions as learner, the roles of computer and student that we see in traditional computer-assisted instruction are reversed. The computer becomes the "learner," and the student becomes the "teacher." The objective is for the student to "teach" the computer to perform some task. To achieve this objective, the student must come to understand some problem or content and be able to communicate this to the computer in a way that the computer will "understand." In other words, the user must learn how to instruct the computer to accomplish some task. This requires organization, logical thinking, and problem-solving skills, and, as a result, many experts believe that this is one of the most valuable ways to use a computer in education.

Using the computer as learner is an open-ended approach that relies on students' abilities to construct their understanding about some content and how to use the computer. In the classroom, you can implement this approach by having students program the computer using a common computer language such as Logo, BASIC, or C. Using Logo, for example, students learn geometry, as well as basic computer programming concepts, by learning to instruct the computer to create geometric designs. A second, more recent, way to implement this approach is to have students develop interactive hypermedia products using a hypermedia authoring tool such as *HyperStudio, Digital Chisel, HyperCard,* or *Toolbook.* Using packages such as these, students must gather content, organize it, put it into the program's hypermedia format, and create mechanisms within the software for others to interact with the content.

We look here at each of these ways that students can learn by creating products on the computer. Begin by reading the scenario that follows. Identify the circumstances in which students are "teaching" the computer.

Scenario: Hypermedia Reports

Peggy Gambrel teaches sixth grade in a self-contained classroom in William McKinley Middle School. Last year, in response to a call from the school for more emphasis on mathematics, science, and technology, she developed a number of new activities for her students. One of these activities was a modification of a history/language arts assignment that she had used in previous years. In the past, Ms. Gambrel had assigned her students the task of writing a report about a famous American "pioneer" (i.e. explorer or scientist such as Meriwether Lewis, Thomas Edison, or George Washington Carver). To fit last year's new theme, she changed the assignment to one in which pairs of students were to do research and create a multimedia report about a famous mathematician or scientist.

At the beginning of the two-and-one-half week activity, Ms. Gambrel made the assignment to her class and paired off the students. Each pair's initial task was to decide on the subject of their report. To help them choose, Ms. Gambrel decorated her room by hanging pictures of famous mathematicians and scientists on the walls. With the help of the school librarian, Ms. Keck, she also gathered a number of print materials about famous scientists and mathematicians. After surveying the available materials, each team wrote the names of their top four preferred choices on a card and turned it in to Ms. Gambrel. By looking through all of the requests, she was able to assign a subject to each team so that there were no duplicates in the class, and every team was able to get its first, second, or third choice.

During the remainder of the first week, students researched their choices. Ms. Gambrel set aside time each day for students to go to the library. All of the students were able to access relevant print materials, and they were also able to go online to find information on the Web. Because McKinley School only has one computer in the library with dialup Internet access, Ms. Keck set up a sign-up system where each team could have one 30-minute block during the week. She helped the students during their searches so that they were able to make productive use of the limited time.

During the second week, students created their multimedia reports using *HyperStudio,* a popular hypermedia authoring tool, using the school's minilab as well as the two computers in their classroom to work on their projects. Ms. Gambrel didn't feel that she was an expert in *HyperStudio* herself, but she could handle the basics. The students had used *HyperStudio* on a couple of occasions earlier in the year, so Ms. Gambrel did not spend time teaching them how to use the software for this activity. The kids just dove right in! Ms. Gambrel gave them some time each day to work on their reports.

All of the teams built *HyperStudio* projects, called *stacks,* consisting of several cards. Ms. Gambrel provided some general guidelines for the multimedia report, but each team had to determine exactly what content to include and how to present it. Ms. Gambrel was amazed at how hard the students worked—much harder, she thought, than when they did their usual written reports—and how creative they were. Each team included textual information about its subject, navigational buttons to allow someone to go through the stack, and multimedia elements. Lauren and Katie, for example, like many of the other students, scanned a picture from a book for their report on Albert Einstein. They also added a sound effect that played each time someone went to a new card in their stack because they thought it sounded "cool." Tim and Jim used a picture of Marie Curie that they found on the Internet for their project. Chris and Sean used *HyperStudio's* ability to record speech to add their own narration to their project. David and Nancy did a particularly interesting thing. Remembering the Logo computer language that they had learned in the fifth grade, these two students used *HyperLogo,* a version of Logo inside *HyperStudio,* to create geometric figures to illustrate their report about Euclid. No two projects were alike.

At the end of the project, the class had a show-and-tell session. Ms. Gambrel hooked one of the computers in her classroom to the TV mounted on the wall so that everyone could see. Each team then presented its multimedia report. The students really enjoyed the assignment, and they loved sharing their projects. When the unit was complete, Ms. Gambrel sent home each team's project on a diskette along with a playback program. Those parents with a computer were able to view their child's work at home. She invited any other parents to stop by the school to see the projects. Ms. Gambrel received notes of thanks from several of the parents. She was pleased with the new class activity and glad that she had tried it.

What does this scenario tell us about using the computer as learner? There are several things to note:

▶ *Students must learn both the content and how to present it.* When the computer functions as learner, students have a two-part task. They must learn the content at hand, and they must learn how to present it or, rather, how to get the computer to present it. This requires organization, logical thinking, and problem solving.

▶ *Students are actively involved.* Although it is certainly not the only way to accomplish this aim, having students create computer-based projects gets them actively involved in learning. It is motivating. It is consistent with a view of learning as construction of understanding.

▶ *There is more than one way to achieve success.* A characteristic of most situations where students "teach" the computer is that there are many ways they can succeed. In the previous scenario, no two students' projects were the same, yet all met the goal. Just as in much of "real-world" problem solving, different approaches can and do work.

▶ *Extensive prior knowledge is not necessarily required.* As with the use of the computer as assistant, teachers are sometimes reluctant to try using the computer as learner without a lot of prior knowledge. However, as with computer productivity tools, a little knowledge can go a long way in the classroom when it comes to using the computer as learner. In this example, Ms. Gambrel didn't feel she was expert with the software, but her students were able to dive in and get the job done.

As we noted above, students can "teach" the computer using either programming languages or hypermedia authoring tools. We look here at one example of each: Logo, a popular programming language for education, and *HyperStudio,* a hypermedia authoring package widely used in schools.

Logo

Logo is a computer language developed by Seymour Papert and his associates at MIT, the Massachusetts Institute of Technology (Papert, 1980). Unlike most computer languages, Logo was created with education in mind. The idea for Logo arose from Papert's work with famed cognitive psychologist Jean Piaget, who believed that learning results from one's interaction with the environment. Piaget saw learning as a constructive process in which the learner plays an active role. Papert, in creating Logo, sought to design a computer environment that could actively engage the learner in constructing understanding.

Papert was also influenced by his association with the artificial intelligence community at MIT. Logo's roots lie in the computer language LISP, a mainstay of artificial intelligence programming. What resulted from this fusion of Piaget's psychology and artificial intelligence programming was a programming language simple enough even for young children yet with sufficient power for complex programming tasks. Because of its ease of use, Logo became a popular computer tool in schools, especially in the elementary grades. Though not as widely used as it once was, Logo remains a viable option for computer-as-learner activities.

The roots of Logo suggest the rationale for its use in the classroom. Advocates of this approach point out that having students learn to "teach" the computer reaps benefits in student learning. As noted, it involves problem solving and the construction of understanding. Further, students who use Logo learn more about the computer itself—how it functions, what it can and cannot do, how it can be controlled. Because programming is an important part of some postsecondary curricula and because some jobs involve programming, learning about it can also prepare students for future study and employment. Many computer scientists fret that too little attention is paid to programming in our K–12 schools today. Finally, knowledge of programming can sometimes come in handy in other contexts. While it is difficult to show that the problem solving one learns from programming transfers to other contexts, there are many computer settings where programming knowledge is of value. For example, a form of the computer language Visual BASIC underlies the popular Microsoft Office suite of productivity packages and can be used to customize how the applications function.

Logo Fundamentals

Logo, like other **programming languages,** consists of a set of instructions that can be assembled, according to particular rules, to tell the computer how to do something. A student can put together individual computer instructions in an organized way to create a program to accomplish something in much the same way that a child might put together building blocks to create a structure. The instructions in Logo resemble natural language (e.g., FORWARD, PENUP) and so are fairly easy for students to understand. Computer languages like Logo that resemble natural language and keep the user from having to understand the inner working of the computer are called **high-level languages.** This is in contrast to lower-level languages such as **machine language,** the binary code that controls the computer at the level of its circuits. Logo programs are automatically translated by the computer into machine language, shielding the user from having to know anything about the grisly details.

When Logo was first developed, users gave simple commands such as FORWARD, LEFT, and RIGHT to a small, mobile robot connected to the computer. This robot, which could be made to draw designs on sheets of butcher paper by means of an attached pen, was dubbed a "turtle." The robot turtle evolved into a graphic figure on the computer's screen that could be programmed to draw geometric designs. This figure became the basis of "turtle geometry" or "turtle graphics," one of the most popular uses of Logo.

In turtle graphics mode, the Logo turtle starts in the center of the computer's display screen, an area designed to match the Cartesian coordinate system familiar to us from mathematics. The built-in commands, or *primitives,* cause the turtle to act. The most common of these are FORWARD (FD), BACK (BK), LEFT (LT), RIGHT (RT), PENUP (PU), and PENDOWN (PD). The student can use these to steer the turtle around on the display screen and create geometric designs.

The creators of Logo have stressed an open and exploratory environment when elementary students use the language. Much of the learning about the language comes from students discovering what the turtle can do. For example, after learning the basic functions of the Logo primitives, a student may discover that the turtle can be made to draw a square on the screen by typing the following commands:

FD 50 RT 90 FD 50 RT 90 FD 50 RT 90 FD 50 RT 90

FD 50 commands the turtle to move forward on the screen 50 "turtle steps" or pixels. RT 90 commands the turtle to turn to the right 90 degrees. Do this four times, and you get a square.

In this case, the student has figured out, either by accident or design, the steps needed to make a square. The series of steps needed to solve a particular problem or perform a particular task on the computer is called an **algorithm.** In order to properly control the machine, the student really has a two-part chore. The first part is figuring out the steps needed, that is, devising the algorithm. This is not a programming task per se but rather a problem-solving task. The second part is coding the algorithm in a computer language. This part of the task demands that the programmer use the proper statements from a particular computer language and the proper **syntax,** the rules for using the computer language. This requires that the student follow certain rules and pay attention to the details. Although this example from Logo is pretty simple, either part of the process can be challenging to younger learners or when the task or problem becomes more complex.

As students' knowledge of Logo grows, they are able to accomplish drawing functions by grouping the commands into small programs called *procedures.* A more sophisticated way of drawing a square, using REPEAT—Logo's way of performing looping or repetition—is shown in Figure 8–7. Once defined, procedures such as SQUARE behave like primitives. Thus, students can use them to build even more complex designs. Spinning the square about one corner can create a pinwheel shape, as shown in the procedure and resulting design in Figure 8–7. From simple

FIGURE 8–7   Using Logo procedures to draw simple shapes that can in turn be used to create more complex figures

```
TO SQUARE
    REPEAT 4 [FD 50 RT 90]
END
```

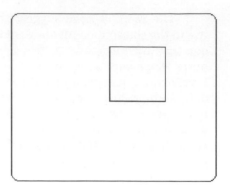

```
TO PINWHEEL
    REPEAT 12 [SQUARE RT 30]
END
```

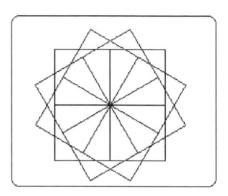

beginnings, a student using Logo can learn to create more and more complex creations.

Logo in the Classroom

You can use Logo for a variety of educational activities or learning objectives in the classroom:

▶ *Introductory computer programming.* As noted, Logo is a popular tool for introducing computer programming to elementary-age students. Simplified versions of Logo have even been used successfully with preschool learners. Because of its simplicity, a student can actually be doing things with Logo only moments after being introduced to it. Yet it has a richness that can permit problem solving and exploration for a long time.

▶ *Problem solving.* Using Logo, students can become acquainted with the computer and with controlling it through a programming language. This involves problem solving. Logo also teaches students that there is more than one way to solve a problem and encourages them to view mistakes as steps on the path to a correct solution.

▶ *Geometry.* Turtle graphics introduces students to many geometric concepts at a much earlier age, and in a much different way, than has been the case in the past. An elementary-age learner may not understand the concept of degrees in the Logo command RIGHT 90, but before long that

student begins to acquire an intuitive sense of degrees and other geometric concepts.

▶ *Art.* Turtle graphics in Logo can provide a natural linkage to art and demonstrate the geometric underpinnings of many designs. Many people liken complex Logo patterns to those produced by the child's art toy, the Spirograph®.

▶ *Microworlds.* Logo can be used to explore small, well-defined environments, called *microworlds,* in a variety of subject areas from mathematics to language to physical science. Microworlds afford the learner the opportunity to gain a rich understanding of one small, well-developed environment.

▶ *Lego Logo. Lego Logo,* in some ways, takes Logo back to its roots. Students use Lego building blocks and small electric motors to construct simple machines that can be controlled via Logo in much the same way that the original Logo turtle was controlled. Students can see real-world manifestations of their programming efforts in contrast to the abstract on-screen turtle.

Hypermedia Authoring

Hypermedia refers to a system of information representation in which the information—text, graphics, animation, audio, and/or video—is stored digitally in interlinked locations called *nodes*. The process of creating hypermedia is called *authoring*. Hypermedia is growing in popularity. Not only are standalone hypermedia authoring tools such as *HyperStudio* for both *MacOS* and *Windows, HyperCard* for the *MacOS*, and *Toolbook* for *Windows* available to schools, but the World Wide Web has made hypermedia a common denominator, of sorts, for much of the computing world. As a result, many schools are now teaching students how to author hypermedia.

The rationale for teaching students to author hypermedia has similarities to that for teaching students to program computers. When developing hypermedia projects, students are actively involved and often highly motivated. Hypermedia development, like computer programming, is consistent with the view of learning as knowledge construction. To develop a hypermedia project, the learner must research, evaluate, organize, and present information. Because hypermedia is rapidly becoming the norm of the computer world, teaching students to author hypermedia can prepare them for future study and work. Further, hypermedia project development serves double duty in the classroom. Not only is the creation of a hypermedia project a learning activity, but the process and the end product can serve as a form of assessment.

Hypermedia Fundamentals

In popular standalone hypermedia programs, nodes are usually referred to as *cards* in a *stack* (like a stack of index cards) or *pages* in a *book* (like a traditional print book). On the Web, we talk about Web pages in a *Website*. The concept is the same. You can think of a hypermedia node as a card or page on which you can put information of various sorts, and the card/page can be linked to one or more other cards/pages of related information. Unlike a print book, however, nodes in hypermedia are often linked to other nodes in a nonlinear fashion.

On any given node, one can place different things, such as text, graphics, and links to other nodes (many times depicted as buttons). Each thing that one can put on a node is an "object." There can be text fields (objects containing text), graphics (picture objects), buttons (linking or action objects), and perhaps other objects such as sounds, videos, and so on. Because they treat things as objects, hypermedia systems have the characteristics of what are known as *object-oriented programming systems* (**OOPS**). In addition, hypermedia systems are **event driven,** which means that they respond to events in the computer environment. For example, when the user clicks on a button or a *hot link* (an active link to an-

other node often appearing as highlighted text), this triggers a *mouse click event*. The hypermedia system can respond to this event with some action, such as navigating to another card or page.

With hypermedia authoring tools, students can create hypermedia products with relative ease. By placing objects (text, pictures) on cards/pages and creating links, it is a simple matter to create functional and effective hypermedia projects. Little if any programming knowledge is needed. However, with most hypermedia authoring tools, programming is available if the student wants to do something more complex. Apple's *HyperCard,* for example, contains a powerful *scripting* (programming) language called HyperTalk. Asymetrix's *Toolbook* uses a scripting language known as OpenScript. Roger Wagner's *HyperStudio* uses a scripting language called *HyperLogo*, a version of the Logo programming language we discussed in the last section. In the next subsection, we focus on *HyperStudio* as an example of a hypermedia authoring tool. *HyperStudio* has become a widely popular hypermedia tool in schools because of its ease of use, its many features, and its availability for different types of computers. In Chapter 9, we will look at tools and techniques for authoring Web-based hypermedia materials.

HyperStudio

HyperStudio is a popular hypermedia authoring tool produced by Roger Wagner Publishing. First developed for the older Apple IIgs computer, the program is now available for both MacOS and *Windows*-based computers. Using it, students can create hypermedia projects that operate on standalone computers. The newest version also provides the capability for sharing *HyperStudio* projects over the Internet. While the complete *HyperStudio* package is needed for authoring, a freely distributable player program can be used to present or play back finished projects on computers that do not have the complete program.

In *HyperStudio,* nodes are referred to as *cards* and complete projects are called *stacks*. The task of creating content on a card is relatively straightforward. When first starting a new stack, the program automatically creates the first card. Additional cards can be added as needed. Through a combination of menu options and tools, hypermedia authors can add objects to a card and subsequently edit them. Authors can add text objects (known as *fields*), graphic objects (pictures or clip art), and *buttons* (objects used for navigation or to invoke actions). Figure 8–8 shows an example of a *HyperStudio* card with a variety of hypermedia objects.

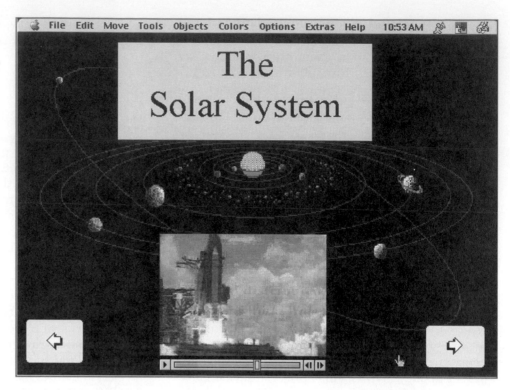

Several options are available in the program to permit authors to create cards with visual interest. The objects on a card rest in layers on top of a background. Authors can paint the background with a color or a pattern or place a graphic in the background to give the card an interesting look. In text objects, the author can control the color of the text and the color of the background field in which the text sits. Buttons can also be colored, and the author can select from a number of available icons to represent buttons. In addition to the ability to import pictures and clip art, *HyperStudio* also provides basic drawing tools so that student authors can create their own illustrations.

HyperStudio also provides a high level of multimedia support. Special multimedia options are made available as actions associated with buttons. Available actions include playing a digital sound, playing a digital movie (e.g., a QuickTime movie), playing a videodisc movie (with a properly attached videodisc player and driver software installed), playing an animation, using a built-in timer function, and using one of several special actions (such as a function that causes credits to roll up the screen like a movie). *HyperStudio* even has some rudimentary test tracking features that can be used for embedded quizzes.

Finally, for students who may not be satisfied with the range of available options in the program, buttons can be programmed using *HyperStudio's*

built-in scripting language, HyperLogo. HyperLogo contains all of the basic features of Logo, as discussed in the preceding section of this chapter. Students can create turtle graphics as they would using a version of Logo itself. However, HyperLogo also gives student authors the power to accomplish things in the *HyperStudio* environment that could not be accomplished otherwise. Figure 8–9 gives an example of a HyperLogo script that would cause a hidden text field to appear in response to a button click.

Hypermedia Authoring in the Classroom
Student development of hypermedia offers many opportunities for classroom activities.

▶ *Hypermedia projects.* Perhaps the most common application of hypermedia authoring in the classroom is student development of hypermedia projects or reports. Hypermedia projects allow students, either individually or in groups, to create reports that summarize a major effort such as a science experiment or interdisciplinary project. Rather than simply writing about it, students can include written work, pictures, sound clips, video, and links to describe what they did and/or to present background information.

▶ *Multimedia presentations.* Students (and teachers) can use hypermedia authoring tools to create multimedia presentations or slide shows.

FIGURE 8–9   A script in *HyperStudio's* HyperLogo can control the appearance of a field. In this example, a click on the Mercury button causes the message "Mercury is correct!" to be placed in a text field named Feedback. *Source: HyperStudio, Roger Wagner Publishing.*

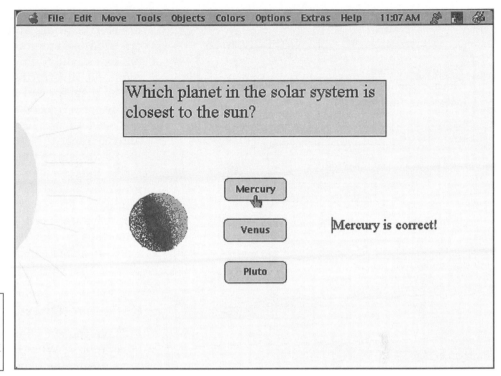

```
HyperLogo script of
button Mercury:

SETFIELDTEXT[]"FEEDBACK
'MERCURY IS CORRECT!'
```

While perhaps not as easy to use for linear presentations as presentation software (e.g., *PowerPoint*), tools such as *HyperStudio* are well suited to branched or linking presentations.

▶ *Nonlinear fiction.* Some teachers have begun to have their students experiment with the possibilities of hypermedia for authoring nonlinear fiction. The branching capabilities of hypermedia offer students the option to create stories that may have more than one ending.

▶ *Portfolios of student work.* Hypermedia authoring tools are excellent for building portfolios of student work in many subjects.

Problems and Pitfalls

Programming is, and probably will remain, a controversial aspect of computers in education for some. Detractors point out that productivity applications become more powerful every day and few students will ever become professional programmers. So, they say, we shouldn't be wasting time teaching kids to program computers. Proponents, on the other hand, stress the problem-solving and practical benefits of learning to program. Logo, they argue, is an excellent tool for doing problem-solving activities and for teaching children about computers. However, investigations of the problem-solving claims of Logo's supporters have led to many questions, and it is difficult to prove that learning to use Logo results in general improvements of students' problem-solving abilities (Littlefield et al., 1988; Maddux, Johnson, & Willis, 1992; Roblyer, Castine, & King, 1988; Singh, 1992). The debate seems likely to continue.

Having students develop hypermedia projects seems to be less controversial than programming today, although its aims are similar. Although it has not been extensively studied, there is evidence that students can benefit educationally from developing hypermedia projects (Ayersman, 1996). Further, it tends to be easier for students to create projects with hypermedia tools than to create computer programs from scratch. However, you must plan and prepare for both programming and hypermedia development. You need to be clear about your goals for using the computer-as-learner approach and plan accordingly.

The developers of Logo stress the importance of having an open, exploratory classroom environment where students have time and opportunity to explore and learn. As a teacher, you need to be comfortable with the open-ended nature of programming and the fact that there is not one right way to do things. However, pure discovery may be too inefficient for some teachers. In addition, as students mature and learn other languages (e.g., BASIC, Pascal, C), most experts believe it is important to adopt a more structured approach to programming instruction. Students need to learn the importance of a **top-down approach,** starting with a general goal and progressively refining until reaching a solution, and

Storyboard Card

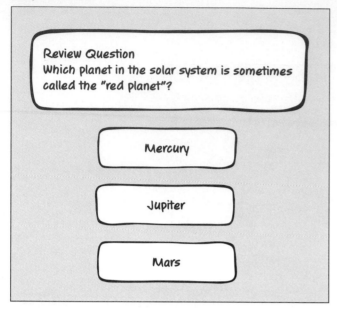

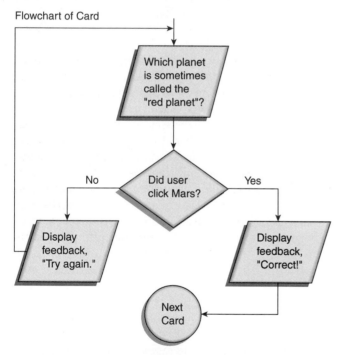

Flowchart of Card

FIGURE 8–10   Sample storyboard card and flowchart of the card for a *HyperStudio* project

before getting on the computer. These two techniques are storyboarding and flowcharting. Software designers often use storyboarding, originally borrowed from animators and filmmakers. **Storyboarding** is a technique for illustrating, on paper, what the computer screen displays will look like in a program. Students can design a *HyperStudio* project, for example, on index cards before making the real thing. They can redesign and rearrange the cards before making the effort to create the project on the computer. Most programmers describe the logic of a program using **flowcharting,** a graphical means of representing the flow of a program. The flowchart illustrates where the links go in a hypermedia stack or a Web page. This can be especially important in a highly linked hypermedia project. Figure 8–10 shows samples of a storyboard card and flowchart of that card for a *HyperStudio* project.

Reflective Questions

▶ Have you ever had occasion to program a computer? What did you think of programming as a learning experience? Why?
▶ Do you think computer programming should be part of the school curriculum? Why or why not?
▶ Think about the last time that you used a prepared hypermedia program or visited a Website. What aspects of the design did you think were effective? What did you think was not effective? Why?

APPLICATIONS IN THE LEARNER-CENTERED CLASSROOM

We hope that this chapter provided you with many good ideas about how your students can learn using computers. Just as there is no one right way to win a game of chess, there is no one right way to help your students learn. Different approaches, like the different chess pieces, have their own strengths and weaknesses. It is the situation, the audience, and the goal that determines which approach to choose.

In chess, the pawn is a relatively weak piece that usually moves forward only a single square. But, in some situations, it is possible to mount a winning attack by making a succession of small pawn moves. In the classroom, a single drill and practice session, like a single pawn on the chessboard, may not accomplish very much. But, many drill and practice sessions, like a sequence of pawn moves, can have a big impact on student learning. The important thing is to match the learning demands of the instructional situation to the particular method of computer use.

they need to adhere to **structured programming** principles, a set of conventions designed to result in organized, easy-to-read, correct programs.

When students develop hypermedia projects, structure and advance planning is just as important. Two forms of advance planning, often used by programmers and instructional designers, are also helpful in getting students to think about their projects

In the classroom, each of the three major categories of computer use discussed in this chapter has its applications. Computer-assisted instruction, depending on the specific type, can help students with everything from low-level, rote learning to application and problem solving. Students can use computer productivity tools for authentic tasks ranging from routine jobs to higher-order thinking and problem solving. Computer-as-learner applications can require students to be organized, to think logically, and to problem solve. It is up to you, the teacher, to determine those uses that best fit the needs of your students and classroom setting.

ONE TEACHER'S STORY

by Janette Moreno

The ways that I use computers with my kids have changed quite a bit over the past few years, although I guess the change was kind of gradual. When I first started teaching, I really only thought about using the computer as a teaching machine. I guess that was the image I had of the computer in education—put a kid in front of a computer and have it teach something. So, I spent a lot of time looking for computer-assisted instruction software packages that I liked, and I did find some things that I was able to use.

About once a week or so, I'd have the kids work on vocabulary exercises, verb conjugation drills, or whatever. It was okay. I think the "drill and kill" helped them, and I still use a lot of that software today. I guess I just got to thinking that there ought to be more that we could do with computers. . . .

So, I started having the kids do other things. Probably the first thing I added was word processing. That was kind of a natural. I just had the kids write a couple of their papers for me using the word processor. Before long, they were illustrating their reports with clip art and other graphics.

Then, a couple of years ago, when we got one of those LCD projection things in the building, I added an assignment to have the kids do an oral report using *PowerPoint*. I was really impressed with how well the kids did with that. They worked really hard and did some great stuff. I had some parents who couldn't believe that it was their kids who did these professional-looking presentations.

Well, that experience gave me enough courage to try hypermedia last year. I had the kids develop hypermedia stacks on cities in Spain and Mexico as one of their projects. I was pretty nervous about it, because I really consider myself a novice with hypermedia. But the students were quick to learn, and they taught me a whole lot about the software. For my part, I had to help them quite a bit with the content and how to organize and present it. I think the hypermedia's nonlinearity was a little bit of a problem for them. But they got through the project all right, and I have ideas for how to make it go better this year.

So today my kids do all sorts of things with the computer. They still use some computer-assisted instruction, but there is so much more going on in the classroom now. I just think computers have so much potential for helping kids to learn, and I feel like we're a lot closer to that potential than when I first started.

SUMMARY

In this chapter we explored ways that students can use computers for learning, examining three basic categories of computer use: computer as teacher, computer as assistant, and computer as learner. Computer as teacher is often labeled computer-assisted instruction (CAI), where the computer delivers instruction to the student. Common forms of CAI include drill and practice, tutorial, simulation, instructional game, and problem solving. Computer as assistant refers to the use of the computer as a productivity tool for common tasks. Typical computer applications in this category include word processor, graphics and desktop publishing, presentation software, database, and spreadsheet. When the computer plays the role of the "learner," it is the student who must "teach" it through the use of a programming language such as Logo or hypermedia authoring tool such as *HyperStudio*. This requires organization and problem solving.

REFLECTIVE ACTIVITIES

▶ Think about the times you used the computer as a tool for learning. Which categories of computer use did you employ? How did you react to them? Why?

▶ Arrange a visit to a school or college that is using computers with students. Take notes about your impressions of the visit. What methods were employed? How did the students react to them? What do you think was being learned?

▶ Find an advertisement for a CAI program in a magazine or catalog. Write to the company for more information or for a demonstration or preview copy of the software. Discuss it with other students when you receive it.

▶ Preview examples of student-created hypermedia, either by contacting a local teacher who has students develop hypermedia or by browsing the Web for examples of students' products. Write down your reactions. What specific learning do you think the students demonstrated?

SUGGESTED RESOURCES

Grabe, M., & Grabe, C. (1997). *Integrating technology for meaningful learning.* Boston, MA: Houghton Mifflin.

Johnson, R. T., Johnson, D. W., & Stanne, M. B. (1985). Effects of cooperative, competitive, and individualistic goal structures on computer-assisted instruction. *Journal of Educational Psychology, 77* (6), 668–677.

Jonassen, D. H. (1996). *Computers in the classroom: Mindtools for critical thinking.* Upper Saddle River, NJ: Merrill/Prentice Hall.

Kulik, C. C., & Kulik, J. A. (1991). Effectiveness of computer-based instruction: An updated analysis. *Computers in Human Behavior, 7,* 75–94.

Lockard, J., Abrams, P. D., & Many, W. A. (1997). *Microcomputers for twenty-first century educators.* New York: Longman.

Papert, S. (1980). *Mindstorms: Children, computers, and powerful ideas.* New York: Basic Books.

Roblyer, M. D., Edwards, J., & Havriluk, M. A. (1997). *Integrating educational technology into teaching.* Upper Saddle River, NJ: Merrill/Prentice Hall.

WEBSITES

HyperStudio
[http://www.hyperstudio.com]
Yahoo Computers and Internet
[http://www.yahoo.com/Computers/]
Yahoo Education
[http://www.yahoo.com/Education/]

CHAPTER 9

Using the Internet and Distance Education

KEY WORDS AND CONCEPTS

Internet
asynchronous
synchronous
listserv
newsgroup
chat room
World Wide Web
Uniform Resource Locator (URL)
hypertext
browser
bookmark
home page
(HTML)

OBJECTIVES

After reading and studying this chapter, you will be able to:

◗ Demonstrate each of the following applications of the Internet:
   1) communication, 2) information retrieval, and 3) information publishing.

◗ Develop a lesson plan incorporating the use of the Internet following the guidelines in Chapter 4 and in this chapter.

◗ Evaluate a variety of Web pages and/or Websites using the Preview Form found in Appendix B.

◗ Describe examples of audio-based, video-based, and computer-based distance education technologies.

◗ Compare and contrast distance education technologies on the basis of capabilities, advantages, and limitations.

PLANNING FOR THE CHAPTER CONTENT

Instructional Technology for Teaching and Learning, will show you how to increase learning by designing lessons that use instructional technology, including computers and other media.

This chapter will focus on *using* instructional technology, specifically the Internet and distance learning. Some of the tools of technology include the methods and media we've discussed. In Chapter 4 you learned how to develop a plan for increasing the level of learning of your students. Chapter 5 addressed ways to select the methods and types of media to use in your plan. Chapter 6 focused on acquiring the specific instructional materials to increase student learning. Chapter 7 focused on using methods and

media. Chapter 8 dealt with using computers. Here we explore two other types of technology—the Internet and distance learning. These technologies incorporate all the planning, methods, media, and computer information discussed throughout the text.

INTRODUCTION

When you go shopping at a grocery store, have you ever thought about the convenience provided? Goods are brought to the store to save you from traveling to many locations around town, as your grandparents and great grandparents did, or even around the world to get the items you want to buy, for example, coffee from Columbia, cheese from Wisconsin, meat from a butcher shop, pineapples from Hawaii, bread from a bakery, and rice from Japan. Just as a grocery store brings items from around the world to one location, the Internet and distance education bring information and resources, including text, sounds, video, and live television, into your classroom.

WHAT IS THE INTERNET AND HOW DO I CONNECT?

In Chapter 3 we introduced computer networks and the Internet. The **Internet** consists of thousands of connected computer networks around the world that connect millions of computers and tens of millions of people. The Internet is also referred to as the "Net," the "Information Superhighway," and "cyberspace."

How is information communicated through the Internet? When you receive information from another computer on the Internet, you are **downloading** the information. When you send information on the Internet, you are **uploading** it. Information is sent through the Internet in **packets** (Figure 9–1). Each packet of an individual message may take separate paths through cyberspace. Packets are reassembled when they arrive at their destination. A **router** regulates traffic on the Internet and determines the most efficient route for each packet. The **backbone** of the Internet is a set of high-speed data lines that connect the major networks. Today most schools are connected to the Internet. The **drop** (connection) may be in the library-media center, the main office, or in classrooms.

Uses of the Internet

You and your students can use the Internet in a wide variety of ways. The most common applications can be grouped into three categories: communication,

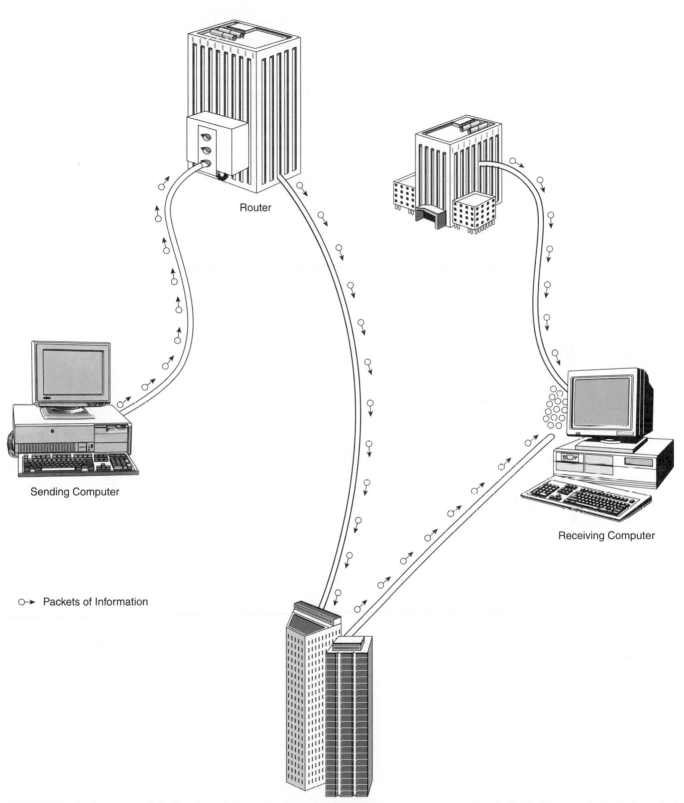

Router

Sending Computer

Receiving Computer

○→ Packets of Information

FIGURE 9–1 Structure of the Internet. Information traveling from one computer to another is divided into packets. Each packet travels independently, often taking different paths. The packets are reassembled at their destination.

Computer Communication over Telephone Lines

For most users, the Internet is accessible from a personal computer over telephone lines on a dialup basis. What is required to make such a connection? In addition to the personal computer itself, one must have a modem, communication software, and a clear telephone line. When two computers communicate, each one must be so equipped (Figure A).

Telephone lines were designed to carry human speech (i.e., sound) between two points. Computers using telephone lines for communication must adapt their information to this format. A *modem* (short for *modulator/dem*odulator) converts a computer's outgoing digital information into analog format (sound) so it can be transmitted over telephone lines, and performs the reverse action on incoming signals. Modems come in both internal (occupying an expansion *bus,* or slot inside the computer) and external varieties. External modems connect by a cable to the computer's serial port. Modems are distinguished, among other things, by their maximum speed of transmission. Speed of transmission is measured by the *baud rate,* which indicates the approximate number of bits transmitted or received each second. For Internet connectivity, 14,400 baud (or what is called a 14.4 k modem) is considered the minimum needed; a 28.8, 33.6, or 56 k modem is preferred. Faster modems exist, but they rely on special connections.

Communication software controls the modem and computer-to-computer communication. The software sets the baud rate and other communication parameters, and it performs "handshaking" with the remote computer to determine exactly how the communication will take place. Most communication software also lets you keep a directory of commonly called numbers. Popular general-purpose computer communication software packages include *Procomm, Crosstalk, QuickLink,* and *Microphone II.* If you subscribe to a commercial service provider such as America Online (AOL) or CompuServe, the service provides communication software specifically designed for its system. AOL, for example, is well known for sending communication disks in the mail to entice people to subscribe to its service.

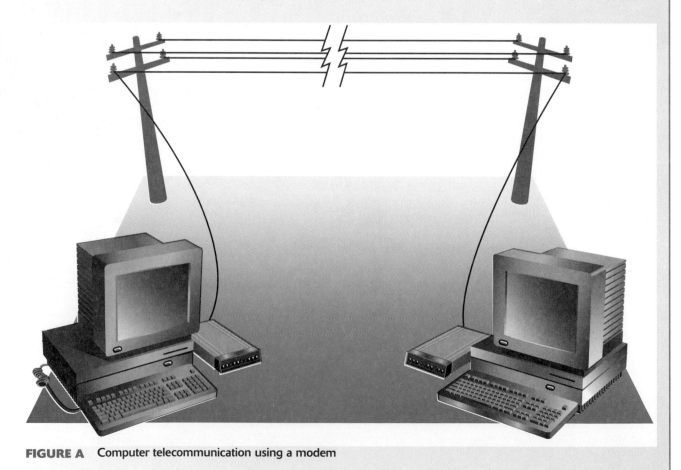

FIGURE A   Computer telecommunication using a modem

information retrieval, and information publishing. We introduce them here, and discuss them at length over the course of this chapter.

Communication
Electronic mail (e-mail) is the most widely used service on the Internet. Anyone with a computer connected to the Internet can communicate with anyone else in the world who is also connected. It is fast, inexpensive, and saves paper. You and your students can also join discussion groups. You can ask questions, discuss problems, and share experiences.

Information Retrieval
There is a lot of interesting and varied information available on the Internet for students and teachers. Most of this information is up to date, available free of charge, and can be accessed in seconds. Computer programs, like word processors, databases, and spreadsheets, as well as lesson plans, are also available.

Information Publishing
You and your students can publish material on the Internet. Publishing on the Internet is quicker than traditional channels. It is also cheaper than "publishing" with a copying machine and sending the documents through the mail. Students' short stories and poems can, with parental approval, be posted on the Internet for the world to read. You can also share your teaching ideas with others in your discipline.

Many think of the Internet as just a transmitter of text material. But graphics, video, sound, and even virtual reality can be sent over the Internet. With a microphone and speaker connected to your computer you can communicate with someone whose computer is similarly equipped as you would during a telephone conversation and not have to pay long distance toll charges. Add an inexpensive camera to each of your systems, and you have a "video phone" (Figure 9–2). The video message can be **asynchronous** (sent like an e-mail and be available when your friend can view it) or **synchronous** (the two of you can communicate in "real time" as you do on a telephone). *Virtual reality* is a computer-generated three-dimensional world. You and your students can enter a virtual world through the Internet and explore ancient ruins, modern cities and museums, and even outer space.

INTERNET APPLICATIONS FOR COMMUNICATION
A valuable aspect of the Internet is its capability of facilitating human interaction and the exchange of data and ideas. You and your students can communicate via the Internet with other students, teachers, and experts in a particular field around the world. The four basic types of communication are e-mail, listservs, newsgroups, and chat groups. Communication by e-mail (electronic mail) is analogous to writing a letter to one person. A listserv is like a bulk mailing. You and your students can subscribe to receive topic-specific information (like magazines) delivered to your electronic doorstep. A newsgroup is a discussion group that allows teachers and students

FIGURE 9–2   A "video phone" can transmit sound and pictures across the Internet

with common interests to communicate with each other. The sites are typically dedicated to a single subject and allow you and your students to read comments and questions, and to post comments, questions, and answers of your own. While newsgroups are asynchronous, individuals using chat rooms communicate instantly (synchronously) by typing back and forth. We look here at each of these four types of communication in more detail.

E-mail

Any communication sent from one individual or group to another over a computer network is called *electronic mail (e-mail)*. It may be sent to or received from another teacher or student in your school or a scientist in Antarctica. Every individual or corporate Internet account holder has at least one unique e-mail address (Table 9–1; also refer back to Chapter 3, Figure 3–11). Because e-mail is transmitted over phone or network lines, it is transmitted in seconds rather than in the days required for postal mail. E-mail is usually a person-to-person communication, and you can provide "enclosures" (called **attachments**) as you would in a letter. In addition, you can send the same letter to multiple individuals as you would copies of a letter sent by the postal service. Using e-mail, you and your students can exchange information with people all over the world. Popular programs for composing, sending, and receiving e-mail include: Qualcomm *Eudora,* Microsoft *Outlook*

TABLE 9–1   *The E-mail Addresses of The Authors of This Text. Feel Free To Communicate With Any of Us*

Author	E-mail Address
Tim Newby	newby@purdue.edu
Don Stepich	D-Stepich@neiu.edu
Jim Lehman	lehman@purdue.edu
Jim Russell	jrussell@purdue.edu

Note: Type all URLs as a single unit, with no internal spaces. Follow all punctuation and capitalization exactly as written, using slashes, hyphens, and underscoring as shown.

Express, and Netscape *Messenger* as well as the e-mail software built into services such as America Online. Free e-mail accounts are even available to individuals on the Web through services such as Yahoo! Mail and MSN Hotmail.

Listservs

One way to receive information over the Internet without having to go look for it is a mailing list. **Mailing lists** use e-mail to deliver topic-specific information to your computer on a regular basis. It is like an electronic magazine. When a mailing list receives a message (information), a copy of the message is sent to everyone on the mailing list. To sub-

TABLE 9–2 *Sample Listservs for Teachers and Students*

List Name	Web Address	Description
Community Learning Network	http://www.cln.org/lists/home.html	Good source for locating educational listservs
San Francisco's Unified School District	http://www.sfusd.kl2.ca.us/resources/listserv.html	Reference for hundreds of educationally oriented listservs
AERA-A	Listserv@asu.edu	AERA division A: Educational Administration Forum
BUGNET	Bugnet@wsuvm1.csc.wsu.edu	Insect education
EDLIST	Desertsky@arizonaone.com	Educators K–12 discussion
ELED-L	Listserv@ksuvm.bitnet	Elementary education list
KIDINTRO	Listserv@sjuvm.stjohns.edu	Pen pal group for children
KIDLIT	Listserv@bingvmb.bitnet	Children's literature
NCTM-L	Listproc@sci-ed.fit.edu	National Council of Teachers of Mathematics discussion
STARNET	Listproc@services.dese.state.mo.us	Student at risk discussion
TEACHNET	Listserv@byu.edu	Exchanging ideas, articles, research, experiences, and questions about teaching
WWWEDU	Listproc@kudzu.cnidr.org	The World Wide Web in Education

Note: Type all URLs as a single unit, with no internal spaces. Follow all punctuation and capitalization exactly as written, using slashes, hyphens, and underscoring as shown.

scribe to a mailing list, all you have to do is to send a message to the **listserv** (the computer that controls, sorts, and distributes incoming information on a particular topic). See Table 9–2 for a small sample of the listservs available for teachers and students. To subscribe to a listserv, contact the computer that administers the list you are interested in. Send an e-mail message with the word "subscribe," the name of the list to which you wish to subscribe, and your name (not your e-mail address). After you send the message, you will receive a confirmation that you are subscribed. Just as you can publish in a journal, you can "post" to a listserv. Likewise, just as you don't have to renew your subscription to a journal, you can stop your subscription to the listserv by sending an "unsubscribe" message to the host computer.

Newsgroups

Newsgroups are like bulletin boards devoted to specific topics. Just as there is probably a bulletin board in your classroom, there are bulletin boards on the Web. **Bulletin board systems** allow you and your students to post information/messages and to read others' messages (Table 9–3). You can "go look at" electronic bulletin boards, just as you might look at a real bulletin board that you pass in the hall each day. For example, you can put a message on the electronic bulletin board for art education and ask for ideas for teaching the color wheel to elementary students. Later that same day or several days later when you log onto that newsgroup, you may find several or tens of suggestions. With a newsgroup you can read all *postings* (questions or information), post your own question or information, and receive answers to your questions. Unlike a listserv, you do not have to subscribe to a newsgroup. You can read and post to any newsgroup you wish to at any time, just as you would a bulletin board in your school.

Chat Rooms

While newsgroups are like bulletin boards, **chat rooms** are like a telephone or CB radio that uses typed words rather than spoken words. Newsgroups are asynchronous, while chat rooms are synchronous. You and your students can "chat" with one person or many people at the same time. You will need a "chat" program on your computer. Like listservs, chat rooms tend to be topic specific (Table 9–4). It can be a time consuming and confusing way to communicate, but most kids love it. It does allow people from all over the world to communicate with each other in real time. However, chat rooms can become addictive and some conversations may

TABLE 9–3　*Sample Newsgroups for Teachers and Students*

Address	Description
K12.ed.math	Mathematics curriculum in K–12 education
K12.ed.music	Music education and performing arts curriculum in grades K–12
K12.ed.comp.literacy	Teaching computer literacy in grades K–12
Alt.parents-teens	Discussions about raising teenagers
Alt.education.distance	Learning over nets via distance
Soc.culture.german	Discussion about German culture and history
Alt.prose	Original writings, fiction and nonfiction

Note: Type all URLs as a single unit, with no internal spaces. Follow all punctuation and capitalization exactly as written, using slashes, hyphens, and underscoring as shown.

TABLE 9–4　*Examples and Sources of Chat Rooms for Teachers and Students*

Name	Web Address	Description
Teachers Net Chatboard	http://www.teachers.net/chatboard/	Dedicated to open discourse among teachers of the world
ESL Chat Central	http://www.eslcafe.com/chat/chatpro.cgi	English as a second language provides forum to chat with ESL/EFL students and teachers from around the world
	K12.chat.senior	Casual conversation for high school students
	K12.chat.elementary	Casual conversation for elementary students, grades K–5
	K12.chat.junior	Casual conversation for students in grades 6–8
	K12.ed.math	Mathematics curriculum in K–12 education

Note: Type all URLs as a single unit, with no internal spaces. Follow all punctuation and capitalization exactly as written, using slashes, hyphens, and underscoring as shown.

not be appropriate for young people, or even for older folks! Just as parents say to their children, "Never talk to strangers," be sure to admonish your students, "Never give out personal information!"

Emoticons are "e-mail body language" and are usually combinations of characteristics that resemble human faces when turned sideways (Table 9–5). Emoticons are used to indicate the writer's feelings because we can't see the writer or hear voice inflection in chat rooms or over e-mail.

Classroom Applications

Learning experiences can be enhanced in a number of ways through the communication application of the Web. Communicating with other individuals and groups allows for the exchange of ideas, insights, and cultures. The following are typical applications of the Web for communication.

▶ Use e-mail "key pals" or electronic pen pals to exchange ideas, cultures, and to learn about and

TABLE 9–5　*Emoticons*

:-)	happy face	:-D	laughing
:-(	sad face	;-)	a wink
:'-(	crying	:-I	indifference
:-X	writer lips are sealed	:->	sarcastic remark
>:->	really devilish remark	:-&	tongue tied
:-/	skeptical	:-O	surprise

from each other. This might occur between two 8-year-olds, or it might be effectively used between students of different countries, or even different age groups (e.g., a college preservice teacher and a group of fifth-grade students).

▶ Use newsgroups involving science experiments in which students from many locations share data. Perhaps, for example, middle school students in New York City could measure air quality data from their city and

TOOLBOX TIPS

Netiquette

The informal rules for appropriate etiquette on the Internet are often referred to as netiquette. The following guidelines apply anytime you or your students are using the Internet (Figure B):

▶ Keep your message short and simple. Try to limit your message to *one* screen. Make it brief, descriptive, and to the point.

▶ Identify yourself as sender. Include your name, school's postal address, and school Internet address. Do not use your or students' home addresses and telephone numbers.

▶ When replying to a message, include the pertinent portions of the original message.

▶ Don't write anything you would not want someone other than the receiver to read. E-mail can be intercepted and/or forwarded.

▶ When joining a newsgroup or listserv, take some time to get acquainted with the topics and typical pattern of postings before contributing your own message. If a FAQ (frequently asked questions) file is available, read it.

▶ Check spelling, grammar, and punctuation. Use lowercase letters except for proper names and beginnings of sentences.

▶ Be sensitive to other people. Treat them with respect and courtesy, especially in reference to social, cultural, and ethnic differences.

▶ Be careful with humor. It is a two-edged sword. The reader doesn't have the benefit of your facial expressions, body language, or tone of voice. You can use "e-mail body language," or emoticons, if you want to clarify your intention.

▶ Cooperate and share. Consider yourself a guest on the system just as if you were in someone's home. In exchange for help and information you receive, be willing to answer questions and to share your resources.

▶ Be certain that your students are aware of netiquette before they use the Internet.

```
Subject: Urban Legend Question
   Date: Wed, 10 Feb 1999 12:06:54 EST
   From: Rjlew98@aol.com
     To: sjackson@cville.k12.in.us, newby@purdue.edu


Hi Sue!

It is Judy from the Tuesday night class (EDCI 560--Purdue).

Regarding the "Urban Legend Question", you will need to write a description of
what an urban legend is or provide an example of a commonly used one.  By
doing this, it will indicate whether you were successful in finding a website
which discussed "Urban Legends".

Feel free to keep your response simple...if you're still not sure...just
include the address of the website that you found on "Urban Legends".

Please let me know if this is still unclear.

Have a great week.

Judy
```

FIGURE B An e-mail message showing proper netiquette

---

compare it with similar data received from students in Mexico City, Mexico, and Sydney, Australia.

▶ Use live chat discussions, in which student teachers discuss problems they are encountering within their current classroom settings with other student teachers or individuals who have been through that experience.

▶ A listserv of individuals within a common group like a gardening club or an afterschool science organization can disseminate information rapidly to all members. For example, the next meeting time, topic of discussion, advance reading, and some reflective questions could be posted on the science club's listserv to allow all members to quickly receive the relevant information and make comments back to the listserv as they deem necessary.

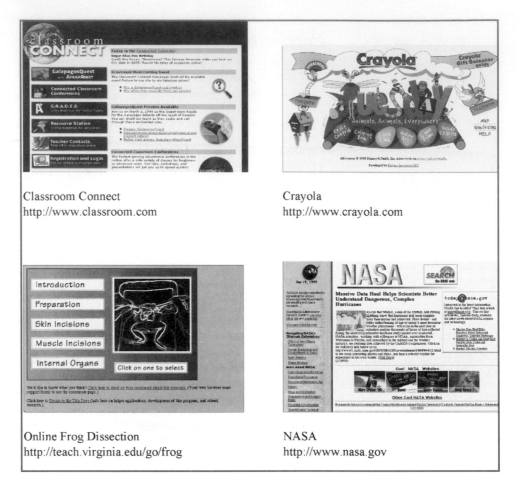

FIGURE 9–3   Websites of interest to teachers and students
Note: Type all URLs as a single unit, with no internal spaces. Follow all punctuation and capitalization exactly as written, using slashes, hyphens, and underscoring as shown.

Classroom Connect
http://www.classroom.com

Crayola
http://www.crayola.com

Online Frog Dissection
http://teach.virginia.edu/go/frog

NASA
http://www.nasa.gov

INTERNET APPLICATIONS FOR INFORMATION RETRIEVAL

Both students and teachers can access valuable resources and a wealth of up-to-date information on the Internet. Students no longer are limited to textbooks and resources in the library. Today you and your students have access to the latest, most up-to-date information located far beyond the walls of the school building (Figure 9–3). The information is available on the Web in the form of databases, documents, government information, online bibliographies, publications, and computer software.

The **World Wide Web** (usually referred to as simply "the Web") is a part of the Internet. Countless documents (including text, graphics, sound, video, and even virtual reality) are stored on computers around the world on documents called **Web pages.** A **Website** is a collection of Web pages maintained by a school, university, government agency, company, or individual. A **Web server** is a computer connected to the Internet that makes Web pages and Websites available to other computers.

Each Web page has a unique address, called a **Uniform Resource Locator (URL).** See Chapter 3, Figure 3–11 for the components of a URL. Web pages are hypertext documents. A **hypertext** document contains highlighted text that connects to other pages on the Web, often at other diverse locations. Hypertext allows you to quickly move from one Web page to another.

One easy way to move around the Web and to locate specific information is a *Web browser.* A **browser** allows you and your students to navigate through information on the Web by choosing nonsequential pathways. The two most common Web browsers are Netscape *Navigator* and Microsoft *Internet Explorer.* Both are available free of charge on the Web if they are not currently on your home or school computer (Netscape *Navigator* at http://home.nctscape.com and Microsoft *Internet Explorer* at http://www. microsoft.com/ie).

While exploring the Web, you may find sites of interest and wish to return to them in the future without having to remember where you were or to retrace your path. A **bookmark** allows you to return to interesting sites without having to remember and retype the URL. Browsers include easy ways to create, store, and retrieve bookmarks. The computer stores the Website address and allows you to easily

TOOLBOX

TIPS

Using Search Engines

Search engines are Websites designed to help people locate information of interest on the Internet. Search engines do not search the Internet in real time. Instead, each search engine maintains a database of information accumulated from the Internet. When you use a search engine and submit a query, the database is searched to yield Web pages, and sometimes other sources of information (e.g., newsgroups), that fit the search criteria. These are returned as a list of "hits," rank ordered according to criteria applied by the search engine. Different search engines maintain different databases of information, and they apply different criteria to rank order the list of potential sites. So, it is a good idea to use those search engines that best fit your needs, or use a variety of search engines when you are looking for information.

Although the specifics of searching for information vary from engine to engine, basic techniques apply across most. Search engines allow you to search for topics using key words. Pick relevant nouns or proper names as key words. Avoid common words (e.g., education, computer) that will return too many hits. Use several key words together to narrow your search (e.g., lesson, biology, plant, elementary). When you want to search for a specific term or phrase, enclose it in quotes (e.g., "lesson plan," "American history"). Many search engines allow you to include key terms with + and exclude other terms with a − (e.g., the key terms "recipe, cookie, +oatmeal, −raisin" would yield a search for cookie recipes containing oatmeal but not raisins). Many search engines permit you to use an asterisk (*) as a wild card at the end of a term to broaden the search (e.g., the key term "planet*" would yield hits for planet, planets, planetary, etc.). Some search engines also allow the Boolean (logical) operators OR and AND to be used with key words to expand or narrow searches, respectively. Popular search engines appear in the following table.

Search Engine	URL
~~Altavista~~ Google	http://www.google.com http://www.altavista.com
Dogpile	http://www.dogpile.com
Excite	http://www.excite.com
Hotbot	http://www.hotbot.com
Infoseek	http://www.infoseek.com
Lycos	http://www.lycos.com
Magellan	http://www.magellan.com
Metacrawler	http://www.metacrawler.com
Snap	http://www.snap.com
Webcrawler	http://www.webcrawler.com
Yahoo	http://www.yahoo.com

Note: Type all URLs as a single unit, with no internal spaces. Follow all punctuation exactly as written.

For more information about how to search the Internet for information, visit the listed search engines and view the guidelines associated with each. You can also visit any of a number of sites that provide information about how to use search engines and locate information on the Web, including the Companion Site for the Official Netscape Guide to Internet Research (http://www.coppersky.com/ongir/), a Guide to Effective Searching of the Internet (http://thewebtools.com/searchgoodies/tutorial.htm), and Search Engine Watch (http://www.searchengine-watch.com/).

recall it using a pull-down menu. Bookmarks may also be filed and divided into many different file folders for easier access if you have a lot of them. For a class, each student may want their own file folder.

Another browser feature is **image capture,** which allows you and your students to "copy" images from others' Web pages and add them to your own.

A reminder about copyright is in order here. *All images on the Internet are copyrighted!* You must have permission to use any image from the Internet (see the discussion on copyright in Chapter 6). You can purchase collections of ready-made images, called *clip art,* which come with permission to use them for certain circumstances. In other cases you and your students must ask for permission from the copyright holder *before* including the image on your own Web page or with any other materials—even for educational purposes.

> **Plug-ins** allow you and your students to display or play certain types of files on the Internet. A plug-in performs tasks the Web browser cannot perform on its own. You must access the appropriate plug-in before you can work with that particular file. For example, Adobe Systems's *Acrobat Reader* lets you view and print Portable Document Format (PDF) files. PDF files are an Internet standard for cross-platform distribution of formatted documents. *Acrobat Reader* is available free of charge at www.adobe.com. Another plug-in, *Crescendo* (available at www.liveupdate.com), lets you listen to background music while viewing text and images on a Web page. Of course, the music must be "programmed" into the Web page by the creator. In order to see some multimedia presentations on the Web, you will need the *QuickTime* plug-in (quicktime.apple.com) or Real Networks's *Real Player* or *G2* standalone helper application (www.real.com). There are literally hundreds of plug-ins available, many at your browser's home Website.

Classroom Applications

The information retrieval aspect of the Internet offers some exciting application possibilities within all classrooms. With access to so much information, you and your students will need to develop skills to be able to effectively wade through all of the possibilities, find that which is most relevant, and determine its quality. Here are just a few ideas of how you can use access to this unlimited information to enhance students' learning experiences:

▶ Conduct online research using databases and other online resources. Here you and your students can access information on almost any topic, from a variety of sources, very quickly. Finding huge amounts of information on topics such as whales, tax laws, soccer rules, trigonometry equations, and kindergarten safety is no longer difficult. Additionally, this information frequently includes visuals, audio, and other media formats beyond text.

▶ Monitor current events through online newspapers and magazines. No longer do students have access to only hometown newspapers and weekly news magazines for current affairs information. Access to the Internet allows you and your students to get up-to-the-minute information on critical news stories and read it from a variety of sources. Now students can access and read what their local newspapers have to say about some current event and immediately compare that with what is being written by the national news organizations and even those from countries around the world.

▶ Access databases of teaching methods, instructional strategies, and lesson plans. Finding information on what to teach and how to teach is now easy. From hands-on science experiments to drama techniques, lesson plans are available to give ideas to both new and experienced teachers.

▶ Retrieve information on possible job opportunities. Information on potential employment, contact personnel, and how to prepare (e.g., résumé development) for job interviews is readily available.

INTERNET APPLICATIONS FOR INFORMATION PUBLISHING

Everyone likes to see his/her writings in "print." You and your students can publish material on the Internet. As we stated earlier, the Internet is a quick and inexpensive method for sharing ideas. Students' short stories and poems can, with parental approval, be posted on the Internet for the world to read. You can also share your teaching ideas with others in your discipline.

The procedures for publishing on the Internet are becoming steadily easier. Publishing on the Internet is almost as easy as generating an e-mail communication. Many schools, teachers, and even students have their own home pages. A **home page** is the main or first page in a Website. People often create personal home pages that show their hobbies, picture, family. It is best *not* to put pictures and personal information of students on Web pages created at school.

The explosive growth of the World Wide Web has led to a surge of interest in Web page authoring in K–12 schools. Many schools now have their own home pages, and an increasing number are using the Web as a vehicle for students to make their work public. As a result, a student's hypermedia project that once may have been seen only by her teacher and classmates may now be available for viewing by anyone in the world. Realistically, of course, the world will probably not beat an electronic path to every school Web page in cyberspace. However, the mere idea that the world can see their work is highly motivating to students, and posting students' hyper-

TABLE 9–6   *Guidelines for Designing Web Pages/Sites*

Start with users.	Know who your users will be and what they are interested in learning.
Identify your purpose.	Describe in writing what you want your users to gain from the Web page/site to keep you on target as you design it.
KISS Principle—Keep It Simple for Students.	Do not assume that users will have the latest and fastest technology to access your Web page/site.
Limit information on each page.	A guideline is about 250 words and a few graphics per page.
Follow guidelines for text development.	See Chapter 6, Figure 6–4, "Guidelines for designing instructional materials."
Use simple graphics that load quickly.	Each page should load in less than 30 seconds using a 28.8 k modem.
Follow guidelines for designing visuals.	See Chapter 6, Figure 6–4, "Guidelines for designing instructional materials."
Limit number of links to other information.	Too many links without structure and guidelines can cause users to get lost in cyberspace.
Provide navigational support.	Don't assume users know as much about the site as you do.
Avoid useless and annoying animation (blinking and movement).	Put your emphasis on the content, not the glitz.

media projects to the Web for all to see does give parents, grandparents, and members of the community an opportunity to keep tabs on what is happening in the school.

When creating Web pages, students may encounter similar difficulties to those they encounter when authoring other forms of hypermedia (see Chapter 8). For example, there is a tendency for students to want to jump right in and begin authoring Web pages without planning. As in other types of development efforts, a little planning at the beginning pays great dividends later on. In addition, as with other forms of visual expression, there is a need for students to adhere to good visual design guidelines (Table 9–6; also see "Toolbox Tips: Guidelines for Designing Graphics," in Chapter 6). In fact, design problems are exacerbated on the Web, because different browsers interpret Web pages in somewhat different ways. It is a good idea when possible for students to check the appearance and functionality of their pages using more than one browser.

It also very important for you and your students to remember that the Web is a public medium of expression. When a student makes a mistake on a paper written in the classroom, probably only the teacher and the student see that error. An error on a Web page has the potential to be seen by many people, which can be very embarrassing for everyone. There is also significant potential for students to get into trouble with copyright infringement on the Web (see the discussion on copyright in Chapter 6). A student who scans a picture from an encyclopedia for a report in class is probably protected under fair use guidelines. But, displaying that scanned picture on the Web without permission would be a clear violation of copyright law. As a general rule, you should assume that material gathered from other sources, including the Web itself, is copyrighted and cannot be displayed on the Web without permission. When in doubt, err on the side of caution.

The hypermedia applications highlighted in Chapter 8, such as *HyperStudio, HyperCard,* and *Toolbook,* now offer tools that make projects developed using these programs available over the Web. However, many schools are turning to the development of Web pages themselves as a way for students to do hypermedia authoring. There are two basic options: Web development tools and authoring in HTML. For a brief overview of Web development tools, see "Toolbox Tools: Web Page Authoring Software." Here, we introduce the basics of HTML, the language of the Web.

Basics of HTML

HTML, Hypertext Markup Language, is the underlying "language" of all Web pages. Each Web page is derived from an HTML document; you can see the document that gives rise to any Web page by choosing the option to view the page source in your Web browser. (This is a great way to learn how to do things.) HTML is not a language in the usual sense of a computer language such as Logo or BASIC. Rather, it is a set of conventions for embedding tags or markup labels within a text file. Because HTML documents are plain text files, you can create them with any text editor, including simple ones such as *Windows WordPad* (or the older *Notepad*) or Apple's *SimpleText*. Alternatively, students can use any word processor to create the HTML document as long as the document is saved in plain text (or ASCII) format. HTML is relatively easy to use and even younger students can learn it.

TABLE 9–7　*Common HTML Tags*

HTML Tags	Function
Organizational	
<HTML> . . . </HTML>	Identifies a Web document
<HEAD> . . . </HEAD>	Specifies the head portion of a Web document
<TITLE> . . . </TITLE>	Defines the title of the page; placed in the head
<BODY> . . . </BODY>	Specifies the body portion of a Web document
Text Formatting	
<H1> . . . </H1>	Largest size heading; others denoted by H2 through H6
<P> . . . </P>	Denotes a paragraph of text
<B> . . . </B>	Specifies boldface
<I> . . . </I>	Specifies italics
<UL> . . . </UL>	Defines an unordered (bulleted) list
<OL> . . . </OL>	Defines an ordered (numbered) list
<LI>	Marks a list item
<CENTER> . . . </CENTER>	Centers text or other elements
 	Creates a line break; new text goes on the next line
Tables	
<TABLE> . . . </TABLE>	Defines a table
<TR> . . . </TR>	Denotes a table row
<TD> . . . </TD>	Denotes an item of table data
Images	
<IMG SRC = "graphic">	Causes an image file to be loaded and displayed
<HR>	Creates a horizontal rule (line) on the page
Links	
<A HREF="url">link text</A>	Defines a link to a particular URL

HTML **tags** tell Web browsers (e.g., Netscape *Navigator* or *Internet Explorer*) how to interpret the text that is marked up. In most cases, the tags tell the browser how to display information on the computer's screen and how to do things like link to other Web pages. Most tags come in pairs, a beginning tag and an ending tag. For example, the tags <B> </B> are used to bracket text that is to be boldfaced (e.g., <B>some text</B> would be displayed by a Web browser as **some text**). All tags are set off by angle brackets (<>). Capitalization of tags is not required, although many people write tags in all capitals to make them easy to see in HTML documents. Tags can be nested within other tags to create compound effects (e.g., <B><I>boldface and italics</I></B> would yield ***boldface and italics***). See Table 9–7 for a list of some of the most common HTML tags.

Tags control a variety of aspects of a Web page. Some tags define the overall organizational structure of a Web document, such as defining the two main divisions of every Web page, the head and the body. Relatively little information typically is found within the head; the title of the page is one example. Most content is located in the page body.

In addition to text formatting, tags also control text layout. For example, one can center or otherwise align page elements, or create tables. Tables are often used on Web pages to control more complex layouts of information.

The <IMG> tag is used to insert a graphic image. Graphic images can also be defined as maps that allow the user to click on an area of the image to invoke a link. Links, connections to other Web pages, are a key feature of most Web pages. Links are accomplished using the anchor tag. The basic format of an anchor tag is

<A HREF="url">the text that signifies the link</A>

Web Page Authoring Software

When the World Wide Web first burst onto the scene a few years ago, tools for creating Web pages were few and far between. As a consequence, many people jumped into learning HTML. While there may still be merit in understanding the fundamentals of HTML, today it is no longer necessary to know HTML inside and out in order to create functional and attractive Web pages. Web page authoring tools allow you to create pages using a simple interface similar to a word processor or presentation package.

There are several categories of Web authoring tools available today, ranging from word processors to HTML editors to products designed to make it easier to manage whole Websites. Among the simplest to use of all of the tools for creating HTML documents is a basic word processor. The latest versions of most popular word processors (e.g., Microsoft *Word,* Corel *WordPerfect*) now provide an option to save documents as HTML. Simply create your document onscreen as you would if you were writing a report, and select the save as HTML option. It is simple and easy. However, word processors were not designed specifically for Web page creation, and they may not be as easy to work with or provide results as good as products designed for that purpose.

A number of programs specifically designed for Web page creation are on the market today. Most of these programs adopt a visual WYSIWYG approach to Web page creation; just design what you want on the display screen, and the software creates the underlying HTML to make it happen. Programs include Adobe *PageMill,* Claris *HomePage,* GoLive *CyberStudio,* Macromedia *Dreamweaver,* Microsoft *FrontPage, NetObjects Fusion,* Netscape *Composer,* and Symantec *Visual Page.* Prices and features vary. While the first products of this type were basically tools for visually designing individual Web pages, more sophisticated features are finding their way into these products. More advanced features include site management tools, such as a visual site map and sitewide spell checking, link testing, and search and replace. Some products are also providing support for the latest developments in Web creation including Java and JavaScript language support, cascading style sheets, and dynamic HTML.

Figure C shows an example screen from Filemaker's Claris *HomePage.* It has become a popular Web development tool in many schools because of its blend of many powerful features and ease of use.

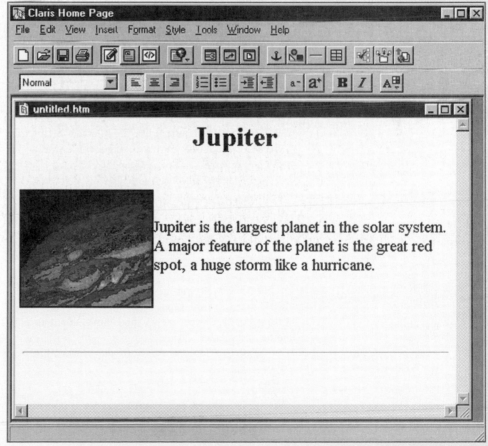

FIGURE C A screen from Claris *HomePage,* a Web page authoring application
Source: Claris Home Page, FileMaker, Inc.

FIGURE 9–4 An example Web page and its corresponding HTML document

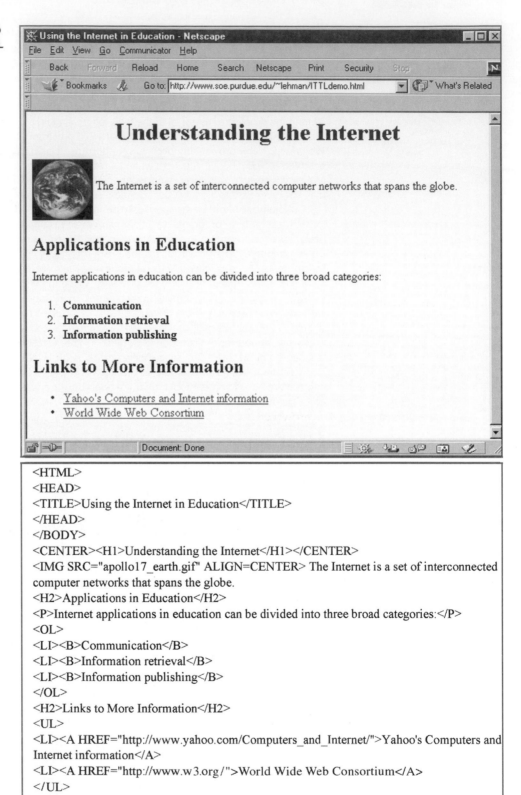

```
<HTML>
<HEAD>
<TITLE>Using the Internet in Education</TITLE>
</HEAD>
</BODY>
<CENTER><H1>Understanding the Internet</H1></CENTER>
<IMG SRC="apollo17_earth.gif" ALIGN=CENTER> The Internet is a set of interconnected
computer networks that spans the globe.
<H2>Applications in Education</H2>
<P>Internet applications in education can be divided into three broad categories:</P>
<OL>
<LI><B>Communication</B>
<LI><B>Information retrieval</B>
<LI><B>Information publishing</B>
</OL>
<H2>Links to More Information</H2>
<UL>
<LI><A HREF="http://www.yahoo.com/Computers_and_Internet/">Yahoo's Computers and
Internet information</A>
<LI><A HREF="http://www.w3.org/">World Wide Web Consortium</A>
</UL>
</BODY>
</HTML>
```

The first part of the expression indicates what URL, or Web location, will be linked to. The text between the tags is what appears in the browser as an active link (usually underlined and often denoted by the color blue). A link to Yahoo's home page might be denoted

<A HREF="http://www.yahoo.com">Visit Yahoo</A>

The text "Visit Yahoo" would appear as a link (probably underlined and blue) on the page in your browser. Clicking on that text would execute the link to the actual Yahoo Website. Links such as this can be embedded in the middle of sentences to make the links appear as natural parts of the text, or you can create lists of links for others to follow.

See Figure 9–4 for a simple example of an HTML document using several common tags with the corresponding Web page that this document creates. There are many more HTML tags than we have space to discuss here. Indeed, HTML itself is not a static set of standards, but is still evolving. In the quest to produce better and more interactive Web pages, efforts are constantly underway to refine and expand HTML. For more information about the latest developments in HTML, visit the World Wide Web Consortium's Website (http://www.w3.org/).

Classroom Applications

Student development of Web pages offers many opportunities for classroom activities that parallel those that we cited for hypermedia authoring packages in the last chapter. Typical applications of the Web for information publishing include the following:

▶ Students can create hypermedia projects or reports on the Web in much the same fashion as they might use a hypermedia authoring tool such as *HyperStudio*. Such projects can contain textual information, pictures, and other multimedia elements. Significantly, on the Web, they can also contain links to further information at that site or on other Websites.

▶ The Web is a great tool for displaying examples of students' work. Parents and members of the community can get a sense of what goes on in the school by seeing posted work. Remember: always get permission from *both* students and their parents/guardians before displaying students' work on the Web.

▶ Learning how to develop Web pages may be an educational goal in and of itself. Students, for example, might learn Web page development skills by helping to construct or maintain a portion of the school's Website. This "win-win"

situation gives students experience and helps schools to maintain a Web presence by using an inexpensive pool of student labor.

Reflective Questions

▶ How might you use the Internet for communication, information retrieval, and information publishing in your teaching?

▶ How might your students use the Internet for communication, information retrieval, and information publishing in your student-centered classroom?

PLANNING FOR THE INTERNET IN THE CLASSROOM

In the next three sections, we use our PIE model, introduced in Chapter 1, as our framework for discussing using the Internet in education. We begin with the P in the model—*planning*.

As we discussed in Chapter 4, you need to develop a plan for using the Internet in the classroom just as you need a plan when using any methods and media. First, you need to consider the characteristics of your students. When using the Internet, you must give special attention to their abilities to access the Internet for communication, information retrieval, and information publishing if they are going to "post" material on a Web page. If your students don't have these skills, you will need to teach them.

In specifying objectives for your students, you will need to determine if using the Internet will enhance their ability to meet the objectives. In many cases, the Internet can provide more up-to-date information on the content you are studying. In other cases, your students will need to communicate with others outside the classroom to meet their objectives.

The learning environment will need to include access to a computer. It may be one computer in the classroom or a computer lab where all students can access the Internet simultaneously.

When selecting methods and media as well as specific instructional materials, you will need to preview the material on the Internet related to content and objectives. This is no different than previewing a videotape before you decide to use it with students. You may choose to see if a lesson plan has already been developed that is appropriate for your students and the content you plan to have them learn (see "Toolbox Tips: Finding Lesson Plans on the Web," in Chapter 4).

Selecting Websites is no different than selecting any instructional materials (textbooks, videotapes, audio recordings, etc.) as described in Chapter 6. See the "Preview Form: Web Pages/Sites" in Appendix B for the criteria for evaluating Internet sites. There are countless Websites for students and teachers. We have included some of our favorites and our students' favorites in Table 9–9.

You can add Internet components to traditional lessons. However, not all lessons benefit from Internet additions. You will need to search for effective Internet resources to add. Go online and search for information on your topic. Be sure to thoroughly explore the site to uncover any inappropriate materials and to find any dead ends. You should also search all links for similar problems.

You should not have students use the Internet just for its own sake. Students should not use the Internet to find information readily available in the classroom. To avoid problems when you implement a lesson, practice to see if the Internet portion of the lesson works. Also see if you have allocated enough class time for the activity. You may even want to have another teacher or colleague review or even do the lesson.

Copyright and Fair Use of Materials on the Web

All materials on the Internet are copyrighted! It is no different from materials published in a textbook. Just because something can be copied electronically doesn't mean it can legally be distributed without the copyright holder's permission. You may use Internet materials personally, but you may not make copies, modify them, or incorporate them into commercial materials without the permission of the copyright holder. Likewise, you should *not* post on a Website any materials (stories, artwork, photographs, poems, etc.) created by your students or photographs of your students *without* the written permission of their parents or guardians. You may want to spend some class time discussing copyright rules and guidelines with your students. Check with your school administration as to the local policies. Refer again to the information on copyright in Chapter 6, and visit the Websites listed in Table 6–1.

IMPLEMENTING THE INTERNET IN THE CLASSROOM

In this section, we discuss *implementation*—the I in our PIE model. When using the Internet with students, you should follow the same general guidelines discussed in Chapter 7: prepare instructional materials, prepare learning environment, prepare learners, and proceed with lesson. Preparation is the key to success! Preparing materials requires that you determine that the Websites you plan to use are still available (Tables 9–8 and 9–9). Some Websites change dramatically over time and others may no longer be available. Check the sites you plan to use a week or so before the planned use date. If possible check them about the same time of day that you plan to have students access them. Some very popular

---

TABLE 9–8 *Websites of Resources and Examples about Using the Web for Educational Purposes*

Name	Web Address	Description
Global School Net Harnessing the Power of the Web	http://www.gsn.org/web/	A tutorial that teaches about integrating the Internet within classroom instruction
Learning Resource Server (LRS)	http://lrs.ed.uiuc.edu/Mining/Overview.html	A series of articles from *The Computing Teacher* about using the Internet in the classroom
Learning Resource Server (LRS)	http://lrs.ed.uiuc.edu/Guidelines/guidelines.html	A collection of a rich variety of guidelines on how to use the Internet in powerful ways for education
Classroom Connect	http://www.classroom.net/resource/lessonplans	Sample lesson plans that integrate classroom use of the Internet
Internet Adventures: K–12 Resources	http://www.xplora.com/~xplora/ancient_civ_newsletter.htm	A comprehensive example of an Internet-based thematic unit of instruction (Ancient Greece)

Note: Type all URLs as a single unit, with no internal spaces. Follow all punctuation and capitalization exactly as written, using slashes, hyphens, and underscoring as shown.

TABLE 9–9 *Popular Educational Websites*

Name	Web Address	Description
AskERIC	http://ericir.syr.edu	Gateway to the information resources of the ERIC system (especially research reports); the link to the Virtual Library connects you to such resources as lesson plans on various subjects.
The CIA World Factbook	http://www.odci.gov/cia/publications/pubs.html/	A well-organized, easy-to-use Website containing maps and data on population, geography, economics, and governments of countries from A through Z
Classroom Connect	http://www.classroom.net	A valuable site for K–12 teachers and students including classroom links, materials for educators, addresses of other educators online, and products to bring the Net into the classroom
CNN Interactive	http://www.cnn.com	An up-to-the-minute source of news, weather, sports, science and technical information, show business, and health
The Crayola Site	http://www.crayola.com/crayola	A colorful site with activities, stories, and games for young people
Department of Education	http://www.ed.gov/	The U.S. Department of Education's Website, with information on its programs and services. This includes research reports, statistics, and news related to educational technology
Discovery Channel School	http://discoveryschool.com	Resources from the Discovery Channel for teachers and students.
ICONnect	http://www.ala.org/ICONN/index.html	Gateway to the American Association of School Librarians' site; the Curriculum Connection link takes you to Web links associated with teaching different school subjects
Kathy Schrock's Guide for Educators	http://discoveryschool.com/schrockguide	Includes a list of Internet sites found to be useful for enhancing curriculum and teacher professional growth
LION (Librarians Information Online Network)	http://www.libertynet.org/~lion/lessons.html	An information resource for K–12 school librarians supported by the School District of Philadelphia. Includes lesson plans for teaching library skills and also for incorporating Internet resources into other subjects
Maps and References	http://www.cgrer.uiowa.edu/servers/servers_references.html	A listing of maps, tutorials, atlases, geographic references, bibliographies, and other resources.
National Education Association	http://www.nea.org/cet/	The NEA's Teaching, Learning, and Technology department includes topics such as software selection and inservice training, plus links to teachers' resources for lesson planning
TeachNet's Teacher-Activities and projects	http://www.teachnet.org/docs/sharing/index.htm	A collection of "battle-tested teacher-designed developed classroom projects" covering the range of K–12 subjects. Supported by TeachNet, the Website of the Education Commission of the States

Note: Type all URLs as a single unit, with no internal spaces. Follow all punctuation and capitalization exactly as written, using slashes, hyphens, and underscoring as shown.

Source. Some of the data for this table are from Instructional Media and Technologies for Learning, 6th ed. (pp. 271–272) by R. Heinich, M. Molenda, J. D. Russell, and S. E. Smaldino, 1999, Upper Saddle River, NJ: Merrill/Prentice Hall. Reprinted by permission.

sites may not be quickly accessible during midmorning or midafternoon because students at other schools also are connected to them.

While preparing your learning environment, check that the computer or computers are working properly and that they have Internet access. In most schools you will have to schedule the computer laboratory if many students are to access the Internet simultaneously. If you are going to access the Internet as a class, be sure that the computer projection equipment is working properly and that all students will be able to see the image and hear the sound.

You will need to prepare your students for the lesson activity whether it is to be done individually, in small groups, or as a class. Discuss the purpose (objectives) of the lesson, provide written guidelines for the activity, and remind them of the copyright guidelines and acceptable use policies for your school.

When the lesson begins, monitor individual students to keep them on task and to be sure that they are following the Internet use guidelines for your school (see "Toolbox Tips: Acceptable Use Policies"). For group use of the Internet, you will be able to monitor what students are doing. Make certain they do not wander off into cyberspace or to an inappropriate site. Just as a student who is directed to find information in a standard encyclopedia may be sidetracked by unrelated pictures and content, students are often distracted on the Internet.

You and your students must have realistic expectations of the Internet. It will not answer all questions and solve all learning problems. The Internet is a learning tool (admittedly a powerful one), and like all tools, you must use it properly. You cannot just turn students loose and hope for the best.

Security

In all cases you should monitor your students when they are using the Web. Discourage students from exploring inappropriate Websites either accidentally or deliberately. The amount and level of your monitoring will be determined by the maturity of your students and local school policies. Instruct students to *not* give out personal information such as phone numbers and addresses. If students are using the Web or Internet for gathering information for a school project, instruct them to receive the information at school using the school's electronic address or postal address.

EVALUATING THE INTERNET IN THE CLASSROOM

We conclude our discussion of using the Internet in education by exploring *evaluation*—the E in our PIE model. How will you and your students know if the Internet lesson was successful? You will need to develop skills in evaluating all media and materials available. This is particularly true of materials on the Internet. For most printed materials, especially textbooks, there are editors who review the materials and make sure what is presented is accurate. You and your students need to understand that what you read on the Internet may not be correct. To assist you, we provide in Appendix B, in the Preview Form: Web Pages/Sites, a set of evaluation questions about the quality of Websites and the manner in which information is presented. However, even if the Web page meets these criteria, it is still no guarantee that the information on it is correct.

One of the most important criteria is to evaluate the content and to separate it from the glitz. It goes back to the old proverb, "Never judge a book by its cover." Many Websites are pretty, but also pretty shallow in terms of content. Inaccurate and inappropriate content beautifully presented is still inaccurate and inappropriate!

Following a lesson, you and your students need to take time to evaluate how the Internet worked (or didn't work) within the lesson. You need to determine if the students learned from the experience. (We will discuss the "Thinking like an evaluator" philosophy in Chapter 10.)

Following each lesson, whether it included the Internet or not, reflectively think of ways in which you could improve it by adding materials and/or experiences. Then focus on how to develop or get the needed materials and/or experiences. Could you achieve this through the Web? As an example, let's consider a lesson about transitive and intransitive verbs. Reflect on how you were taught about them. After reviewing how you learned (which perhaps included something from the Web), think of ways in which your teacher could have improved the lesson. For example, your students could go to the Online Writing Lab at Purdue University (http://owl.english.purdue.edu) and get online help with this topic. Perhaps you want to visit this site and consider ways to embellish such a lesson with resources from the Internet.

The Internet is a tool, a very powerful tool, for teachers and students to bridge distances and enhance learning opportunities. From anywhere in the world, with access to the Internet one can visit the Louvre, check out exhibits of the Library of Congress, or tour the treasures of the Smithsonian Institution. But, the

TOOLBOX

TIPS

Acceptable Use Policies

Some information on the Web is inappropriate for students. What you might consider appropriate might be considered inappropriate by parents or your school administration. It is the responsibility of your school board to establish acceptable use policies for your district. Acceptable use policies are signed agreements among students, parents/guardians, and the school administration outlining what is considered to be proper use of the Internet and Web by all persons involved (Figure D). Locate and read your local policies very carefully *before* you use the Internet or Web with your students. Protocol will vary from one community to another.

Internet Use Agreement

The intent of this contract is to ensure that students will comply with all Network and Internet acceptable use policies approved by the District. In exchange for the use of the Network resources either at school or away from school, I understand and agree to the following:

A. The use of the network is a privilege which may be revoked by the District at any time and for any reason. Appropriate reasons for revoking privileges include, but are not limited to, the altering of system software, the placing of unauthorized information, computer viruses or harmful programs on or through the computer system in either public or private files or messages. The District reserves the right to remove files, limit or deny access, and refer the student for other disciplinary actions.

B. The District reserves all rights to any material stored in files which are generally accessible to others and will remove any material which the District, at its sole discretion, believes may be unlawful, obscene, pornographic, abusive, or otherwise objectionable. Students will not use their District-approved computer account/access to obtain, view, download or otherwise gain access to, distribute, or transmit such materials.

C. All information services and features contained on District or Network resources are intended for the private use of its registered users. Any use of these resources for commercial-for-profit or other unauthorized purposes (i.e. advertisements, political lobbying), in any form is expressly forbidden.

D. The District and/or Network resources are intended for the exclusive use by their registered users. The student is responsible for the use of his/her account/password and/or access privilege. Any problems which arise from the use of a student's account are the responsibility of the account holder. Use of materials, information, files, or an account by someone other than the registered account holder or accessing another person's account without permission is forbidden and may be grounds for loss of access privileges.

E. Any misuse of the account will result in suspension of the account privileges and/or other disciplinary action determined by the District. Misuse shall include, but not be limited to:

   1) Intentionally seeking information on, obtaining copies of, or modifying files, other data, or passwords belonging to other users.

   2) Misrepresenting other users on the Network.

   3) Disrupting the operation of the Network through abuse of or vandalizing, damaging, or disabling the hardware or software.

   4) Malicious use of the Network through hate mail, harassment, profanity, vulgar statements or discriminatory remarks.

   5) Interfering with others' use of the Network.

   6) Extensive use for noncurriculum-related communication.

   7) Illegal installation of copyrighted software.

   8) Unauthorized down-sizing, copying, or use of licensed or copyrighted software or plagiarizing materials.

   9) Allowing anyone to use an account other than the account holder.

   10) Using the Internet without a teacher's permission.

   11) Violating any local, state, or federal statutes.

FIGURE D Sample statement of Acceptable Use Policy from Crawfordsville (IN) School Corp. *Source:* Crawfordsville Community School Corporation, Crawfordsville, IN 47933.

Internet is not the only tool that allows students and teachers to overcome the barriers of distance. We next turn our attention to the full range of distance education technologies that are helping to change the face of teaching and learning today.

Reflective Questions

▶ Why is planning important when using the Internet? What are the potential hazards and pitfalls if you do not plan properly?

▶ What implementation strategies for the Internet are different from implementation strategies for other media?

▶ Why is evaluation necessary before, during, and after using the Internet? What evaluation strategies are most appropriate when using the Internet?

Problems and Pitfalls

The Internet is a rich source of information for students and teachers. It can also provide quick communication and a place to display ("publish") materials. However, these benefits have a downside as well. There is a financial cost to access the Internet. Costs vary greatly from school to school depending on arrangements with local Internet Service Providers (IPS). Once the connection is there and paid for, there still may be a problem gaining access. Frequently a Website may be busy or not available when you or your students want to access it. This is especially true for popular educational sites during the school day. Other times the school's connection to the Internet may be down.

Many educators believe that the biggest problem with the Internet is students deliberately or accidentally gaining access to inappropriate material. To discourage this—it can never be totally prevented—requires close monitoring. Students also may choose to "play" on the Internet. They gain access to age-appropriate materials not relevant to lesson content. For example, a student may access the "Hot Wheels" Website during a social studies class studying World War I.

DISTANCE EDUCATION

Distance education refers to an organized instructional program in which teacher and learners are physically separated. It addresses problems of educational access. Obviously, distance itself can be a major barrier to individuals seeking education. People in rural or remote locations are often at a disad-

vantage educationally compared with those in urban areas. Resources may be scarce, and, in the worst cases, there may not be enough teachers to reach the students. A small, rural school may not be able to justify the cost of a teacher to provide advanced physics instruction or teach Japanese to a handful of students. Problems of access may be manifested in other ways as well. For example, learners who are homebound due to illness or physical disability may not be located far from an educational institution, but they are effectively isolated. Adults who wish to pursue education may lack the time needed to pursue traditional coursework at a local school or college. For them, home study may be the only option. Distance education can overcome many of these problems of access and provide educational opportunities.

Distance Education Technologies

The earliest efforts at distance education involved correspondence study in which individuals used self-study printed materials. While useful and still in existence today, print-based correspondence study is limited, especially because of the limited interaction between instructor and learners. Over the years, various technologies have been employed to enhance distance education, including radio, television, and the telephone. Today a variety of telecommunication technologies are available for support of distance education. Often, a key element of these technologies is their ability to enhance communication between teacher and learners. We look at three broad categories of distance education technologies: audio-based, video-based, and computer-based.

Audio-Based Technologies

Radio is an audio-based technology with which all of us are familiar. It has the capability to reach a relatively broad geographical region at relatively low cost when compared to a delivery technology such as television. It can provide a standardized message to a large audience, and it has clear utility in areas such as music, discussion, dramatic presentation, and language learning. However, radio broadcasts adhere to a fixed schedule, and this can be a disadvantage compared with more flexible media such as audiocassettes. In addition, without special measures, radio is a one-way medium; it sends a message from the instructor to the learners, but it doesn't allow learners to send messages back to the instructor. Today radio rarely plays an overtly instructional role in this country, although educational and informational programming are staples of the National Public Radio network. However, in some developing countries where schools are scattered across isolated geographical regions, radio is used successfully for instruction.

Audio teleconferencing is a distance education technology that overcomes the one-way limitation of radio. It is an extension of a basic telephone call that permits instruction and interaction between individuals or groups at two or more locations. By using a speakerphone or more sophisticated audio equipment (e.g., microphones, amplifiers, noise filters, high-quality speakers), members of the audience can both hear and be heard. This allows for true, live, two-way interaction between two or more physically separated sites.

Audio teleconferencing is a popular and convenient way to conduct meetings or simple instructional sessions in situations where the time and cost of travel cannot be justified. When only dialogue is needed—for example, for discussion or consultation—it is ideal. A literature teacher might use it to have her students interact with the author of a book the class has recently read. A foreign-language teacher might use it to permit students to interact with a native speaker of the language. Audio teleconferencing offers the advantage of true interaction; people can talk to one another. Its chief limitation is that it is an audio-only medium. Visual elements are absent, unless print-based or graphical materials are distributed to the participating sites in advance.

Video-Based Technologies

Video overcomes the lack of visual elements in audio-based distance education technologies. Video may be delivered over distances using a variety of means, including broadcast television, satellite and microwave transmission, and closed-circuit and cable systems. The key distinction among the various delivery systems is the degree of interactivity afforded. Options include one-way video and audio, one-way video with two-way audio, and two-way video and audio.

Video, like radio, often involves one-way transmission of information, with limited opportunities for interaction. This mode of information delivery is typical of broadcast television, and experiments in the use of television for education date back many years. Today, many schools make use of programming developed by the Public Broadcasting System as well as special programming designed specifically for schools, such as Whittle Communication's *Channel One* and CNN's *CNN Newsroom*. The obvious advantage of one-way video for distance education is its ability to cost effectively reach a mass audience with both video and audio information. Its chief limita-

tions are time dependence (i.e., programs are broadcast at certain times, whereas videocassettes can be used at any time that is convenient) and the lack of interaction between instructor and learners.

One solution to the interactivity problem associated with one-way video is to provide two-way audio accompaniment. This approach is common where video is used to deliver formal instruction, as in video-based courses. Audio "talkback" capability usually is added by means of a simple telephone connection, perhaps with a speakerphone, between the originating video location and the receiving sites. With this talkback capability, students can call the instructor with questions or comments. In other words, talkback capability allows students to be active participants rather than passive receivers of a video-based message. This is a significant advantage compared to one-way video. Limitations include the added cost of talkback capability, the instructor's lack of visual contact with callers, and problems of access that can arise when many receiving sites attempt to call a single originating site.

The latest development in video-based distance education is **two-way interactive video.** With this technology, both sending and receiving sites are equipped with cameras, microphones, and video monitors. Some means of transmission—satellite, microwave, cable, fiber optic, or digital-grade telephone line—links the two (or sometimes more) sites together. As a result, a high level of interaction is possible, with audio and video information traveling in both directions. This is the closest approximation to face-to-face instruction yet achieved by technological means. Figure 9–5 shows an example of a two-way, interactive video classroom.

Clearly, two-way interactive video overcomes many of the limitations of one-way distance education technologies. It promises to offer situations where an expert teacher at one location can teach a class that is physically dispersed, complete with visual feedback and interchange among sites. Experiments in the use of two-way interactive video in K–12 schools are underway at many sites, and considerable enthusiasm surrounds the potential of this medium. However, it is important to recognize that this technology is still in its infancy. Video compression, which is needed to support two-way video transmission over telephone lines, is technically difficult and can result in problems with picture quality. In addition, two-way interactive video equipment can be quite complex and expensive to set up and operate. Schools interested in exploring this technology should consult experts in the field for advice about the best ways to proceed.

FIGURE 9–5   A two-way, interactive video classroom

Computer-Based Technologies

Computers represent one of the newest tools for distance education. Just as audiocassettes and videocassettes can be used to supplement print-based correspondence study, computer diskettes or CD-ROMs with instructional software can be mailed to learners for correspondence study on home computers. However, this approach doesn't use computers as telecommunication tools. There are, however, ways to use computers to augment audio and video telecommunication, as well as ways to use them as telecommunication tools in their own right.

Audiographics refers to the use of audio teleconferencing along with the transmission of still pictures and graphics. Several techniques can be used to accomplish the transmission of images to accompany an audio teleconference. These include slow-scan video, fax, and electronic graphics tablets. At heart, each of these is really a computer-based technology, and, in fact, the most sophisticated audiographics systems include an integrated computer. Audiographics enhances the basic audio teleconference by adding the capability of using images. However, the addition of audiographics capability significantly increases the cost of audio teleconferencing equipment. Also, when images are transmitted over standard telephone lines, voice interaction can be interrupted on many audiographics systems, and transmission time can be lengthy.

Audio teleconferencing now can be conducted over the Internet using computers. Recent developments in Internet-based telephony make it possible to conduct telephone calls that are routed across the Internet. To accomplish this, one must have the appropriate hardware and software. While some systems require that both parties be online before a connection can be established, the newest developments allow an individual to place a call, much as one normally would, with the call routed across the Internet instead of across standard telephone circuits. This option is less expensive than a telephone call, especially for international calling, but there can be lags in response time and degradation of audio quality from the transmission across the Internet.

Computers can also be used to enhance both one-way and two-way video teleconferencing. With special computer-based hardware, a computer signal can be "gen-locked," or integrated into a video signal. This permits a computer to be used as a presentation tool in video-based distance education (see Chapter 8 for a discussion of the computer as a presentation tool). With this technique, you can use the computer like a slide projector to present computer text and/or graphics, or like a sketch pad to dynamically create drawings. If the aim of the distance education is to teach or demonstrate a particular computer application, this too can be accomplished. Of course, this capability adds to the cost of a video conferencing system, and there is some loss of resolution when a computer display is converted into video.

Computers can also be used for what is known as **desktop video conferencing.** With appropriate hardware and software—an appropriate network or modem connection, a microphone, speakers, and a small video camera—computers can communicate via both audio and video across the Internet. This is the computer equivalent of video conferencing or what is sometimes called *video phone* technology. Popular software for desktop video conferencing includes: White Pine's *CUSeeMe* and Microsoft's *NetMeeting*. While functional, this technology is currently limited because it requires a lot of bandwidth.

Image sizes are typically quite small, and transmission rates are slow, resulting in jerky images. For best results, special high-speed connections, such as over ISDN digital telephone lines, are needed. However, as the technology matures, it promises to become an important option for distance education.

Desktop video conferencing is one way to use computers as devices for distance education. **Computer-mediated communication (CMC)** is the term given to any use of the computer as a device for mediating communication between teacher and learners and among learners, often over distances. Common CMC applications include e-mail, computer conferencing, and the Web. E-mail permits personal communication between teacher and learners and among individual learners. Increasingly, e-mail is providing a kind of "electronic office hours," whereby students can keep in contact with teachers.

Computer conferencing systems, like audio and video conferencing, permit two or more individuals to engage in dialogue. However, computer conferencing is a text-based asynchronous communication medium; people do not interact with one another at the same time. Instead, these systems allow individuals who have access to an appropriate personal computer or terminal to type messages and post them to the conference at any time and from any place that is convenient for them. The computer maintains and organizes the messages posted by the participating individuals. So, a computer conference resembles an ongoing conversation, in printed form, where participants can drop in and out at any time without missing anything. Some conferencing systems operate on a dedicated computer that users access through a dialup or network connection; there are also Web-based conferencing systems.

When synchronous or same-time interaction is desired, computers support what is commonly referred to as a *chat* function. As discussed earlier, individuals interact by typing messages back and forth to one another. This can be done one-to-one. Alternatively, a chat room allows multiple individuals to interact simultaneously. Chat room interactions resemble CB radio traffic, except in printed form. Chat rooms have become popular on the Internet as places for electronic socializing. They can be used in the classroom, for example, to permit students to interact with students from another school about a science experiment or other project, or to allow students to interact online with an expert such as a book author.

Of course, the Web with its abundance of resources is quickly becoming a key component of many distance education experiences, even those that rely on other delivery systems, such as video. The Web can deliver content, provide links to information at other locations, and serve as a focal point for a distance education experience. Web courses and programs are proliferating rapidly at the college level, and they are beginning to appear in K–12 education as well.

Computer-mediated communication, whether via the Web or a dedicated computer system, can remove barriers both of distance and of time. Students can take classes from anywhere that there is a network or telephone connection and, for asynchronous approaches, at any time that is convenient to them. Further, because the Internet is now reaching into millions of homes, schools, and places of work around the world, this technology has the potential to inexpensively reach almost anywhere. However, it requires computer access and familiarity for effective use. In addition, some content cannot effectively be taught via this medium. For example, you would not want to fly in a plane that has been serviced by a mechanic who has only learned about aircraft engines on the Internet. However, as the Internet continues to expand, it is likely that increasing use will be made of computer-based distance education, both alone and in conjunction with other distance education media.

Classroom Uses of Distance Education Technologies

Distance education technologies can be used for most educational goals that one would have in a typical classroom. Some common applications of distance education technologies include the following:

▶ Reaching individuals isolated by distance or geographical barriers
▶ Reaching nontraditional populations of learners (e.g., adult learners, homebound individuals)
▶ Providing instruction in specialized subject areas, such as advanced physics or foreign languages, for which a local teacher might not be available
▶ Bringing experts or other special individuals into the classroom from a distance (e.g., having the author of a children's book interact with a class of elementary students who have just finished reading the book)
▶ Linking two classrooms together so that students can interact with one another to learn, solve problems, and communicate

▶ Allowing teachers to consult with experts at remote locations regarding teaching practices, curriculum, research, and so on

Problems and Pitfalls

Distance education technologies offer many exciting opportunities for educators and for learners. However, they are not without cost, both in monetary terms and in difficulty. All distance education technologies entail some real monetary cost. In the case of simpler technologies, such as audio teleconferencing, this may be only the cost of a long-distance telephone call. That alone, however, may be a problem in some schools. More advanced distance education technologies, such as two-way interactive video, can be very costly. The equipment needed is expensive, and the recurring costs associated with actually connecting two sites can be quite high. Distance education technologies can be technically complex as well. While an audio teleconference may not be too difficult to set up, video conferencing requires expert assistance and may involve the coordinated efforts of local personnel, vendors, telephone company technicians, and others.

Distance education requires careful planning. This is true even for simpler forms of distance education. Most distance education media require advance scheduling of equipment and facilities. Materials may need to be prepared in advance and sent to participants or remote sites. In many cases, teachers need to redesign curriculum and learning activities to accommodate or take advantage of the distance education medium. Teachers may need training to effectively use distance education technologies. Learners may need assistance in learning via these unfamiliar means, and provisions for assisting participants need to be made. These may involve onsite coordinators, telephone help, e-mail, and the like. In short, there is a lot to distance education, and teachers and schools shouldn't expect to engage in it without significant effort. As with any other educational enterprise, distance education requires time, effort, commitment, and resources. The technology is only a tool that helps schools meet existing needs.

Reflective Questions

▶ Have you ever participated in a distance learning experience? Reflect on what it was like. What did you like about it? What didn't you like?
▶ Why is planning so important in distance education? What problems can result from inadequate planning?

APPLICATIONS IN THE LEARNER-CENTERED CLASSROOM

In this chapter we have discussed the use of both the Internet and various forms of distance education. The use of these technologies has increased the ability to communicate. Although many individuals immediately grasp the convenience of quick communication that electronic mail provides, there are other benefits you also should recognize. For example, within the learner-centered classroom, an emphasis on social and cultural diversity is possible (Wagner & McCoombs, 1995). As students work within cooperative groups, they come to learn how individuals can work together to accomplish tasks. Likewise, through the use of technology, those cooperative groups may come to include individuals that actually reside and live at great distances away from each other, but are attempting to work together. It is conceivable that small groups of students may include individuals from all parts of the world and across many different cultures. This may allow students to learn to appreciate a wider variety of views of the world around them. They may come to see potential solution paths that previously they did not think possible.

ONE TEACHER'S STORY

by Janette Moreno

I recently had a wonderful opportunity to use the Internet and distance education technologies to provide my advanced Spanish students with a unique educational experience. Our class had spent several weeks studying the cultures of northern and southern Spain. They had read a number of things, and browsed the Web to look at sites from Spain including Spanish newspapers online. The students had enjoyed learning about the different areas of Spain, so I decided to capitalize on their enthusiasm and provide them with the opportunity to interact directly with people living in those areas.

When I was in high school, I had a pen pal in Barcelona. We used to write and send each other things like coins, stamps, photographs, and postcards. I always regretted that I never met Juanita, or even spoke with her. I have no idea where she might be today. But it made me think, with the technologies we have today, that my students ought to be able to do more than I did.

I decided to get in touch with my old professor, Señor Diego, and his wife, who is a high school English teacher in Seville. I e-mailed them one day, and we decided to see if we could do a "real-time" conversation between the students in Señora Diego's English class and the students in my Spanish Conversation class. It sounded neat to both of us, and so I started to look into it.

I talked to our technology coordinator, to the principal, and to a bunch of other people. The bottom line was that a video teleconference was just going to cost too much. The school wouldn't do it, even if we technically could. The technology coordinator told me that video conferencing on the computer was an option, but wouldn't be very good for a whole class of students. So I decided to try an audio teleconference. My principal okayed that when the Spanish Club agreed to pay for the call. So, I e-mailed Señora Diego and we arranged the day and time, being sure to account for the time difference with Seville.

About a week later, using a speakerphone I borrowed from the media center, I called Señora Diego at the arranged time. I had had my students prepare questions for the Spanish kids, and they all took turns asking and answering questions. My kids spoke Spanish, and her kids spoke English. It was pretty crazy, but somehow they all managed to understand each other. I think they thought it was pretty cool.

As a followup activity, my students and her students became e-mail pen pals or, what do you call them, keypals. So, the students got to practice their writing skills as well as their speaking skills. They were really motivated to do well because they knew someone real was on the other end. I think the neatest thing is that a lot of the kids continued to correspond with each other throughout the year and beyond. One of my former students stopped by this fall to tell me that she had finally met her Spanish pen pal last summer when her family took a trip to Spain. Pretty neat, huh?

SUMMARY

In this chapter we examined three applications of the Internet for instructional purposes: communication, information retrieval, and information publishing. We related Internet use to the PIE model—planning for the Internet, implementing the Internet, and evaluating the Internet. In spite of its potential access to inappropriate material for your students, they and you can facilitate their learning by accessing the seemingly endless amount of information available. The Internet contains lesson plans and materials for you to use in promoting learning as well as instructional materials and information in a wide variety of formats (text, audio, and video) that your students can use individually, in small groups, or as a class to increase their knowledge and skills and to change their attitudes and perceptions of the world around them.

We also examined distance education, any organized instructional program in which the teacher and learners are physically separated. Distance education addresses problems of educational access caused by distance, disability, or work and family obligations among others. Technology is often used in distance education to facilitate communication between teacher and learners. We examined the characteristics of three categories of distance education technologies: audio-based, video-based, and computer-based.

REFLECTIVE ACTIVITIES

▶ E-mail one of the authors of this text with a question or comment (see Table 9–1).
▶ Preview several Web pages/sites related to the subject matter you teach or plan to teach. Use the Preview Form found in Appendix B.
▶ Sit in on a distance education class at your school or a nearby college or university. What evidence do you see that the instructor relies on planning, implementation, and evaluation in this setting?

SUGGESTED RESOURCES

Books

Ackerman, E. (1995). *Learning to use the Internet: An introduction with examples and exercises.* Wilsonville, OR: Franklin, Beedle, & Associates.

Gardner, P. (1996). *Internet for teachers & parents.* Westminster, CA: Teacher Created Materials.

Kehoe, B., & Mixon, V. (1997). *Children and the Internet: A Zen guide for parents and educators.* Upper Saddle River, NJ: Prentice Hall PTR.

Lamb, A., Smith, N., & Johnson, L. (1996). *Surfin' the Internet: Practical ideas from A to Z.* Emporia, KS: Vision to Action.

Miller, E. B. (1997). *The Internet resource directory for K–12 teachers and librarians,* 1996–97. Englewood, CO: Libraries Unlimited.

Rivard, J. D. (1997). *Quick guide to the Internet for educators.* Needham Heights, MA: Allyn & Bacon.

Ryder, R. J., & Hughes, T. (1997). *Internet for educators.* Upper Saddle River, NJ: Prentice Hall.

Sharp, V. F., Levine, M. G., & Sharp, R. M. (1997). *The best Web sites for teachers.* Eugene, OR: International Society for Technology in Education.

Videos

Distributed by AECT

Exploring Internet Resources. (1997). 60 minutes.
Integrating Internet Resources. (1997). 60 minutes.
Creating Internet Resources. (1997). 60 minutes.

The Internet Revealed **Series produced by Classroom Connect (1995)**

The Amazing Internet. 17 minutes.
Internet E-Mail. 27 minutes.
Searching the Internet. 24 minutes.
Discovering the World Wide Web. 38 minutes.

PBS Series, aired in February and March, 1997

A Teacher's Guide to the Information Highway. (2/27/97). University of Wisconsin.
Internet for Teachers. (3/19/97). White Rain Films.
Distanc e Learning Today. (3/19/97). Minnesota Satellite & Technology.
Transforming Teaching and Learning Through Electronic Visualization. (3/21/97). Mississippi State University.

Produced/Distributed by Educational Video Network

Internet for Educators. (1996). Part 1, 35 minutes; Part 2, 35 minutes.
Video Guide to the Internet. (1994). 45 minutes.

Produced/Distributed by Films for the Humanities & Science

The Internet: How to Plug In. (1996). 30 minutes.
Your School and the Internet. (1996). 45 minutes.

Produced/Distributed by Insight Media

How to Use the Internet in the Classroom. (1995). 30 minutes.
Inside the Internet. (1996). 20 minutes.
Internet for the Educator. (1996). 48 minutes.
Netscape—The Easiest Way to Surf the Internet. (1995). 40 minutes.
Teaching and the World Wide Web: Global Online Projects. (1995). 70 minutes.
Understanding the Internet. (1996). 30 minutes.

CD-ROM

CD-ROM distributed by Insight Media

Educator's World Wide Web Tourguide. (1995).

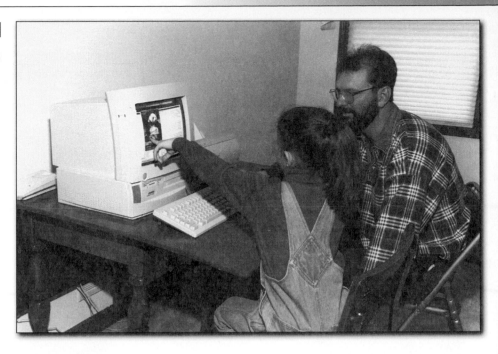

EVALUATION

Evaluation is, and probably always will be, anxiety provoking. That is, most of us feel a little nervous when someone says, "Next week, you will be tested on . . ." or "It's time to assess your skill level in . . ." or even "Demonstrate how well you've mastered the goal of . . ." Why? Because evaluation is the major way we receive information about our levels of competency and skill—and that information may reveal some of our inadequacies. In a commercialized world that constantly promotes perfection, being shown that you have more to learn is about as much fun as a two-hour root canal procedure.

If evaluation is that unpleasant, why bother with it? Although many students may think that tests are created merely as a way for teachers to inflict pain and suffering, in most cases there is a good reason for their use. That reason centers around the *feedback* they provide. By obtaining feedback about your current level of performance, you can make the changes needed to reach your specific goal.

When individuals realize the value of feedback, evaluation becomes a desirable tool for facilitating improvement. Recall the opening pages of Chapter 1, where we described a master cabinetmaker and explained some of the differences between experts and novices. One of the critical differences mentioned was the way experts constantly engage in self-evaluation. Their goal is to change or eliminate small imperfections early on, so they do not become big problems later. This is the true essence of evaluation—helping learners to assess where they are and then envisioning what their next steps might be.

In Chapter 10 the focus is on evaluation as a tool for improvement. It looks at evaluating both students and instructional materials. In both cases we discuss various instruments you can use to supply feedback *as* learning is occurring (or supposed to be occurring) as well as *after* learning has occurred. Additionally, you will see how the computer can be an important assistant in your evaluation process.

CHAPTER 10

Evaluation of Students and Materials

KEY WORDS AND CONCEPTS

Evaluation
Cycle of continuous improvement
Pretest
Formative evaluation
Summative evaluation
Pilot test
Triangulation

OBJECTIVES

After reading and studying this chapter, you will be able to

▶ Describe the purposes of evaluating student learning and the effectiveness of instruction before, during, and after a learning experience.
▶ Identify and describe a variety of techniques for evaluating both students and instruction and describe their advantages and limitations.
▶ Use a list of developmental guidelines to construct and/or assess a set of evaluation instruments.

PLANNING FOR THE CHAPTER CONTENT

Instructional Technology for Teaching and Learning, will show you how to increase learning by designing lessons that use instructional technology, including computers and other media.

This chapter will focus on using evaluation as a tool to increase learning. In this chapter we explore methods designed to measure how well students have learned and how effective your instruction is. With this information, you will be able to make changes in instruction in order to increase its effectiveness, efficiency, and appeal.

This chapter expands the PIE model, as shown in the following outline:

Plan
Implement
Evaluate—students and instruction
  Before
  During
  After

INTRODUCTION

Evaluation is a common activity. As an example, recall the last time that you took a shower. Did you just take off your clothes, step in, turn on the water, lather up, rinse off, and step out? Probably not. Most of us have learned not to stand in front of a shower and then turn it on. Instead, we first stand off to the side, run the water for a moment, and then check its temperature with our hand or foot. If the water is too hot or too cold, we adjust it until it feels "just right." Likewise, during the shower, we monitor the temperature and adjust it whenever it feels too hot or too cold. During a typical shower we may also find ourselves thinking about whether we have rinsed all the soap off, left enough hot water for the next person in the family, and stayed in the shower long enough to wake up, sing, and think about the day's activities.

This example illustrates the basic purpose of evaluation: to make sure that we are getting what we want and, if not, to figure out what we can do so that we can get what we want in the near future.

In this chapter, we describe evaluation in terms of *what* it is, *why* you should do it, and *how* to do it.

WHAT IS EVALUATION?

Evaluation is the process for gathering information about the worth or quality of something as a way of making decisions designed to increase its worth or quality.

Within education, evaluation is an ongoing process. Recall again your most recent shower, described in the introduction. Note that evaluation in this case did not occur at a single point in time. Evaluation occurred before, during, and after the shower. This is typical of good evaluation, in the classroom as well as the bathroom.

In discussing the PIE model in Chapter 1, we described evaluation as a time to reflect on both successes and problems, resulting in information you can use to improve the quality of instruction. Seen in this way, a thorough evaluation considers all instructional components—objectives, activities, methods, media, and materials—as well as the way you combine and present them to students to help them learn. This reflection can occur at any point in the learning process. This translates into a **cycle of continuous improvement,** represented graphically in Figure 10–1.

There are two important characteristics of this cycle. First, evaluation is an integral part of planning and implementing instruction, rather than something that simply gets tacked on to the end of the process. Evaluation is an important part of "reflection in action" (Schön, 1983), in which instructional experts continually monitor their efforts to help their students learn, looking for and incorporating ways to better match instruction to them. Second, evaluation allows you to make adjustments as

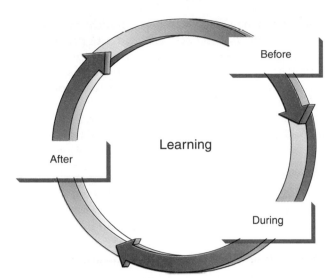

FIGURE 10–1   The cycle of continuous improvement

you gain information from one part of the learning process. You can use the information as the input for the next part of the process, following it with more evaluation and adjustment. This cycle repeats throughout the instructional process.

Naturally, evaluation takes a somewhat different form at different points in the cycle. Evaluation *before* instruction has a future orientation: How will it work? This encourages *pre*planning by providing a framework for making conscious estimates about the effectiveness, efficiency, and appeal of instruction. Evaluation *during* instruction has a present orientation: How is it working? Continuing the evaluation during the lesson allows you to revise instruction in time to benefit current students. Evaluation *after* the instruction has a past orientation: How did it work? This encourages conscious reflection about the effectiveness, efficiency, and appeal of the instruction so you can improve it for the next time.

Evaluation also can focus on both learning and instruction. We commonly think of teachers evaluating their students in order to give them a grade. But teachers also naturally evaluate their own instruction. As a result, evaluation can focus on determining both how well students have learned the desired material and how effectively the instruction helped them learn.

WHY EVALUATE?

This is not always as simple a question as it seems. Sometimes, evaluations indicate that "all is well." However, evaluations often point out problems and weaknesses, and indicate the time and effort that you must devote to making changes. This isn't always something to look forward to.

So, if evaluation often points out your weaknesses and increases your workload, why would you want to do it? The answer lies in the fact that evaluation provides information you can use to guide your efforts to improve. In addition, the amount of information increases as you repeat the cycle. Throughout the cycle, the consistent purpose of the evaluation is to increase the amount of student learning that takes place by continually evaluating the instruction in terms of its effectiveness (Does it lead students to their learning goals?), efficiency (Does it make good use of available time and resources?), and appeal (Does it hold students' interest and maintain their motivation?). As you repeat the cycle your evaluation gains power, like the proverbial snowball rolling downhill. It should come as no surprise that instruction that has been used (and evaluated) several times often works better than instruction being used for the first time. Through repeated evaluation, information accumulates and trends—both positive and negative—become identifiable. Based on emerging trends, you can update content; revise methods, media, activities, and materials; and add new ones. Thorough and continuous evaluation contributes to this in the following ways:

▶ Identifying areas of the content that are unclear, confusing, or otherwise not helpful
▶ Identifying areas of the content that have the highest priority for revision because they (1) are the most critical aspects, (2) are the most difficult to learn, or (3) are likely to have the greatest impact on learning
▶ Providing a rationale and evidence in support of making specific revisions

Thinking like an evaluator, therefore, means that you view evaluation as a way to improve and that you seek, rather than avoid, opportunities to evaluate your efforts.

Evaluation takes on slightly different purposes depending on whether the focus is on student learning or the effectiveness of the instruction. We focus first on student learning.

Evaluating the learner. During a recent parent-teacher conference, Ms. Sara Powley, the ninth-grade English teacher at McCutcheon High School, explained some of the assignments and tests her students had completed. Her comments focused on the first essay examination. She explained that, for many students, this was the first exam they had taken that relied entirely on essay questions. She described how well the students had done and to what extent they had achieved the intended objectives. This particular evaluation method, Ms. Powley explained, had been helpful in a number of different ways. First, she thought that it had served as a great motivator. It gave students a reason to think about what they had discussed in class and to assimilate information from many different topics. Second, it provided information about how well students were able to recall, analyze, and integrate critical information. Third, students' answers provided an indication of their writing skills. Fourth, the exam gave students the chance to determine how well their study habits were working. By comparing *how* they had studied with *what* had been asked on the exam, they could judge if their efforts had been successful. Finally, the exam provided Ms. Powley with a way to give students useful feedback. Her extensive comments on the essays highlighted strengths and weaknesses of students' work.

Before instruction, evaluation (often called a **pretest**) can serve the following purposes:

▶ Identify students' preinstructional knowledge and skill levels. This indicates (1) whether students have the prerequisite knowledge and skills and (2) whether they already know the lesson content.

▶ Focus learners' attention on the important topics you will cover. In this way, the students are primed to notice those important topics when they come up during the instruction (Fleming, 1987).

▶ Establish a point of comparison with postinstruction knowledge and skills. One word of caution: Tell your students that you predict lower scores on a pretest since they are taking it prior to the lesson. Be sure they understand that you are not holding them responsible for content you have not yet taught them.

For example, our English teacher, Ms. Powley, could have given her English class an essay pretest as a way of identifying the students' prerequisite knowledge and showing the students what they would be expected to learn. For those students who had already mastered the content, Ms. Powley could have provided some enrichment activities.

During instruction, evaluation (often called **formative evaluation**) serves the following purposes:

▶ Determine what students have learned to that point. Both teachers and students can use this information to determine if new content can be introduced or if additional practice is needed to master the previous content.

▶ Supply feedback as the learning process occurs. This feedback both can increase students' confidence by indicating that they have mastered content to that point and can correct problems *before* they become thoroughly ingrained.

▶ Identify when and what type of additional practice may be needed. As students progress, evaluation ensures that they are integrating the new knowledge and skills with previously learned information and that they can apply this learning when needed.

▶ Refocus students' attention. In the event that students lose sight of their goals and objectives, a formative evaluation can be an effective tool for refocusing their attention.

For example, Ms. Powley evaluated how well students were learning new information throughout the course. Her formative evaluations often consisted of asking students to write a paragraph or two summarizing a new topic. As Ms. Powley pointed out, her reasons for evaluation during instruction were to (1) find out how well students were assimilating the information and (2) encourage the students to monitor their own learning.

After instruction, evaluation (often called **summative evaluation**) serves the following purposes:

▶ Measure what students have learned. This is the most frequent use of formal evaluation. Along with demonstrating their learning, summative evaluation gives students the opportunity to think about and synthesize what they have learned.

▶ Make specific decisions about grades, accreditation, advancement, or remediation.

▶ Review important knowledge and skills and **transfer** them to new and different situations. The value of new knowledge and skills increases when it can be used in a variety of contexts and a summative evaluation can facilitate this transfer.

For example, Ms. Powley used the essay exam to determine how well her students could perform following instruction. The exam indicated how much improvement they had made and whether they could advance to the next unit of instruction.

Evaluating the instruction. As an example of the continuous cycle of improvement when the focus is on the effectiveness of the instruction, consider the following high school history class. Each semester, Mrs. Singleton teaches a twelfth-grade U.S. history course to about 25 students. One of the units in the course focuses on the broad impact of various social issues that took shape during the 1960s, including desegregation and civil rights, the Cold War, poverty and the Great Society, and the space race. As part of her research, Mrs. Singleton previewed the *American History Videodisc* produced by the Instructional Resources

TABLE 10–1 *Key Questions for Evaluating Learning and Instruction*

	Evaluating Learning	Evaluating Instruction
Before Instruction	Do students have the prerequisite knowledge and skills?	How well is the instruction likely to work?
	Do students already know the content they are slated to learn?	Will the instruction hold student interest?
	What is the student's current level of performance (baseline)?	Is there an alternative way to organize the instruction to make better use of available time and resources?
During Instruction	Are students ready for new content or is additional practice and feedback needed?	What obstacles are students encountering and how can they be overcome?
	In what specific areas do students need additional practice and feedback?	What can be done to maintain student motivation?
	What types of remediation or enrichment activities may be necessary for students?	How can these students be helped to better progress through the instruction?
After Instruction	Have students learned what was intended?	What improvements could be made in the instruction for future use? What revisions have the highest priority?
	Can students be accredited or "passed"?	Did students find the instruction interesting, valuable, and meaningful?
	What will be needed to help students generalize what they have learned and transfer it to new situations?	Were the selected instructional methods, media, and materials effective in helping students learn?

Corporation. The videodisc contains a collection of photographs and short video clips that can be randomly accessed with a bar code reader and shown on a monitor connected to a videodisc player. The photographs and video clips are arranged chronologically and described in an accompanying catalog. Mrs. Singleton thinks the images on the disc will help make her presentation of the events of the 1960s less abstract and will stimulate discussion among her students.

Before the lesson (often called a **pilot test**), Mrs. Singleton discusses the visual images she has selected with Ms. Fellows, who also teaches history at the school. They discuss which issues might be most interesting to students, which are most likely to be confusing to students, and what possible directions students might take in their discussion of the issues. Based on this conversation, Mrs. Singleton decides to add a few images to her initial presentation and to identify a second set of images that matches the directions students are likely to take in their discussion.

During the lesson (formative evaluation), Mrs. Singleton begins by showing a few selected images related to each issue, briefly describing each image. She begins the discussion by asking, "Which of these events had the greatest impact on American society during the 1960s?" Mrs. Singleton closely monitors the discussion as it progresses. She uses images from the videodisc, including the second set she had selected, to focus the discussion when it gets off track,

to provide additional information when students request it, and to provide visual support to students making critical points.

After the lesson (summative evaluation), Mrs. Singleton assigns students the task of selecting one of the issues presented in class and writing an essay about the breadth and depth of its impact. As she reads the essays, she notes that, in general, they are thoughtful and insightful and that they include more specific references to people, places, and events than had been the case when she had taught the lesson without the videodisc. She determines from this that the videodisc presentation is worth trying again, and she decides to expand its use. She considers using the videodisc to link the social issues of the 1960s and the 1930s to encourage students to compare the two periods. She makes notes on her lesson plan about the issues and questions that generated a lot of discussion, the types of images that might help bridge the two periods, and possible adaptations to the essay assignment.

Before she teaches the lesson during the next year, Mrs. Singleton reviews her notes and incorporates them into a revised instructional plan, emphasizing the link between the 1960s and the 1930s. She selects a new set of photographs and video clips to show to students, revises the question she will ask to begin the discussion, and modifies the essay assignment.

Table 10–1 summarizes the key questions that you should consider for each aspect of evaluation.

HOW TO EVALUATE

Now that you understand what evaluation is and why you should do it, we look at specific techniques you can use to conduct the actual evaluation. There are three basic principles to keep in mind as you select and use these techniques. First, continuous improvement requires continuous information. Recall that the purpose of evaluation is to increase the amount of student learning through ongoing self-renewal. To be effective, therefore, evaluation isn't simply tacked on to the end of the learning process. Instead, continuous improvement depends on a steady stream of information flowing before, during, and after every period of instruction. Over time this information may become increasingly detailed and the refinements in the instruction may become increasingly small, but these small refinements are no less important to student learning than the earlier, larger refinements (for a fuller discussion, see Stiggins, 1997).

Second, encourage and teach students how to evaluate for themselves. We most often think of evaluation as being done by the teacher. Teachers, as instructional experts, are responsible for evaluation. However, throughout the cycle of evaluation, students can often evaluate their own learning and the instruction implemented to help them learn. They may need help in identifying the best techniques to use, and guidance in how to use those techniques, but they can often be effective evaluators.

Before the lesson, students can ask, What will work best for me? This will encourage them to think strategically, identifying the instructional methods, media, activities, and materials that are most likely to help them achieve the learning goals. *During* the lesson, students can ask, Is this working for me? This will encourage them to think about what they are learning and what they are having trouble with, thus helping to identify where they need additional information and/or different study techniques. *After* the lesson, students can ask, Did this work for me? This will encourage them to think about their own skills as learners and about the learning strategies they use. They can then make a conscious effort to add to their repertoire of learning strategies and become more effective learners. Finally, *before* the next lesson, students can ask, What will work best for me now? This will encourage them to think ahead about their newly developed learning skills and strategies, identifying ways the instructional methods, media, activities, and materials can be matched to their particular skills and strategies.

Third, information will carry more weight when it has been "triangulated" (Kemp, Morrison, & Ross, 1998). **Triangulation** refers to the process of obtaining information from multiple techniques or sources.

All information is useful. However, information is strengthened when supported by information from other techniques or sources. Similarly, information is weakened when contradicted by information from other techniques or sources. Therefore, rather than relying on a single source of information, when possible gather information from several different sources.

Techniques to Evaluate Student Learning

It would be wonderful if, as shown in Figure 10–2, all learners could be plugged into a machine that would overtly indicate when learning had occurred. Although it isn't quite that easy, there are means that you can use to help identify when, and to what degree, learning has occurred.

This section will give you an overview of different techniques you can use to evaluate student learning, some of their advantages and limitations, and some guidelines for their selection and use. The first group of instruments will focus on traditional means of gathering evaluation data (e.g., multiple-choice, essay, and true-false items), and the second will be devoted to alternative evaluation techniques (e.g., portfolios, logs, journals). We have included both types for a very important reason: different instruments will give different types of feedback. Just as we have shown the need for you to know a variety of instructional methods and media to ensure the ap-

FIGURE 10–2 Evaluation would be much easier if student learning could be overtly measured by a "learn-o-meter"

propriate learning of individual students, you need to know different forms of evaluation instruments to be able to determine which will deliver the best possible information. You must understand the types from which to choose and under which conditions each is most appropriate. For example, many educators feel that standard evaluation instruments (e.g., multiple choice, true-false) will not always produce the full information about student learning they need during the learning process. In some cases, then, alternative forms (e.g., portfolios, journals) may prove more beneficial. Again, you must understand the learners, the situation, and the type of outcome (feedback) that you desire before you can choose a proper evaluation instrument. In all cases, however, you are in a much better position when you know the different varieties and their individual strengths and limitations.

Standard Evaluation Techniques

True-False.   This technique consists of statements in which a choice is made between two alternatives—generally either true or false, agree or disagree, or yes or no. Examples:

▶ Slavery was the main cause of the American Civil War.
▶ In the sentence, "The old woman and her husband walked slowly up the stairs," the word *slowly* is an adjective.

Advantages of true-false items:

▶ These items and their answers tend to be short, so you can ask more items within a given time period.
▶ Scoring is relatively easy and straightforward.

Limitations of true-false items:

▶ There is no real way to know why a student selected the incorrect answer, thus it is difficult to review students' responses and diagnose learning problems.
▶ There is a tendency to emphasize rote memorization. It is difficult to design true-false items that measure comprehension, synthesis, or application.

Matching.   In this type of evaluation, students are asked to associate an item in one column with a number of alternatives in another column. Example:

▶ Match the following wars with their main causes.

Wars

_____   1.   American Revolutionary War
_____   2.   American Civil War
_____   3.   Spanish-American War

Main Causes
   a. Failure of the British to sign commercial agreements favorable to the United States.
   b. Use of yellow journalism to sway public opinion about the need for humanitarian intervention and the annexation of Cuba by the United States.
   c. The Nullification Controversy, in which South Carolina declared the U.S. tariff laws null and void.
   d. Imposition of taxation without proper representation of those being taxed.

Advantages of matching items:

▶ Matching items are well suited for measuring students' understanding of the association between pairs of items.
▶ Students can respond rapidly, thus allowing for more content coverage.

Limitations of matching instruments:

▶ They are frequently used to associate trivial information.
▶ They measure students' ability to recognize, rather than recall, the correct answer.

Completion/Short Answer.   This type of item asks students to recall a particular short answer or phrase. Completion and short-answer instruments are similar. A completion item requires students to finish a sentence with a word or short phrase; a short-answer item poses a question they can answer in a word or phrase. Examples:

▶ A major cause of the American Civil War was the _____ .
▶ The Nullification Controversy was a major cause of which American war? _____

Advantages of completion and short-answer items:

▶ These items work well when students are expected to recall specific facts such as names, dates, places, events, and definitions.
▶ The possibility of guessing a correct answer is eliminated.
▶ More items can be used because this type of item usually takes less time to read and answer than other types. This allows you to cover a larger amount of content.

Limitations of completion and short-answer instruments:

▶ It is difficult to develop items that measure higher-level cognitive skills.
▶ They can be difficult to score. For example, which is the correct answer for the following item?:

Abraham Lincoln was born in _____ (Kentucky, a bed, a log cabin, 1809).

Multiple Choice.   The multiple-choice item is one of the most frequently used evaluation techniques. Each item is made up of two parts: a stem and a number of options or alternatives. The **stem** sets forth a problem, and the list of options contains one alternative that is the correct or "best" solution. All incorrect or less appropriate alternatives are called **distractors,** or **foils.** Examples:

▶ Which of the following was a major cause of the American Civil War?
  a. Failure of the British to sign commercial agreements favorable to the United States.
  b. Use of yellow journalism to sway public opinion about the need for humanitarian intervention and the annexation of Cuba by the United States.
  c. The Nullification Controversy, in which South Carolina declared the U.S. tariff laws null and void.
  d. Imposition of taxation without proper representation of those being taxed.
▶ If one frequently raises the cover of a container in which a liquid is being heated, the liquid takes longer to boil because
  a. boiling occurs at a higher temperature if the pressure is increased.
  b. escaping vapor carries heat away from the liquid.
  c. permitting the vapor to escape decreases the volume of the liquid.
  d. the temperature of a vapor is proportional to its volume at constant temperature.
  e. permitting more air to enter results in increased pressure on the liquid.

Advantages of multiple-choice items:

▶ You can use them with objectives ranging from simple memorization tasks to complex cognitive manipulations.
▶ You can use them to diagnose student learning problems if incorrect alternatives are designed to detect common errors.
▶ You can construct them to require students to select among alternatives that vary in degree of correctness. Thus students are allowed to select the "best" alternative and aren't left to the absolutes required by true-false or matching instruments.

Limitations of multiple-choice instruments:

▶ They are often difficult and time consuming to write. Determining three or four plausible distracters is often the most arduous part of the task.

▶ Students may feel there is more than one defensible alternative. This may lead to complaints of the answer being too discriminating or "picky."

Essay.   The essay item asks students to write a response to one or more questions. For elementary students an answer may consist of a single sentence. For older students the responses may range from a couple of sentences to several pages. Essay items can be used to compare, justify, contrast, compile, interpret, or formulate valid conclusions—all of which are higher-level cognitive skills. Example:

▶ Why does the single issue of slavery fail to explain the cause of the American Civil War?

Advantages of essay items:

▶ You can use them to measure desired competency at a greater depth and in greater detail than with most other items.
▶ They give students the freedom to respond within broad limits. This can encourage originality, creativity, and divergent thinking.
▶ They effectively measure students' ability to express themselves.

Limitations of essay instruments:

▶ They are difficult and time consuming to score, and scoring can be biased, unreliable, and inconsistent.
▶ They may be difficult for students who misunderstand the main point of the question, who tend to go off on tangents, or who have language and/or writing difficulties.
▶ They provide more opportunity for bluffing.

Figure 10–3 presents guidelines for developing these standard types of evaluation items.

Alternative Evaluation Techniques

Alternatives are available to the traditional evaluation techniques described previously. In particular, the performance and portfolio techniques have gained popularity in recent years. We here outline their purpose, advantages and limitations, and some guidelines for their use. Following this we describe additional techniques: interviews, journals, writing samples, open-ended experiences, and long-term projects. (See Stiggins, 1997, for more on all of these alternatives.)

Performance.   The purpose of a performance evaluation is to measure skills (usually psychomotor or physical) needed to accomplish a specific task. Within a per-

General guidelines	❑ Relate all items to an objective.
	❑ Provide clear, unambiguous directions.
	❑ Make sure all options appear on the same page.
	❑ Make sure the vocabulary is suitable for students.
	❑ Avoid lifting statements verbatim from the instructional materials.
True-False	❑ Select items that are unequivocally true or false. Avoid words such as *always, all,* and *never.*
	❑ Avoid multiple negatives (e.g., "It was not undesirable for the First Continental Congress to meet in response to the Intolerable Acts of the British Parliament").
	❑ Make sure the evaluation has approximately the same number of true and false answers.
Matching	❑ Explain to students the basis for matching and whether options may be used more than once or if more than one option is given for any of the questions.
	❑ Provide extra alternatives in the answer column to avoid selection by elimination.
	❑ Provide between six and eight associations within a single question.
	❑ Arrange the answer choices in a logical manner (alphabetical, chronological, etc.).
Multiple choice	❑ Avoid opinion items.
	❑ Include graphics, charts, and tables within items whenever possible.
	❑ Present one problem or question in the stem, and make sure it presents the purpose of the item in a clear and concise fashion.
	❑ Make sure the stem contains as much of the question or problem as possible. Do not repeat words in each option that you could state once in the stem.
	❑ Use negatives sparingly. If the word *not* is used in the stem, highlight it to make sure students do not overlook it.
	❑ Provide only one correct or clearly best answer.
	❑ All alternatives should be homogeneous in content and length and grammatically consistent with the stem.
	❑ Provide three to five alternatives for each item.
	❑ Write alternatives on separate lines beginning at the same point on the page.
	❑ Ensure that all alternatives are plausible.
	❑ Compose incorrect alternatives by including common misconceptions.
Completion and short answer	❑ Write the item specifically enough that there is only one correct answer.
	❑ Omit only key words from completion items.
	❑ Put the blanks near the end of the statement rather than at the beginning.
	❑ Avoid writing items with too many blanks.
	❑ Require a one-word response or at most a short phrase of closely related words.
	❑ Use blanks of the same length to avoid providing clues as to the length of the correct response.
Essay	❑ Phrase each question so students clearly understand what you expect. For example, include specific directions using terms such as *compare, contrast, define, discuss,* or *formulate.*
	❑ Provide as many essay items as students can comfortably respond to within the time allowed.
	❑ Avoid using items that focus on opinion and attitudes—unless the learning goal is to formulate and express opinions or attitudes.
	❑ Begin, when possible, with a relatively easy and straightforward essay item.
	❑ Minimize scoring subjectivity by preparing a list of key points, assigning weights to each concept, scoring all papers anonymously, and scoring the same question on all papers before moving on to the next question.

FIGURE 10–3   Development guidelines for standard evaluation items

formance situation, students are required to perform some feat or demonstrate some skill they have learned, such as delivering a persuasive speech, calculating an arithmetic average, performing a successful ceiling shot in racquetball, or parallel parking a car. Unlike the previous techniques, learners in this situation must demonstrate not only that they know *what* to do but also that they know *how* to do it. Regarding the Civil War topic previously presented, for example, you may ask a student to present a persuasive speech explaining why the Southern states were justified in seceding from the Union. Figure 10–4 shows a performance checklist

FIGURE 10–4   Performance checklist for evaluating the front crawl swimming stroke
Source: Courtesy of the American Red Cross. All rights reserved in all countries.

Swimming stroke: Front Crawl	
Component	Level V
Body Position	❏ Body inclined less than 15°
Arms	❏ Elbow high during recovery ❏ Hand enters index finger first ❏ Arm fully extended at finish of pull ❏ Arms pull in "S" pattern
Kick	❏ Emphasis on downbeat ❏ Relaxed feet with floppy ankles
Breathing/Timing	❏ Head lift not acceptable during breathing ❏ Continuous arm motion in time with breathing

used by water safety instructors to evaluate swimming performance.

Advantages of performance assessment:

▶ This technique allows for the objective evaluation of a performance or product, particularly when using a checklist.
▶ Students actually get to demonstrate, rather than simply describe, the desired performance.
▶ With the use of a performance checklist, students can practice the performance before the test and receive reliable feedback from other students, parents, teachers, or themselves.

Limitations of performance assessment:

▶ This format can be time consuming to administer (usually one student at a time).
▶ It may require several individuals or judges (e.g., skating and diving competitions) to assess the abilities of the performers.
▶ Increased setup time with specialized equipment at a specialized location is often required.

Portfolio.   Arter and Spandel (1992) define the student **portfolio** as "a purposeful collection of student work that tells the story of the student's efforts, progress, or achievement" (p. 36). The portfolio is a rich collection of work that demonstrates what students know and can do. For years, artists have used portfolios to highlight the depth and breadth of their abilities. Similarly, students may use portfolios to illustrate their unique problem-solving or critical-thinking skills, as well as their creative talents (e.g., writing, drawing, design). Additionally, portfolios can be used to demonstrate the evolution students went through to achieve their current performance level. Unlike the end-of-the-unit objective evalua-

tion, the portfolio is designed to capture a greater range of students' capabilities and to indicate how those capabilities developed and grew over time. Not only does the portfolio convey to others the students' progression, it also serves as a vehicle for students to gauge their own development and to envision what additional things they might learn. In our discussion of constructivist theory in Chapter 2, we explained that this theory deals with the creation of meaning and understanding by the student. Portfolios (as well as journals, logs, long-term projects, etc.) can effectively show how and to what degree that meaning and understanding have developed. Moreover, the portfolio itself offers a means by which learners can reflect and gain greater insights as they think about what they have accomplished and what additional things they can do.

As suggested by D'Aoust (1992), portfolios may be structured around the exemplary "products" of students' work (i.e., including only those of the best quality) or around the "process" by which students arrived at current levels of performance (i.e., pieces from the beginning, middle, and end of the course that show the progression of students' abilities), or they could include a mixture of both. In either case, a major benefit comes from actually putting it together. "Students cannot assemble a portfolio without using clearly defined targets (criteria) in a systematic way to paint a picture of their own efforts, growth, and achievement. This is the essence of assessment. Thus, portfolios used in this manner provide an example of how assessment can be used to improve achievement and not merely monitor achievement" (Arter & Spandel, 1992, p. 37).

Within the classroom setting, the portfolio is becoming more and more accepted as a means of

Performance test guidelines	❑ Specify exactly what learners are to do (through a demonstration and/or explanation), the equipment and materials that will be needed, and how performances will be assessed.
	❑ Develop and use a checklist based on acceptable performance standards. In most cases, the checklist should include some type of scoring system.
	❑ Make sure the checklist outlines all the critical behaviors that should be observed. List behaviors that should *not* be observed on a separate part of the checklist.
	❑ Be sure that, if a sequence of behaviors is needed to complete a task successfully, it is highlighted in some way.
	❑ Keep the scoring system as simple as possible.
	❑ Give a copy of the checklist and scoring system to students before they begin to practice the skill. Have them refer to it as they are learning the skill.
	❑ Use video- and/or audiotape to record performances. This may be extremely helpful when behaviors occur very quickly or in rapid succession. The tapes are also an effective means for supplying feedback to students.
Portfolio guidelines	❑ Many different skills and techniques are needed to produce an effective portfolio. Students need models of finished portfolios as well as examples of how others develop and reflect on them.
	❑ Students should be involved in selecting the pieces to be included in their portfolios. This promotes reflection on the part of students.
	❑ A portfolio should convey the following: *rationale* (purpose for forming the portfolio), *intents* (its goals), *contents* (the actual displays), *standards* (what are good and not-so-good performances), and *judgments* (what the contents tell us).
	❑ Portfolios should contain examples that illustrate growth.
	❑ Student self-reflection and self-evaluation can be promoted by having students ask, What makes this my best work? How did I go about creating it? What problems did I encounter? What makes my best piece different from my weakest piece?
	❑ All pieces should be dated so that progress can be noted over time.
	❑ Students should regularly be given time to read and reorganize their portfolios.
	❑ The portfolio should be organized, inviting, and manageable. Plan a storage system that is convenient for both you and your students.
	❑ Students should be aware of the criteria used for evaluating the portfolio.

FIGURE 10–5   Development guidelines for performance and portfolio evaluation

student assessment. Some states, such as Vermont, now have a mandated statewide portfolio assessment program. Other states, such as Indiana, will invoke similar programs in the near future.

Advantages of portfolio assessment:

▶ It provides a broad picture of what students know and can do.
▶ It can portray both the process and the products of student work, as well as demonstrate student growth.
▶ It actively involves students in assessing their own learning and actively promotes reflection on their work and abilities.

Limitations of portfolio assessment:

▶ The work in the portfolio may not be totally representative of what students know and can do.
▶ The criteria used to critique the product may not reflect the most relevant or useful dimensions of the task.

▶ The conclusions drawn from the portfolio can be heavily influenced by the person doing the evaluation.

Figure 10–5 presents a set of guidelines to consider when developing either performance or portfolio evaluation instruments.

Interviews and Oral Evaluations.   Interviews and oral evaluations are generally conducted face to face, with one person asking questions and the other responding. To conduct an interview or oral evaluation, first design a set of questions covering a specific set of objectives. The questions may be very structured (i.e., requiring a specific response) or fairly unstructured (i.e., open-ended questions that allow for lengthy, detailed answers). As with the questions for an essay evaluation, the person conducting the interview or oral evaluation (normally you, the teacher) asks a question and allows the student to respond. For purposes of clarification, students may take (or be asked to take) the opportunity to explain their

Electronic Portfolios

There are many advantages for using portfolios. The problems that often occur, however, have to do with two basic questions. First, Is the portfolio constructed in a manner that is useable and valuable for student assessment? Second, once it is assembled, how is it stored so that it can be expanded and used whenever needed?

Today there are several software programs that are available to assist in the development of portfolios. Scholastic's *Electronic Portfolio,* for example, is a program to develop an electronic cumulative record that can be used for each student every year, from prekindergarten through grade 12. Within programs such as this, you or your students can build the portfolio from within the program itself or import work from other programs or through scanned images. Once stored, the portfolio can be searched and sorted based on a table of contents, by subject, project, or theme.

With this program, you can include images and photographs of the student and sample work, include videos of the student as well as those produced by the student, and record all of the information that is standard in a cumulative record. This capacity enables you to capture and monitor both the learning process and samples of work within the same portfolio. The electronic portfolio provides teachers, students, and parents with access to rapid evaluation of student progress and comprehensive capacities for reporting and monitoring student performance. The program provides you with the ability to transfer selected pieces or entire portfolios onto VHS videotape for presentation in the classroom, to pass on to next year's teachers, or to be viewed at home.

Today, storage of the portfolio has also become more simplified. Where once you had to create folders of materials for each student and store them in some file drawer or closet, much of the information can now be stored electronically on CD-ROM. In particular, the CD-R (CD-Recordable) and CD-RW (CD-Rewritable) formats are capable of storing huge amounts of information. Unlike the standard prerecorded CD-ROM, a CD-R allows the user to select information and "burn" or write it on the CD. A CD-RW permits information to be written, erased, and rewritten. CD-R and CD-RW recorders are now relatively inexpensive peripherals for computers. This technology allows you to record huge amounts of written text, scanned pictures, other digital images, and even videos. With this amount of storage space, it is possible for you to place on a single CD-ROM the entire school portfolio of a student from kindergarten to twelfth grade. Recordable DVD formats also are available and will become affordable in the near future. These will provide even greater storage capacity. So, storage capacity will no longer be a barrier to maintaining student portfolios.

---

answers in more depth and detail. You may record the response on video- or audiotape, or transcribe the main point. Because this form of evaluation is conducted orally between two or more individuals, you also can conduct it over the telephone. As our expertise with e-mail increases, adaptations that incorporate this technology will become prevalent. Interviews allow for more in-depth, on-the-spot questioning if needed. However, they can take a lot of time to complete and they may be somewhat unreliable.

Logs and Journals. Logs and journals are written records that students keep as they work through a long-term experience. For example, students in a discussion group might take time at the end of each session to write out their thoughts and experiences about what happened in the group. How well was the topic covered? What feelings did the discussion provoke? There is value in organizing one's thoughts and pre-

senting them logically in writing. There is also value in rereading the journal later and reflecting. Just as students can reflect on their experiences, so too you can use the journal or log as a means to evaluate what they experienced. This is a good instrument to use during the formative stages of learning.

Writing Samples. This evaluation technique is frequently combined with the portfolio. It generally consists of the student selecting one or more samples from different writing assignments and submitting them for evaluation. The samples may be selected as the student's "best work" as a means to demonstrate the progression that has occurred over a specific period of time. This technique is frequently used by businesses and by graduate school selection committees.

Open-Ended Experiences. This type of evaluation technique generally is not focused on a single "correct"

TABLE 10–2   *Examples of the Application of Different Alternative Evaluation Instruments*

Alternative Evaluation Instrument	Application Examples
Portfolio	Evaluate the improvement of writing skills over the course of a semester by having 11th-grade English students create a portfolio of their best writing samples at the end of the first week, at the end of the first 9 weeks, and at the end of the semester.
	Have student teachers compile a portfolio of their teaching philosophy with accompanying documents and examples to illustrate the implementation of their philosophy during the semester of classroom teaching.
Interviews and Oral Examinations	Interview third-year Spanish students about different cultural aspects of Mexico. All questions and responses are to be given in Spanish.
	Ask preschool children to complete a sorting task and then explain how they actually accomplished the task.
Logs and Journals	Have students within a fifth-grade "Conflict Resolution" program keep a journal about what they learned in class and how they used the techniques with their family and friends.
	Have students in a high school psychology class keep a daily journal of interactions between themselves and their friends, including descriptions of the "most significant interaction to happen each day" and thoughts on why it was important.
Writing Samples	Evaluate potential graduate student applicants' writing and organizational skills by having them submit three or four papers from their undergraduate classes.
	Assess the abilities of candidates for the school newspaper by having them submit short articles about recent school events.
Open-Ended Experiences	Evaluate students on their ability to research and then debate the pros and cons of corporal punishment (e.g., spankings) used within the school systems of other countries.
	Assess student understanding of the concept of supply and demand by having them set up a classroom store and demonstrate what would happen given different conditions (e.g., competition from other classes, lack of product, increased costs of product).
Long-Term Projects	In a project on the Native American tribes of Indiana, group students into tribes of Miami, Potowatami, and Delaware Indians and have them develop reports and skits on the village life of their tribe. This could include designing a model of the village, preparing food similar to what their tribe would eat, and dressing in authentic attire.
	After a science unit on sound, have students in a fourth-grade class develop different ways in which the principles of frequency and pitch can be demonstrated.

answer. Here students are placed in a novel situation that requires a performance, and that performance is judged by how they respond and react. Many results from a continuum of possible "correct" outcomes may be produced. Examples include mock trials, debates, and different types of simulated experiences.

Long-Term Projects. Term papers, science fair projects, and unit activities (e.g., mini-societies, dramatic reenactments, trade fairs) are all examples of long-term projects. They can require extended research and library work and often involve the use of cooperative groups. As stated by Blumenfeld et al. (1991), "Within this framework, students pursue solutions to nontrivial problems by asking and refining questions, debating ideas, making predictions, designing plans and/or experiments, collecting and analyzing data, drawing conclusions, communicating their ideas

and findings to others, asking new questions, and creating artifacts" (p. 371). This technique generally requires the use of checklists with important attributes that must be exhibited within the project. Frequently, the effectiveness of this project is enhanced through the use of journals or logs.

Table 10–2 gives application examples of this and other alternative evaluation instruments.

Planning Evaluation

After considering different types of evaluation instruments, we are ready to plan evaluation. Think back to the instructional plan described in Chapter 4. Evaluation is an integral part of that plan. In Chapter 4, we emphasized the importance of planning so that your final instructional materials accomplish the desired learning goals. Likewise, forethought and planning are required to properly measure learning. The following suggestions outline important considerations for planning and implementing an evaluation. Do not interpret the following to be a "cut-in-stone" prescription of exact steps to follow. These are guidelines, proven helpful in the past, that you can adapt to your specific situation.

1. Ask yourself the following question: What is it that students are supposed to have learned? The easiest and quickest way to answer this question is to refer to the objectives. As explained in Chapter 4, objectives, instruction, and evaluations should all be parallel. This means that the evaluation instruments should measure what you taught during your instruction and that instruction should be developed from the objectives.

2. Determine the relative importance of each objective. Make decisions on how many questions to ask related to the different objectives and how much time you will need to evaluate each one. In most cases, those decisions are closely aligned with the relative importance of each objective.

3. Based on the objectives, select the most relevant evaluation technique(s) and construct the evaluation items. These items should reflect the principles of good evaluation item construction discussed earlier. It is critical that the conditions and the behaviors mentioned in the objectives match those within the evaluation item. Be sure to consider other techniques you could use to evaluate the given objective.

4. Assemble the complete evaluation. As you bring together all of the individual items, it is important to consider the following:
   a. Group questions according to item type (e.g., multiple choice, true-false) so students don't have to continuously shift response patterns.
   b. Do not arrange items randomly. Try to list items in the order the content was covered or in order of difficulty. When possible, place easier questions first to give students confidence at the outset of the test.
   c. Avoid using a series of interdependent questions in which the answer to one item depends on knowing the correct answer to another item.
   d. Reread the examination and make sure items do not provide clues or answers to other items.

5. Construct the directions for the complete evaluation and any subparts. Make sure you include the full directions on the type of response required. You may also wish to include information regarding the value of each item or subpart of the evaluation. This is useful to students as they determine how much emphasis they should place on any one item.

6. If possible, have a content expert or another teacher check the items to be sure they are accurate and valid. This is helpful with both the items and the directions.

7. If possible, try out the exam on a few students who are similar to the ones you are actually evaluating. This tryout will ensure that the directions are clear, that the vocabulary is at the correct level, that the test length is appropriate, and that the scoring system is adequate.

8. Finally, consider what will occur after the evaluation is over. Evaluate the evaluation. Ask yourself the following questions: How well did the students do? Were there any particular problems? What should I change before using this evaluation again? How should this evaluation and the suggested changes be filed and retrieved when I need it in the future?

Summary of Student Evaluation Techniques

We have suggested a number of different techniques that you can use to evaluate what your students have learned. It is important, however, to realize that in most cases this information is most effectively used by the learners themselves. For the cycle of continuous improvement to function appropriately, students must know how well they are performing and what adjustments they need to make in order to achieve your learning objectives. These evaluation techniques will help learners gain that information if they are constructed and delivered in the proper manner, at the proper time, and coupled with timely feedback about the results. Review the information found in Figure 10–6. This figure relates important questions about student evaluation to the PIE model. These questions are focused on learners and what they can do. What needs to occur during planning, implementation, and actual evaluation?

Techniques to Evaluate Instruction

In this section we describe a collection of techniques that you can use to generate information in order to evaluate your instruction.

Tests

We use the term *test* here in a generic sense to refer to any of the variety of standard and alternative evaluation techniques you can use to assess students' knowledge and skills. As noted, evaluation techniques can

FIGURE 10–6 Evaluation of student learning within the PIE model

Planning	❑ How well did students plan and prepare themselves for the learning experience? ❑ What could they have done to be better prepared? ❑ What obstacles did they encounter that they should have planned for but did not? ❑ Did students understand what they were supposed to learn, what the learning required? ❑ Did the students plan to invest enough effort into their learning experience to achieve the lesson objective?
Implementation	❑ Did students monitor their progress during the lesson? ❑ Did they actually implement changes in their learning strategies as they noticed a need? ❑ Did they understand what they were learning, how it related to previous materials, and perhaps what would come afterwards? ❑ Did they know whether they were investing sufficient effort to achieve the lesson objective? ❑ Did they monitor their own levels of motivation and make appropriate changes, if needed, to increase them?
Evaluation	❑ Do students have a good idea of how well they have learned? ❑ Do they have confidence in what they have learned? ❑ Can they reiterate what they have learned? ❑ Have students recorded the lesson's events in some way and brainstormed how to improve their learning if they encounter this type of experience again?

identify what students know before beginning instruction, assess their growing knowledge and skills during instruction, and measure what they have learned at the end of instruction. Since evaluation techniques focus primarily on student learning, which is invariably the purpose of instruction, they provide a direct measure of a lesson's effectiveness. As a result, it is usually beneficial to you to use test results as a part of evaluating your own teaching.

As an example, Ms. Estes has her fourth-grade students play the computer game *Where in the World is Carmen Sandiego?* At the beginning of the lesson, Ms. Estes gives students a pretest, an assortment of matching, multiple-choice, and short-answer items, to find out how much they already know about geography. Then, at the end of the lesson, when everyone has completed the game, she gives them a posttest to find out how much their knowledge of geography has grown. Ms. Estes finds that virtually all students score much higher on the posttest than on the pretest. She determines from this that the game has been a valuable addition to her students' learning experience and decides to make it a permanent part of the lesson.

Student Tryout

A **student tryout** refers to having a "test run" of some instructional activity, method, media, or material with a small group of students before using it on a large scale. In a sense, a tryout is a rehearsal or practice runthrough intended to identify any problems that might come up when you actually teach using the particular lesson. A tryout has two distinct advantages. First, it is an opportunity to test your assumptions about the usefulness of the materials. Second, it helps you find any problems in the materials so you can "fix" them before using the materials in the "real" classroom.

Mr. Hughes has developed a board game to use in his eighth-grade social studies class. However, before he uses the game in the class, he decides to try it out. He enlists the help of his 14-year-old daughter and several of her friends, asking them to play the game as though they were his students. He notices from this that the rules of the game are clear and that the game seems to engage their interest. However, he also notices that his tryout learners seem to become bored with the game if it slows down for any reason. He determines from this that the game is potentially useful as long as sessions are kept brief, so he decides to use it as a relatively short review activity.

Direct Observation

As may be clear from the term, **direct observation** refers to watching students as they go through some part or parts of the lesson, often when group activities

Computer-Managed Instruction

Computers are excellent tools for working with all kinds of information—text, graphics, and data in various forms—so it should come as no surprise that computers can be very valuable teacher tools for managing the information associated with student progress. **Computer-managed instruction (CMI)** is the term given to this use of the computer. While CMI can vary from simple grade keeping to quite complex applications, any form of CMI has something to do with student record keeping, performance assessment, monitoring of student progress, or evaluation. We look briefly here at some simple tools for evaluating student progress.

TEST GENERATORS

Computer programs that are used to create tests are called **test generators.** Most test generators use a database of prepared test items; many textbooks now come with such databases to help you prepare tests. The database of test items may be coded into various categories, including book chapter, topic, objective, level of difficulty, type of item, and so on. Alternatively, the software may allow you to create their own test items. Most test-generator programs accommodate different question types, including multiple choice, true-false, matching, and even essay. Examples of test generators include *Quiz Writer Plus, Test Quest,* and *Test Writer.*

The chief advantage of test-generator programs is that you can easily create multiple forms of the same test. With a sufficiently large database of items, the program can select from among several items for a given chapter and objective to create multiple unique forms of a test.

TEST SCORING

Another area where computers can save time in the testing process is in test scoring. For some time, colleges and universities have utilized test-scoring services. With the advent of personal computers and readers designed to accommodate computer scoring sheets, test scoring capability has come to K–12 schools as well. Most test-scoring devices use special scoring sheets or cards, often called *scan sheets* or *bubble sheets,* on which students mark their answers to multiple-choice or true-false items. By optically scanning the sheets and comparing the students' selections to the key, the machine can identify whether items are answered correctly or incorrectly. Simple test-scoring machines scan each sheet and print the student's score on the sheet itself. More sophisticated machines can feed the results to an attached personal computer. The computer then can provide additional information, such as a list of student names and their scores, descriptive statistics such as the class average and range, more sophisticated statistics such as t-scores (scores adjusted for the variation within the class), and an item analysis of the test items used. These can assist you in evaluating both the students and the test itself.

GRADEBOOK PROGRAMS

One of the most widely used of all basic CMI applications is the **computer gradebook** program. Computer gradebook programs are designed to resemble their paper-based kin, but with greater capability. Essentially, computer gradebooks are database programs that can store and manipulate students' grades. Most gradebook programs allow you to work with a variety of common functions, such as creating a new class, entering student names for a class, adding categories of grades, entering student scores for particular categories, editing entries, calculating grades, printing reports, and saving to and retrieving from disk. Good gradebook programs allow categories of grades to be weighted to suit your grading scheme. Most accept either letter grades or numerical scores. Some include additional features such as attendance tracking, the ability to add comments to students' records, and even the capacity to print seating charts.

Computer gradebooks offer some significant advantages over their paper-based counterparts. One is time savings. Although it may take a little more time to set up a computer gradebook, this is more than offset by the time savings later. At the end of the grading period, you can generate grades at the touch of a button without the need for tedious manual calculations. Student records are also readily available at any time. If a student's parents stop by for a conference, it is a simple matter to retrieve the records and get an exact, up-to-the-minute picture of their child's status in the class. Finally, computer gradebooks offer the advantage of accuracy. As long as the program is set up correctly, the computer will not make errors in calculation (as a human might) that could result in an erroneous grade. Standalone computer gradebook programs include *Grade Machine, Gradebook Plus, Making the Grade,* and *Classmaster.* Gradebook programs are also part of more comprehensive student management systems such as *Columbia* and *MacSchool.*

are involved. The primary advantage of observing students is that you gain information about the process of your instruction as well as the products of their learning. With careful observation you will learn how students actually use materials and how they respond to different parts of the lesson, and can identify places where you may need to give them more information or guidance.

Students in Mr. Lockwood's high school art appreciation class are learning about the different forms of creative art through a cooperative learning activity. Mr. Lockwood has divided the students into groups. Each group contains a student who plays a musical instrument, a student who paints, and a student who sculpts. The students' task is to use research as well as their own experience to identify the similarities and differences among these art forms. From this they are to identify the essential characteristics of the concept "art." Much of their research occurs outside of class, but the groups meet during the class period to discuss what they have found. Mr. Lockwood routinely listens as they talk, making sure that he spends time with each group. For the most part, he lets the students do their own work. However, because individual students have different experiences, each group is examining somewhat different issues and coming to different conclusions. As a result, Mr. Lockwood is modifying the activity "on the fly" and pushing the groups in somewhat different ways. He challenges some groups to incorporate a broader range of creative arts to test their emerging definition. He helps other groups narrow their focus on the important similarities among the arts as a way of developing a definition.

Talking with Students

Talking with students may take a variety of forms. It may involve a relatively formal discussion with a student or group of students, or it may consist of a relatively informal chat with them. Whether formal or informal, talking with students has the advantage of going straight to the source to find out what they think about instruction. As a result, it is an excellent source of information about the appeal of particular materials. You can learn a great deal, from the students' perspective, about how well the materials worked and how interesting they were. This encourages students to reflect on their own learning and to think about what helps them learn. It also helps communicate to your students your interest in them. Students get the message that you are committed to helping them learn.

The fifth-grade Elementary Ecology Club is taking a field trip to a creek near the school, and the club's advisor decides to ask club members to research the source of oil floating in the water and to determine what may be done about it. Each member of the group is given a specific task to perform. After completing the research, preparing a report, and delivering it to the public health department, the advisor decides to spend a club meeting discussing the project. He asks members specific questions to identify which parts of the project were easy and challenging, fun and boring, and informative and uninformative. Based on the discussion, the advisor determines that the project is a useful learning experience for students and decides that the club should do similar projects on a regular basis.

Peer Review

Peer review refers to asking a colleague or colleagues to examine all or part of the materials for a lesson, to comment on their usefulness, and to suggest ways to improve the lesson. This is a little like getting a second opinion before having surgery. The idea is to have another set of eyes look at the materials. This has two distinct advantages. First, it helps identify trouble spots that you may miss. Sometimes, when a lesson is relatively new, you aren't sure what to look for. On the other hand, sometimes you are so familiar with a lesson that you look past existing problems, just as you can sometimes read past your own spelling errors. In either case, you may overlook inaccuracies, inconsistencies, and other potential problems. Second, a review by a colleague will provide a fresh perspective on the materials, offering new insights on student responses to the lesson, ways to update the content, and so on.

Mr. Crawford has developed a slide-tape presentation for his fifth- and sixth-grade Spanish class. He took the slides during his trip to Spain, and has added Spanish music and his own narration describing the various people, places, and activities he photographed. Before showing the slides to his class, Mr. Crawford invites Mrs. Rivera, who also teaches Spanish, to review the presentation. Mr. Crawford is particularly interested in whether he has chosen slides that will be interesting to students, whether he has adequately matched the slides and his narration, and whether the technical quality of the slides and the tape is sufficient. Mrs. Rivera agrees that the slides add a personal touch to the lesson, which will increase its relevance to the students. However, in some parts she feels the students will become confused by the lack of explanation about locations and landmarks. Based on this review, Mr. Crawford decides to rearrange the slides and to add more narration at several points.

Classroom Observation

Classroom observation refers to inviting a colleague into the classroom to watch the lesson in process, comment on how well the materials and activities work, and suggest improvements. Like peer review, classroom observation provides another set of eyes that can offer a different perspective and help find problems in the implementation of the instruction that you may otherwise overlook.

Nancy Borelli uses a presentation with a larger-than-life model to teach her vocational school students how an automobile carburetor works. Because this is a relatively new part of the lesson, Nancy is interested in getting some feedback, so she asks Ted Morrison to observe her presentation. Ted, who teaches construction methods, frequently uses models in his classes, and Nancy is particularly interested in how effectively she uses the model carburetor during her presentation. After observing Nancy's class, Ted makes a number of suggestions that allow Nancy to improve this specific presentation and her use of models in general.

Teacher Preview

Regardless of the content area, a variety of instructional materials may already be available from several different sources. Some have been produced commercially, some have been produced by teachers and published in professional journals or on the Internet, and some you may have produced yourself during previous terms. **Previewing** materials refers to the process of reading or working through specific instructional materials prior to using them (Heinich, Molenda, Russell, & Smaldino, 1999). In Chapter 6, we described the instructional materials acquisition process, noting that your students, content, instructional method, and instructional setting are all important considerations when selecting materials. A thorough preview is the necessary first step in determining how well specific materials match these considerations and, therefore, in deciding whether to use the materials as they are, use a part or parts of them, use them with some modifications or adaptations, or not use them at all.

Mr. McCormick has found a piece of computer software titled *Discover—A Science Experiment,* which he thinks would be useful in his first-year high school biology class. However, before he makes a final decision he previews the software by working through the entire program himself. As he works through the exercises in the program, he makes notes on a preview form for computer software (see Appendix B). He is particularly interested in how well the program matches the objectives he has for the lesson, encourages collaborative hypothesis testing, and pre-

sents realistically complex problems, as well as how likely it is to hold his students' interest. Based on his preview, Mr. McCormick determines that the exercises in the software match his learning objectives and are engaging, interesting, and reasonably complex. He decides to use it in class, adding only his own introduction to the lesson and the software.

Reflection

In many cases, experience is the best gauge of whether something worked. As described in Chapter 1, *reflection* refers to the process of thinking back over what happened during a lesson, using your own experience and expertise to identify the parts of the lesson that did and did not work.

For example, in her middle school U.S. history class, Mrs. Chan uses a debate as part of a lesson. She selects two teams of students and asks them to debate the question, "Were the causes of the Civil War primarily economic or political?" The rest of the class observes the debate, evaluates the two teams on their presentation of facts and arguments, and selects a "winner." Later in the term, Mrs. Chan reflects on this activity. She reviews the notes she had made on her lesson plan, specifically considering the clarity and scope of the debate topic, the time allotted to the debate, and the amount of participation of students who were not on one of the debate teams. From her reflection, Mrs. Chan determines that, while it had been interesting, there had been too many students in the class not involved in the debate. She concludes that this activity is not a good match for the large classes she often teaches, so she decides to save the activity for a time when she has a smaller class.

Figure 10–7 presents guidelines to consider when using these evaluation techniques.

Summary of Techniques to Evaluate Instruction

We have suggested a number of techniques you can use to evaluate how well your instruction has helped students learn. Your students, too, can use these techniques. Review the information found in Figure 10–8, relating evaluation of the instruction to our PIE model. What needs to occur during planning, implementation, and actual evaluation? These questions are focused on the instruction and what you can do to improve it.

APPLICATIONS IN THE LEARNER-CENTERED CLASSROOM

This chapter has examined the evaluation of student learning and instructional materials. Throughout, we have stressed the need to develop an attitude of "seeking continuous improvement." A key to this im-

Guidelines for direct observation of students	❑ Prior to the observation, identify anything that is of particular interest in your evaluation of the materials. You'll want to pay particular attention to these aspects of the materials during the observation.
	❑ Observe a range of students. Although it's relatively easy to observe students who ask for help, or who are particularly active, it's important to observe as many different types of students as is practical.
	❑ Be as unobtrusive as possible; avoid letting your observation interfere with students' use of the materials.
	❑ Rather than trust your memory, make notes about what seems to work well, what doesn't seem to work well, and for what types of students it seems to work or not work.
Guidelines for talking with students	❑ Prior to talking with students, identify anything of particular interest in your evaluation of the materials. You'll want to pay particular attention to these aspects of the materials during the discussion.
	❑ Talk with a range of students. Although it's relatively easy to talk with students who express themselves easily or who are opinionated, it's important to talk with as many different types of students as is practical.
	❑ Keep the discussion short and focused. To keep the discussion on track, ask about specific aspects of the materials.
	❑ Use your listening skills. Try to avoid being defensive about the instruction. Remember that you're trying to find out what students think. Use open-ended questions, paraphrasing, and other active listening techniques to encourage students to talk. Clarify their comments when necessary.
Guidelines for peer review	❑ Prior to asking a colleague to review your materials, identify anything of particular interest in your evaluation. Give this information to your colleague; you'll want him or her to pay particular attention to these aspects of the materials during the review.
	❑ Ask colleagues who are familiar with the topic, the students, and/or the methods or media in the lesson.
	❑ Try to get a perspective that is different than your own by (1) asking more than one colleague to review the materials, when practical; (2) asking someone who is likely to hold a view of the content, the students, instructional methods, and so on, that is different than yours; and (3) asking the colleague(s) to make a conscious effort to look at the materials in different ways.
	❑ Use your listening skills. Explain your rationale, when necessary, but try to avoid being defensive about the materials. Remember that you're trying to get a second opinion. Use open-ended questions, paraphrasing, and other active listening techniques to encourage your colleague(s) to talk. Ask for clarification when necessary.
Guidelines for classroom observation	❑ Prior to asking a colleague to observe your classroom, identify anything of particular interest in your evaluation. Give this information to your colleague; you'll want him or her to pay particular attention to these aspects of the materials during the observation.
	❑ Ask colleagues who are familiar with the topic, the students, and/or the methods or media used in the lesson.
	❑ Arrange to talk with the observer after the lesson. Make this conversation unhurried.
	❑ Encourage the observer to use a "good news–bad news" format to make it easy to consider both the strengths of the lesson and the areas where you could improve it.

FIGURE 10–7 Techniques for evaluating the effectiveness of instruction

provement is feedback. Feedback allows you to make judgements about the current status of a learning experience and how to make it more effective, efficient, and appealing. Likewise, it is important for learners to develop an attitude of continually searching for ways to improve their own learning.

When analyzing the most effective skills of expert learners, the ability to self-monitor comes to the forefront. Self-monitoring requires learners to search out and obtain feedback in order to note what they have completed correctly and what they need to change. You want to have students continually look for ways to get feedback so they can make improvements in their own performances. For example, Olympic divers, figure skaters, and gymnasts learn to constantly ask coaches, review event videos, and seek judges' comments to attain feedback that may lead to very small, but critical, changes in their performance.

FIGURE 10–8 Evaluation of instruction within the PIE model

Planning	❑ Was the planning of the instructional materials effective and efficient?
	❑ How could you have planned the instructional experience in a better/more efficient/effective manner?
Implemention	❑ How well was the instructional experience carried out?
	❑ Did the feedback from students indicate that they were motivated by the materials?
	❑ Did students achieve the desired results?
Evaluation	❑ How could you have improved the instructional materials?
	❑ Were the materials evaluated properly?
	❑ Were the correct criteria for evaluation used?

Likewise, students in your classroom should monitor their own behavior and seek advice, guidance, and feedback so that they may continually improve their learning.

To develop this "attitude," emphasize to your students how such feedback is obtained and why it is valuable. Develop specific experiences focused on acquiring feedback and making changes to help students learn of its value. For example, have students reflect in journals or through some other means about feedback they received, what additional feedback they would have wanted, why it was important, and how the lesson could change and improve because of it. Likewise, periodic discussions on the value of feedback can encourage students to actively seek it.

Just as you want your students to desire feedback, you yourself should work toward continually improving your instructional materials. You should always try to plan, select, develop, and deliver lessons using methods that give you feedback on what is working and where to devote your efforts to improve.

ONE TEACHER'S STORY

by Janette Moreno

I always try to think about "continuous improvement" for both my students and my instructional materials. From the beginning days of the course I tried to model this behavior. For example, before students start their first project, I usually try to model for them what it will entail. Immediately after this, I stop everything and ask them to tell me what was good and what could be improved about the way I explained the project. Usually, they don't really know what to say—they aren't used to *giving* feedback. But after a couple of tries and with some coaching they begin to give me some serious things to

consider. I then try to implement as many of the changes as are possible. I can't tell you how many improvements I have made over the years by listening to the feedback that my students have offered.

Once this modeling has occurred, my students have a basic understanding of why they need assessment. Assessment soon becomes an important part of learning for them instead of something to try to avoid.

Something else that I have found extremely effective is helping students see their progress. I have found that often they forget to note that they have learned. One of the best tools that I have encountered is the portfolio. We collect periodic pieces of each student's best work and put them into a portfolio. At one time, this was a hassle just storing all of the stuff for my students, but now I quickly store most of it on the computer using a digital camera, scanner, and word processor. At the end of the year (or any other time that it is needed), I can take their work and put it on a recordable CD-ROM and then they have a permanent record. It makes it great for students (and parents, administrators, etc.) to be able to sit down at the computer screen and review all that they have done. I find that this leads to some real insights as you see a student note what has and hasn't changed over the course of a semester. Likewise, I am able to store some of the best examples of different projects and show other classes what they can strive to accomplish.

SUMMARY

In this chapter we described evaluation as a "cycle of continuous improvement" in which you can use a variety of evaluation techniques before, during, and after a learning experience. We discussed different techniques to evaluate both how much students have learned (including both standard and alternative evaluation techniques) and how effective your instruction is. For each technique, we described its advantages, and offered a set of practical guidelines for its use.

REFLECTIVE ACTIVITIES

▶ Review an examination that you took recently. Select one of the items on the exam and ask yourself the following questions:

a. Does this item relate to the desired learning objectives? If not, describe why you think this item was included.

b. Do you think this item has or has not been constructed properly? How would you improve it?

c. Could the same type of information be obtained through another type of evaluation? If yes, describe the possible alternatives and your rationale for each.

▶ Form a small group and discuss the advantages and limitations of standard evaluation techniques. Then compare them to the advantages and limitations of the alternative techniques described in this chapter.

▶ As stated in the text, some states now require the use of portfolios as the key measure of student achievement. Debate with another student the pros and cons of such a requirement.

▶ Think about the evaluation techniques described in this chapter. Which do you think would be the easiest or most natural for you to use as a teacher? Why? Which would be the most difficult for you to use? Why?

▶ Talk to several teachers about how they evaluate their instruction. Do they evaluate before, during, and after instruction? What techniques do they use? How does their evaluation help them in their role as instructional experts?

SUGGESTED RESOURCES

Blumenfeld, P. C., Soloway, E., Marx, R. W., Krajcik, J. S., Guzdial, M., & Palinscar, A. (1991). Motivating project-based learning: Sustaining the doing, supporting the learning. *Educational Psychologist, 26,* 369–398.

McMillan, J. H. (1997). *Classroom assessment: Principles and practices for effective instruction.* Boston: Allyn & Bacon.

Stiggins, R. J. (1997). *Student-centered classroom assessment* (2nd ed.). Upper Saddle River, NJ: Merrill/Prentice Hall.

Worthen, B. R., White, K. R., Fan, X., & Sudweeks, R. R. (1999). *Measurement and assessment in schools* (2nd ed.). New York: Longman.

TECHNOLOGY AND LEARNING TODAY AND TOMORROW

Throughout this textbook we have discussed how you can use instructional technology to identify and produce principles and processes, as well as hardware products that both you and your students can use to increase learning effectiveness, efficiency, and appeal. We have attempted to demonstrate the importance of such tools for both you and your learners. When considering the individual differences in learners, the varying content, environment, and constraints in today's world, learning is an ever increasingly complex activity. As we progress into the twenty-first century, that complexity will not diminish. Individuals will require skills with advanced instructional tools and techniques to succeed, to be able to function and solve the complex problems of an advanced society.

Where are we going? What skills and tools will you need to be successful in the future? To be prepared, it is important that you have a vision of the future. We conclude the text with a look at the past, present, and future of instructional technology. The highlights of the past

help to illustrate how we have progressed to our current position, but even more importantly, they help us predict what will be the challenges and needs of the future. Although predicting exactly what the future will bring is not a simple task, of these you can rest assured: Change will be a constant, and you will be continually learning.

New problems will confront us as we go about teaching and learning in the future, likewise new tools and techniques will be introduced. It is up to us to develop the mindset and skills needed to confront the challenges, make the needed changes, and find creative solutions. Instructional technology will play a vital role in providing tools and techniques to facilitate learning so that we can solve all upcoming problems no matter how complex.

Chapter 11 concludes the text with a look at the past, present, and future of instructional technology. The highlights of the past help to illustrate how we have progressed to this point, but even more importantly, they help us to project the changes that are on the horizon. This is a great asset as we envision and plan for the future.

C H A P T E R 11

Issues and Directions in Instructional Technology

OUTLINE

KEY WORDS AND CONCEPTS

Artificial intelligence (AI)
Intelligent tutoring system
Speech recognition
Virtual reality (VR)
Java

OBJECTIVES

After reading and studying this chapter, you will be able to

▶ Discuss the evolution of the fields of instructional design, instructional media, and instructional computing, and describe the contributions of prominent individuals or projects to the development of those fields.

▶ Describe the status of instructional technology and its role in education today.

▶ Discuss important issues related to instructional technology that face schools today.

▶ Identify significant trends in instructional technology and speculate about their impact in the future.

▶ Describe a vision for the future of education and schooling, based on the changes now occurring in technology.

PLANNING FOR THE CHAPTER CONTENT

Instructional Technology for Teaching and Learning, will show you how to increase learning by designing lessons that use instructional technology, including computers and other media.

In Section I of the text, we introduced you to instructional technology and a systematic approach to planning, implementing, and evaluating instruction. In Section II, we focused on planning for instruction. In Section III, we looked at implementing the plan. In Section IV, we examined evaluation. Throughout the book, we stressed appropriate applications of media. We also focused a great deal of attention on the personal computer, because it is a powerful tool that teachers can use throughout the instructional process and that learners can use as a tool for constructing understanding and for communicating. In this final chapter, we look back on instructional technology in the past to get some perspectives on where we are today. We examine the field today and consider the important issues facing us. Finally, we look to the future and try to envision what teaching and learning will be like in the years to come.

INTRODUCTION

One of the most enduring legends of the Old West is that of the Pony Express. Most of us have images of daring young Pony Express riders, braving the elements and the constant threat of attack, racing across the plains to deliver the mail. Leaping from exhausted horses to fresh ones along the trail, the riders battled time and their own exhaustion to carry the mail from Missouri to California in a record-breaking 6 to 10 days. The Pony Express was truly a marvel of its day.

Do you know that the Pony Express actually operated for only 18 months? Why did this legendary mail service exist for such a short time? To understand what happened to the Pony Express, we need a little historical perspective. Prior to its creation, communication between the east and west coasts of North America was slow indeed. Ships had to travel the long route around South America or transport materials overland across Panama (the canal was not yet built) to another waiting ship. Stagecoaches, though faster than ships, still required 20 days to carry mail from Missouri to California. The Pony Express, with its relays of riders, was a much faster way to deliver the mail. For a time, at least, it fulfilled a need. But, in 1861, the whole concept of communication was radically altered; overland telegraph connections across America were completed. In a flash, technology transformed life. Communication was achieved in a whole new way, and the Pony Express faded into memory.

Just as a historical perspective helps us understand what happened to the Pony Express, a historical perspective allows us to better understand instructional technology and its role in education. The saga of the Pony Express underscores the importance of knowing where you are and where you might be going. Had the owners of the Pony Express realized that the critical issue for their business was really communication (not just mail delivery), they might have predicted the impact of the telegraph on that business and taken steps to adapt. We are in the business of teaching and learning. Today, new technologies have the potential to transform that business. If we are to avoid going the way of the Pony Express, we need to understand what is happening in order to prepare for the future.

As with almost any field of study, there is a tendency for students new to the field to view the discipline in static terms—as an established body of knowledge, practices, rules, and procedures. Of course, no discipline, including instructional technology, is static. As with any other field, what we know today has accumulated over many years as the result of the dedicated work of many individuals. Instructional technology, too, has a past! Likewise, the discipline is not standing still. Like any other field, it is growing and evolving. Undoubtedly, instructional technology will be different in the future than it is today. We need to understand this continuum from past to present to future.

We begin this chapter with a historical perspective of instructional technology. We examine the roots of instructional design, instructional media, and instructional computing. We then turn our attention to the present and beyond. What is the status of instructional technology today? What are the issues that confront us? Can we identify trends and/or new directions? Can we extrapolate to the future? What changes might we reasonably expect, and how might these changes affect education and schooling in the future?

INSTRUCTIONAL TECHNOLOGY IN THE PAST

The roots of instructional technology run deep, and a complete exposition of the history of the field is well beyond the scope of this text. For the historical account that follows, the authors are indebted to the work of Anglin (1991), Gagné (1987), Shelly and Cashman (1984), and particularly Saettler (1990). Interested readers are encouraged to consult these references for more information.

The beginnings of instructional technology can be traced back as far as the ancient Greeks. Indeed, the word *technology* comes from the Greek *technologia*, meaning systematic treatment or craft. The Sophists, from whom we derive the term *sophisticated*, were a group of Greek teachers who were known for their clever arguments and oratorical style. Sophists often tutored groups of youths using a formal rhetorical style and thus can probably lay claim to being the first instructional technologists. Sophist teachings influenced the likes of Socrates, Plato, and Aristotle and, as a result, helped to form the basic philosophical foundations of Western thought.

While we can see the bases for instructional technology in the ideas of the ancient Greeks, the modern history of instructional technology is one that falls largely within the twentieth century. Figure 11–1 presents an overview of developments in instructional design, instructional media, and instructional computing in the twentieth century. We begin here by looking at the modern foundations of instructional design.

Instructional Design Roots

While many early contributions might be cited, probably the single most influential figure in the early history of the instructional design field was Edward L. Thorndike, who joined the faculty of Teachers College of Columbia University in 1899. Thorndike, pictured in Figure 11–2, conducted scientific investigations of learning, first on animals and then on humans. As a result of his experiments, he developed what is considered by many to be the first scientific theory of learning. Thorndike's view of learning was founded on the basic notion that organisms establish a connection between stimulus and response. Every action has a consequence, and that consequence influences whether or not the action will be repeated. In a nutshell, when a particular action yields a satisfying result, it is more likely to be repeated in similar circumstances. When an action leads to a dissatisfying or unpleasant consequence, repetition is less likely.

From an educational standpoint, Thorndike's work suggested that teachers needed to make explicit appropriate connections (e.g., between the stimulus 2 + 2 and the response 4), reward students for making the proper connections, and discourage inappropriate connections. These concepts are evident in classrooms even today. Thorndike also did pioneering work on educational measurement and the design of educational media. He cast a long shadow on the history of the instructional design field.

In the 1920s, Thorndike's idea of applying empirical methods to educational problems was expanded. Franklin Bobbitt, an advocate of schooling for practical ends, suggested that the goals of schooling should be based on analysis of the skills necessary for successful living. This laid the foundation for the practice of analyzing tasks in order to design better instruction and established the link between instructional outcomes and instructional practices. The early part of the century also gave rise to efforts to individualize instruction. Frederic Burk and his associates developed individualized instruction programs that laid the foundations for later work.

In the 1930s, Ralph W. Tyler, at The Ohio State University, as part of his eight-year study, focused on the use of *objectives* to describe what students were expected to learn. He found that schools often failed to specify objectives or specified them poorly. Resolving to address this problem, he refined the process of writing instructional objectives. By the end of his study, Tyler established that instructional objectives could be clearly stated in terms of student behaviors and that the use of clearly specified objectives made it possible to formatively evaluate instructional materials.

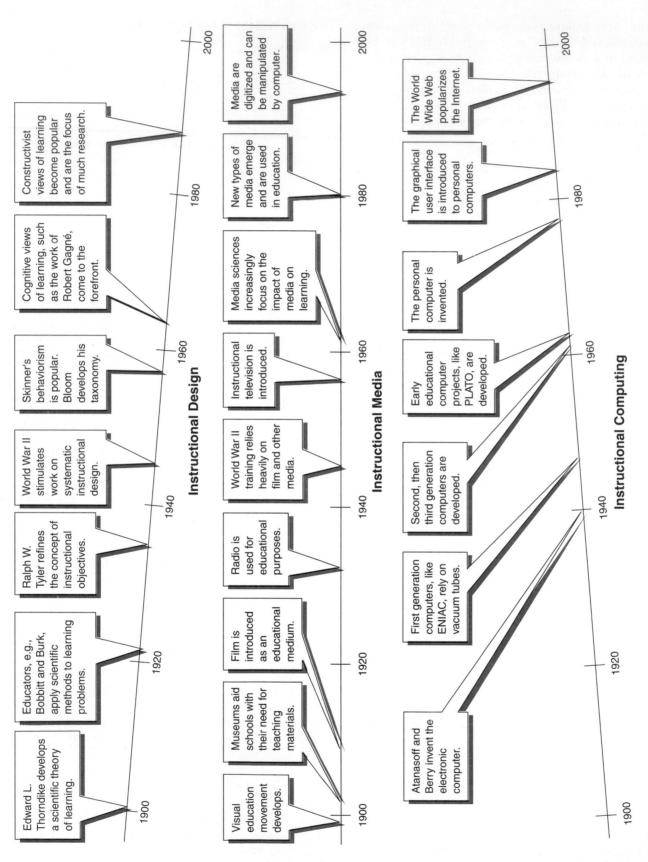

FIGURE 11–1 Converging timelines of developments in instructional design, instructional media, and instructional computing

FIGURE 11–2 Edward L. Thorndike (left) developed one of the first scientifically based theories of learning and is often viewed as the "father of instructional technology"

World War II gave a big boost to the field of instructional design. The need to rapidly train tens of thousands of new military personnel created a heightened interest in applying educational research in a systematic way. Many educational researchers participated in the war training effort, and this helped to advance systematic efforts to design instruction. During the war, the fruits of this effort were seen primarily in increased use of educational media to train military personnel. However, after the war, interest in instructional design greatly increased.

The 1950s and 1960s were a period of intense activity in the emerging field of instructional design. In 1956 Benjamin Bloom and his colleagues published the *Taxonomy of Educational Objectives,* a hierarchical scheme for categorizing educational objectives that is now familiar to most students of education. Bloom's taxonomy proved to be very useful for specifying instructional objectives and for designing instruction to attain those objectives. During this time B. F. Skinner's theory of operant conditioning, commonly referred to as *behaviorism,* was one of the dominant views in instructional design. As we mentioned in Chapter 2, Skinner's approach, which was an extension of the ideas originally put forth by Thorndike, focused on the role of reinforcement in connecting stimulus and response. Skinner maintained that learning could be maximized by carefully controlling reinforcement. These ideas gave rise to a systematic approach to designing, developing, evaluating, and revising instruction.

In the 1960s the field moved forward on several fronts. Work by Robert Gagné and other cognitive scientists helped to bring a more cognitive orientation to instructional design. Gagné specified the instructional conditions necessary for learners to achieve specific outcomes and focused more attention on understanding what happens inside the minds of learners. In addition, the term *instructional system* began to be used to describe systematic instructional design efforts. Because the federal government provided significant support for research and development in the field during this period, instructional design became much more widely used and studied.

By the end of the 1960s, instructional design was established as a discipline in its own right. The decades after the 1960s gave rise to refinements and expansions of the field. Cognitive theories of learning became increasingly influential. Instructional design degree programs were developed on many college campuses. Models of instructional design were developed and tested by various theorists in the field. Instructional design proliferated in military and business training, and its influence began to be felt in K–12 teaching.

Instructional Media Roots

In many ways, instructional media and instructional design developed along separate but converging pathways. Although the use of real objects, drawings, and other media has been a part of instruction at least since the dawn of civilization, the history of instructional media, like that of instructional design, is mostly confined to the twentieth century.

In North America, museums were one of the most significant early influences on instructional media. While this may seem odd, museums have a long history of cooperating with schools and assuming an instructional role in their communities. In 1905 the St. Louis Educational Museum became the first school museum to open in the United States. A forerunner of what is now called a media center, the museum housed collections of art objects, models, photographs, charts, real objects, and other instructional materials gathered from collections around the world. These materials were placed at the disposal of teachers in the St. Louis schools. The basic idea was to bring the world to the child. Weekly deliveries of instructional materials to the schools were first accomplished by horse and wagon (Figure 11–3) and later by truck. A catalog of materials, organized by course of study, was provided to teachers so that they could request specific materials. In 1943 the museum was renamed the Division of Audio-Visual Education for the St. Louis schools. Similar initiatives were undertaken in other U.S. cities.

FIGURE 11–3 The St. Louis Educational Museum first used a horse and wagon to deliver instructional materials to teachers

Even before the beginning of the twentieth century, there was widespread interest in what was then called visual instruction or visual education. The principle behind this movement was that pictures more closely represent real objects than do words; therefore, in school settings dominated by verbal information, pictures should make many topics more accessible to learners. Magic lanterns that projected slides (Figure 11–4), and stereopticons, early visual display devices, were popular means of illustrating public lectures and could be found in schools prior to the start of the twentieth century. In 1904 the state of New York organized the first visual instruction department, which was responsible for collecting and distributing lantern slides to schools. By 1920 visual instruction departments had been formed at a number of universities. These were the beginnings of what later became audiovisual and media science departments.

Films also came into classrooms early in the twentieth century. Indeed, pioneers of the motion picture viewed the medium primarily in educational terms, although films soon gravitated toward the theatrical and entertaining. Thomas Edison developed a series of historical and scientific films for school use. Some theatrical films were also used educationally—for example, to show productions of dramatic plays. The first educational film catalog to be published in the United States appeared in 1910, and later that same year the first public school system (Rochester, New York) adopted films for regular instructional use. Film continued to evolve as an educational medium throughout the century.

There were also early efforts by schools to use audio as an instructional medium. During the 1920s

FIGURE 11–4 The magic lantern was an early audiovisual device used in schools

and 1930s, radio was the focus of a number of educational experiments. In 1929, one of the first major initiatives, the Ohio School of the Air, was launched with the cooperation of the state government, The Ohio State University, and a Cincinnati radio station. Although it survived for less than a decade, it

FIGURE 11–5 Training of U.S. military personnel during World War II made extensive use of media such as film

established a model for similar efforts in other locations and demonstrated that radio could be a useful educational medium.

During World War II, educational films and other media became an integral part of the training effort for the war. During the war years, the U.S. government produced more than 800 training films and filmstrips, purchased tens of thousands of projectors, and spent about one billion dollars on training films (Figure 11–5). This rapid deployment of large quantities of mediated instruction influenced the field and contributed to the perception that media can be very useful for education and training.

In the 1950s, television took center stage as an important new medium on the educational scene. The first nonexperimental educational television station was launched by Iowa State University in 1950. Others quickly followed suit. In 1952 the Federal Communications Commission set aside 242 television channels for public (then called *educational*) television stations. This action helped to spur an already growing interest in the use of television for education. Today we see educational television in the form of the latest National Geographic special, much of the Public Broadcasting System's (PBS) programming, newsmagazines, the *Discovery Channel,* the *Learning Channel,* the *History Channel,* and similar programming. In schools, initiatives such as *Channel One,* which provides a synopsis of news programming, have had some impact. Although instructional television has never achieved the success in the classroom predicted by its early advocates, it has remained an available and much-used medium of instruction. Video continues to evolve and affect schooling, although video in schools today often means VCRs or distance education.

In the 1950s and 1960s, the educational media field began to shift its focus from hardware to the role of media in learning. Systematic studies were undertaken to establish how the attributes or features of various media affected learning. Various theories or models of communication were developed that incorporated the role of media. These models helped to move audiovisual specialists to consider all of the components involved in the communication process. As a result, audiovisual studies began to be conceptualized as something broader than just media. A convergence of audiovisual sciences, communication theories, learning theories, and instructional design began. This marked the beginnings of instructional technology as we have defined it in this book.

As media use increased during the 1970s and 1980s, the field continued to change and mature. Media specialists became important members of the school community. Interest grew in new forms of media, and the movement to redefine the nature of

FIGURE 11–6   ENIAC was the first large-scale, general-purpose electronic digital computer

audiovisual sciences and media studies, which began at the end of World War II, continued. Media came to be viewed not in isolation but as one part of a larger educational technology process. As instructional design developed into a field of study, media science matured in ways that increasingly acknowledged its link to instructional design and communication.

Instructional Computing Roots

Computers are relatively recent innovations. The first all-electronic digital computer was invented in 1939 by John Atanasoff and Clifford Berry at Iowa State University. The first large-scale, general-purpose electronic digital computer, called ENIAC, was put into service by John W. Mauchly and J. Presper Eckert at the University of Pennsylvania in 1946 (Figure 11–6). This huge device, weighing 30 tons and occupying the space of a small house, used vacuum tube technology to calculate trajectory tables for military artillery. By today's standards, this behemoth had relatively little computing power.

Following ENIAC, computer technology developed at a dizzying pace. The history of computer development has been divided into four generations, with each generation being based on a different underlying technology. First-generation computers, like ENIAC, relied on vacuum tube technology. The second generation, which emerged in the late 1950s and early 1960s, was based on transistors, devices that replaced vacuum tubes and were smaller, faster, cheaper, and more reliable. The third generation fol-

lowed rapidly on the heels of the second in the 1960s; it used solid-state technology or integrated circuits (ICs). ICs replaced discrete transistors and other electrical components with circuits etched onto tiny wafers of silicon called *chips*. The fourth generation, which arrived in the 1970s, relied on large-scale integration (LSI) and very large-scale integration (VLSI). One of the most significant developments of the fourth generation was the invention of the **microprocessor,** a single silicon chip that included all of the key functions of a computer, first developed by engineers at Intel Corporation. This development made possible the invention of the personal computer. In 1977, Apple, Commodore, and Tandy/Radio Shack all marketed ready-to-run personal computers. This launched a revolution in the computer industry.

Since their inception, the capabilities of personal computers have continued to develop at a dramatic pace. In 1981 IBM introduced its version of the personal computer, adding a stamp of business legitimacy to what had up until then been considered a hobbyist's plaything. In 1984 Apple introduced a dramatically redesigned personal computer, called the Macintosh. It featured a graphical-user interface (GUI) and the use of a mouse as a pointing device. With the subsequent release of Microsoft *Windows,* this approach came to dominate personal computing. Peripherals such as laser printers, modems, and so forth expanded the power and capabilities of personal computers. In the 1990s, the Internet, which had quietly existed as the province of researchers for many years, exploded onto the

FIGURE 11-7   A PLATO terminal gave the user access to a variety of CAI programs in one of the largest instructional computing projects ever

originally used with PLATO, called TUTOR, was used as the basis for subsequent personal computer authoring packages. PLATO itself continues today as a corporate training system.

The impact of early computer projects like PLATO was limited, in part, because these projects were initially conducted using terminals on mainframe computers or minicomputers, which were not widely accessible. The emergence of the personal computer in the late 1970s promised to change that. Indeed, some developments in instructional computing did come about as a result of a successful transition from large computers to personal computers. For example, Seymour Papert and his associates at MIT began work on the Logo computer language in the 1970s on large computers. Logo was quickly adapted for personal computers and became one of the early successes in instructional computing. The Minnesota Educational Computing Consortium (MECC), one of the first large-scale state initiatives involving educational uses of computers, also began with large computers and terminals. MECC quickly moved into the personal computer arena, however, and was instrumental in helping to spur and shape the early growth of instructional computing.

The 1980s saw a dramatic rise in the number of personal computers in U.S. schools. Between 1981 and 1987, the percentage of U.S. schools with one or more computers earmarked for instruction rose from 18 percent to 95 percent (Office of Technology Assessment, 1988). Figure 11-8 illustrates the growth of computers in schools.

When personal computers were first introduced to schools, there were few productivity tools and little educational software. As a result, much of the early use of personal computers focused on programming and learning about computers. The concept of computer literacy, analogous to reading and writing literacy, was put forth. Early computer literacy courses and curricular integration plans focused on the development of computer knowledge and programming skills among students. Some authorities in the field predicted that a new discipline, computers and programming, would soon be taught alongside reading, writing, and arithmetic in the schools. While this view did not prevail, the interest in computers in education grew.

As the use of personal computers proliferated and their capabilities grew, more and more software became available. CAI programs in various subject areas appeared. While software quality was often an issue in the early days of personal computers, the number of available titles expanded and the quality improved

personal computing scene with the popularity and growth of the World Wide Web. Personal computers, which had once been isolated machines, became linked to one another in record numbers. Networked personal computers emerged as the dominant form of computer technology.

Meanwhile, efforts to infuse computers into education were underway. Actually, the first efforts to use computers for education came in the early 1960s, well before the personal computer. At Stanford University, Patrick Suppes and his associates initiated a computer-assisted instruction (CAI) project. Working with elementary students, the Stanford team developed drill and practice and tutorial applications, first in mathematics and then in a number of curricular areas, that ran on mainframe computer terminals. These carefully developed and researched programs became models for many later developers of instructional computer software.

Also in the early 1960s, the PLATO project was initiated at the University of Illinois. Probably the best-known and largest CAI effort ever, PLATO (Programmed Logic for Automatic Teaching Operation) resulted in the development of hundreds of quality software programs in a variety of subject areas (Figure 11-7 shows an old PLATO terminal). Many courses at the University of Illinois relied on PLATO for instruction, and the system was used at other campuses as well. Much of the courseware originally developed for PLATO was ultimately adapted for personal computers, and the authoring language

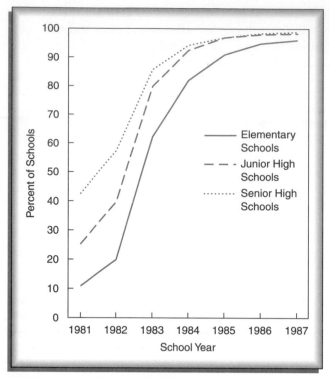

FIGURE 11–8 Increase during the 1980s in the number of schools with personal computers

over time. Powerful productivity applications such as word processors, electronic spreadsheets, and database managers were developed for personal computers. As a result, more attention began to be focused on the use of the computer for personal productivity. By the end of the 1980s, most experts in instructional computing had abandoned the idea of computer literacy as a separate field of study and instead had adopted a more comprehensive view of curricular integration that included the use of computers and computer tools in authentic subject-area contexts. Thus greater attention was given to those uses of the computer that were carefully integrated into specific subject areas—for example, using word processing to teach writing, or using the Logo computer language as part of the study of elementary mathematics.

From its inception in the late 1970s to the 1990s, the personal computer underwent a remarkable transformation, from a novelty that could only be used for simple programming to a widespread, multipurpose, powerful personal productivity and educational tool. Instructional computing as a field of study was transformed along with the personal computer. It changed from a narrow focus on computers and programming to a broader perspective of the computer as a tool to be integrated into the instructional process. Like instructional design and

media sciences, instructional computing emerged as a discipline in its own right.

Reflective Questions

▶ Think about your own schooling in the past. How were instructional design, media, and computers used when you first attended school? How have things changed today?
▶ What developments in media or computing have you observed in the last ten years? Have these developments become available in education?

INSTRUCTIONAL TECHNOLOGY TODAY

Instructional design, media, and computing began as separate disciplines, and each has been around as a field of study for a century or less. Yet, each has a history, and that history helps us to see where we are today. So, we now shift our focus to the present. Where is instructional technology today?

Instructional Technology Status

Instructional technology continues to grow and evolve. Today we can see a convergence of the disciplines of instructional design, media sciences, and instructional computing into a single discipline that we call *instructional technology*. When we looked at the past of instructional technology, we examined its three component disciplines separately. We did so because these three disciplines arose and to a large extent developed separately. But, you can see the seeds of convergence in the historical record. Instructional design and media began to merge years ago when E. L. Thorndike experimented on the impact of pictures in textual presentations. During the World War II training effort, this merging accelerated with the development of mass-mediated instruction such as training films. After the war, instructional design and media studies took off, and media became key elements of instructional design models. Instructional computing was implicitly linked to instructional design and media from its inception, and explicit connections were made in early projects such as PLATO.

Today, there is renewed interest in applying our understanding of instructional design and media utilization to teaching and learning. For example, distance learning programs are rapidly expanding in part because of the new opportunities that multimedia computers and the Internet bring. Figure 11–9 illustrates this idea of converging disciplines. We see

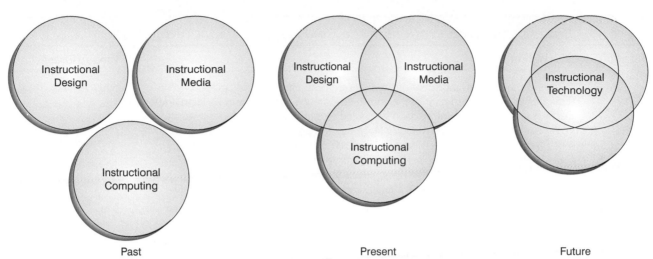

Past   Present   Future

FIGURE 11–9   Intersections of instructional design, instructional media, and instructional computing in the past, present, and future

the disciplines drawing close today, and we predict even greater convergence in the future. That was one of the main reasons we created this book!

Today, there are many exciting developments taking place in instructional technology. For one thing, we see new developments related to the applications of learning theories. In Chapter 2, we introduced you to some of the basic theoretical perspectives of learning and their implications for instruction. As we explained, the field was founded on the works of Edward L. Thorndike and B. F. Skinner, researchers who took a behavioral approach to learning. However, beginning in the 1960s and 1970s, cognitive theories of learning, such as the information processing perspective, began to hold sway. Today, constructivism is the focus of much research. The basic concept of this theoretical perspective is that knowledge cannot be transmitted to learners; rather, they must construct knowledge for themselves, usually within a social context. Although instructional technology remains linked in many people's minds to its behavioral roots, it is safe to say that the great majority of instructional technologists today accept the cognitive view, and the constructivist perspective is where much of the current research and development in the field is taking place. Although the application of the constructivist perspective to the practice of designing, implementing, and evaluating instruction is not always clear, there seems to be a shift today from a more teacher-centered perspective to a more learner-centered perspective. As in any other vibrant field of study, the work today of instructional technology researchers and practitioners is helping to shape the future.

Major developments are taking place with respect to media. In fact, we are in the midst of what is probably the most profound change in media in history. Where once media developed separately—each with its own technological basis, vocabulary, and experts—today all media are converging in the computer. Media are going digital! It is difficult to overstate the significance of the digital revolution. Traditional ways of handling text—typing, mimeographs, and printing—are giving way to word processing and desktop publishing. Computer graphics and newer technologies such as Kodak's PhotoCD are turning traditional visuals digital. Audio CDs, digital audiotape (DAT), and computer audio digitizers are making sound digital. Telephone networks are converting to digital. Even video is being digitized, and new digital high-definition television (HDTV) is just around the corner. The advantages of this approach are considerable. Digital media can be reproduced flawlessly. They can be recorded on computer-readable media such as diskettes, CD-ROMs, and DVDs. They can be sent anywhere in the world by computers over the Internet without loss of information. Additionally, computers can be used to process, transform, or otherwise manipulate the media in myriad ways. The Information Superhighway is being built on the foundations of digital multimedia!

The emergence of the Internet as the Information Superhighway is another key trend of today. While personal computers were once isolated desktop machines, networking is common today and increasing globally at a phenomenal rate. It is as though our planet is growing its own nervous system. The Internet brings unprecedented opportunities for teaching and learning. It brings up-to-the-minute multimedia resources into classrooms, it provides a vehicle for communication among schools

TABLE 11–1   *Professional Organizations in the Field of Instructional Technology*

Organization	Description	Web Address
AACE	Association for the Advancement of Computing in Education. This organization is dedicated to the advancement of the knowledge, theory, and quality of learning and teaching at all levels with information technology. It publishes a number of journals: *WebNet Journal: Internet Technologies, Applications & Issues, Journal of Computers in Mathematics and Science Teaching, Journal of Interactive Learning Research, Journal of Educational Multimedia and Hypermedia, International Journal of Educational Telecommunications, Journal of Technology and Teacher Education, Information Technology in Childhood Education Annual,* and *Educational Technology Review.*	http://www.aace.org/
AECT	Association for Educational Communications and Technology. This organization provides leadership in educational communications and technology by linking professionals holding a common interest in the use of educational technology and its application to the learning process. It publishes *TechTrends* and *Educational Technology Research and Development.*	http://www.aect.org/
ALA	American Library Association. This group of library and media specialists provides leadership of the development, promotion, and improvement of library and information services and the profession of librarianship to enhance learning and ensure access to information for all. It publishes the *American Library Association Archives.*	http://www.ala.org/
ASTD	American Society for Training and Development. This professional organization focuses on the field of workplace learning and performance. It publishes *Training & Development Magazine* and *Technical Training Magazine.*	http://www.astd.org/
IICS	International Interactive Communications Society. This group is dedicated to the advancement of interactive systems and the people who produce them in a variety of multimedia-related fields.	http://www.iics.org/
ISPI	International Society for Performance Improvement. This organization is dedicated to improving human performance in the workplace in systematic and reproducible ways. It publishes *Performance Improvement Journal* and *Performance Improvement Quarterly.*	http://www.ispi.org/
ISTE	International Society for Technology in Education. This organization focuses on helping K–12 classroom teachers and administrators share effective methods for enhancing student learning through the use of new classroom technologies. It publishes *Learning & Leading With Technology* and *Journal of Research on Computing in Education.*	http://www.iste.org/

and between schools and their communities, and it provides a forum for students to publish their work. Computers and the Internet are bringing tremendous new opportunities to schools.

Today, instructional technology and its influence have never been greater. Instructional technology programs abound in colleges and universities. A number of professional organizations are devoted strictly to the issues and concerns that confront instructional technology (Table 11–1). In the military and in business training settings, the systematic design and implementation of instruction has been widely embraced, and the interconnectedness of the disciplines is evident in the widespread use of mediated instruction delivered via video, multimedia computer software, and intranets and the Internet. Schools are investing millions of dollars in the nuts

and bolts of instructional technology—computers and allied technologies. But, the influence of instructional technology on K–12 education remains an open question. Are we getting a return on our investment? Some schools are moving forward with innovative programs, but others seem mired in nineteenth-century approaches. We now turn our attention to the schools. What is the status of instructional technology in schools today?

Instructional Technology in the Schools of Today

Instructional technology, at least in some respects, is evident in schools today as never before. Of course, the instructional process has always been there. Teachers have always been instructional experts,

FIGURE 11–10   Common computer laboratory layouts

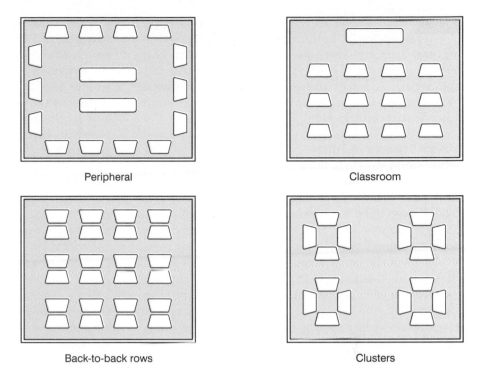

Peripheral

Classroom

Back-to-back rows

Clusters

even if many in the past may not have viewed the process from a perspective such as the PIE model. However, in days past, the tools available to teachers were few. Today, computers and other educational technologies are on the increase in schools. However, access to particular technologies and their use varies. Using data from national reports (Educational Testing Service, 1996; National Center for Education Statistics, 1998; Office of Technology Assessment, 1995), what follows is what you might find in a "typical" school today. We follow this section with a discussion of model schools that have embraced technology as a central feature of reform.

Typical Schools of Today

In the typical school of today, you will find one computer for every 8 to 10 students on average; the ratio is a little better in schools with below-average enrollments and a little worse in schools with greater numbers of poor and minority students. Computers capable of running modern multimedia applications are less common, perhaps only one for every 20 to 25 students. The computers are more likely than not to be found in a lab, although in elementary schools, especially, classroom placement is common. Many different configurations for computer laboratories are common in schools, and these configurations are suited to different instructional purposes. Four of these are shown in Figure 11–10. As shown in the figure, the peripheral layout works

well for monitoring laboratory activities. The classroom layout is effective for teaching computer applications. The back-to-back rows layout maximizes utilization of space in individualized student work situations. The cluster layout supports small-group activities well.

It is a tossup whether our typical school will have a local area network (LAN). It probably will have a link to the Internet, but Internet access may be available at only a few locations within the school. Some video technologies will be evident. You are almost certain to find one or more VCRs. There will probably be cable TV. You might find videodisc technology, but satellite access is not nearly as likely. Access to instructional technologies in the typical school of today is much better than it was in the past, but it is still a long way from ideal.

Having access to certain technologies, of course, does not guarantee their use. According to some estimates, students in the typical school today use computers for only a few hours per week. When they do use computers, the most common application across classes and grade levels is word processing. In the elementary school, drill and practice associated with basic skills such as mathematics facts is also common, while at the secondary level a lot of computer time is devoted to having students learn about computers (e.g., computer applications or programming classes). The relatively low level of student use is not surprising when you consider that only a minority of teachers are themselves real users of the technology. Given the variety of applications available for teaching and learning that we have introduced in this book, this picture of the "typical" school is rather disappointing. A lot of the potential of instructional technologies is going untapped. However, some schools are trying to change all that.

Model Schools of Today

What kinds of things have been done in schools that have set out to make instructional technology a special focus? What can we learn from model schools of today? Over the past decade or so, a number of school projects emphasizing instructional technology have been developed. We will briefly highlight a few here.

One of the longest-running efforts involving instructional technology in the schools is Apple's Classrooms of Tomorrow (ACOT) project. First initiated in 1985, the basic goal of the ACOT project is to investigate what happens to students and teachers when they have access to technology whenever they need it. Since its inception, the project has involved a number of schools across the country, and a number of findings have emerged from the ACOT school environments.

In the technology-rich ACOT classrooms, students tend to work collaboratively more than in traditional classrooms. They are comfortable with technology and use it for creating and communicating. Social skills improve. The technology tools afford students the opportunity to represent information in multiple ways and to analyze that information. Students tend to become independent learners, and they often become recognized for their own areas of expertise within the classroom. Teachers too are influenced by the ready access to technology. They tend to move through stages from learning about the technology, to adopting technology to support traditional teaching, to adapting it to classroom practices, to appropriating it for project-based and cooperative student work, to inventing new uses for it. In the process, teachers tend to become more collaborative and guiding in their teaching. And, because both teachers and students are learning and doing new things, less traditional forms of assessment, such as portfolios, come to be used. In the ACOT classrooms, a transformation of teaching and learning occurs with instructional technology serving as a catalyst.

Similar themes emerge from other model school projects. The Saturn School of Tomorrow, a magnet middle school, opened in 1989 in St. Paul, Minnesota. Designed to emphasize individualized instruction and student accountability for learning, students in consultation with parents and advisors develop their own personal growth plans. Textbooks are replaced by technology and community-based resources for learning. Other innovative ideas include an extended school year, linkages with local businesses, student cohort groups, and an absence of traditional grading. Of course, technology plays a key role in the school too. Originally, the school emphasized an integrated learning system (ILS) so that students could master basic skills in mathematics and language arts while pursuing their individualized growth plans. However, the most effective and enduring uses of technology have proved to be those in which students use the technology as a tool in their own projects and investigations. This result mirrors what was observed in the ACOT classrooms.

Peakview Elementary School in Aurora, Colorado, another example of a technology-focused model school, opened in 1991. Like the Saturn School, at Peakview textbooks have been eliminated in favor of technology and other resources, and students progress through the school in teams. As in other model projects, students use technology extensively as a tool for such work as research and writing. Students work collaboratively to do research and to create projects using technologies such as multimedia authoring packages, videodiscs, and CD-ROMs. Assessment is performance based. Teachers use the technology to adapt to individual students' interests and needs. They also use the computer as a productivity tool and report increased time devoted to teaching, greater effectiveness, and increased satisfaction. Teachers function as collaborators and guides as students take significant responsibility for their own learning.

What can we learn from these examples? In these settings, the barrier of lack of access to instructional technology was removed. The results were strikingly similar in each case. The process of teaching and learning itself became transformed. These model school technology sites have the following in common:

▶ Technology is used as a tool for creative expression, information access, communication, and collaboration.
▶ Teachers are models, guides, collaborators, and sometimes learners.
▶ Students are active and collaborative learners, and sometimes teachers.
▶ Assessments are performance based (e.g., portfolios).

As access to technology continues to expand, and schools set out to take advantage of technology, we can probably expect to see these characteristics in more classrooms in the future.

1. Create a technology committee with representation from all school constituents.
2. Develop a vision of education and articulate a role for technology in that vision.
3. Assess ongoing technology implementation efforts.
4. Identify general goals and plan how to achieve them over 3 to 5 years.
5. Develop specific objectives and have teachers create implementation plans.

FIGURE 11–11 Important steps in school technology planning

Issues Today

Typical schools of today face many challenges as they attempt to transform themselves into model school sites for tomorrow. Instructional technology brings many benefits, but not without problems. What issues do schools face as they attempt to integrate instructional technology? We have touched on a number of these issues throughout this book. Here we briefly summarize some of the most important.

Planning for Instructional Technology

Throughout this text, we have stressed the importance of planning. When it comes to instructional technology, planning is no less important for schools and schools districts than it is for individual educators. How should schools plan for instructional technology? Figure 11–11 provides an overview.

The first step is to create a district-level or building-level technology committee. The committee should have representation from all of the constituent groups: teachers representative of various grade levels, disciplines, and schools; administrators; parents; the community; the school board; and even students, assuming an adequate level of understanding and maturity.

The first task of any school's technology committee is to develop a vision of education and to articulate a role for technology in that vision. What separates model schools from the typical schools of today is not just access to instructional technologies but a *vision* for their use. The technology committee should identify the school's general educational goals for all students and how technology can facilitate the achievement of those goals. The vision statement will begin to drive the plan for the integration of instructional technologies.

The technology committee should then evaluate the school's or district's ongoing implementation efforts—including cataloging hardware and software resources, identifying current uses of technology, as-

sessing faculty and staff proficiencies, and evaluating students' uses of technology (Billings, 1985). Then, the committee can get more specific about what sorts of technology should be implemented, at what grade levels, in what curricular areas, and how.

The committee then should begin the process of planning for the future. It should identify general goals and plan for how to achieve them. Technology implementation efforts should be planned over a reasonable, short-term period. In most cases, a three- to five-year plan is desirable. This looks far enough into the future to provide useful guidance, but not so far that conditions are likely to change dramatically because of changes in the technology. To ensure that the plan stays on course, however, it is important to have clearly achievable objectives for each year of the multiyear plan. Observable progress is key to the plan's success.

In the end, specific technology objectives must be associated with the general goals outlined by the committee. Actual implementation of particular objectives is best left to the discretion of local committees of teachers. Teachers have a tremendous amount of autonomy in their classrooms—their own ways of doing things. A decentralized approach that emphasizes shared leadership in achieving technology goals and objectives generates a sense of ownership and involvement across a broad base of faculty. At this point, we are back to the planning issues we discussed in Chapter 4. Individual teachers must make specific lesson plans to help students accomplish the learning goals and objectives.

We have emphasized in this text the importance of instructional planning—the P in the PIE model. As the preceding discussion illustrates, in the school of today instructional technology planning should extend from the district level all the way to the individual teacher. At the district level, key decisions that can support the classroom teacher take place, e.g., the acquisition and placement of computer hardware, the acquisition of software licenses. Individual teachers are then free to plan lessons based on the available resources and the characteristics of their students.

Support for Technology

Successful schools have technology specialists who can help teachers with the process of implementing instructional technology. Until recently, most of the specialized work related to instructional media in the schools was performed by **library/media specialists.** Library/media specialists help students and teachers to become effective users of ideas and information by providing access to materials, providing instruction to

FIGURE 11–12   A school technology specialist, a library/media specialist, or technology coordinator helps teachers and students effectively use instructional technology

develop users' interest in as well as competence to find and use information and ideas, and working with teachers to design learning strategies to meet the needs of individual students.

Over the past decade or so a new category of specialist has also emerged in the schools—the computer or technology coordinator. The **technology coordinator** is a specialist and resource person who handles computers and related technologies for a school building or district (Figure 11–12). In some school districts, the position of technology coordinator is a full-time post. Indeed, some larger school districts employ a technology support staff of several individuals. Many schools today also support building-level coordinators. At the building level, and at the district level in smaller school districts, it is common for the technology coordinator to be a teacher who has expertise in the use of computers and who assumes these duties on a part-time basis. Part-time coordinators usually receive some release time and/or extra compensation for their activities. Perhaps you will find yourself serving as a part-time coordinator one day.

The job of a technology coordinator varies considerably from school to school. In some cases, responsibilities are distributed among a number of persons, while in other cases one person does it all. It is common for a technology coordinator to do any or all of the following:

- Work with administrators and the district's technology committee to develop and implement a technology plan

- Work with teachers to support and promote technology integration
- Plan and oversee hardware and software purchases and installations
- Install and maintain the school's computer network
- Maintain up-to-date records of the school's hardware and software
- Arrange for, or conduct, repairs of equipment
- Assemble and disseminate information about instructional technologies
- Write grants to seek support for the school's technology activities
- Provide inservice training for faculty and staff

Although typical schools today devote only a small portion of their technology budgets to faculty and staff training, regular inservice education is needed to keep teachers up to date in educational technology. Inservice training should be considered as part of overall technology planning. It should be regular and ongoing. It should derive from the school's technology plan. It should help teachers to utilize technology effectively within the framework of both the plan and their own classroom goals and objectives.

Several approaches to inservice education for instructional technology are common. Single, focused presentations or workshops on a topic (sometimes referred to as "one-shot" inservice sessions) can be useful for raising faculty awareness and stimulating interest, but they are unlikely to have a long-term impact without followup activities. More successful programs involve a series of activities, with opportunities for guided practice, exploration, and feedback. Better inservice training experiences use local computer experts and teachers, provide hands-on experience, are conducted in a nonthreatening environment and at convenient times for teachers, present information in steps with opportunities for practice and mastery, and provide followup support and feedback. Good inservice education is a key component of successful implementation of instructional technology in schools today.

Equity and Other Issues of Access

Equity is another key issue for all schools planning for instructional technology. It seems likely that access to technology and opportunity to learn to use it appropriately will be a key factor for individual students' economic success both now and in the future. Unfortunately, socioeconomic differences have the potential to create a serious gap when it comes to technology. While students from wealthier households are likely to have access to a computer at home today, this is not true of students from poorer households. Schools have a responsibility to help remedy this problem by providing access to all students.

However, the situation in U.S. schools mirrors that of society as a whole. Poorer school districts and those with higher percentages of minority students have fewer computers per capita and are less likely to have Internet connections than wealthier districts. Fortunately, the ratio of students to computers continues to improve, and efforts to bring the Internet to every school in the United States are well underway. Of course, this is a problem that schools cannot solve alone. Government, communities, and businesses must help schools provide needed access to technology.

However, even when access is not an issue, there are concerns about equity within schools. Less wealthy and less able students are more likely to experience computers as a tool for things such as remediation and drill and practice over basic skills, while more affluent and more capable students tend to have more opportunities to use computers in creative and open-ended ways. Schools and teachers need to avoid the stereotype that certain students can't use technology in creative ways. *All* students can benefit from such applications.

There are also gender inequities with regard to technology. Boys tend to be more involved with computers, both in school and out, than girls, and girls tend to exhibit less confidence with computers than boys. There is some evidence that these tendencies can be ameliorated by involving girls with computers at an early age and maintaining that involvement

throughout the school curriculum. Teachers need to be sensitive to possible gender bias and encourage girls to participate fully. Schools need to plan their curricula so that both girls and boys have opportunities to be involved with instructional technology throughout their schooling.

Schools and teachers also need to guard against other biases in access to technology. In some schools, available computers are monopolized by a minority of users. This may result from preferential laboratory scheduling for certain classes, historical patterns of use, or other reasons. To some extent, this is natural. But, when prioritizing access to available equipment, schools should make an effort to encourage a spectrum of users. Teachers, too, sometimes unconsciously stack the deck against certain students. Some teachers, for example, may provide access to a classroom computer as a reward for students getting their work done early. While this may occasionally be all right, it can create a pattern where the same speedier students are rewarded time after time, and other students are left out. Teachers must take care to provide equitable access to all students.

Finally, schools today must also be concerned with how students access information and what information they access on school computers. Probably the most important example today is the Internet. As we pointed out in Chapter 9, there is much on the Internet that is unsuitable for school children and much potential for misuse. As a result, it is incumbent upon schools to educate students and to develop and implement acceptable use policies regarding the Internet.

Legal, Ethical, and Security Issues

Schools and teachers must also be concerned with a range of potential legal and ethical issues associated with instructional technologies. In Chapter 6, we discussed one of these—copyright—and how it affects teachers and schools. Schools should have a clearly stated policy regarding copyright, and this policy should be made known to every teacher and student. Schools and teachers have a responsibility to model proper use of instructional technology within the confines of copyright law. This includes the use of copyrighted materials and application of fair use guidelines. Certainly, an important part of this modeling also includes a stance of zero tolerance for software piracy, the illegal copying of computer software. Teachers have often been guilty of illegally copying software, often rationalizing that limited school budgets and high software costs make it justified. It does not! Illegal copying of software is theft. Teachers must not do it, and they must educate their students about illegal software copying.

Computer Viruses

Computer viruses can create significant problems both for individual users and in school laboratories. In the biological realm, viruses are tiny particles that infect organisms; they can be benign or disease causing. A virus invades a cell, taking it over to make more viruses, and releasing the copies to start a new cycle of infection. In the computer world, the term **virus** refers to a computer program that functions in a manner similar to a biological virus. A computer virus invades software, usually without any overt sign, and directs the computer to copy the virus and pass it on. Like natural viruses, computer viruses can have effects ranging from fairly benign (e.g., a prankish message appears on the infected computer's screen) to quite serious (e.g., the contents of the computer's hard disk are damaged or erased). Computer viruses have become a common problem for computer users in many settings, including schools.

Take the following precautions to reduce problems due to computer viruses:

▶ Use antivirus software (e.g., Norton *AntiVirus, PCSafe, Virex, VirusSafe Firewall, VirusScan*) on personal and school computers to check for and eliminate known viruses. Regularly update this software, because antivirus programs have limited effectiveness against new or unknown viruses.

▶ Avoid downloading software from bulletin boards and Internet sites that may not be trustworthy; this is a common source of infection. If you do download software, scan the downloaded files with antivirus software before use.

▶ In schools, establish practices that reduce the spread of viruses. Discourage or prohibit students from bringing their own software to school. Restart each computer between users, and set up your antivirus software to perform a scan automatically when the computer starts up or when a diskette is inserted.

Many viruses pose real threats to computer data. However, there are also many reports of viruses, often circulated on the Internet, that are groundless. These virus hoaxes warn of catastrophic results often from just reading an e-mail message with a particular subject heading (e.g., Good Times, Penpal Greetings). While some security problems with popular e-mail programs have been reported, manufacturers have patched many of these potential security holes, and there have been no reports of viruses that can infect a computer through the simple act of reading an e-mail message. E-mail attachments, on the other hand, can contain executable programs, and these can be infected by a virus, such as the Melissa virus of 1999, which had a massive corrupting effect on personal, educational, and corporate e-mail programs in the United States and many other countries. It is good practice to scan e-mail attachments with antivirus software before use. For more information about real viruses and virus hoaxes, visit the Computer Incident Advisory Capability Website, operated by the U.S. Department of Energy (http://ciac.llnl.gov/).

Teachers must also help students learn to use computers and other technologies in proper ways. This can sometimes be difficult when the computer culture itself glorifies questionable behavior. **Hackers,** individuals who gain access to computer systems without authorization, usually for the intellectual challenge and thrill, are viewed as heroes—sort of latter-day Robin Hoods—by many members of the computing community. While hackers are often not malicious, they can create problems on accessed computer systems, either intentionally or unintentionally. In addition, it is a small step from hacking into a computer for fun to hacking into one for the purpose of stealing information or committing some other type of computer crime. Schools and teachers need to help students understand that this type of activity is wrong.

Viruses represent another threat in the school computer environment. While schoolage students are rarely responsible for creating viruses, they can certainly be responsible for infecting school computers. Viruses are easily spread from infected disks to school computers, and they can often unknowingly be downloaded from sites on the Internet. To avoid virus problems, both schools and individuals should use antivirus software. For more information on viruses and virus protection, see "Toolbox Tips: Computer Viruses."

Finally, schools must address issues related to privacy. Certainly, one concern that has been around for a number of years is security of student data. Schools and teachers often keep grades and other student records on the computer. These should not be accessible to students. But, perhaps a bigger concern today is the access to personal information that is possible through the Internet. Many Internet sites collect personal information; this is of such concern that lawmakers have drafted legislation to make it illegal for Websites to collect information from children. Individuals bent on exploitation may try to gather information from young people in chat rooms or online forums. Finally, schools that post information about students on the school Website may inadvertently allow pedophiles or others to locate the students. Care must be exercised. Students should be educated about the risks of giving out information on the Internet and taught to use precautions. Schools and teachers should not post student information or products to a Website without first getting the approval of both the students and their parents/guardians. When it comes to protecting privacy, it is best to err on the side of caution.

Reflective Questions

▶ Have you been in a classroom recently where you thought the teacher made particularly good use of technology? What made it such a good use? What sorts of technology were available? What sorts of things did the teacher do?

▶ Have you had a personal problem with any of the issues discussed (equity, viruses, privacy) associated with computer use in schools? How was your problem resolved, if it was?

INSTRUCTIONAL TECHNOLOGY IN THE FUTURE

Predicting the future is always a risky business (Figure 11–13). Conditions change, new developments occur, and old patterns fail to hold true. Nonetheless, developments in instructional technology over the past 100 years certainly do suggest some trends. If we assume that these trends will continue, then we are able to make some predictions. The implications of these trends may not always be clear, but it is possible, at least in some cases, to see the direction in which we are headed. And knowing which way we are going helps us to chart our course.

Technology Trends

We have discussed some of the trends that we see occurring in instructional technology today. Instructional technology, itself, as a discipline is drawing together instructional design, media, and computing. As a field of study, its focus is shifting from a teacher-

---

"Heavier-than-air flying machines are impossible."
—Lord Kelvin, president, Royal Society, 1895

"I think there is a world market for maybe five computers."
—Thomas Watson, chairman of IBM, 1943

"There is no reason for any individuals to have a computer in their home."
—Ken Olsen, chairman and founder of Digital Equipment Corp., 1977

FIGURE 11–13 Even the best of thinkers have trouble predicting the future *Note: Quotations are from "The Past Imperfect," Time, July 15, 1996, p. 54. Reprinted by permission.*

---

centered to a more learner-centered perspective. Media are converging; they are all becoming digital. As a result, computers are becoming key tools in work, education, and life. Computers are no longer isolated desktop machines. The Internet has created an Information Superhighway that interconnects people and provides resources the world over. The times they are a-changing!

Computers, in some form, seem likely to continue to play a prominent role in the future. The developments that led to the personal computer and to the increases in computer capability that have occurred over the last two decades seem likely to continue unabated for a number of years. This means that personal computers will continue to become more powerful, faster, smaller, and less expensive. RAM and hard disk storage capacities will continue to soar. Eventually progress in the electronics industry will probably slow. The tiny circuits that are packed onto computer chips can only get so small. But these fundamental obstacles have not yet caused significant problems, and researchers are already at work on ways to get around some of the problems that are beginning to loom. This means that we can look forward to more, and better, computer technology in the future.

The developments in computer power will support the continuation of media convergence that is underway today. It seems likely that, in the near future, it will be common for computers to support audio and full-screen, full-motion video as well as text and true-color graphics. Functions that are now managed by separate devices—television, radio, telephone, fax machine, and so on—may be merged into a single, multipurpose information machine, the computer (or information appliance) of the future. Alternatively, computer processing may proliferate. Just as computer chips inhabit everything from microwave ovens to cars today, in the future we may have a world full of "smart" devices powered by microchips.

With declining size and cost, computers should become more portable and more commonplace. Many experts foresee a future in which small but powerful computers will become standard school equipment for every learner. We may see very powerful computers no larger than a textbook. Network connections wired into the school or home, or wireless connections of some kind, would allow these computers to stay tapped permanently into the global information network. Such devices may completely replace textbooks, paper, and pencils.

Developments in the Internet, the Information Superhighway, will continue as well. In the near future, we will see increasingly interactive Websites being developed. *Streaming audio* and *video*, audio and video sent out on request over the Internet, will improve; eventually we may be able to expect on-demand audio and video capable of high-fidelity sound and television-quality images. *Bandwidth*, the capacity to carry information, will expand to permit more and more complex forms of information exchange on the Internet. The move to expand bandwidth is already underway with the development of the Internet 2, a second-generation network backbone that will support significantly greater data transfer rates among education institutions and research centers. Growth in the number of users and sites will continue. Increasingly, the world will get online.

Horizon Technologies

The trends that we note here are ones that are fairly apparent. We see these things happening today, and it seems likely that they will continue in the future. Other technologies are emerging in importance today. Many of these technologies are not yet fully functional or widely implemented. But, the nature of these technologies suggests that they could become increasingly important to teaching and learning. We call these *horizon technologies*, because, like the horizon, we can see them in the distance but we are not altogether sure what they will look like when we get closer. We examine a few of these horizon technologies here.

Artificial intelligence (AI) is a branch of computer science concerned with the design of computers and software that are capable of responding in ways that mimic human thinking. AI has actually been around as a field of study for some time now. The early promise of "intelligent" machines that can truly think like people has not been realized. However, we include it as a horizon technology because several branches of AI research have shown success, and we expect to see further developments in the future.

One successful result of AI research has been the development of expert systems. *Expert systems* are programs that embody the knowledge and skills of an expert in a particular discipline. They have already proven to be successful in fields as diverse as oil exploration and medical diagnosis. In education, the concept of the expert system led to the development of **intelligent tutoring systems,** sometimes called *intelligent computer-assisted instruction* (ICAI). These programs have been developed in mathematics, geography, and computer science, to name just a few subjects. Intelligent tutoring systems usually combine detailed information about the subject area and a database of common student mistakes with a model of student performance to diagnose a given student's level of understanding and provide instruction designed to meet that student's specific needs. They embody the expertise of a tutor within a particular content domain. We may see more of these programs in the future as well as the adaptation of techniques from these programs to more common instructional software.

AI has been influential in other areas as well. One of the most significant results of AI research has been the improvement of speech recognition systems. **Speech recognition** systems translate speech into text on the computer screen; some support basic computer commands (e.g., opening or closing applications) issued by voice. Several speech recognition systems are on the market now. Examples include Dragon Systems's *Naturally Speaking* and IBM's *ViaVoice*. The day when we can routinely communicate with our computers via voice, just like on *Star Trek* or *2001: A Space Odyssey*, may not be far off.

Another emerging area of computer development is virtual reality. **Virtual reality (VR)** refers to a computer-generated, three-dimensional, visual representation of an environment that responds to the user's motion within it. Today, VR systems consist of a computer linked to special headgear and bodysuits or gloves worn by the user (Figure 11–14). The headgear projects the image of a three-dimensional world before the user and senses the motion of the user's head so that as the head turns, the image the user sees also turns appropriately. With a sensor-equipped glove, the user can reach out and touch or grab objects in the virtual environment.

While VR technology is fairly crude now, it has already gained popularity as an arcade attraction. As it improves, we can envision a variety of educational applications. It may be possible for students to take virtual field trips—re-creations of historical events, travel to faraway places, or journeys inside the human body. Or, students may be able to perform

FIGURE 11–14   One day, virtual reality gear like this may allow students to take virtual field trips

FIGURE 11–15   Classrooms of today do not look much different from this classroom of the nineteenth century

virtual tasks such as mixing dangerous chemicals or learning how to perform an operation without the risk and expense of the real thing. Virtual reality could make simulations incredibly lifelike. The possibilities are truly exciting.

As we suggested, developments in the Internet seem certain to continue at a rapid pace. Several Web technologies are under development today that promise to have a greater impact in the future. New ways of defining Web pages, that go by labels such as cascading style sheets, DHTML (dynamic HTML), and XML (Extensible Markup Language), are being developed. These promise to make Web pages more interactive and flexible. In addition, developments continue with **Java,** a computer language designed to make it easy to create programs that one can distribute over the Web and which can operate on any computer platform. As these technologies mature, the Web promises to become an even more exciting place than it is today.

So, we foresee a future in which the electronics technology that is driving many of the dramatic changes today will continue to develop. Powerful computing tools will become commonplace, and the interconnectedness of computers will continue. It seems certain that this will change the ways that we work, play, and learn.

Learning and Education in the Future

How will these predicted changes affect education and schooling in the future? This is the most difficult thing of all to predict; our crystal ball is rapidly fading to black! The difficulty lies in the fact that education is a complex social, cultural, and political phenomenon. While it is relatively simple to predict that present technological trends will one day result in a computer capable of interacting vocally with humans, it is far less certain how, if at all, such a development may impact the educational enterprise. However, with trepidation, we will forge ahead.

In many ways, public education in the United States has been a tremendous success. Yet despite this success—or perhaps because of it—the history of education and schooling shows remarkable resistance to change. If you ever saw a picture of a nineteenth-century classroom, you probably noticed a teacher in the front of the room, students with books at neat rows of benches and worktables, and a potbellied stove in the corner. Except for the use of individual desks and more modern heating systems, not a lot has changed in present-day classrooms. Most classrooms today still look like and to a large extent function as they did over one hundred years ago (Figure 11–15). Even the summer vacation common to most school calendars is a vestige of a bygone era when children were needed during the summer to work on the family farm. Do schools today prepare students for the Information Age that is upon us?

Over the years, many educational innovations with promises of dramatic change have come and gone. Instructional television is certainly a case in point. During the 1950s, advocates of instructional television envisioned a radical change in education and schooling as a result of this innovation. Although instructional television did not disappear, it never lived up to the expectations created by early advocates. Today, some people think that the computer and related technologies represent a similar "flash in the pan" for schools. Critics charge that despite investments of huge sums of money, computers have not delivered the expected educational improvements. Perhaps, say some, computers will simply fade into a minor role in the classroom, as did instructional television. Education and schooling will continue unaffected. This is one extreme position.

Yet it would be foolish to deny that dramatic changes are taking place in society. The Information Age is here now. Computers have brought about significant changes in the workplace, and they are becoming more common in homes every day. The beginnings of media convergence are here, and there is no denying that major corporations are investing significant sums of money to get on and make use of the Information Superhighway. Major changes *are* occurring!

Lewis Perelman, the author of the controversial book, *School's Out* (1992), makes a strong case for educational transformation. He suggests that schools and education today are already obsolete and that the only way to proceed is to scrap the current system altogether. He argues that with computers, knowledge acquisition and storage is no longer a simply human process. Whereas learning was once thought of as something that happens only in school, now it occurs everywhere, and is lifelong. Further, with the growth of the Information Superhighway, learning is something that can happen anytime and anywhere. To put it simply, according to Perelman, schools are no longer needed, and, to make matters worse, they are getting in the way of the truly necessary changes. This is another extreme position.

So it seems that we have two possibilities before us for education and schooling in the future. On one hand, perhaps the status quo will continue; nothing will change. On the other, changes may be so dramatic that they completely alter what we think of as education and schooling today. What will happen?

While either of the extremes described here might come to pass, we envision a more moderate course. It is clear that individual learning is already developing into a lifelong commitment. The days when a person could expect to get a high school diploma, go to work for the local company, and retire 45 years later without ever having cracked a book again are long gone. It is also clear that the tools are here now, or will be here soon, to free learning from the confines of the school building. Soon the world's knowledge may be traveling into every household via a thin fiber-optic cable or through the airways. Will this mark the demise of schooling and education as we have known it? While it could, the social and political ramifications of such an eventuality would be considerable. Alternatively, this may provide the impetus needed to truly change schools to become centers of lifelong learning for the Information Age.

We envision a future between the two extremes. We envision a future where teachers and learners embrace and integrate instructional technology and use it to improve both teaching and learning. To be sure, this will mean that there must be some significant changes in education. The following are possible outcomes of this process of change:

▸ Multimedia learning resources, available via information networks, will proliferate and become a central feature of education.

▸ Students will become active learners, collaborating with one another and with more experienced members of society, to seek out information and gain knowledge.

▸ Learning increasingly will take place in authentic contexts. Students will work on real problems, finding their own answers.

▸ Teachers' roles will tend to shift from "the sage on the stage" to the "guide on the side." Instead of conveying information, they will help learners make use of new information tools to find, analyze, and synthesize information; to solve problems; to think creatively; and to construct their own understandings.

▸ Education will become a lifelong process, important and accessible to all, and schools will become centers of learning—not just for children, but for all members of the community.

▸ The boundaries separating schools from each other and from the community will blur or disappear. Using distance learning technologies, including the Internet, students may learn from teachers at other locations and collaborate with students at other locations. Teachers will learn alongside students. Students will learn from other students or from members of the community. Communities themselves will change as technology enables collaboration over distances.

▸ The artificial divisions of grade levels will disappear. Education will focus increasingly on authentic performance-based forms of assessment. Students will be judged by their ability to find and use information to solve genuine problems.

This is a future that is not just about instructional technology. Education and schooling are bigger than that. However, without instructional technology, it will be very hard for us to get where we need to go. We see a future that is *enabled* by instructional technology.

APPLICATIONS IN THE LEARNER-CENTERED CLASSROOM

Throughout this chapter we have encouraged reflection on the past of instructional technology, the present, and where we are going in the future. It is appropriate that we finish this "in the learner-centered classroom" section of the text by stressing the importance of reflection. We live in a society that seems to be moving ever faster. That speed often leaves us with the feeling that no time exists to adequately reflect on what has occurred and what we have experienced.

As a teacher, reflection needs to play a key role in improving what we do and how we do it for our students. Likewise, we need to reflect so that we can engender within ourselves what it is that we enjoy about learning and about coaching learning in others. For our students, reflection needs to be skill they learn so that they can come to fully understand their experiences and learn from their mistakes as well as their triumphs. Although most reflection is a mental activity, we can engender it by encouraging the use of reflective writing experiences, the use of journals, and the use of electronic key pals to discuss and answer questions pertaining to learning experiences. Additionally, our use of probing questions can help students begin that reflective process. Questions such as, What is the value of the experience? What did you learn from this experience? What would have helped you learn even more? Were you motivated by the experience? In what ways?

As a reflective conclusion to this section, think about the following key principles, which we have introduced throughout the text. Each should play an important role in your learner-centered classroom:

▶ Encourage exploration and learner activity.
▶ Use problems that are realistic and meaningful.
▶ Encourage collaboration between students. Encourage them to learn from each other. Social and cultural diversity often proves beneficial in determining unique problem solutions.
▶ Do not be afraid to learn from your students. Teachers generally learn the most—so let them teach you.
▶ Goals and planning are important for both teachers and learners.

▶ Learners are individuals and may require unique learning methods and media to come to a full understanding of any given lesson or experience.
▶ Self-reflection, monitoring, motivation and the use of feedback are needed skills of the expert learner. Every individual must learn them through use and exercise.

ONE TEACHER LOOKS TO THE FUTURE

by Janette Moreno

I have wonderful ideas for my future students. Some, I am sure, are just dreams, but dreaming is where the rest of this story began! So, why not dream? You know, I used to dream about all the wonderful things I would teach my students when I found time, or when they were ready to learn it, or when I had more resources, and so on and so forth. I finally realized that I'll never be able to teach my students everything they need to know! We just can't keep up with all the information that's out there anymore. But I *can* help my students become good learners—expert learners, even—by showing them all the possible ways they can learn and by exciting them about learning. And that's where technology comes in. It's so easy now for students to explore what's interesting, relevant, and meaningful to them and to do so in exciting and challenging ways. If I can excite my students about learning now, they won't be thinking about the day they can stop! They won't *want* to stop learning.

Another dream that's already coming true is being able to include every student in every learning activity I design. In the past, I've been frustrated when I couldn't include a few students in the school in certain activities and learning projects because of handicaps, language differences, or disabilities. But technology can often help eliminate those differences. Computers with touch screens, specialized keyboards, speech synthesizers, speech recognition, and other amazing capabilities are reaching more and more students. It's becoming possible to give all students opportunities to work at their own pace on problems that have relevance in their own lives.

I also look forward to accessing an ever-expanding number of information resources across the world. I've already started using the Internet and distance education technologies to introduce my students to information resources, other students, teachers, researchers, and community leaders. But, I know I'm just scratching the surface. I know my classes can do even more. I'm especially hopeful that these interchanges will help expand my students' understanding of both the amazing similarities and the wonderful differences between themselves and others throughout the world. I know it sounds corny, but I really think these exchanges over the Internet may help to bring a little more peace and understanding to this world.

I used to worry that all this powerful technology would eventually just replace me, but I really don't think that anymore. My role is changing, certainly, but I think it's become more meaningful. I actually feel like I have *more* opportunities to be a good teacher, as well as an amazing range of choices for reaching students. Technology has definitely increased the potential I have for helping all my students!

Isn't it amazing how quickly we can become comfortable with new tools and devices? I remember how scared I was even turning the computer on, but now I can't imagine being without one. It's my all-purpose information tool—worldwide resources at my fingertips! And kids today hardly blink an eye at all these capabilities. They seem as natural to them as the telephone was to me and videotape and CD players are to you.

It's exciting dreaming about our future classrooms and the growing possibilities for our students. What do you think it will be like for you and your students in the next 10 or 20 years? Whatever changes you foresee, be sure you're a part of them. Don't be afraid to jump in! The future starts right now!

SUMMARY

In this chapter we examined the past, present, and future of instructional technology. The modern era of instructional design and media began near the start of the twentieth century with the work of pioneers such as Edward Thorndike and with the school museum movement. Because of the need for effective and efficient training of military personnel during World War II, the fields received a major boost. Following the war, instructional design and media became established fields of study. Instructional computing began with early computer-assisted instruction experiments on mainframe computers, such as the PLATO project. Computers proliferated in education following the development of the personal computer in the late 1970s.

Today, instructional design, instructional media, and instructional computing are all established disciplines and are converging through the capabilities of the computer. Media are becoming digital, and the computer offers new capabilities for planning, implementing, and evaluating instruction. While the typical school of today may not utilize instructional technology fully, model schools have made great strides. As schools move toward the future, they must address issues such as planning for instructional technology, support for instructional technology, equity, and legal/ethical issues.

Trends that we see today are likely to continue in the future. There will be even greater convergence of instructional design, media, and computing. Computer networking will expand, and computer capabilities will grow. While education and schooling may ultimately either ignore these innovations or become totally transformed by them, we see a middle course in which instructional technology empowers both teachers and learners.

REFLECTIVE ACTIVITIES

- Visit a museum or read a book that includes displays, photographs, or other information about schools and classrooms of the past. For contrast, visit a classroom today. What similarities do you see between past classrooms and those of today? What differences do you see?
- What evidence do you see for a convergence of instructional design, instructional media, and instructional computing today?
- How do you think computers will be different in 5 years? 10 years? 50 years?
- Create a scenario for a day in the life of a restructured school in the future. What will it be like? How will education and schooling be different in an ideal future?
- Contact to one of the professional organizations listed in Table 11–1 and request information about the organization and its membership.
- Think about your own future and instructional technology. What resources can support your personal growth and development?

SUGGESTED RESOURCES

Anglin, G. J. (Ed.). (1991). *Instructional technology: Past, present, and future.* Englewood, CO: Libraries Unlimited.

Educational Testing Service, Policy Information Center. (1996). *Computers and classrooms: The status of technology in U.S. schools.* Princeton, NJ: Educational Testing Service. Available on the World Wide Web: http://www.ets.org/research/pic/compclass.html

Gagné, R. M. (Ed.). (1987). *Instructional technology: Foundations.* Hillsdale, NJ: Lawrence Erlbaum Associates.

National Center for Education Statistics. (1998, March). *Internet access in public schools.* Washington, DC: U.S. Department of Education. Available on the World Wide Web: http://nces.ed.gov/

Office of Technology Assessment, U.S. Congress. (1995, April). *Teachers and technology: Making the connection* (Report No. OTA-EHR-616). Washington, DC: U.S. Government Printing Office.

Perelman, L. J. (1992). *School's out.* New York: Avon.

Presidents' Committee of Advisors on Science and Technology, Panel on Educational Technology. (1997, March). *Report to the President on the use of technology to strengthen K–12 education in the United States.* Washington, DC: U.S. Government Printing Office.

Saettler, P. (1990). *The evolution of American educational technology.* Englewood, CO: Libraries Unlimited.

Shelly, G. B., & Cashman, T. J. (1984). *Computer fundamentals for an information age.* Brea, CA: Anaheim.

WEBSITES

Media Lab at MIT [http://www.media.mit.edu/]

Yahoo Computers and Internet [http://www.yahoo.com/Computers/]

Yahoo Education [http://www.yahoo.com/Education/]

APPENDIX A

Understanding Computer Systems

Here we present the components of a typical personal computer system and some basic computer terminology. Figure A–1 presents diagrammatic and pictorial representations of a computer system.

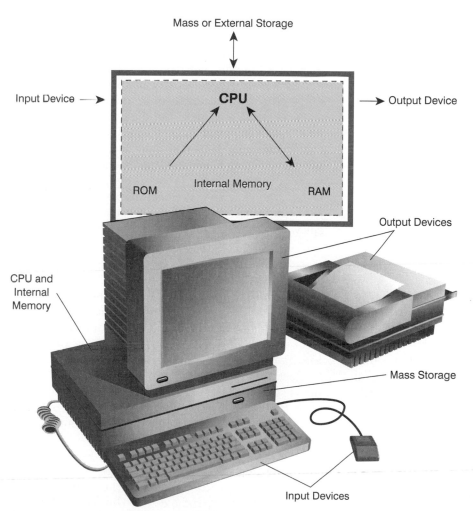

FIGURE A–1 Diagrammatic and pictorial representations of a typical personal computer system (*Note:* the dashed box represents the computer proper in the computer system)

CPU

At the core of any computer system is the central processing unit, or **CPU.** The CPU is the "brain" of the machine. It controls the functions of the rest of the system, and it performs the calculations that make the computer a prodigious number cruncher. In most personal computers today, the CPU resides on a single computer chip, a little square of silicon with tiny electronic circuits etched onto it, called a *microprocessor.* Different personal computers are distinguished from one another, in part, by the particular microprocessor each uses. The powerful versions found in personal computers today have millions of electrical components and are capable of millions of mathematical operations every second.

Personal computers are digital machines; that is, they work with numbers. At their most basic level, personal computers do their work using just zeros and ones. Zeros and ones are the language the computer "understands," that is, machine language. People represent this information using the binary numbering system. The smallest amount of information the CPU can deal with is a single zero or one, that is, a single binary digit, or **bit** for short. By itself, a single bit is not very exciting. However, put some bits together, and you've got something! A collection of eight bits is used by the computer to code each basic symbol needed to represent such things as a letter of the alphabet, a numeral, or a punctuation mark. In computer terminology, this collection of eight bits is called a **byte.** There is a unique byte for every letter, numeral, and symbol the computer can represent. In a way, bytes are the intelligible common denominator of the computer world.

INTERNAL OR MAIN MEMORY

To do its work, the CPU has to have information to process. This information is stored inside the machine in the internal or main memory. The CPU in a personal computer maintains an intimate working relationship with the internal memory of the machine. There are two basic varieties of memory found in most personal computers: **read-only memory (ROM)** and **random-access memory (RAM).**

ROM is the permanent memory that is built into the computer at the factory. ROM is referred to as "read only" because the computer can retrieve, that is to say read, the information that is stored there, but it cannot change that stored information. The computer retreives important information from ROM to help it to operate, but users do not directly work with ROM.

RAM is the computer's working memory. It is referred to as "random access" because the computer can rapidly retrieve information from or put information into any spot in it directly. When you use a personal computer, RAM is your personal workspace. For example, when you are word processing, your computer copies your word processing software from disk into a section of RAM. The document that you write with your word processor occupies another block of RAM as you compose it. The beauty of RAM is that its contents can change, as needed, to perform different tasks. However, common RAM is *volatile;* that means that its contents disappear as soon as the power is turned off (or otherwise interrupted). Mass or external storage, which we will discuss shortly, is used to store the contents of RAM so that you do not lose work between computer sessions.

The functionality of personal computer systems depends, in part, on the quantity of RAM storage available. The metric abbreviations K for kilo (thousand), M for mega (million), and b for byte have been adopted to describe the how many bytes of storage are available. So, a computer that has 640 Kb of RAM can store roughly 640,000 bytes of information in working memory, while one with 32 Mb (i.e., 32 megabytes) of RAM can store approximately 32 million bytes. To put these quantities in perspective, consider that a typical double-spaced, typewritten page requires about 2 Kb of storage. In modern personal computer systems, it is useful to have many Mb of available RAM to support the operating software of the computer, to use large software applications, to work with large documents or other types of files, and, especially, to work with more than one software application at one time.

INPUT DEVICES

In addition to its working relationship with internal memory, the CPU maintains contact with the various devices connected to the computer. Collectively, these devices are referred to as **peripherals.** Peripherals include input and output devices (collectively referred to as **I/O devices**), as well as mass storage devices. The computer communicates with these devices through electronic go-betweens called **interfaces.** We begin by looking at input devices.

The CPU processes information. Somehow information has to get into the computer for processing. Information that goes into the computer is referred to as **input,** and a device that generates input is called an *input device.* Several types of input devices now are common on personal computers.

The most common input device is the keyboard. The computer keyboard resembles the keyboard of a typewriter but has a few extra keys, such as Control and Escape, that provide for additional functions. Most personal computers today also have a mouse. The **mouse** is a pointing device. When it is moved along a flat surface such as a desktop, an arrow moves across the display screen in the same direction. The mouse can be used to select, enter, and move information on the display screen. Today's graphically oriented software relies on the mouse for many functions. On some computer systems trackballs, joysticks, or touch pads function in much the same manner as a mouse.

A variety of other input devices are available. Oversized keyboards and special input pads are available for use with younger learners or those with impaired motor skills. For learners with severe impairments, a range of augmentative communication devices can provide access to the computer. Artists may use graphics tablets to enter artwork. Musicians may use musical instrument digital interface (MIDI) devices. Microphones can be used to input speech. For multimedia work, optical scanners allow material from printed sources such as books to be entered into the computer, and video and audio digitizers capture these types of media for the computer to use.

OUTPUT DEVICES

If you can put information into the computer, you must also be able to get information out. Information that comes out of the computer is called **output.** Common output devices include a display screen or monitor, printer, and speakers.

The display screen or **monitor** is the most common output device on personal computers. Most desktop personal computers come equipped with a television-like display often called a **CRT** (cathode-ray tube). Laptop computers, on the other hand, use liquid crystal display (LCD) screens. LCD screens, unlike bulky CRT displays, are compact, flat units.

Computer displays, whether CRT or LCD, are distinguished from one another by size, resolution, and color capability. Size, as in TV sets, is measured diagonally in inches. Desktop computer monitors often measure 15" or more, while laptop screens are smaller. *Resolution* refers to the clarity of the displayed image. Higher-resolution monitors yield sharper graphics and better text readability. Color capability varies. While some computer displays today are monochrome (i.e., black and white), most are capable of displaying up to millions of colors.

Printers provide printed output, commonly referred to as **hard copy.** Three types of printers are common in personal computer systems: dot matrix, inkjet, and laser printers.

▸ **Dot matrix printers** are so named because a set of tiny pins strikes the page to form the image of each letter out of a matrix of dots. While capable of doing a passable job of printing both text and graphics, they are slow and noisy. These printers are often used as workhorse printers in school computer laboratories but are little used in personal computer systems today.

▸ **Inkjet printers** form letters on the page by shooting tiny electrically charged droplets of ink. They are a step up from dot matrix printers and can produce high-quality text and graphics printing. They are faster and quieter than dot matrix printers, although operating costs (e.g., ink cartridges) are higher. Additionally, excellent color printing is available at reasonable cost with ink jet printers.

▸ **Laser printers** are the cream of the printer options. They combine laser and photocopying technology to produce very high quality output, comparable to that produced in typesetting. They can produce text as well as high-quality graphics. Laser printers can achieve print densities of 1200 dots per inch or more for very finely detailed images. They are very fast and quiet. Their chief disadvantage is cost; they are expensive to buy and to operate, and color laser printers are much more expensive than their inkjet counter parts.

While display monitors and printers are the most common output devices, there are others. Plotters, like printers, are used for creating hard copy mainly of drawings such as CAD (computer-aided design) blueprints. Audio speakers have become an increasingly important output device. They make the sounds of multimedia software accessible. Sometimes, audio speakers are built into the monitor, but other times they are separate peripherals. Finally, we should briefly mention modems. Modems are actually both input and output devices. They permit personal computers to communicate with other computers via phone lines. We discuss modems, and how to use them to connect your computer to the Internet, in Chapter 9.

MASS STORAGE

Mass storage (also called *external storage*) refers to those I/O devices that permit information to be stored over long periods of time. Sometimes mass storage is thought of as external or auxiliary memory. Alternatively, you might think of it like a library for housing software. You access mass storage, like you go to the library, to get information or tools you need to work with at a particular time. Because the contents of RAM disappear after a working session on the computer is finished, mass storage provides a means for keeping work and bringing it back into memory when needed at a later time. We examine here the most popular mass storage devices.

Most personal computers today rely on floppy disks (or diskettes) for small-scale mass storage. The typical personal computer system today comes equipped with at least one floppy disk drive. The **floppy disk** is a flexible magnetic storage medium similar to magnetic tape, and a floppy disk drive works somewhat like a tape recorder. But, unlike linear tape, floppy disks can be randomly accessed, making storage and retrieval of information much easier and faster. While once there were a variety of sizes and capacities of floppy disks (older computers used a 5.25 inch size), today almost all personal computers use 3.5" floppy disks that hold up to 1.44 Mb of data.

Floppy disks are a convenient, portable storage medium for personal computers, but they are not suitable when storage requirements are large. It takes a lot of floppy disks to store 500 Mb of data! Large storage requirements call for a **hard** or **fixed disk.** Hard disks, which are also a magnetic storage medium, are so named because the disks are rigid, and can be manufactured to very fine tolerances for large storage capacities and very rapid access. While floppy disks can be inserted into and removed from disk drives, hard disks are *fixed;* they stay within sealed units inside the case of the computer system so that they are protected from dust, smoke, and other harmful contaminants. Hard disks come in various sizes and capacities. Today, most have capacities of gigabytes (or billions of bytes, abbreviated Gb). Personal computers today come with a hard disk built in. Commonly used software is kept on the hard disk for ready access.

While hard disk drives are the primary mass storage device for personal computers, there are other options. One drawback of hard disks is their lack of portability. This problem has been addressed by the development of removable mass storage systems with much larger capacities than floppy disks. A variety of removable large-scale storage options (e.g., Zip, Jaz, SuperDisk, SyJet) are available today. The Iomega Zip drive is one of the most popular; it uses a removable cartridge about the same size as a floppy disk that is capable of storing up to 250 Mb of data. Zip drives and other large-scale removable storage devices are popular computer system accessories on many systems.

Optical storage technologies provide another solution for large-scale storage needs. A single **CD-ROM,** a medium derived from the audio CD, can store about 650 Mb of data. A CD-ROM drive is a very popular mass storage peripheral, and many software programs are now distributed on CD-ROM. While CD-ROM is a read-only medium—that is, the computer can retrieve prerecorded data from a CD-ROM but cannot record information onto it—a one-time recordable format, called CD-R, is available for personal computer systems. CD-R provides a convenient option for archiving information or making what amounts to single copies of personally produced CD-ROMs. Another alternative, CD-RW, is capable of multiple rewrites, and is becoming available in educational settings.

A new medium similar to CD-ROM is DVD. **DVD,** which stands for *digital video disk* or *digital versatile disk,* is an emerging standard for digital information storage and delivery. While the same size as CD-ROMs, DVD disks have a greater storage capacity (4.7 to 17 Gb) and therefore can meet very large-scale storage needs. DVD disks are now being used for distribution of movies on disk as well as large-scale storage applications like those for CD-ROM.

SOFTWARE

Finally, it is important to recognize that software is an essential component of any computer system. As we noted above, the software is what makes the hardware work. Software, within the limitations set by the capabilities of the hardware, determines what the computer can do. Like the music you play on a stereo system, it is the software that gives the hardware real meaning.

With a stereo system, software may consist of the individual songs recorded on a medium such as a tape or CD. In a computer system, software takes the form of computer programs, sets of instructions to the computer's CPU that tell it how to perform a particular task, such as processing text or presenting a computer-based lesson. Most programs are loaded from disk into the machine's RAM for use as needed. There are two basic categories of software: systems software and applications software.

Systems Software

Systems software is the basic operating software that tells the computer how to perform its fundamental functions. For example, the computer has to be told what to do when the power is turned on, how to retrieve a program from disk, and how to save your word processing document. These functions are all carried out by the systems software.

The basic systems software is called the **operating system (OS).** The OS acts as the master control program for the computer. In some personal computers, part of the OS may be permanently stored in ROM. In most, only very rudimentary startup instructions are kept in ROM, and the remainder of the OS is loaded from disk into RAM when the computer starts up.

Different computers use different operating systems, and the characteristics may vary considerably. Older IBM–PCs and compatibles used an operating system called PC–DOS or MS–DOS that still has a presence today. MS-DOS was popular but awkward because of its reliance on text commands for carrying out computer functions. For example, to copy a particular file (and verify the accuracy of the copy) from the computer's hard disk to a floppy disk using MS-DOS, one had to type a relatively cumbersome command such as: COPY C:\thisfile.txt A: /V. The latest trend in operating systems is the **graphical user interface (GUI).** First popularized by the Apple *MacOS* and now seen in Microsoft *Windows,* the GUI makes use of graphical symbols instead of text commands to control common machine functions such as copying files and working with disks. With a graphical operating system, the same disk copying task given above is as simple as using the mouse to click and drag an icon representing the file to be copied from the hard drive onto an icon representing the floppy drive. The operating system then automatically performs the copying and verification.

Applications Software

Applications software includes programs designed to perform specific functions for the user, from processing text to doing calculations to presenting a lesson on the computer. Thus, applications software includes the common computer tools (word proces-

sors, databases, etc.) as well as all educational software. Although applications software interacts frequently with the OS because of the OS's role in controlling the machine, it is through the applications software that most of the real work gets done.

PUTTING IT ALL TOGETHER

When the computer operates, it carries out a complex set of actions that involves interplay among the various components of the system and the person using the computer. Suppose that you wish to use your word processing software to compose a letter. When you sit down at your personal computer and turn it on, the ROM is tapped to provide the computer's basic startup information. On many personal computers, a brief check of all systems is conducted to make sure everything is operating properly. Your operating system is then loaded into RAM, where it assumes control of your computer.

To begin your word processing session, you might type the name of your application, or, more likely, use your mouse to click on the icon (pictorial representation) for the software. This input passes to the CPU and on to the OS, which acts on it by instructing the computer to copy the word processing program from your computer's hard disk into working memory. The word processing program then assumes control of your interactions with it.

As you begin to type, each keystroke sends a signal to the CPU. The word processing software keeps the information in RAM and displays the contents of your letter on the monitor. When you finish, you select the print option from the word processor. The OS handles sending a copy of your letter to your printer, and the hard copy emerges. Finally, you save a copy of your letter to a diskette for later reference or editing. Again, the computer system, operating system software, and word processing software work in concert to carry out the desired action. The whole process involves a complicated interplay of many different components. Fortunately, most of the time this process works so well that we never even notice it is happening.

B

Preview Forms for the Review of Instructional Materials

Preview Form: Real Objects and Models

Title/Description _____   **Producer** _____

Source _____   **Date** _____   **Cost** _____

Criteria   *Comments*

Relevance to objectives

Likely to arouse/maintain interest

Sturdy, stable, not easily broken

Ease of use, manipulable

Ease of storage

   Not dangerous (real objects)

   Shelf life (real objects)

Degree of realism (models)

Accuracy (models)

Preview Form: Text

Title _____   Producer _____

Source _____   Date _____   Cost _____

Criteria   *Comments*

Photographs, diagrams, drawings

Use of color, layout

Relevance to course objectives

Up to date, accurate (copyright date)

Free of objectionable bias

Reading level (easy to read)

Likely to stimulate/maintain student interest

Table of contents, glossary, index

Special features

Adjunct materials (student manual, teacher's guide)

Organization, scope, and sequence

Chapter summaries/reviews

Study questions

References (complete and up to date)

Preview Form: Visuals

Title _____   **Producer** _____

Source _____   **Date** _____   **Cost** _____

Criteria   *Comments*

Relevance to objectives

Authenticity/accuracy of visual

Likely to arouse/maintain interest

Likely to be comprehended clearly

Technical quality (durability)

Legibility for use (size and clarity)

Simplicity (clear, unified design)

Appropriate use of color

Appropriateness of accompanying verbal information

Timeliness (avoids out-of-date elements, such as dress)

Preview Form: Overhead Transparencies

Title _____   Producer _____

Source _____   Date _____   Cost _____

Criteria   *Comments*

Relevance to objectives

Accuracy of information

Likely to arouse/maintain interest

Likely to be comprehended clearly

Technical quality (e.g., easy to read)

Promotes participation/involvement

Evidence of effectiveness (e.g., field-test results)

Free from objectionable bias

Provisions for discussion/follow-up

Preview Form: Slides and Filmstrips

Title _____ Producer _____

Source _____ Date _____ Cost _____

Minutes _____

Criteria   *Comments*

Relevance to objectives

Accuracy of information

Likely to arouse/maintain interest

Likely to be comprehended clearly

Technical quality

Promotes participation/involvement

Evidence of effectiveness (e.g., field-test results)

Free from objectionable bias

Provisions for discussion/follow-up

Preview Form: Audio

Title _____   Producer _____

Source _____   Date _____   Cost _____

Minutes _____

Criteria	Comments

Relevance to objectives

Accuracy of information

Likely to arouse/maintain interest

Technical quality

Promotes participation/involvement

Evidence of effectiveness (e.g., field-test results)

Free from objectionable bias

Pacing appropriate for audience

Clarity of organization

Appropriate vocabulary level

Preview Form: Video and Film

Title _____   **Producer** _____

Source _____   **Date** _____   **Cost** _____

Format _____   **Minutes** _____

Criteria   *Comments*

Relevance to objectives

Accuracy of information

Likely to arouse/maintain interest

Technical quality

Promotes participation/involvement

Evidence of effectiveness (e.g., field-test results)

Free from objectionable bias

Pacing appropriate for audience

Use of cognitive learning aids (e.g., overview, cues, summary)

Preview Form: Computer Software

Title _____ Producer _____

Source _____ Date _____ Cost _____

Format _____ Equipment needed _____ Minutes _____

Criteria   *Comments*

Relevance to objectives

Accuracy of information

Likely to arouse/maintain interest

Ease of use

Appropriate color, sound, graphics

Frequent, relevant practice (active participation)

Feedback provides remedial branches

Free of technical flaws (e.g., dead ends, infinite loops)

Clear, complete documentation

Evidence of effectiveness (e.g., field-test results)

Preview Form: Multimedia

Title _____   **Producer** _____

Source _____   **Date** _____   **Cost** _____

Format _____

Equipment Required _____

Criteria	*Comments*
Relevance to objectives	
Accuracy of information	
Likely to arouse/maintain interest	
Ease of use	
Level of interactivity	
Appropriate use of color, graphics, sound	
Appropriate use of individual media	
Coordination of visuals, sound, text	
Technical quality	
Evidence of effectiveness	

Preview Form: Web Pages/Sites

Title _____   Producer _____

Source _____   Date _____   Cost _____

Criteria   *Comments*

Material appropriate for students

Content relevant to objectives

Information reliable, up to date, and accurate

Value of content vs. glitz ("bells and whistles")

Ease of navigation

Appropriate reading level for users

Site supporters

Author cites other authorities

Site provides useful links to other sites

Note: You may also want to refer to Chapter 9, Table 9–6, "Guidelines for Designing Web Pages/Sites" for other criteria.
Newby/Stepich/Lehman/Russell, Instructional Technology for Teaching and Learning: Designing Instruction, Integrating Computers, and Using Media, *Appendix B (A Merrill Publication), © 2000 by Prentice-Hall, Inc., Upper Saddle River, NJ 07458. Permission to reproduce this form is granted by the publisher to teachers and students for classroom and/or personal use provided the handout is distributed free of charge and not included in a coursepack. Permission must be obtained from the publisher for all other usage.*

ISTE Foundations in Technology and Standards for Basic Endorsement

ISTE RECOMMENDED FOUNDATIONS IN TECHNOLOGY FOR ALL TEACHERS*

FOUNDATIONS

The ISTE Foundation Standards reflect professional studies in education that provide fundamental concepts and skills for applying information technology in educational settings. All candidates seeking initial certification or endorsements in teacher preparation programs should have opportunities to meet the educational technology foundations standards.

A. Basic Computer/Technology Operations and Concepts. Candidates will use computer systems to run software; to access, generate and manipulate data; and to publish results. They will also evaluate performance of hardware and software components of computer systems and apply basic troubleshooting strategies as needed.
   1. operate a multimedia computer system with related peripheral devices to successfully install and use a variety of software packages.
   2. use terminology related to computers and technology appropriately in written and oral communications.
   3. describe and implement basic troubleshooting techniques for multimedia computer systems with related peripheral devices.
   4. use imaging devices such as scanners, digital cameras, and/or video cameras with computer systems and software.
   5. demonstrate knowledge of uses of computers and technology in business, industry, and society.
B. Personal and Professional Use of Technology. Candidates will apply tools for enhancing their own professional growth and productivity. They will use technology in communicating, collaborating, conducting research, and solving problems. In addition, they will plan and participate in activities that encourage lifelong learning and will promote equitable, ethical, and legal use of computer/technology resources.
   1. use productivity tools for word processing, database management, and spreadsheet applications.

All of the following was obtained from the ISTE website: http://www.iste.org/Resources/Projects/TechStandards/found.html

2. apply productivity tools for creating multimedia presentations.
3. use computer-based technologies including telecommunications to access information and enhance personal and professional productivity.
4. use computers to support problem solving, data collection, information management communications, presentations, and decision making.
5. demonstrate awareness of resources for adaptive assistive devices for student with special needs.
6. demonstrate knowledge of equity, ethics, legal, and human issues concerning use of computers and technology.
7. identify computer and related technology resources for facilitating lifelong learning and emerging roles of the learner and the educator.
8. observe demonstrations or uses of broadcast instruction, audio/video conferencing, and other distant learning applications.

C. Application of Technology in Instruction. Candidates will apply computers and related technologies to support instruction in their grade level and subject areas. They must plan and deliver instructional units that integrate a variety of software, applications, and learning tools. Lessons developed must reflect effective grouping and assessment strategies for diverse populations.

1. explore, evaluate, and use computer/technology resources including applications, tools, educational software and associated documentation.
2. describe current instructional principles, research, and appropriate assessment practices as related to the use of computers and technology resources in the curriculum.
3. design, deliver, and assess student learning activities that integrate computers/technology for a variety of student group strategies and for diverse student populations.
4. design student learning activities that foster equitable, ethical, and legal use of technology by students.
5. practice responsible, ethical and legal use of technology, information, and software resources.

All of the following was obtained from the ISTE website: http://www.iste.org/Resources/Projects/TechStandards/basic.html

STANDARDS FOR BASIC ENDORSEMENT IN EDUCATIONAL COMPUTING AND TECHNOLOGY LITERACY

1.0 Prerequisite Preparation - Foundations. Professional studies culminating in the educational computing and technology literacy endorsement, prepare candidates to use computers and related technologies in educational settings. All candidates seeking initial certification or endorsements in teacher preparation programs should have opportunities to meet the educational technology foundations standards.

1.1 Basic Computer/Technology Operations and Concepts.
Candidates will use computer systems to run software; to access, generate and manipulate data; and to publish results. They will also evaluate performance of hardware and software components of computer systems and apply basic troubleshooting strategies as needed.
  1.1.1 operate a multimedia computer system with related peripheral devices to successfully install and use a variety of software packages.
  1.1.2 use terminology related to computers and technology appropriately in written and oral communications.
  1.1.3 describe and implement basic troubleshooting techniques for multimedia computer systems with related peripheral devices.
  1.1.4 use imaging devices such as scanners, digital cameras, and/or video cameras with computer systems and software.
  1.1.5 demonstrate knowledge of uses of computers and technology in business, industry, and society.

1.2 Personal and Professional Use of Technology.
Candidates will apply tools for enhancing their own professional growth and productivity. They will use technology in communicating, collaborating, conducting research, and solving problems. In addition, they will plan and participate in activities that encourage lifelong learning and will promote equitable, ethical, and legal use of computer/technology resources.
  1.2.1 use productivity tools for word processing, database management, and spreadsheet applications.

1.2.2 apply productivity tools for creating multimedia presentations.

1.2.3 use computer-based technologies including telecommunications to access information and enhance personal and professional productivity.

1.2.4 use computers to support problem solving, data collection, information management, communications, presentations, and decision making.

1.2.5 demonstrate awareness of resources for adaptive assistive devices for student with special needs.

1.2.6 demonstrate knowledge of equity, ethics, legal, and human issues concerning use of computers and technology.

1.2.7 identify computer and related technology resources for facilitating lifelong learning and emerging roles of the learner and the educator.

1.2.8 observe demonstrations or uses of broadcast instruction, audio/video conferencing, and other distant learning applications.

1.3 Application of Technology in Instruction. Candidates will apply computers and related technologies to support instruction in their grade level and subject areas. They must plan and deliver instructional units that integrate a variety of software, applications, and learning tools. Lessons developed must reflect effective grouping and assessment strategies for diverse populations.

1.3.1 explore, evaluate, and use computer/technology resources including applications, tools, educational software and associated documentation.

1.3.2 describe current instructional principles, research, and appropriate assessment practices as related to the use of computers and technology resources in the curriculum.

1.3.3 design, deliver, and assess student learning activities that integrate computers/technology for a variety of student grouping strategies and for diverse student populations.

1.3.4 design student learning activities that foster equitable, ethical, and legal use of technology by students.

1.3.5 practice responsible, ethical and legal use of technology, information, and software resources.

2.0 Specialty Content Preparation in Educational Computing and Technology Literacy. Professional studies in educational computing and technology provide concepts and skills that prepare teachers to teach computer/technology applications and use technology to support other content areas.

2.1 Social, Ethical, and Human Issues. Candidates will apply concepts and skills in making decisions concerning social, ethical, and human issues related to computing and technology.

2.1.1 describe the historical development and important trends affecting the evolution of technology and its probable future roles in society.

2.1.2 describe strategies for facilitating consideration of ethical, legal, and human issues involving school purchasing and policy decisions.

2.2 Productivity Tools. Candidates integrate advanced features of technology-based productivity tools to support instruction.

2.2.1 use advanced features of word processing, desktop publishing, graphics programs and utilities to develop professional products.

2.2.2 use spreadsheets for analyzing, organizing, and displaying numeric data graphically.

2.2.3 design and manipulate databases and generate customized reports.

2.2.4 use teacher utility and classroom management tools to design solutions for a specific purpose.

2.2.5 identify, select, and integrate video and digital images in varying formats for use in presentations, publications, and/or other products.

2.2.6 apply specific-purpose electronic devices (such as a graphing calculator, language translator, scientific probeware, or electronic thesaurus) in appropriate content areas.

2.2.7 use features of applications that integrate word processing, database, spreadsheet, communication, and other tools.

2.3 Telecommunications and Information Access. Candidates will use telecommunications and information access resources to support instruction.

2.3.1 access and use telecommunications tools and resources for information sharing, remote information access and retrieval, and multimedia/hypermedia publishing.

2.3.2 use electronic mail and web browser applications for communications and for research to support instruction.

2.3.3 use automated on-line search tools and intelligent agents to identify and index desired information resources.

2.4 Research, Problem Solving, and Product Development.
Candidates will use computers and other technologies in research, problem solving, and product development. Candidates use a variety of media, presentation, and authoring packages; plan and participate in team and collaborative projects that require critical analysis and evaluation; and present products developed.

2.4.1 identify basic principles of instructional design associated with the development of multimedia and hypermedia learning materials.

2.4.2 develop simple hypermedia and multimedia products that apply basic instructional design principles.

2.4.3 select appropriate tools for communicating concepts, conducting research, and solving problems for an intended audience and purpose.

2.4.4 participate in collaborative projects and team activities.

2.4.5 identify examples of emerging programming, authoring, or problem-solving environments.

2.4.6 collaborate in on-line workgroups to build bodies of knowledge around specific topics.

2.4.7 use a computer projection device to support and deliver oral presentations.

2.4.8 design and publish simple on-line documents that present information and include links to critical resources.

2.4.9 develop instructional units that involve compiling, organizing, analyzing, and synthesizing of information and use technology to support these processes.

2.4.10 conduct research and evaluate on-line sources of information that support and enhance the curriculum.

3.0 Professional Preparation.
Professional preparation in educational computing and technology literacy prepares candidates to integrate teaching methodologies with knowledge about use of technology to support teaching and learning.

3.1 Teaching Methodology.
Candidates will effectively plan, deliver, and assess concepts and skills relevant to educational computing and technology literacy across the curriculum.

3.1.1 design and practice methods and strategies for teaching concepts and skills related to computers and related technologies including keyboarding.

3.1.2 design and practice methods and strategies for teaching concepts and skills for applying productivity tools.

3.1.3 design and practice methods/strategies for teaching concepts and skills for applying information access and delivery tools.

3.1.4 design and practice methods and strategies for teaching problem-solving principles and skills using technology resources.

3.1.5 observe in a K-12 setting where K-12 computer technology concepts and skills are being taught.

3.1.6 practice methods and strategies for teaching technology concepts and skills in a lab and classroom setting.

3.1.7 identify and support implementation and revision of computer/technology literacy curriculum to reflect on-going changes in technology.

3.1.8 design and implement integrated technology classroom activities that involve teaming and/or small group collaboration.

3.1.9 identify activities and resources to support regular professional growth related to technology.

3.1.10 describe student guidance resources, career awareness resources, and student support activities related to computing and technology.

3.1.11 compare national K-12 computer/technology standards

with benchmarks set by local school districts and critique each.

3.1.12 identify professional organizations and groups that support the field of educational computing and technology.

3.1.13 design a set of evaluation strategies and methods that will assess the effectiveness of instructional units that integrate computers/technology.

3.2 Hardware/Software Selection, Installation and Maintenance.

Candidates will demonstrate knowledge of selection, installation, management, and maintenance of the infrastructure in a classroom setting.

3.2.1 develop plans to configure computer/ technology systems and related peripherals in laboratory, classroom cluster, and other appropriate instructional arrangements.

3.2.2 identify and describe strategies to support development of

school/laboratory policies, procedures, and practices related to use of computers/technology.

3.2.3 research, evaluate, and develop recommendations for purchasing instructional software to support and enhance the school curriculum.

3.2.4 research, evaluate, and develop recommendations for purchasing technology systems.

3.2.5 design and recommend procedures for the organization, management, and security of hardware and software.

3.2.6 identify strategies for troubleshooting and maintaining various hardware/software configurations.

3.2.7 identify and describe network software packages used to operate a computer network system.

3.2.8 configure a computer system and one or more software packages.

GLOSSARY

Acceptable use policy An agreement signed by all participants defining proper Internet usage guidelines.

Acronym A type of mnemonic in which a single word is made up of the first letters of a group of words.

Acrostic A type of mnemonic in which letters in the new information are used as the first letters of the words in a sentence or phrase.

Advance organizer An outline, preview, or other such preinstructional cue used to promote retention of content to be learned.

Algorithm A series of steps needed to solve a particular problem or perform a particular task.

Analogy A statement that likens something new to something familiar. Analogies are typically used either to make abstract information more concrete or to organize complex information.

Antecedent An event, object, or circumstance that prompts a behavior.

Application activity A type of instructional activity that provides students with an opportunity to practice using what they are learning.

Applications Software programs designed to perform a specific function for the user, such as processing text, performing calculations, and presenting content lessons.

Artificial intelligence (AI) A branch of computer science concerned with the design of computers and software that are capable of responding in ways that mimic human thinking.

ASCII format American Standard Code for Information Interchange; the standard way of representing text, which allows different computer brands to "talk" to one another. Sometimes referred to as plain text or unformatted text.

Assistive technology Computer hardware and software that supports students with special needs.

Asynchronous Not occurring at the same time.

Attachments E-mail additions; may be either documents, graphics, or software.

Attention The process of selectively receiving information from the environment.

Attitudes A type of learning that refers to feelings, beliefs, and values that lead individuals to make consistent choices when given the opportunity.

Audio Spoken words or sounds, either live or recorded.

Audio teleconferencing A distance education technology that uses a speakerphone to extend a basic telephone call and permits instruction and interaction between individuals or groups at two or more locations.

Audiographics The use of audio teleconferencing accompanied by the transmission of still pictures and graphics via slow-scan video, fax, or an electronic graphics tablet.

Audiotape Acetate on which sounds are recorded using magnetic signals, usually stored in a cassette case.

Authoring systems Computer programs that permit the development of interactive, computer-based applications without a need for programming knowledge.

Backbone The set of high-speed data lines connecting the major networks that make up the Internet.

Baud rate The communication speed between a computer and a device (such as a modem), roughly equivalent to bits per second.

Behavior A response made by an individual.

Bit The smallest amount of information that the CPU can deal with; a single binary digit.

Bitmapped graphics Sometimes called paint or raster graphics, in which each pixel directly corresponds to a spot on the display screen. When scaled to larger sizes, this type of graphic looks jagged.

Bookmark A way to store addresses of frequently used Websites on your computer.

Browser A computer application for accessing the World Wide Web.

Bulletin board system A computer network software tool that allows individuals to "post" messages and to read messages posted by others.

Byte A collection of eight bits, equivalent to one alphanumeric character.

Case study A type of problem solving that requires students to actively participate in real or hypothetical problem situations that reflect the types of experiences actually encountered in the discipline under study.

CD see Compact disc.

CD-ROM (Compact disc—read-only memory) Digitally encoded information permanently recorded on a compact disc.

Cell A single block in a spreadsheet grid, formed by the intersection of a row and a column.

Chat room On computer networks, a location for person-to-person real-time (synchronous) interaction by typing messages.

Classroom observation A form of evaluation that involves having a knowledgeable person come into the classroom to watch a lesson in process, to comment on how well the materials and activities work, and to make suggestions for improvements.

Clip art Already-created graphics designed to be added to word processing or desktop publishing documents or to computer-based instruction.

Compact disc (CD) A 4.72-inch-diameter disc on which a laser has digitally recorded information such as audio, video, or computer data.

Computer A machine that processes information according to a set of instructions.

Computer conferencing An asynchronous communication medium in which two or more individuals exchange messages using personal computers connected via a network or telephone lines.

Computer gradebook A computer database program that can store and manipulate students' grades.

Computer program A set of instructions that tells the computer how to do something.

Computer software See Software.

Computer system A collection of components that includes the computer and all of the devices used with it.

Computer-assisted instruction (CAI) See Computer-based instruction.

Computer-assisted learning (CAL) See Computer-based instruction.

Computer-based instruction (CBI) The use of the computer in the delivery of instruction.

Computer-managed instruction (CMI) The use of the computer in the management of instruction, including applications such as student record keeping, performance assessment, and monitoring students' progress.

Computer-mediated communication (CMC) The use of the computer as a device for mediating communication between teacher and students and among students, often over distances. Electronic mail and computer conferencing are two types of application software commonly used in CMC.

Concept map A graphical representation of interrelated concepts that students can use as a learning aid or that teachers can use as an aid in content organization.

Conditional information A type of information that describes the potential usefulness of facts, concepts, and principles.

Conditions A portion of the instructional objective that indicates under what circumstances students are expected to perform.

Consequence An event, object, or circumstance that comes after a behavior and is attributable to the behavior.

Contingencies The environmental conditions that shape an individual's behavior.

Cooperative learning An instructional method that involves small heterogeneous groups of students working toward a common academic goal or task. Its use promotes positive interdependence, individual accountability, collaborative/social skills, and group processing skills.

Copyright The legal rights to an original work produced in any tangible medium of expression, including written works, works of art, music, photographs, and computer software.

Corrective feedback Feedback that tells students specifically what they can do to correct their performance.

CPU The central processing unit, or brain, of the computer, which controls the functions of the rest of the system and performs all numeric calculations.

Criteria A portion of the instructional objective that indicates the standards that define acceptable performance.

CRT Television-like display screen that uses a cathode ray tube.

Cursor A highlighted position indicator used on the computer screen.

Cursor control The use of directional movement keys or a mouse to position the cursor anywhere within a document for the purposes of editing.

Cycle of continuous improvement   The continuous evaluation of instruction before, during, and after implementation, which leads to continual revision and modification in order to increase student learning.

Database   An organized collection of information, often stored on computer.

Database management system (DBMS)   Software that enables the user to enter, edit, store, retrieve, sort, and search through computer databases.

Datafile   The collection of all related records in a database.

Declarative information   A type of information that includes facts, concepts, principles, and the relationships among them.

Demonstration   An instructional method that involves showing how to do a task as well as describing why, when, and where it is done. Provides a real or lifelike example of the skill or procedure to be learned.

Designing instruction   The process of "translating principles of learning and instruction into plans for instructional materials" and activities (Smith & Ragan, 1999, p. 2).

Desktop publishing (DTP)   Computer application software that gives users a high degree of control over the composition and layout of material on a printed page, including both text and graphics.

Digital camera   A camera that stores pictures in computer-compatible digital format rather than on film.

Digital Versatile Disc (DVD)   see Digital video disc.

Digital Video Disc (DVD)   A compact disc format for storing motion video and computer data.

Digitizer   A device that allows audio as well as still or motion video to be captured in a form that the computer can use.

Direct observation   A form of evaluation that involves watching students as they work through some part(s) of the lesson.

Discovery   An instructional method that uses an inductive, or inquiry, method to encourage students to find "answers" for themselves through the use of trial-and-error problem-solving strategies.

Discussion   A dynamic instructional method in which individuals talk together, share information, and work cooperatively toward a solution or consensus. This method encourages classroom rapport and actively involves students in learning.

Display boards   Classroom surfaces used for writing and displaying information, including chalkboards, multipurpose boards, bulletin boards, magnetic boards, and flip charts.

Distance education   An organized instructional program in which the teacher and learners are physically separated by time or by geography.

Distractors   The incorrect or less appropriate alternative answers for a given multiple-choice question. Also called *foils*.

Domain   A major category of locations on the Internet. Major domains include com (company), edu (educational institution), gov (government), mil (military), net (network), and org (organization).

Dot matrix printer   A low-cost, versatile printer in which a set of tiny pins strikes the page to form the image of each letter out of a matrix of dots.

Downloading   Receiving information over a network from another computer.

Drill and practice   A series of practice exercises designed to increase fluency in a new skill or to refresh an existing one. Use of this approach assumes that learners have previously received some instruction on the concept, principle, or procedure to be practiced.

Drop   Point of actual physical connection between a computer and external network access lines.

DVD   see Digital video disc.

Electronic mail (e-mail)   Electronically transmitted private messages that can be sent from individuals to other individuals or groups.

E-mail address   A unique electronic address for an individual or organization, analogous to a postal address.

E-mail   see Electronic mail.

Emoticons   Combinations of type characters that resemble human faces when turned sideways. Used to indicate emotion or intent on e-mail or in chat rooms.

Encoding   The process of translating information into some meaningful form that can be remembered.

Evaluation   The third phase in the Plan, Implement, Evaluate model. Focus is on assessment techniques used to determine the level of learning learners have achieved and/or the effectiveness of the instructional materials.

Evaluation activity   A type of instructional activity designed to determine how well students have mastered lesson objectives.

Event driven   Computer actions or programs, such as hypermedia software, that respond to events in the environment; for example, a mouse action event that occurs when the user clicks on a button.

FAQ   Acronym for "frequently asked questions." Used on the Internet to disseminate basic information and to reduce repetitive queries.

Feedback   Information provided to students regarding how well they are doing during practice.

Field   Each individual category of information recorded in a database.

File server   A computer dedicated to managing a computer network and providing resources to other computers on the network (the clients). The file server is usually faster and has larger storage capabilities than the client machines.

Fixed disk   See Hard disk.

Flat filer   A type of DBMS that works with a single datafile at a time.

Floppy disk/diskette   A magnetic storage medium for computer data that allows users to randomly access information.

Flowcharting   A graphical means of illustrating the logical flow of a computer program.

Focusing question   A question typically used at the beginning of a lesson to direct students' attention to particularly important aspects of the new information.

Foils   See Distractors.

Font   The appearance of the text itself, which can be altered through the selection of various typefaces and sizes of type. These include many typefaces common to the printing field, such as Times, Helvetica, Geneva, and Courier.

Formative evaluation   A form of assessment that indicates whether or not students have learned what they must know before progressing to the next portion of the instruction.

Formula   A mathematical expression that directs an electronic spreadsheet to perform various kinds of calculations on the numbers entered in it.

ftp (file transfer protocol)   The standard method for sending or retrieving electronic files on the Internet.

Game   An activity in which participants follow prescribed rules as they strive to attain a goal.

Gopher   Software, invented at the University of Minnesota, for accessing information resources on the Internet. Gopher software relies on a client-server model and a hierarchical menu system to permit users to easily "go for" information located on many computers throughout the world.

Grammar checker   Ancillary feature of word processors that identifies a range of grammatical and format errors such as improper capitalization, lack of subject-verb agreement, split infinitives, and so on.

Graphic   Any pictorial representation of information such as charts, graphs, animated figures, or photographic reproductions.

Graphical user interface (GUI)   The use of graphical symbols instead of text commands to control common computer functions such as copying programs and disks.

Graphics tablet   A computer input device that permits the development of graphic images by translating drawing on the tablet into onscreen images.

Hacker   An individual who gains access to computer systems without authorization.

Hard copy   A printed copy of computer output.

Hard disk   A large-capacity magnetic storage medium for computer data. Also called a *fixed disk,* it remains sealed within the case of most computers to protect it from dust, smoke, and other contaminants.

Hardware   The physical components of the computer system.

Heuristic   A rule of thumb or flexible guideline that can be adapted to fit each instructional situation.

High-level language   A computer language that contains instructions that resemble natural language and that does not require knowledge of the inner workings of the computer to use successfully.

Highlighting   Various techniques designed to direct attention to certain aspects of information, including the use of **bold,** underlined, or *italicized* print; color, labels, and arrows for pictorial information; and speaking more loudly or more slowly to highlight verbal information.

Home page   The preliminary or main Web page of a particular Website.

HTML   See Hypertext Markup Language.

Hypermedia   A system of information representation in which the information—text, graphics, animation, audio, and/or video—is stored in interlinked nodes.

Hypertext   An associational information-processing system in the text domain. In a hypertext system, text information is stored in nodes, and nodes are interconnected to other nodes of related information.

Hypertext Markup Language (HTML)   The authoring "language" used to define Web pages.

I/O device   Any computer input or output device.

Icon   A small pictorial or graphical representation of a computer hardware function or component, or a computer software program, commonly associated with a graphical user interface.

Image capture   The software capability to copy images from Web pages or computer applications and store them on your own computer.

Imagery   A type of mnemonic in which mental pictures are used to represent new information.

Implementation   The second phase of the Plan, Implement, Evaluate model. Focus is on the use of instructional materials and activities designed to help students achieve the outcomes specified in the instructional plan.

Individualized education program (IEP)   An instructional plan for an individual student (usually one with special needs) that describes the student's current level of proficiency and also establishes short- and long-term goals for future focus. An IEP is typically developed through a conference with the student's teachers and parents and other appropriate individuals.

Information activity   A type of instructional activity designed to help students understand, remember, and apply new information.

Inkjet printer   A type of printer that forms letters on the page by shooting tiny electrically charged droplets of ink.

Input   Information entered into the computer for processing.

Input device   Hardware such as a keyboard, mouse, or joystick through which the user sends instructions to the computer.

Instruction   The selection and arrangement of information, activities, methods, and media to help students meet predetermined learning goals.

Instructional activity   Something done during a lesson to help students learn. There are five types of instructional activities: motivation, orientation, information, application, and evaluation activities.

Instructional appeal   The interest, or value, that instructional materials or activities have for the learner.

Instructional computing   The use of the computer in the design, development, delivery, and evaluation of instruction.

Instructional design   "The systematic process of translating principles of learning and instruction into plans for instructional materials and activities" (Smith & Ragan, 1999, p. 2).

Instructional effectiveness   A measure of the difference between what learners know before and after instruction; for example, Posttest − Pretest = Achievement.

Instructional efficiency   A measure of how much learners achieve per unit of time or dollar spent; for example, (Posttest − Pretest) /Time, or (Posttest − Pretest) /Cost.

Instructional game   An instructional approach that provides an appealing environment in which learners invest effort to follow prescribed rules in order to attain a challenging goal.

Instructional materials   The specific items used in a lesson and delivered through various media formats, such as video, audio, print, and so on.

Instructional media   Channels of communication that carry messages with an instructional purpose; the different ways and means by which information can be delivered to or experienced by a learner.

Instructional method   A procedure of instruction selected to help learners achieve objectives or understand the content or message of instruction (e.g., presentation, simulation, drill and practice, cooperative learning).

Instructional plan   A blueprint for instructional lessons based on analyses of the learners, the context, and the task to be learned. Planning involves "the process of deciding what methods of instruction are best for bringing about desired changes in student knowledge and skills for a specific course content and a specific student population" (Reigeluth, 1983, p. 7). The instructional plan also includes the selection of appropriate media.

Instructional technology   "Applying scientific knowledge about human learning to the practical tasks of teaching and learning" (Heinich et al., 1993, p. 16).

Integrated learning system (ILS)   A single networked delivery system that combines sophisticated computer-assisted instruction (CAI) with computer-managed instruction (CMI).

Intellectual skills   A type of learning that refers to a variety of thinking skills, including concept learning, rule using, and problem solving.

Intelligence   The adaptive use of previously acquired knowledge to analyze and understand new situations.

Intelligent tutoring system   Combines detailed information about a subject area and common student mistakes with a model of student performance to diagnose a given student's level of understanding. Also provides instruction designed to meet that student's individual needs. Sometimes called intelligent computer-assisted instruction (ICAI).

Interactive media   Media formats that allow or require some level of physical activity from the user, which in some way alters the sequence of presentation.

Interactive multimedia   Multimedia that allows user interactions so that the user can determine the direction of the program or presentation.

Interactive videodisc   A video playback system involving computer control of a videodisc player, where video is displayed in response to user choices.

Interface   An electronic go-between by which the computer communicates with a peripheral device.

Internal memory   Storage inside the computer. The CPU in a personal computer retrieves and deposits information in the computer's internal memory. Also called *main memory*.

Internet   A network of computer networks that links computers worldwide.

Intrinsic motivation   Motivation in which the act itself is the reward.

Java   A computer language, often associated with the Internet, designed to create applications capable of operating across different hardware platforms.

Keyboard   The most common input device; resembles the key layout of a typewriter.

Key word   A type of mnemonic in which an unfamiliar new word is linked to a similar-sounding familiar word, which is used to create a visual image that incorporates the meaning of the new word.

Knowledge   A type of learning that refers to the ability to recall specific information.

Label   Text used to name parts of an electronic spreadsheet.

Laser printer   A printer that combines laser and photocopying technology to produce very high-quality output, comparable to that produced in typesetting. Laser printers can produce text as well as high-quality graphics and can achieve print densities of up to 1200 dots per inch for very finely detailed images.

LCD panel/projector   A liquid crystal display device used with a computer or VCR for large-group display.

LCD screen   Liquid crystal display screen, commonly used in laptop computers and also in conjunction with display panels and projectors as large-group display devices for computer output.

Learner-centered instruction   "Actively collaborating with learners to determine what learning means and how it can be enhanced within each individual learner" (Wagner & McCombs, 1995, p. 32). An emphasis is placed on drawing on the learner's own unique talents, capacities, and experiences.

Learning "Learning is a persisting change in human performance or performance potential [brought] about as a result of the learner's interaction with the environment" (Driscoll, 1994, pp. 8–9). To change (or have the capacity to change) one's level of ability or knowledge.

Learning environment The setting or physical surroundings in which learning takes place, including the classroom, science or computer laboratory, gymnasium, playground, and so on.

Learning in context The application of knowledge to solve problems or complete tasks that are realistic and meaningful.

Learning style An individual's preferred ways for "processing and organizing information and for responding to environmental stimuli" (Shuell, 1981, p. 46).

Learning theory A set of related principles explaining changes in human performance or performance potential in terms of the causes of those changes.

Library/media specialist A school specialist who helps students and teachers to become effective users of ideas and information by providing access to materials, providing instruction, and working with teachers to design learning strategies to meet the needs of individual students.

Liquid crystal display (LCD) See LCD screen.

Listserv Also called a *mail server*, this is the computer or software that operates an e-mail discussion list on the Internet. Interested individuals subscribe to the list and subsequently receive all e-mail that is sent to the listserv.

Local-area network (LAN) A computer network covering a limited geographical area, such as a single building or even a single room within a building.

Logo A computer language developed by Seymour Papert and based on the learning theories of Jean Piaget; it is widely used in schools, particularly at the elementary level.

Machine language The binary code that controls the computer at the level of its circuits.

Macro A shortcut to encoding a series of actions in a computer program. Provides the means to perform a number of separate steps through a single command.

Mailing list Software that uses e-mail to deliver topic-specific information to a targeted group of respondents.

Mainframe computer The largest and most powerful class of computers; these have very large storage capacities and very fast processing speeds, and they are often used to support large numbers of users simultaneously.

Mass storage Input/output devices that provide for storage and retrieval of programs and other types of data that must be stored over a long period of time. Also referred to as *external* or *auxiliary* memory.

Medium/media see Instructional media.

Megabyte Approximately a million bytes, or 1,000 kilobytes.

Methods see Instructional methods.

Microprocessor A single silicon chip that contains all of the CPU circuits for a computer system.

Minicomputer A member of the second class of computers; features intermediate storage capacities and processing speeds and simultaneous use by as many as several dozen users.

Mnemonic Any practical device used to make information easier to remember, including rhymes, acronyms, and acrostics.

Model A three-dimensional representation of a real object; it may be larger, smaller, or the same size as the object represented.

Modem A combination input and output device that allows a computer to communicate with another computer over telephone lines. A modem (short for *modulator-demodulator*) converts digital computer information into sound (and vice versa) for transmission over telephone lines.

Monitor A video or computer display device. The most common output device for personal computers.

Motivation An internal state that leads people to choose to work toward certain goals and experiences. Defines what people will do rather than what they can do (Keller, 1983).

Motivation activity A type of instructional activity that leads students to want to learn and to put in the effort required for learning.

Motor skills A type of learning that refers to the ability to perform complex physical actions in a smooth, coordinated manner.

Mouse A pointing device used to select and move information on the computer display screen. When the mouse is moved along a flat surface such as a desktop, an arrow moves across the display screen in the same direction. The mouse typically has one to three buttons that may be used for selecting or entering information.

Multimedia Sequential or simultaneous use of a variety of media formats in a single presentation or program. Today this term conveys the notion of a system in which various media (e.g., text, graphics, video, and audio) are integrated into a single delivery system under computer control.

Netiquette Rules for polite social behavior while communicating over a network.

Newsgroup On computer networks, a discussion group created by allowing users to post messages and read messages among themselves.

Objective A statement of what learners will be expected to do when they have completed a specified course of instruction, stated in terms of observable performances.

One-computer classroom Classroom equipped with a single computer.

OOPS   Object-oriented programming systems, where each thing that one sees on the computer screen is treated as an object, and each object can have a programming code associated with it.

Operating system (OS)   The master control program for a computer system.

Orientation activity   A type of instructional activity that helps students understand what they have previously learned, what they are currently learning, and what they will be learning in the future.

Output   Information that comes out of the computer.

Output device   The hardware that receives and displays information coming from the computer.

Overhead transparencies   Acetate sheets whose images are projected by means of a device that transmits light through them and onto a screen or wall.

Packet   A chunk of information routed across the Internet.

Parallel   The extent of the match among the components of an instructional plan. Objectives and instructional activities must work together to create an effective plan.

Peer review   A form of evaluation that involves asking a colleague to examine all or part of an instructional lesson and make suggestions for improvement.

Performance   A portion of the instructional objective that indicates what students will do to demonstrate that they have learned.

Peripheral   Any of various devices that connect to the computer, including input devices, output devices, and mass storage devices.

Personal computer   Members of the third class of computers; these are the smallest, least powerful, and least expensive, intended for use by individuals.

PhotoCD   A CD format developed by Kodak that can store high-quality images made from 35-millimeter photographic negatives or slides.

Pilot test   An evaluation of instruction conducted before implementing the instruction.

Pixel   A single dot, or picture element, on the computer screen.

Planning   The first phase of the Plan, Implement, Evaluate model. Focus is on the design of instructional materials based on the learners, content, and context.

Plug-in   Small software program that works with a Web browser to perform tasks that the browser cannot perform on its own.

Portfolio   "A purposeful collection of student work that tells the story of the student's efforts, progress, or achievement" (Arter & Spandel, 1992, p. 36).

Prerequisites   The knowledge and skills students should have at the beginning of a lesson.

Presentation   An instructional method involving a one-way communication controlled by a source that relates, dramatizes, or otherwise disseminates information to learners, and which includes no immediate response from, or interaction with, learners (e.g., a lecture or speech).

Presentation software   Computer software designed for the production and display of computer text and images, intended to replace the functions typically associated with the slide projector and overhead projector.

Pretest   Preinstructional evaluation of students' knowledge and/or skills to determine students' level of performance before instruction.

Preview   A form of evaluation that involves reading, viewing, and/or working through specific instructional materials prior to using them (Heinich et al., 1999).

Printer   A device that provides printed output from the computer.

Printer driver   Software that ensures that an application's formatting commands are correctly translated into printer actions. Most word processors, for example, provide a number of different printer drivers to support different models of printers.

Problem solving   An instructional method in which learners use previously mastered skills to reach resolution of challenging problems. Based on the scientific method of inquiry, it typically involves the following five steps: (1) defining the problem and all major components, (2) formulating hypotheses, (3) collecting and analyzing data, (4) deriving conclusions/solutions, and (5) verifying conclusions/solutions.

Problem-solving software   Computer applications designed to foster students' higher-order thinking skills, such as logical thinking, reasoning, pattern recognition, and use of strategies.

Process technologies   Instructional technologies that are less tangible than hardware technologies (e.g. computer systems) and that include instructional strategies, methods, and techniques.

Programming   The process of creating a computer program. See computer program.

Programming language   A set of instructions that can be assembled, according to particular rules and syntax, to create a working computer program.

RAM   See Random-access memory.

Random-access memory (RAM)   The computer's working memory. In a personal computer, RAM provides a temporary work space that allows you to change its contents, as needed, to perform different tasks. Common RAM is volatile, which means that its contents disappear as soon as the power is turned off (or otherwise interrupted).

Read-only memory (ROM)   The permanent memory that is built into the computer at the factory, referred to as "read only" because the computer can read the information that is stored there but cannot change that stored information. ROM contains the basic instructions the computer needs to operate.

Real objects   Actual materials, not models or simulations.

Record   A collection of related fields that is treated as a logical unit in a database.

Reinforcing feedback Feedback used to recognize good performance and encourage continued effort from students. Takes the form of verbal praise or a "pat on the back."

Relational database A type of computer database that permits the interrelation of information across more than one datafile.

Reliability "The degree to which a test instrument consistently measures the same group's knowledge level of the same instruction when taking the test over again" (Gentry, 1994, p. 383).

Repurposing Creating a computer program to control a videodisc so that the content can be used in ways other than originally intended.

Retrieval Identifying and recalling information for a particular purpose.

Rhyme A type of mnemonic which uses words spoken in a rhythm or in verse to help remember information.

ROM See Read-only memory.

Router A computer that regulates Internet traffic and assigns data transmission pathways.

Scanner A device that uses technology similar to a photocopying machine to take an image from a printed page and convert it into a form the computer can manipulate.

Search and replace A common feature of word processors that allows the user to locate the occurrence of any word or phrase within a document and substitute something else.

Search engine A Website that maintains a database of Internet accessible information that can be searched to locate information of interest.

Server See File server.

Simulation An instructional method involving a scaled-down approximation of a real-life situation that allows realistic practice without the expense or risks otherwise involved. Similar to problem solving, simulations often include case studies and/or role plays.

Slides A small-format (e.g., 35mm) photographic transparency individually mounted for one-at-a-time projection.

Software The programs or instructions that tell the computer what to do, usually stored on diskette or CD-ROM.

Speech recognition Artificial intelligence based computer technology in which oral speech is converted by the computer into text.

Spelling checker A common ancillary feature of word processors that searches through a document and reports any instances of text that do not match a built-in dictionary.

Spreadsheet A general-purpose computer calculating tool based on the paper worksheet used by accountants.

Stem The part of a multiple-choice assessment instrument that sets forth the problem that will be "answered" by one option from a list of alternatives.

Storyboarding A technique for illustrating, on paper, what the screen displays in a computer program will look like before they are actually programmed.

Structured programming A set of programming conventions designed to result in organized, easy-to-read, and correct programs. It relies on a top-down method, modular program design, a limited set of program constructs, and careful documentation of the program.

Student tryout A "test run" of an instructional activity, approach, media, or materials with a small group of students before using it on a large scale (Mager, 1997).

Summative evaluation Assessment that occurs after instruction that measures what students have learned.

Supercomputers The most powerful and fastest of the mainframe computers.

Synchronous Occurring at the same time.

Syntax Rules for using computer languages.

Systems software The basic operating software that tells the computer how to perform its fundamental functions.

Tags Elements of HTML that are used to define properties of Web pages, for example, the tags <B> and </B> denote the beginning and end of boldfaced text.

TCP/IP Transmission Control Protocol/Internet Protocol—the communication standard used by computers on the Internet.

Technology "The systematic application of scientific or other organized knowledge to practical tasks" (Galbraith, 1967, p. 12). Technology performs a bridging function between research and theory on one side and professional practice on the other.

Technology coordinator A specialist and resource person who handles computers and related technologies for a school building or district.

Telnet A standard method for directly connecting to and using the resources of a remote computer on the Internet.

Template A prepared layout designed to ease the process of creating a product in certain computer applications, e.g., a slide design and color scheme for presentation software or a spreadsheet with appropriate labels and formulas but without the data.

Test generator A computer program used to create assessment instruments.

Text A combination of alphanumeric characters and numbers used to communicate.

Text justification The positioning of text in a word processed document. This includes text that is centered, aligned with respect to the right margin (right justified), and aligned with respect to the left margin (left justified). Left justified, the most common, aligns text flush with the left margin, leaving a "ragged" right margin.

Text selection The ability to choose portions of a word processing document for subsequent editing through the use of cursor movement keys or the mouse. Selection is sometimes called *highlighting* because selected text is usually rendered in special colors designed to stand out from surrounding material.

Theory   A set of related principles explaining observed events/relationships. Theories typically make predictions in the form of "If . . . , then . . . " statements that can be tested.

Top-down approach   An approach to problem solving and computer programming that begins by outlining the basic solution at a fairly high level of abstraction and then breaks that outline down into its component parts until they can be coded.

Transfer   The use of prior knowledge in new situations or as it applies to new problems.

Triangulation   The process of obtaining information from more than one technique or source in order to strengthen individual findings.

Tutorial   An instructional method in which a tutor—in the form of a person, computer, or special print materials—presents the content, poses a question or problem, requests learner response, analyzes the response, supplies appropriate feedback, and provides practice until the learner demonstrates a predetermined level of competency.

Two-way interactive video   A distance education technology in which sending and receiving sites are equipped with cameras, microphones, and video monitors and linked via some means of transmission (e.g., satellite, microwave, cable, fiber-optic cable).

Type style   Application of different features to any word processing font, including **boldface,** *italics,* underline, and others.

Undo   A software feature that allows the user to recover from an error; for example, if you select and delete the wrong block of text, the undo command restores the text to the document.

Uniform Resource Locator (URL)   The unique address for every Internet site or World Wide Web page, containing the protocol type, the domain, the directory, and the name of the site or page.

Uploading   Sending information over a network to another computer.

URL   See Uniform resource locator.

Vector graphics   Also called *draw graphics,* in which the computer "remembers" the steps involved in creating a particular graphic image on the screen, independent of a particular screen location or the graphic's size.

Video   The display of recorded pictures on a television-like screen. Includes videotapes, videodiscs, and CDs.

Video digitizer   An add-on device for the computer that takes video from standard video sources and captures it as a computer graphic or motion video.

Video teleconferencing   A distance education technology that uses one-way video with two-way audio or two-way video between sites.

Videodisc   A video storage medium composed of recorded images and sound, similar to the CD. Depending on format, a videodisc can hold from 30 to 60 minutes of motion video images, up to 54,000 still images, or a combination of motion and still images. As with the CD, the videodisc can be indexed for rapid location of any part of the material.

Videotape   A video storage medium in which video images and sound are recorded on magnetic tape. Popular sizes include one-inch commercial tape, three-quarter-inch U-matic, half-inch VHS or S-VHS, and 8-millimeter.

Virtual reality (VR)   A computer interface that simulates an interactive environment that appears to the observer as another reality. A VR system uses special hardware and software to project a three-dimensional visual representation of an environment and responds to the user's motion within that environment.

Virus   A computer program that infects a computer system, causing damage or mischief. Like a biological virus, it causes the host computer to make copies of the virus, which can then spread to other computers over networks, through online services, or via infected diskettes.

Visual   Combination of graphics and text presented in a two-dimensional format.

Web   See World Wide Web.

Web browser   Application program designed to access the Internet and navigate its nonsequential pathways.

Web page   A hypertext document on the World Wide Web, somewhat analogous to a printed page.

Web server   A computer connected to the Internet that makes Web pages and Websites available to other computers.

Website   A set of interrelated Web pages usually operated by a single entity (e.g., company, school, organization, or individual).

Web use policy   See Acceptable use policy.

Wide-area network (WAN)   A computer network covering a broad geographical area, such as between buildings, campuses, or even across hundreds or thousands of miles. Often involves the interconnection of multiple local-area networks.

Word processing   Using a word processor.

Word processor   A computer program for writing that supports the entry, editing, revising, formatting, storage, retrieval, and printing of text.

Word wrap   A feature of a word processor that automatically shifts the next whole word to the next line of the document when a line of text in a computer document is filled.

World Wide Web (WWW or the Web)   An information retrieval system on the Internet that relies on a point-and-click hypertext navigation system.

WYSIWYG   What You See Is What You Get—a standard for word processor displays where what shows on the computer display is what the document will look like when it is printed.

REFERENCES

Ackerman, E. (1995). *Learning to use the Internet: An introduction with examples and exercises.* Wilsonville, OR: Franklin, Beedle, & Associates.

Anglin, G. J. (Ed.). (1991). *Instructional technology: Past, present, and future.* Englewood, CO: Libraries Unlimited.

Arter, J. A., & Spandel, V. (1992). Using portfolios of student work in instruction and assessment. *Educational Measurement: Issues and Practice, 11*(Spring), 36–44.

Asimov, I. (1984). *Asimov's guide to science* (2nd ed.). New York: Basic Books.

Ault, C. R. (1985). Concept mapping as a study strategy in earth science. *Journal of College Science Teaching, 15*(1), 38–44.

Ausubel, D. P. (1968). *Educational psychology.* New York: Holt, Rinehart, & Winston.

Ausubel, D. P., Novak, J. D., & Hanesian, H. (1978). *Educational psychology: A cognitive view.* New York: Holt, Rinehart & Winston.

Ayersman, D. J. (1996). Reviewing the research on hypermedia-based learning. *Journal of Research on Computing in Education, 28*(4), 500–525.

Baine, D. (1986). *Memory and instruction.* Englewood Cliffs, NJ: Educational Technology.

Bangert-Drowns, R. L. (1993). The word processor as an instructional tool: A meta-analysis of word processing in writing instruction. *Review of Educational Research, 63*(1), 69–93.

Barell, J. (1995). *Teaching for thoughtfulness: Classroom strategies to enhance intellectual development.* White Plains, NY: Longman.

Barenholz, H., & Tamir, P. (1992). A comprehensive use of concept mapping in design instruction and assessment. *Research in Science and Technological Education, 10*(1), 37–52.

Becker, H. (1992). Computer-based integrated learning systems in the elementary and middle grades: A critical review and synthesis of evaluation reports. *Journal of Educational Computing Research, 8*(1), 1–41.

Bell-Gredler, M. E. (1986). *Learning and instruction: Theory into practice.* Upper Saddle River, NJ: Merrill/Prentice Hall.

Billings, K. J. (1985). *An evaluation handbook for a computer education program.* Eugene, OR: ICCE.

Block, J.H. (1983). Differential premises arising from differential socialization of the sexes: Some conjectures. *Child Development, 54,* 1335–1354.

Blumenfeld, P. C., Soloway, E., Marx, R. W., Krajcik, J. S., Guzdial, M., & Palinscar, A. (1991). Motivating project-based learning: Sustaining the doing, supporting the learning. *Educational Psychologist, 26,* 369–398.

Borko, H., & Livingston, C. (1992). Cognition and improvisation: Differences in mathematics instruction by expert and novice teachers. *American Educational Research Journal, 26,* 473–498.

Brooks, J. G., & Brooks, M. G. (1993). *In search of understanding: The case for constructivist classrooms.* Alexandria, VA: American Society for Curriculum Development.

Brown, J. S., Collins, A., & Duguid, P. (1989). Situated cognition and the culture of learning. *Educational Researcher, 18*(1), 32–42.

Bruer, J. T. (1993) *Schools for thought: A science of learning in the classroom.* Cambridge, MA: MIT Press.

Bruner, J. S. (1961). The act of discovery. *Harvard Education Review, 31*(1), 21–32.

Clark, C. M. & Yinger, R. J. (1987). Teacher planning. In J. Calderhead

(Ed.), *Exploring teachers' thinking* (pp. 84–103). London: Cassell.

Cochran-Smith, M. (1991). Word processing and writing in elementary classrooms: A critical review of related literature. *Review of Educational Research, 61*(1), 107–155.

Cognition and Technical Group at Vanderbilt. (1993). Designing learning environments that support thinking: The Jasper series as a case study. In T. M. Duffy, J. Lowyck, & D. H. Jonassen (Eds.), *Designing environments for constructive learning* (pp. 9–36). Berlin: Springer-Verlag.

Collins, A., Brown, J. S., & Holum, A. (1991). Cognitive apprenticeship: Making thinking visible. *American Educator, 15*(3), 6–11, 38–46.

Collis, B. (1990). *The best of research windows: Trends and issues in educational computing.* Eugene, OR: International Society for Technology in Education. (ERIC Document Reproduction Service No. ED 323 993)

Dallmann-Jones, A. S. (1994). *The expert educator: A reference manual of teaching strategies for quality education.* Fond du Lac, WI: Three Blue Herons.

D'Aoust, C. (1992). Portfolios: Process for students and teachers. In K. B. Yancey (Ed.), *Portfolios in the writing classroom* (pp. 39–48). Urbana, IL: National Council of Teachers of English.

Deaux, K. (1984). From individual differences to social categories: Analysis of a decade's research on gender. *American Psychologist, 39,* 105–116.

Derry, S., & Murphy, D. A. (1986). Designing systems that train learning ability: From theory to practice. *Review of Educational Research, 56*(1), 1–39.

Dewey, J. (1897). My pedagogic creed. *School Journal, 54,* 77–80.

Dick, W., & Reiser, R. A. (1989). *Planning effective instruction.* Upper Saddle River, NJ: Prentice Hall.

Driscoll, M. P. (1994). *Psychology of learning for instruction.* Boston: Allyn & Bacon.

Duffy, T. M., Lowyck, J., & Jonassen, D. H. (1993). Introduction. In T. M. Duffy, J. Lowyck, & D. H. Jonassen (Eds.), *Designing environments for constructive learning* (pp. 1–5). Berlin: Springer-Verlag.

Educational Products Information Exchange. (1990). *Report of computer-based integrated instructional systems.* Water Mill, NY: Author.

Educational Testing Service, Policy Information Center. (1996). *Computers and classrooms: The status of technology in U.S. schools.* Princeton, NJ: Educational Testing Service. Available on the World Wide Web: http://www.ets.org/research/pic/compclass.html

Ehrman, L., Glenn, A., Johnson, V., & White, C. (1992). Using computer databases in student problem solving: A study of eight social studies teachers' classrooms. *Theory and Research in Social Education, 20*(2), 179–206.

Eisner, E. (1985). *The educational imagination: On the design and evaluation of school programs* (2nd ed.). New York: Macmillan.

Ertmer, P. A., & Newby, T. J. (1993). Behaviorism, cognitivism, constructivism: Comparing critical features from an instructional design perspective. *Performance Improvement Quarterly, 6*(4), 50–72.

Ertmer, P. A., & Newby, T. J. (1996). The expert learner: Strategic, self-regulated, and reflective. *Instructional Science, 21*(4), 1–24.

Fennema, E. (1987). Sex-related differences in education: Myths, realities, and interventions. In V. Richardson-Koehler (Ed.). *Educator's Handbook: A research perspective.* New York: Longman.

Fleming, M. L. (1987). Displays and communication. In R. M. Gagné (Ed.), *Instructional technology: Foundations.* (pp. 233–260) Hillsdale, NJ: Lawrence Erlbaum Associates.

Gagné, R. M. (Ed.). (1987). *Instructional technology: Foundations.* Hillsdale, NJ: Lawrence Erlbaum Associates.

Galbraith, J. K. (1967). *The new industrial state.* Boston: Houghton Mifflin.

Gardner, H. (1983). *Frames of mind: The theory of multiple intelligences.* New York: Basic Books.

Gardner, H. (1985). *The mind's new science: A history of the cognitive revolution.* New York: Basic Books.

Gardner, P. (1996). *Internet for teachers & parents.* Westminster, CA: Teacher Created Materials.

Gentry, C. G. (1994). *Introduction to instructional development: Process and technique.* Belmont, CA: Wadsworth.

Grabe, M., & Grabe, C. (1997). *Integrating technology for meaningful learning.* Boston, MA: Houghton Mifflin.

Gredler, M. E. (1997). *Learning and instruction: Theory into practice.* Upper Saddle River, NJ: Merrill/Prentice Hall.

Heinich, R., Molenda, M., Russell, J. D., & Smaldino, S. (1993). *Instructional media and technologies for learning* (4th ed.). Upper Saddle River, NJ: Merrill/Prentice Hall.

Heinich, R., Molenda, M., Russell, J. D., & Smaldino, S. (1999). *Instructional media and technologies for learning* (6th ed.). Upper Saddle River, NJ: Merrill/Prentice Hall.

Honebein, P. C., Duffy, T. M., & Fishman B. J. (1993). Constructivism and the design of learning environments: Context and authentic activities for learning. In T. M. Duffy, J. Lowyck, & D. H. Jonassen (Eds.), *Designing environments for constructive learning* (pp. 87–108). Berlin: Springer-Verlag.

Hunter, M. (1982). *Mastery teaching.* El Segundo, CA: TIP.

Jacobsen, D., Eggen, P., & Kauchak, D. (1993). *Methods for teaching: A skills approach* (4th ed.). Upper Saddle River, NJ: Merrill/Prentice Hall.

Johnson, R. T., Johnson, D. W., & Stanne, M. B. (1985). Effects of cooperative, competitive, and individualistic goal structures on computer-assisted instruction. *Journal of Educational Psychology, 77*(6), 668–677.

Jonassen, D. H. (1991). Evaluating constructivist learning. *Educational Technology, 31*(9), 28–33.

Jonassen, D. H. (1996). *Computers in the classroom: Mindtools for critical thinking.* Upper Saddle River, NJ: Merrill/Prentice Hall.

Jonassen, D. H., Peck, K. L., and Wilson, B. G. (1999). *Learning with technology: A Constructivist approach.* Upper Saddle River, NJ: Merrill/Prentice Hall.

Kauchak, D., & Eggen, P. D. (1989). *Learning and teaching: Research based methods.* Boston: Allyn & Bacon.

Kearny, C., Newby, T., & Stepich, D. (1995). *Building bridges: Creating instructional analogies.* Presentation at the Annual Convention of the National Society for Performance and Instruction, Atlanta, GA, March.

Kearny, L. (1996). *Graphics for presenters: Getting your ideas across.* Menlo Park, CA: Crisp.

Kehoe, B., & Mixon, V. (1997). *Children and the Internet: A Zen guide for parents and educators.* Upper Saddle River, NJ: Prentice Hall.

Keller, J. M. (1983). Motivational design of instruction. In C. M. Reigeluth (Ed.), *Instructional design theories and models: An overview of their current status* (pp. 383–434). Hillsdale, NJ: Lawrence Erlbaum Associates.

Kemp, J. E., Morrison, G. R., & Ross, S. M. (1998). *Designing effective instruction.* (2nd ed.). Upper Saddle River, NJ: Merrill/Prentice Hall.

Knirk, F. G., & Gustafson, K. L. (1986). *Instructional technology: A systematic approach to education.* Ft. Worth, TX: Holt, Rinehart & Winston.

Kozma, R. (1991). Learning with media. *Review of Educational Research, 61*(2), 179–211.

Kulik, C. C., & Kulik, J. A. (1991). Effectiveness of computer-based instruction: An updated analysis. *Computers in Human Behavior, 7,* 75–94.

Lamb, A., Smith, N., & Johnson, L. (1996). *Surfin' the Internet: Practical ideas from A to Z.* Emporia, KS: Vision to Action.

Leshin, C. B., Pollock, J., & Reigeluth, C. M., (1992). *Instructional design strategies and tactics.* Englewood Cliffs, NJ: Educational Technology.

Littlefield, J., Delclos, V., Lever, S., Clayton, K., Bransford, J., & Franks, J. (1988). Learning LOGO: Method of teaching, transfer of general skill, and attitudes toward school and computers." In R. Mayer (Ed.), *Teaching and learning computer programming* (pp. 111–135). Hillsdale, NJ: Lawrence Erlbaum Associates.

Lockard, J., Abrams, P. D., & Many, W. A. (1997). *Microcomputers for twenty-first century educators.* New York: Longman.

Maddux, C. D., Johnson, D. L., & Willis, J. W. (1992). *Educational computing. Learning with tomorrow's technologies.* Boston: Allyn & Bacon.

Mager, R. F. (1997). *Preparing instructional objectives* (3rd ed.). Belmont, CA: Pitman.

Maor, D., & Taylor, P. C. (1995). Teacher epistemology and scientific inquiry in computerized classroom environments. *Journal of Research in Science Teaching, 32*(8), 839–854.

McCutcheon, G. (1980). How do elementary school teachers plan? The nature of planning and influences on it. *Elementary School Journal, 81*(1), 4–23.

McKeachie, W. J. (1994). Why classes should be small, but how to help your students be active learners even in large classes. In W. J. McKeachie (Ed.), *Teaching tips* (pp. 197–210). Lexington, MA: Heath.

McMillan, J. H. (1997). *Classroom assessment: Principles and practice for effective instruction.* Boston: Allyn & Bacon.

Miller, E. B. (1997). *The Internet resource directory for K–12 teachers and librarians,* 1996–97. Englewood, CO: Libraries Unlimited.

National Center for Education Statistics. (1998, March). *Internet access in public schools.* Washington, DC: U.S. Department of Education. Available on the World Wide Web: http://nces.ed.gov/

Niemiec, R., & Walberg, H. J. (1987). Comparative effects of computer-assisted instruction: A synthesis of reviews. *Journal of Educational Computing Research, 3*(1), 19–37.

Office of Technology Assessment, U.S. Congress. (1988, September). *Power on! New tools for teaching and learning* (Report No. OTA-SET-380). Washington, DC: Government Printing Office.

Office of Technology Assessment, U.S. Congress. (1995, April). *Teachers and technology: Making the connection* (Report No. OTA-EHR-616). Washington, DC: U.S. Government Printing Office.

Ormrod, J. E. (1995). *Educational psychology: Principles and applications.* Upper Saddle River, NJ: Merrill/Prentice Hall.

Palinscar, A. S. (1986). Metacognitive strategy instruction. *Exceptional Children, 53*(2), 118–124.

Papert, S. (1980). *Mindstorms: Children, computers, and powerful ideas.* New York: Basic Books.

Perelman, L. J. (1992). *School's out.* New York: Avon.

Phillips, D. C. (1995). The good, the bad, and the ugly: The many faces of constructivism. *Educational Researcher, 24*(7), 5–12.

Presidents' Committee of Advisors on Science and Technology, Panel on Educational Technology. (1997, March). *Report to the President on the use of technology to strengthen K–12 education in the United States.* Washington, DC: U.S. Government Printing Office.

Reigeluth, C. M. (1983). Instructional design: What is it and why is it? In C. M. Reigeluth (Ed.), *Instructional-design theories and models: An overview of their current status* (pp. 3–36). Hillsdale, NJ: Lawrence Erlbaum Associates.

Reiser, R. A., & Dick, W. (1996). *Instructional planning: A guide for teachers.* Boston: Allyn & Bacon.

Reynolds, A. (1992). What is competent beginning teaching? A review of the literature. *Review of Educational Research, 62*(1), 1–35.

Rivard, J. D. (1997). *Quick guide to the Internet for educators.* Needham Heights, MA: Allyn & Bacon.

Robinson, P. W. (1981). *Fundamentals of experimental psychology.* Upper Saddle River, NJ: Merrill/Prentice Hall.

Roblyer, M. D., Castine, W., & King, F. (1988). *Assessing the impact of computer-based instruction: A review of recent research.* New York: Haworth.

Roblyer, M. D., Edwards, J., & Havriluk, M. A. (1997). *Integrating educational technology into teaching.* Upper Saddle River, NJ: Merrill/Prentice-Hall.

Rogoff, B. (1990). *Apprenticeship in thinking: Cognitive development in social context.* New York: Oxford University Press.

Rothwell, W. J., & Kazanas, H. C. (1992). *Mastering the instructional design process: A systematic approach.* San Francisco: Jossey-Bass.

Ryder, R. J., & Hughes, T. (1997). *Internet for educators.* Upper Saddle River, NJ: Prentice-Hall.

Saettler, P. (1990). *The evolution of American educational technology.* Englewood, CO: Libraries Unlimited.

Salend, S. J. (1994). *Effective mainstreaming: Creating inclusive classrooms* (2nd ed.). Upper Saddle River, NJ: Merrill/Prentice Hall.

Sardo-Brown, D. (1990). Experienced teachers' planning practices: A U.S. survey. *Journal of Education for Teaching, 16*(1), 57–71.

Satterthwaite, L. (1990). *Instructional media.* Dubuque, IA: Kendall/Hunt.

Schmitt, M. S., & Newby, T. J. (1986). Metacognition: Relevance to instructional design. *Journal of Instructional Development, 9*(4), 29–33.

Schön, D. A. (1983). *The reflective practitioner: How professionals think in action.* New York: Basic Books.

Seels, B. B., & Richey, R. C. (1994). *Instructional technology: The definition and domains of the field.* Washington, DC: Association for Educational Communications and Technology.

Sharp, V. F., Levine, M. G., & Sharp, R. M. (1997). *The best Web sites for teachers.* Eugene, OR: International Society for Technology in Education.

Shelly, G. B., & Cashman, T. J. (1984). *Computer fundamentals for an information age.* Brea, CA: Anaheim.

Shuell, T. J. (1981). Dimensions of individual differences. In F. H. Farley & N. J. Gordon (Eds.), *Psychology and education: The state of the union* (pp. 32–59). Berkeley, CA: McCutchan.

Simonson, M. R., & Thompson, A. (1997). *Educational computing foundations.* Upper Saddle River, NJ: Merrill/Prentice Hall.

Singh, J. (1992). Cognitive effects of programming in Logo: A review of literature and synthesis of strategies for research. *Journal of Research on Computing in Education, 25*(1), 88–104.

Skinner, B. F. (1968). *The technology of teaching.* New York: Appleton-Century-Crofts.

Skinner, B. F. (1984). The shame of American education. *American Psychologist, 39,* 947–954.

Slavin, R. E. (1990a). *Cooperative learning: Theory, research, and practice.* Upper Saddle River, NJ: Merrill/Prentice Hall.

Slavin, R. E. (1990b). Research on cooperative learning: Consensus and controversy. *Educational Leadership, 47*(4), 52–54.

Smith, P. L., & Ragan, T. J. (1999). *Instructional design.* Upper Saddle River, NJ: Merrill/Prentice Hall.

Stepich, D. A., & Newby, T. J. (1988). Analogical instruction within the information processing paradigm: Effective means to facilitate learning. *Instructional Science, 17,* 129–144.

Sternberg, R. J., & Detterman, D. K. (1986). *What is intelligence? Contemporary viewpoints on its nature and definition.* Norwood, NJ: Ablex.

Stiggins, R. J. (1997). *Student-centered classroom assessment* (2nd ed.). Upper Saddle River, NJ: Merrill/Prentice Hall.

Sullivan, H., & Higgins, N. (1983). *Teaching for competence.* New York: Teachers College Press.

Taylor, R. P. (Ed.). (1980). *The computer in the school: Tutor, tool, tutee.* New York: Teachers College Press.

Teague, F. A., Roger, D. W., & Tipling, R. N. (1994). *Technology and media: Instructional applications.* Dubuque, IA: Kendall/Hunt.

Tessmer, M. (1990). Environment analysis: A neglected stage of instructional design. *Educational Technology Research and Development, 38*(1), 55–64.

Thorndike, E. L. (1931). *Human learning.* New York: Century.

Volker, R., & Simonson, M. (1995). *Technology for teachers.* Dubuque, IA: Kendall/Hunt.

Wagner, E. D., & McCombs, B. L. (1995, March–April). Learner centered psychological principles in practice: Designs for distance education. *Educational Technology, 35,* 32–35.

Wasserman, S. (1992). *Asking the right question: The essence of teaching.* Bloomington, IN: Phi Delta Kappa.

Watson, J. B. (1924). *Behaviorism.* New York: Peoples' Institute.

Weinstein, C. E., & Van Mater Stone, G. (1993). Broadening our conception of general education: The self-regulated learner. *New Directions for Community Colleges, 81,* 31–39.

West, C. K., Farmer, J. A., & Wolff, P. M. (1991). *Instructional design: Implications from cognitive science.* Upper Saddle River, NJ: Merrill/Prentice Hall.

Wittrock, M. C. (1990). Generative processes of comprehension. *Educational Psychologist, 24,* 345–376.

Woolfolk, A. E. (1990). *Educational psychology* (4th ed.). Upper Saddle River, NJ: Merrill/Prentice Hall.

Woolfolk, A. E. (1998). *Educational psychology* (7th ed.). Boston: Allyn & Bacon.

Worthen, B. R., White, K. R., Fan, X., & Sudweeks, R. R. (1999). *Measurement and assessment in schools* (2nd ed.). New York: Longman.

Yelon, S. L. (1991). Writing and using instructional objectives. In L. J. Briggs, K. L. Gustafson, & M. H. Tillman (Eds.), *Instructional design: Principles and applications* (2nd ed.) (pp. 75–122). Englewood Cliffs, NJ: Educational Technology.

Yelon, S. L. (1996). *Powerful principles of instruction.* White Plains, NY: Longman.

NAME INDEX

SUBJECT INDEX